75



# THE FOREST OF SYMBOLS

*Aspects of Ndembu Ritual*

Side view of Chizaluki. The designs on the mask are in white, red, and black.

# THE FOREST OF SYMBOLS

## *Aspects of Ndembu Ritual*

VICTOR TURNER

*Cornell Paperbacks*

CORNELL UNIVERSITY PRESS

ITHACA AND LONDON

First published 1967 by Cornell University Press
Published in the United Kingdom by Cornell University Press Ltd.,
2–4 Brook Street, London W1Y 1AA.

*First printing, Cornell Paperbacks,* 1970
*Second printing,* 1972

International Standard Book Number 0–8014–9101–0
Library of Congress Catalog Card Number 67-12308

PRINTED IN THE UNITED STATES OF AMERICA
BY VAIL-BALLOU PRESS, INC.

To Monica Wilson

# Acknowledgments

FOR permission to reprint these essays the author makes grateful acknowledgment to Oliver and Boyd Ltd. ("Symbols in Ndembu Ritual"); to the International African Institute, which retains the world rights ("Ritual Symbolism, Morality, and Social Structure among the Ndembu" and "Witchcraft and Sorcery: Taxonomy versus Dynamics"); to the Association of Social Anthropologists of the Commonwealth ("Color Classification in Ndembu Ritual: A Problem in Primitive Classification"); to The American Ethnological Society ("Betwixt and Between: The Liminal Period in *Rites de Passage*"); to Dr. Joseph Casagrande ("Muchona the Hornet, Interpreter of Religion"); to the *Anthropological Quarterly* ("Themes in the Symbolism of Ndembu Hunting Ritual"); to Mr. Barrie Reynolds and the National Museums of Zambia ("Lunda Medicine and the Treatment of Disease"); and to The Macmillan Company ("A Ndembu Doctor in Practice").

The opportunity to write "Color Classification," "Themes in the Symbolism of Ndembu Hunting Ritual," "Lunda Medicine," and "A Ndembu Doctor in Practice" was afforded me by a fellowship at the Center for Advanced Study in the Behavioral Sciences (Ford Foundation). "Symbols in Ndembu Ritual" was written when I was a recipient of a Simon Research Fellowship at the University of Manchester.

My thanks are due to many people and institutions. My wife has worked with me from the beginning of this venture, in the field, until its completion in book form. Without her constant help and encouragement it would not have taken shape. I am deeply grateful to my many Ndembu friends and informants whose names appear in the text. My former colleagues in the Department of Social Anthropology at the University of Manchester, notably Professor Max Gluckman, have commented on many of these articles before publication. My fieldwork was conducted while I was a Research Officer of the Rhodes-Livingstone Institute, a body which continued to make its informational resources available to me after the termination of my employment.

V. T.

*Ithaca, New York*
*April 1966*

# Contents

# Illustrations

# *Diagrams*

# THE FOREST OF SYMBOLS

## *Aspects of Ndembu Ritual*

# Correspondances

La Nature est un temple où de vivants piliers
Laissent parfois sortir de confuses paroles;
L'homme y passe à travers des forêts de symboles
Qui l'observent avec des regards familiers.

Comme de longs échos qui de loin se confondent
Dans une ténébreuse et profonde unité,
Vaste comme la nuit et comme la clarté,
Les parfums, les couleurs et les sons se répondent.

Il est des parfums frais comme des chairs d'enfants,
Doux comme les hautbois, verts comme les prairies,
—Et d'autres, corrompus, riches et triomphants,

Ayant l'expansion des choses infinies,
Comme l'ambre, le musc, le benjoin et l'encens,
Qui chantent les transports de l'esprit et des sens.

Charles Baudelaire

# Introduction

PROFESSIONAL colleagues in America and Britain have encouraged me to bring together in a single volume a set of articles and papers hitherto widely scattered in journals and anthologies. All these publications deal specifically or indirectly with aspects of the ritual system of the Ndembu people of northwestern Zambia (formerly Northern Rhodesia) in south-central Africa. These anthropological studies are arranged in two sections: (1) mainly theoretical treatments of symbolism and witchcraft; and (2) descriptive accounts of aspects of ritual. The descriptive studies have been augmented by an extensive account of the Ndembu boys' circumcision rites (*Mukanda*), never before published, which includes a theoretical section on the manipulation of ritual in contexts of local political struggle. This distinction between sections is nowhere clear-cut, for the theoretical part contains much descriptive material, and the descriptions are interwoven with theoretical passages. The essays in each section appear in the order in which they were written, to enable the reader to follow developments and modifications in the author's ideas and handling of data. Unavoidably, there is a measure of repetition, but where the same material appears in different articles it is almost always to illustrate different aspects of theory or to raise new problems.

Since an account of the main features of Ndembu local and kinship organization has already been presented in my study of Ndembu village life, *Schism and Continuity in an African Society* (1957), this introduction will be limited to an abbreviated restatement of the salient features of village and vicinage structure and to an outline of the ritual system. It is in these contexts that the particular studies of both the "practice" and "manipulation" of ritual (Spiro 1965, 105) by Ndembu acquire much of their significance.

In many parts of Zambia the ancient religious ideas and practices of the Africans are dying out through contact with the white man and his ways. Employment in the copper mines, on the railway, as domestic servants and shop assistants; the meeting and mingling of tribes in a nontribal environment; the long absence of men from their homes—all these factors have contributed to the breakdown of religions that stress the values of kinship ties, respect for the elders, and tribal unity. However, in the far northwest of the Territory, this process of religious disintegration is less rapid and complete; if one is patient, sympathetic, and lucky one may still observe there the dances and rituals of an older day. In Mwinilunga, for instance, where I did two and a half years' fieldwork as a research officer of the Rhodes-Livingstone Institute, I was able to attend many rituals of the Ndembu people and obtain material on others from informants. Gradually I became aware of a vast and complicated system of ceremonial practices going on around me somewhat as one picks out the skyline of a distant city in the growing dawn. It was an astonishing and enriching experience to note the contrast between the relatively simple and monotonous economic and domestic life of these hunters and hoe cultivators and the ordered arrangement and colorful symbolism of their religious life.

To underline the contrast mentioned, let us take a brief look at the Ndembu in their daily, secular existence. There are about eighteen thousand of them in Mwinilunga District, dispersed in scattered villages of about a dozen huts, over seven thousand square miles or so of deciduous woodland, cut up by hundreds of streams and young rivers flowing down towards the Zambezi. The Ndembu live to the west of the Lunga River, which divides the district roughly from north to south, and the Kosa live to the east of it, both groups calling themselves Lunda and claiming to have come from the land of the great Congo chief, Mwantiyanvwa. In the two centuries following this supposed migration, both Kosa and Ndembu Lunda seem to have lost what central authority and military organization they may have possessed at first and to have broken up into small, virtually independent chiefdoms. In the late nineteenth century, Kanongesha the Ndembu and Musokantanda the Kosa, senior chiefs, whose ancestors had led the respective war parties from Mwantiyanvwa, were still respected by their junior chiefs but had little direct control over them. Considerable intermarriage took place with the simply organized

Mbwela and Lukolwe peoples whom the first Ndembu had conquered. Later, Ovimbundu slave traders and Lwena and Chokwe slave raiders from Angola, encouraged by the Portuguese, completed the disintegration of these virtually isolated outposts of Mwantiyanvwa's empire, now grown weak in the homeland itself. Later still, under British rule, a hierarchy was established consisting of a chief (the Native Authority) and four subchiefs. Formerly, these subchiefs belonged to a class of senior village headmen who held renowned historical titles but had little real power. However, the Ndembu, like *émigré* aristocrats at Cannes or Biarritz, in their talk by the village fires still live in the strenuous and heroic past. Whatever time and raids have done to them, they say, "We are the people of Mwantiyanvwa," and that is that!

On their well-wooded plateau the Ndembu practice a form of subsistence cultivation in which cassava growing is associated with hunting. In addition to cassava, finger millet is grown by small circle ash-planting methods mainly for beermaking, and maize is cultivated in streamside gardens for food and beer.

They are a matrilineal, virilocal people, with high personal spatial mobility, and they inhabit small villages with cores of male matrikin of whom the oldest member of the senior genealogical generation is usually the headman.

Among the Ndembu, not only villages but individuals and families have high rates of mobility. Men, of their own choice, and women, through marriage, divorce, widowhood, and remarriage, each of which normally entails a change in domicile, are constantly moving from one village to another, although usually men go where they have kin. This is possible since kin groups get widely dispersed over the region. We have, then, a society whose villages move widely and frequently over space and often tend to split, even to fragment, through time. Individuals circulate continually through these moving villages. It is not surprising that many Central Africanists, who work in areas characterized by much residential mobility, should have become interested in problems of social dynamics and in processes of adjustment, adaptation, and change.

## *Village Structure*

Although the majority of local groups in Ndembu society are relatively transient and unstable, the organizational principles on which they are formed and re-formed are persistent and enduring.

Particular villages break up and divide or disperse, but the structural form of the Ndembu village remains. If we look at a large sample of particular Ndembu villages, we can abstract from their concrete variations a general or normal form. From informants' comments on the rules they believe should govern village residence, an anthropologist is able to assess somewhat the extent and mode of conformity between statistical and ideal norms of village structure. On the whole, I found that most Ndembu villages are "on the ground," much as informants thought they ought to be. Nevertheless, I found also that the principles on which they are built up are often situationally incompatible, in the sense that they give rise to conflicts of loyalties. People who observe one set of norms find that this very observance makes them transgress equally valid rules belonging to another set.

Two major principles influence the residential pattern: matrilineal descent and virilocal marriage. Matriliny governs prior rights to residence, succession to office, and inheritance of property. A man has a right to reside with his matrilineal kin, primary or classificatory. He may reside in his father's village if his mother lives there, or, if she does not, as a privilege granted him by his father, by virtue of that father's rights as a member of the village matrilineage, a man has the right to be considered as a candidate for the headmanship of his matrilineal village and is entitled to share in the property of a deceased matrilineal kinsman. On the other hand, a man has the right to take his wife to reside in his own village. From this might arise the difficult situation where women, on whom the social continuity of villages depends, do not live in these same villages but in their husbands' villages. This difficulty would be reduced if there was a clearly defined custom whereby boys went to live in their mothers' brothers' villages at a given age, say at puberty. Among Ndembu there is no such custom, and the outcome is left uncertain. The onus of choice is thrown on the individual. Men try to keep their sons with them as long as they can, and indeed the father-son relationship is highly ritualized, especially in the hunters' cults and in the circumcision ceremony. The upshot is that there are strong patrifocal tendencies in a matrilineal society.

## *Matriliny and Virilocality: Some Implications*

An over-all picture emerges of mobile groups of male matrilineal kinsmen, changing residential sites about twice every decade, in competition with one another for women and their children. Young children usually remain with their mothers, who are granted their custody after divorce. To obtain the allegiance of the children, their maternal uncles must win over the children's mothers. A contradiction thus tends to arise between a man's role as a husband and a father who wishes to retain his wife and children with him, and his role as uterine brother and uncle, whereby he seeks to win the residential allegiance of his sister and her children. This struggle, veiled though it often is and mitigated by customs enjoining friendship between in-laws of the same generations, is reflected in a divorce rate exceptionally high even for Central Africa. The importance of matriliny also appears in the custom whereby widows return to the villages of their uterine or close matrilineal kin after their husbands' deaths. There is no levirate or widow inheritance among free Ndembu. Thus, in practice, at any given time, the matrilineal structure of a village is made up not only of relationships between male matrilineal kin, but also between these men and a variable number of matrilineal kinswomen who have returned to them after divorce or widowhood, bringing their children.

Let me put the matter in another way. In discussion with me, Ndembu emphasized the solidarity between two kinds of male kin: between fathers and sons and between brothers. These are the relationships, for example, that receive ritual recognition in the boys' circumcision ritual (see below pp. 155, 233). Often, two or three full brothers are circumcised at the same lodge—and this is one reason for the wide age range of the novices (between seven and seventeen)—or the oldest brother will act as guardian to his novice younger brothers. Not infrequently, a father will act as guardian. This official attends to the needs of the novices, instructs them in various matters, and also chastises them for breaches of lodge discipline.

The father's role in the ritual is important. He must refrain from sexual intercourse altogether until his sons' scars are healed. It is said that in the past a man would kill a circumciser who maimed his son. On the other hand, the mother's brother—sister's son relationship is not ritualized at all circumcisions, nor need the mother's brother practice sexual continence until the circumcision scars are healed. Hunting rituals also emphasize the father-son bond. As I have said, I see in all this a patrifocal element in a basically matrilineal society. There is a masculine ideal, never completely realized in practice, of a community of male kin, consisting of full brothers, their wives, and sons. Matriliny however, strongly ritualized in the girls' puberty ceremony and in many cults connected with female fertility, prevents the full pragmatic realization of this ideal model. Ndembu say that they trace descent through women, because "the mother's blood is self-evident and manifest, whereas one can never be sure who is the begetter." Matriliny provides a more certain basis for tracing descent; one knows undeniably just who are one's maternal kin. Thus, matrilineal kinship provides the framework for persisting groups and controls succession and inheritance within such groups. Nevertheless, given matriliny, a Ndembu village can continue through time only if sisters' sons come to live in it. Concomitantly, sons must leave the village, to replenish the villages of their maternal uncles. The village still remains essentially a structure of relationships between male kinsmen, but matriliny determines the form of the majority of these relationships. The unity of brothers is still stressed, but the brothers who live together are uterine brothers, children of the same mother. They may in addition be seminal brothers, sons of the same father, but the uterine link is crucial for coresidence. Many adult sons reside with their fathers, but after the death of the latter they must go where they have matrilineal kin.

At any given time, sisters and adult sisters' daughters of the senior male generation reside in the village. During their reproductive period these women are residents only in the intervals between successive marriages, but after the menopause they may stay there permanently. Sisters' sons and sisters' daughters' sons tend to accumulate in each village, sometimes along with their mothers and sometimes remaining behind after their mothers have married out again. As a result, any actual village contains a number of adult persons related by primary or classificatory matrilineal ties and a smaller number of persons linked to the village matrilineage through their fathers. Male kin preponderate over female kin by more than two to one. In other words, each real village tends in its structure to represent a compromise between matriliny and patrilocality (which I here take to mean residence with one's own father). Patrilocality owes its importance to virilocal marriage, and it is this form of marriage that enables uterine brothers to reside together. If marriage were uxorilocal, uterine brothers would be dispersed through the villages of their wives.

## *Some Kinds of Ritual*

Broadly speaking, Ndembu rituals fall into two main types: life-crisis rituals and rituals of affliction. Both these terms require some explanation.

### LIFE-CRISIS RITUALS

What, for instance, is a life-crisis? Briefly, it is an important point in the physical or social development of an individual, such as birth, puberty, or death. In most of the world's simpler societies and in many "civilized" societies, too, there are a number of ceremonies or rituals designed to mark the transition from one phase of life or social status to another (see below pp. 93 ff.). We have christening and graduation ceremonies, for example, the first to indicate the arrival of a new social personality on the human scene, the second to celebrate the successful outcome of a long and often painful learning process and the launching of a new breadwinner. These "crisis" ceremonies not only concern the individuals on whom they are centered, but also mark changes in the relationships of all the people connected with them by ties of blood, marriage, cash, political control, and in many other ways. When a Ndembu woman bears her first child, a boy, let us say, she may be presenting her brother, a village headman, with an heir, while husband becomes a father and her mother a grandmother, with all the changes in behavior and status involved in these new relationships. Therefore her society itself undergoes changes along with her own important passage from young wife to mother. Whatever society we live in we are all related to one another; our own "big moments" are "big moments" for others as well.

#### *Initiation Ceremonies*

Although both boys and girls undergo initiation ceremonies, the form and purpose of the ceremonies differ widely in either case. Boys, for instance, are circumcised, but there is no cliterodectomy of girls. Boys are initiated collectively, girls individually. Boys are initiated before and girls at the onset of puberty. The main purpose of boys' initiation is to inculcate tribal values, hunting skill, and sexual instruction; that of girls' initiation is to prepare them for marriage, which follows immediately in the great majority of cases. Boys are secluded and taught in the bush; a grass hut is built in the village itself for girls. Other striking differences exist and will be brought out in the descriptions below. The main points to notice, however, are the contrast between the group nature of the boys' ceremony and the individual treatment of the girls; the emphasis on obedience to the discipline of the elders and endurance of hardship for the boys as contrasted with the emphasis on sex and reproduction and the freedom from manual work associated with the girls' ceremony, and the bush setting of the former as compared with the domestic and village setting of the latter.

With regard to the difference between the collective nature of the boys' and the individual nature of the girls' ceremonies, the comment of a Ndembu woman is perhaps illuminating. "If many girls and their instructresses were away at once for a long time, who would work in the gardens, fetch water and cook for the men?" Since the agricultural work of men was in the past confined to clearing and burning the bush and some preliminary hoeing in the early rains and since they did no preparation or cooking of food, but spent most of their time in irregular hunting and shooting, their withdrawal in large numbers from economic activities would not produce such a marked effect.

In a sense, *Mukanda,* the boys' circumcision ceremony, qualifies a man for entrance into the hunting cults and *Nkang'a,* the girls' puberty ritual, prepares a woman to take part in the fertility cults. However, the life-crisis rituals are common to all Ndembu and automatic, while hunting and fertility cults depend upon the affliction of individuals by individual shades and are not automatic.

It is interesting that the main theme of *Mukanda* should be productive activity (i.e., hunting), while that of *Nkang'a* should be reproductive activity. Women's economic activity, which is, when all is said and done, essential to the existence of the community, is hardly ritualized at all, while that of men is steeped with ritual. Hunting and sex for men, sex and motherhood for women seem to be the values underlined most strongly in life-crisis rituals, with respect for elders and superiors, dramatically and awesomely embodied in the boys' *makishi,* a constant element in both.

*Funeral Ceremony*

As in most societies the amount of "pomp and circumstance" at a funeral depends on the wealth and importance of the dead person. Professor Radcliffe-Brown has said that funerals are concerned more with the living than the dead. It has been mentioned previously that in all life-crisis rituals changes take place in the relationships of all those people closely connected with the subject of the ritual. When a person dies, all these ties are snapped, as it were, and the more important the person the greater the number and range of ties there are to be broken. Now a new pattern of social relationships must be established: if the dead person was, for instance a headman, a successor has to be found for him, his heirs must divide his inheritance among them, someone must be responsible for his debts, the fate of his widow must be decided, and everyone who stood in a particular relationship with him must know where they stand with regard to his heirs and successor. Before all these things can be done, a period of adjustment must take place, an interval during which society passes gradually from the old to the new order. Among the Ndembu this period coincides with the time that a mourning camp, *Chipenji* or *Chimbimbi*, lasts.

It is during this period that the shade of the dead is thought to be most restless, forever trying to revisit the scenes and communicate with the people it knew best alive. Ndembu believe that without the ritual of mourning the shade would never lie quietly in the grave, but would be constantly interfering in the affairs of the living, jealous of every new adjustment, such as the remarriage of its widow or the appointment of a successor of whom it would have disapproved, and indeed it might afflict with illness all those people who should have honored its memory by holding a funeral gathering but omitted to do so.

### RITUALS OF AFFLICTION

Now what is meant by "rituals of affliction"? The answer to this question points out the major theme of Ndembu religious life. For some reason, Ndembu have come to associate misfortune in hunting, women's reproductive disorders, and various forms of illness with the action of the spirits of the dead. Furthermore, whenever an individual has been divined to have been "caught" by such a spirit, he or she becomes the subject of an elaborate ritual, which many people from far and near attend, devised at once to propitiate and to get rid of the spirit that is thought to be causing the trouble. These statements give rise to a further chain of questions. What sort of "spirits" are said to afflict the living, those of relatives, of strangers, "nature spirits," or demons? The answer is simple and unambiguous. They are the spirits of deceased relatives. The Ndembu term for such a spirit is *mukishi*, plural *akishi*. I would like to make it clear that *akishi*, "spirits," must not be confused with *makishi* (singular *ikishi*, Lwena *likishi*), which means "masked dancers at initiation or funeral ceremonies" or the costumes in which they appear. For the sake of convenience, I will use Professor Wilson's term "shade" rather than "spirit" or "ancestor spirit" for *mukishi*. Rightly or wrongly, "ancestor spirit" suggests "remote or distant ancestor" to most people, and these uneasy inhabitants of the "unquiet grave" are always the spirits of those who played a prominent part in the lifetime of the persons they are troubling.

Why do the shades "come out of their graves," as the Ndembu put it, to plague their kinsfolk? Various reasons are alleged, the most important being that the latter have "forgotten" them or that they have acted in a way that the shades have disapproved of. "Forgetting" implies neglect to make an offering of beer or food at the *muyombu* trees planted as living shrines in the center of villages or omitting to mention their names while praying there. It may also mean neglecting to pour blood from one's latest kill down an opening made in a hunter's grave, "for the shade to eat." It may simply consist in forgetting the dead "in one's heart." "Disapproved conduct" may mean causing a quarrel in the kin-group, going away from the dead person's village to live elsewhere or disobeying a wish expressed in his or her lifetime. Whatever the reason, there is usually thought to be something rather distinctive and important in being "caught by a *mukishi*." To begin with, one becomes the central figure of a great ritual gathering, all of whom earnestly desire that one should get better or have better luck. Then, if one has undergone successful treatment, one is entitled to become a minor "doctor" (*chimbuki*) when the same ritual is performed for other people, perhaps progressing in time to the role of principal doctor. Thus, the way to religious fame is through affliction. I have often heard doctors or diviners reply to the question "How did you learn your job?" by the words, "I started by being sick myself," meaning that the shade of one of their relatives afflicted them with illness. There is then a double meaning in being caught by a shade. One is punished for neglect of their memory, but at the same time one is chosen or "elected" to be a go-between in future rituals that put the living into communication with the dead. If the ritual fails in its purpose and one's sickness or bad luck continues, it may be a sign that one has not properly atoned for one's offense. It may mean, on the other hand, that one is being attacked by the witchcraft of the living.

What are the ways in which a shade comes to afflict one? They fall roughly into three main types: (1) the shade of a hunter may cause his kinsman to miss his aim, fail to find animals to shoot, or drive animals out of range; (2) the shade of a woman may cause her kinswoman to have various reproductive troubles ranging from sterility to suffering a series of miscarriages; (3) shades of both sexes may cause their living kin of both sexes to become ill in various ways, such as "wasting away," "sweating and shivering," or "pains all over the body," to use Ndembu descriptions of symptoms. To these three modes of affliction correspond three principal kinds of ritual to remove them, which may be described as: hunting cults, fertility cults, and curative cults. The first is performed for men, the second for women, and the third for both sexes. The mode of affliction and the rite to dispel it are both known by the same name. For instance, if a woman suffers from prolonged and painful menstruation she is said to have been "caught by a shade which has come out in *Nkula,*" and the rite to rid her of the shade is also called Nkula. Within each cult are a number of separate rituals, those of the hunting cult being arranged in a graded order while those of the other cults have no fixed order of performance. The afflicting shade in a given ritual is said to have been itself afflicted in the same way while it was alive. Thus, patient, leading "doctor" and lesser "doctors," and the shade itself belong to a single, sacred community consisting of the elect and the candidate for election.

*Hunting Cults*

The high value set on hunting as a male occupation has already been pointed out in connection with boys' initiation where the basic values of the Ndembu people are taught and expressed.

To us, hunting is merely an economic or sporting activity, in which, granted a natural talent in the beginning, skill is increased with practice. The Ndembu do not look on it in this way. A young man receives a "call" to be a great hunter, much as a person has a call to become a missionary in our own society, that is, he receives a message from a supernatural source telling him that he has a vocation. In the case of the Ndembu youth, the message comes in the form of dreams about the shade of a famous hunter relative, accompanied by bad luck at hunting. On consulting a diviner, he learns that the shade wishes him to become a famous hunter and that he must enter the hunters' cult by having the first of its rituals performed for him. From that time forward the same sequence continues—bad luck and dreams followed by ritual to win the favor of the shade, followed in turn by greater success at hunting—until the hunter is acknowledged to be a master of his profession. Huntsmanship may thus be seen as acquirement of increasing supernatural power through successive degrees of initiation into a cult of the hunter shades. This power enables the hunter "to see animals quickly," "to draw them to where he is," and "to become invisible to them" (see pp. 289, 295).

*Women's Fertility Cults*

When I was in Mwinilunga I attended many rituals concerned with women's reproductive disorders and heard of many more. In a sample of nineteen women whose ritual histories I recorded, not one had failed to have such a ritual performed for her and one old woman had been the subject of four separate rituals. Is there any medical basis for these widespread cults connected with reproductive troubles? My evidence is slight but suggestive. Figures supplied to me by the lady doctor at Kalene Mission Hospital in August, 1951, revealed that out of ninety women accepted as normal pregnancy cases, sixteen, or nearly 18 per cent, underwent abnormal deliveries. My wife was asked to assist at half a dozen cases of prolonged childbirth or miscarriages in the villages adjoining our camp in about three months. Many women showed clear signs of anemia and some revealed that they had frequent periodic troubles. It may well be that the modern prevalence of these disorders is associated on the one hand with the shortage of meat and fish in many areas, such as the northwest corner of the district where game has almost disappeared, and on the other with the low protein value of the staple crop, cassava, which has only one-eighth the protein value of millet. Ndembu do not keep cattle and their small stock is not adequate for their meat requirements.

However, although these fertility (or rather contra-infertility) rituals were increasing in the 1950's, most of them seem to have existed in the far past, coming, as Ndembu say, "from Mwantiyanvwa." The theme of affliction crops up again. The woman who has miscarriages, abortions, or an excessive menstrual discharge, or who is sterile, is thought to have offended a shade who comes out of the grave and "sits" in her body until propitiated by one or another of the women's rituals prescribed by a diviner. I found that a woman's mother's mother was by a long way the most frequently offended shade, afflicting women in twelve out of twenty-five cases where I could trace the relationship. After her came a woman's own mother, in five instances, and next her older sister, in two. This seemed significant in view of the fact that women, through whom succession and inheritance are reckoned, go to their husbands' villages after marriage, often far away from their own villages, and may in the course of time cease to remember their older kin on the mother's side who have died. Moreover, when they were young girls they would have spent most of their time in their father's villages where they would have been living with their mothers. Yet, in spite of spending so much of their lives away from their "own" villages, they are still expected to send their sons back to them in the course of time, and if they themselves are divorced or widowed their matrilineal villages are regarded as their sanctuaries until remarriage. It would seem, therefore, that being "caught" by a matrilineal shade serves as a sharp reminder that their own first loyalty is to their matrilineal villages and that they bear children not for their husbands, but for their mother's brothers and brothers "back home." We find that "forgetting" the shade is the usual cause of affliction.

Four rituals are performed for women with reproductive troubles: (1) *Nkula,* when a woman has an excessive flow of blood at menstruation (see below pp. 41–42); (2) *Wubwang'u,* when a woman has had or expects to have twins, or when she seems to be sterile; (3) *Isoma,* when a woman has had a number of stillbirths or abortions; and (4) *Chihamba,* which can be performed for sickness as well as for reproductive disorders and for men as well as women. *Nkula, Wubwang'u* and *Chihamba* can also be performed for ailing children, in which case mother and child are treated together. Often the husband is treated with the wife, "to make him sacred and taboo (*kumbadyi nakwajila*)," for he must eat with her and sleep with her, and intimate contact between sacred and profane persons or things is thought to be dangerous or at the least to nullify the effects of the treatment. Each of these rituals has three well-marked phases: (1) *Ilembi* or *Kulembeka,* consisting of a treatment and dance to make the subjects "sacred"; (2) a period of seclusion, during which they are partially or entirely separated from everyday existence and have to observe certain food taboos; and (3) *Ku-tumbuka,* a further treatment and dance which celebrates the end of seclusion and prepares the patients to enter ordinary life again.

The principal doctor at each ritual is a man, though they are women's rituals. However he must have been made "sacred," either as a brother, child, or husband of a woman undergoing a particular ritual, before he could have been taught the medicines and procedure appropriate to it. Each doctor (*chimbuki* or *chimbanda*) tends to specialize in one or another ritual, although some doctors know the techniques of many. Usually he has a leading woman doctor as assistant and a throng of minor doctors who are women supposed to have been cured by previous rituals of the same type. An initial payment—in the 1950's from 2*s.* 6*d.* to 4*s.*—is made to the male doctor to secure his services; food and beer are given to the women doctors. If a cure is effected and the woman successfully bears children, the doctor is paid 10*s.* or £1, which he may divide among his assistants as he thinks fit. The patient herself and her husband usually provide the money. Holding a ritual is an expensive business in terms of Ndembu wealth. It costs 3*s.* 6*d.* in diviner's fees, over a pound for the doctor, and a great expenditure of cash, time, and labor to provide food and beer for the assistants and the general gathering. In addition, the rules of seclusion often forbid a woman to draw water, work in her cassava gardens, and carry the roots to her kitchen, thus depriving her family of her economic services for several months.

Each separate performance of *Ku-lembeka* and *Ku-tumbuka* has three main stages: (1) the collection of medicines; (2) the construction of a shrine; and (3) a long period of drumming, singing, and dancing, interspersed with treatment of the patient by the doctors, who wash her with medicine, address the afflicting shade at the shrine, and perform various ritualistic actions. The patient usually sits passively before the shrine but may on occasion join the circle of women dancing around her or even dance by herself.

Each type of ritual has its own special drum rhythm, its own "theme song," its own combination of medicines, and its own stylized behavior, expressed in dancing and gestures, and its own type of shrine and ritual apparatus.

Three main categories of people usually take part in these rituals: (1) men and women who have been patients themselves for the particular ritual and hence can act as major or minor doctors (*ayimbuki*), (2) matrilineal and patrilineal kin of the wife and husband patients (the term for "patient" is *muyeji* and is also used for an unlucky hunter who is being treated in a *Wuyang'a* ritual; it really means "a person afflicted by the shade of one of his or her relatives"); and (3) other Ndembu, who may or may not be related to the patients but come to take part in the dancing and drinking, for each ritual, especially the final phase, is the occasion for a public festivity, a general tribal gathering recruited, perhaps, from several distinct chiefdoms. If the headman of the village where the ritual is being performed knows the techniques and medicines, he will act as principal doctor, but the doctor need not necessarily be related to the patients.

As a general rule, membership of the cult gives one a more important role in the ritual than kinship with the patient.

*Curative Cults*

*Chihamba* (Turner 1962a) and *Kalemba* seem to be the only truly indigenous Ndembu cults to cure sickness or disease, unless we include the antiwitchcraft ritual of *Kaneng'a*. Other cults I have seen or heard of, such as *Kayong'u, Tukuka,* and *Masandu,* are of Lwena (Luvale), Luchazi, or Chokwe origin and are characterized by hysterical tremblings, "speaking with tongues" in foreign languages, and other symptoms of dissociation. In these introduced cults the doctor gives medicine to himself as well as to the patient and both give way to paroxysms of quivering, very unpleasant to behold. In *Tukuka* and *Masandu* women play a far more prominent role than in the traditional Ndembu rituals. These two rituals are becoming very popular in northwest Mwinilunga and are often performed for persons suffering from tuberculosis. The shades who cause the disease are said to be those of Europeans or of members of other tribes like the Lwena and part of the treatment consists of giving the patient European foods, served by a "houseboy," miming European dancing in couples, wearing European dress, and singing up-to-date songs such as "We are going in an airplane to Lumwana."

*Kayong'u* (see below pp. 142–145) is often performed for patients with breathing difficulties, and part of the treatment consists in placing the patient under a blanket with a steaming pot of leaf medicines and making him inhale the steam. It is also performed for a person who has dreamed that a shade wishes him to become a diviner.

*Kalemba* is not often seen nowadays, and I have no reliable information about it, except that it was a women's ritual, and a woman dancer-doctor, with her face covered in white clay and carrying a *lwalu* basket containing specimens of all the Ndembu food crops, performed a solo dance.

*Ihamba* is described below (pp. 362–392). Although it appears to be of Lwena-Chokwe origin, it has been incorporated into the *Wuyang'a* hunters' cult. It, too, has become popular in the northwest where there are many villages and little game. It gives nonhunters a kind of vicarious participation in the hunters' cult and illustrates the tenacity with which a people will hold on to their cherished values even when their material basis has gone.

## BIBLIOGRAPHY

Spiro, M. 1965. "Religion: Problems of Definition and Explanation" in *Anthropological Approaches to the Study of Religion*. A. S. A. Monograph No. 3. London: Tavistock Publications.

Turner, V. W. 1957. *Schism and Continuity in an African Society: A Study of Ndembu Village Life*. Manchester University Press.

——. 1962. *Chihamba, the White Spirit* (Rhodes-Livingstone Paper 33). Manchester University Press.

# PART I

## CHAPTER I

# Symbols in Ndembu Ritual*

AMONG the Ndembu of Zambia (formerly Northern Rhodesia), the importance of ritual in the lives of the villagers in 1952 was striking. Hardly a week passed in a small neighborhood, without a ritual drum being heard in one or another of its villages.

By "ritual" I mean prescribed formal behavior for occasions not given over to technological routine, having reference to beliefs in mystical beings or powers. The symbol is the smallest unit of ritual which still retains the specific properties of ritual behavior; it is the ultimate unit of specific structure in a ritual context. Since this essay is in the main a description and analysis of the structure and properties of symbols, it will be enough to state here, following the *Concise Oxford Dictionary*, that a "symbol" is a thing regarded by general consent as naturally typifying or representing or recalling something by possession of analogous qualities or by association in fact or thought. The symbols I observed in the field were, empirically, objects, activities, relationships, events, gestures, and spatial units in a ritual situation.

Following the advice and example of Professor Monica Wilson, I asked Ndembu specialists as well as laymen to interpret the symbols of their ritual. As a result, I obtained much exegetic material. I felt that it was methodologically important to keep observational and

* Read at a meeting of the Association of Social Anthropologists of the Commonwealth in London, March 1958. First published in *Closed Systems and Open Minds: The Limits of Naivety, in Social Science,* M. Gluckman, ed. (Edinburgh: Oliver and Boyd, 1964).

interpretative materials distinct from one another. The reason for this will soon become apparent.

I found that I could not analyze ritual symbols without studying them in a time series in relation to other "events," for symbols are essentially involved in social process. I came to see performances of ritual as distinct phases in the social processes whereby groups became adjusted to internal changes and adapted to their external environment. From this standpoint the ritual symbol becomes a factor in social action, a positive force in an activity field. The symbol becomes associated with human interests, purposes, ends, and means, whether these are explicitly formulated or have to be inferred from the observed behavior. The structure and properties of a symbol become those of a dynamic entity, at least within its appropriate context of action.

## *Structure and Properties of Ritual Symbols*

The structure and properties of ritual symbols may be inferred from three classes of data: (1) external form and observable characteristics; (2) interpretations offered by specialists and by laymen; (3) significant contexts largely worked out by the anthropologist.

Here is an example. At *Nkang'a,* the girl's puberty ritual, a novice is wrapped in a blanket and laid at the foot of a *mudyi* sapling. The *mudyi* tree *Diplorrhyncus condylocarpon* is conspicuous for its white latex, which exudes in milky beads if the thin bark is scratched. For Ndembu this is its most important observable characteristic, and therefore I propose to call it "the milk tree" henceforward. Most Ndembu women can attribute several meanings to this tree. In the first place, they say that the milk tree is the "senior" (*mukulumpi*) tree of the ritual. Each kind of ritual has this "senior" or, as I will call it, "dominant" symbol. Such symbols fall into a special class which I will discuss more fully later. Here it is enough to state that dominant symbols are regarded not merely as means to the fulfillment of the avowed purposes of a given ritual, but also and more importantly refer to values that are regarded as ends in themselves, that is, to axiomatic values. Secondly, the women say with reference to its observable characteristics that the milk tree stands for human breast milk and also for the breasts that supply it. They relate this meaning to the fact that *Nkang'a* is performed when a girl's breasts begin to ripen, not after her first menstruation, which is the subject of another and less elaborate ritual. The main theme of *Nkang'a* is indeed the tie of nurturing between mother and child, not the bond of birth. This theme of nurturing is expressed at *Nkang'a* in a number of supplementary symbols indicative of the act of feeding and of foodstuff. In the third place, the women describe the milk tree as "the tree of a mother and her child." Here the reference has shifted from description of a biological act, breast feeding, to a social tie of profound significance both in domestic relations and in the structure of the widest Ndembu community. This latter meaning is brought out most clearly in a text I recorded from a male ritual specialist. I translate literally.

The milk tree is the place of all mothers of the lineage (*ivumu,* literally "womb" or "stomach"). It represents the ancestress of women and men. The milk tree is where our ancestress slept when she was initiated. "To initiate" here means the dancing of women round and round the milk tree where the novice sleeps. One ancestress after another slept there down to our grandmother and our mother and ourselves the children. That is the place of our tribal custom (*muchidi*),[1] where we began, even men just the same, for men are circumcised under a milk tree.

This text brings out clearly those meanings of the milk tree which refer to principles and values of social organization. At one level of abstraction the milk tree stands for matriliny, the principle on which the continuity of Ndembu society depends. Matriliny governs succession to office and inheritance of property, and it vests dominant rights of residence in local units. More than any other principle of social organization it confers order and structure on Ndembu social life. Beyond this, however, "*mudyi*" means more than matriliny, both according to this text and according to many other statements I have collected. It stands for tribal custom (*muchidi wetu*) itself. The principle of matriliny, the backbone of Ndembu social organization, as an element in the semantic structure of the milk tree, itself symbolizes the total system of interrelations between groups and persons that makes up Ndembu society. Some of the meanings of important symbols may themselves be symbols, each with its own system of meanings. At its highest level of abstraction, therefore, the milk tree stands for the unity and continuity of Ndembu society. Both men and women are components of that spatiotemporal continuum. Perhaps that is why one educated Ndembu, trying to cross the gap between our cultures, explained to me that the milk tree was like the British

[1] *Muchidi* also means "category," "kind," "species," and "tribe" itself.

flag above the administrative headquarters. "*Mudyi* is our flag," he said.

When discussing the milk tree symbolism in the context of the girls' puberty ritual, informants tend to stress the harmonizing, cohesive aspects of the milk tree symbolism. They also stress the aspect of dependence. The child depends on its mother for nutriment; similarly, say the Ndembu, the tribesman drinks from the breasts of tribal custom. Thus nourishment and learning are equated in the meaning content of the milk tree. I have often heard the milk tree compared to "going to school"; the child is said to swallow instruction as a baby swallows milk and *kapudyi*, the thin cassava gruel Ndembu liken to milk. Do we not ourselves speak of "a thirst for knowledge"? Here the milk tree is a shorthand for the process of instruction in tribal matters that follows the critical episode in both boys' and girls' initiation—circumcision in the case of the boys and the long trial of lying motionless in that of the girls. The mother's role is the archetype of protector, nourisher, and teacher. For example, a chief is often referred to as the "mother of his people," while the hunter-doctor who initiates a novice into a hunting cult is called "the mother of huntsmanship (*mama dawuyang'a*)." An apprentice circumciser is referred to as "child of the circumcision medicine" and his instructor as "mother of the circumcision medicine." In all the senses hitherto described, the milk tree represents harmonious, benevolent aspects of domestic and tribal life.

However, when the third mode of interpretation, contextual analysis, is applied, the interpretations of informants are contradicted by the way people actually behave with reference to the milk tree. It becomes clear that the milk tree represents aspects of social differentiation and even opposition between the components of a society which ideally it is supposed to symbolize as a harmonious whole. The first relevant context we shall examine is the role of the milk tree in a series of action situations within the framework of the girls' puberty ritual. Symbols, as I have said, produce action, and dominant symbols tend to become focuses in interaction. Groups mobilize around them, worship before them, perform other symbolic activities near them, and add other symbolic objects to them, often to make composite shrines. Usually these groups of participants themselves stand for important components of the secular social system, whether these components consist of corporate groups, such as families and lineages, or of mere categories of persons possessing similar characteristics, such as old men, women, children, hunters, or widows. In each kind of Ndembu ritual a different group or category becomes the focal social element. In *Nkang'a* this focal element is the unity of Ndembu women. It is the women who dance around the milk tree and initiate the recumbent novice by making her the hub of their whirling circle. Not only is the milk tree the "flag of the Ndembu"; more specifically, in the early phases of *Nkang'a,* it is the "flag" of Ndembu women. In this situation it does more than focus the exclusiveness of women; it mobilizes them in opposition to the men. For the women sing songs taunting the men and for a time will not let men dance in their circle. Therefore, if we are to take account of the operational aspect of the milk tree symbol, including not only what Ndembu say about it but also what they do with it in its "meaning," we must allow that it distinguishes women as a social category and indicates their solidarity.

The milk tree makes further discriminations. For example, in certain action contexts it stands for the novice herself. One such context is the initial sacralization of a specific milk tree sapling. Here the natural property of the tree's immaturity is significant. Informants say that a young tree is chosen because the novice is young. A girl's particular tree symbolizes her new social personality as a mature woman. In the past and occasionally today, the girl's puberty ritual was part of her marriage ritual, and marriage marked her transition from girlhood to womanhood. Much of the training and most of the symbolizm of *Nkang'a* are concerned with making the girl a sexually accomplished spouse, a fruitful woman, and a mother able to produce a generous supply of milk. For each girl this is a unique process. She is initiated alone and is the center of public attention and care. From her point of view it is *her Nkang'a,* the most thrilling and self-gratifying phase of her life. Society recognizes and encourages these sentiments, even though it also prescribes certain trials and hardships for the novice, who must suffer before she is glorified on the last day of the ritual. The milk tree, then, celebrates the coming-of-age of a new social personality, and distinguishes her from all other women at this one moment in her life. In terms of its action context, the milk tree here also expresses the conflict between the girl and the moral community of adult women she is entering. Not without reason is the milk tree site known as "the place of death" or "the place of suffering," terms also applied to the site where boys are circumcised, for the girl novice must not move a muscle throughout a whole hot and clamant day.

In other contexts, the milk tree site is the scene of opposition between the novice's own mother and the group of adult women. The mother is debarred from attending the ring of dancers. She is losing her child, although later she recovers her as an adult co-member of her lineage. Here we see the conflict between the matricentric family and the wider society which, as I have said, is dominantly articulated by the principle of matriliny. The relationship between mother and daughter persists throughout the ritual, but its content is changed. It is worth pointing out that, at one phase in *Nkang'a,* mother and daughter interchange portions of clothing. This may perhaps be related to the Ndembu custom whereby mourners wear small portions of a dead relative's clothing. Whatever the interchange of clothing may mean to a psychoanalyst—and here we arrive at one of the limits of our present anthropological competence—it seems not unlikely that Ndembu intend to symbolize the termination for both mother and daughter of an important aspect of their relationship. This is one of the symbolic actions—one of very few—about which I found it impossible to elicit any interpretation in the puberty ritual. Hence it is legitimate to infer, in my opinion, that powerful unconscious wishes, of a kind considered illicit by Ndembu, are expressed in it.

Opposition between the tribeswomen and the novice's mother is mimetically represented at the milk tree towards the end of the first day of the puberty ritual. The girl's mother cooks a huge meal of cassava and beans—both kinds of food are symbols in *Nkang'a,* with many meanings—for the women visitors, who eat in village groups and not at random. Before eating, the women return to the milk tree from their eating place a few yards away and circle the tree in procession. The mother brings up the rear holding up a large spoon full of cassava and beans. Suddenly she shouts: "Who wants the cassava of *chipwampwilu?*" All the women rush to be first to seize the spoon and eat from it. "*Chipwampwilu*" appears to be an archaic word and no one knows its meaning. Informants say that the spoon represents the novice herself in her role of married woman, while the food stands both for her reproductive power (*lusemu*) and her role as cultivator and cook. One woman told my wife: "It is lucky if the person snatching the spoon comes from the novice's own village. Otherwise, the mother believes that her child will go far away from her to a distant village and die there. The mother wants her child to stay near her." Implicit in this statement is a deeper conflict than that between the matricentric family and mature female society. It refers to another dominant articulating principle of Ndembu society, namely virilocal marriage according to which women live at their husbands' villages after marriage. Its effect is sometimes to separate mothers from daughters by considerable distances. In the episode described, the women symbolize the matrilineal cores of villages. Each village wishes to gain control through marriage over the novice's capacity to work. Its members also hope that her children will be raised in it, thus adding to its size and prestige. Later in *Nkang'a* there is a symbolic struggle between the novice's matrilineal kin and those of her bridegroom, which makes explicit the conflict between virilocality and matriliny.

Lastly, in the context of action situation, the milk tree is sometimes described by informants as representing the novice's own matrilineage. Indeed, it has this significance in the competition for the spoon just discussed, for women of her own village try to snatch the spoon before members of other villages. Even if such women do not belong to her matrilineage but are married to its male members, they are thought to be acting on its behalf. Thus, the milk tree in one of its action aspects represents the unity and exclusiveness of a single matrilineage with a local focus in a village against other such corporate groups. The conflict between yet another subsystem and the total system is given dramatic and symbolic form.

By this time, it will have become clear that considerable discrepancy exists between the interpretations of the milk tree offered by informants and the behavior exhibited by Ndembu in situations dominated by the milk tree symbolism. Thus, we are told that the milk tree represents the close tie between mother and daughter. Yet the milk tree separates a daughter from her mother. We are also told that the milk tree stands for the unity of Ndembu society. Yet we find that in practice it separates women from men, and some categories and groups of women from others. How are these contradictions between principle and practice to be explained?

## *Some Problems of Interpretation*

I am convinced that my informants genuinely believed that the milk tree represented only the linking and unifying aspects of Ndembu social organization. I am equally convinced that the role of the milk tree in action situations, where it represents a focus of specified groups in opposition to other groups, forms an equally important component of its total meaning. Here the important question must be asked, "meaning for whom?" For if Ndembu do not recognize the discrepancy between their interpretation of the milk tree symbolism and their behavior in connection with it, does this mean that the discrepancy has no relevance for the social anthropologist? Indeed, some anthropologists claim, with Nadel (1954, 108), that "uncomprehended symbols have no part in social enquiry; their social effectiveness lies in their capacity to indicate, and if they indicate nothing to the actors, they are, from our point of view, irrelevant, and indeed no longer symbols (whatever their significance for the psychologist or psychoanalyst)." Professor Monica Wilson (1957, 6) holds a similar point of view. She writes that she stresses "Nyakyusa interpretations of their own rituals, for anthropological literature is bespattered with symbolic guessing, the ethnographer's interpretations of the rituals of other people." Indeed, she goes so far as to base her whole analysis of Nyakyusa ritual on "the Nyakyusa translation or interpretation of the symbolism." In my view, these investigators go beyond the limits of salutary caution and impose serious, and even arbitrary, limitations on themselves. To some extent, their difficulties derive from their failure to distinguish the concept of symbol from that of a mere sign. Although I am in complete disagreement with his fundamental postulate that the collective unconscious is the main formative principle in ritual symbolism, I consider that Carl Jung (1949, 601) has cleared the way for further investigation by making just this distinction. "A sign," he says, "is an analogous or abbreviated expression of a *known* thing. But a symbol is always the best possible expression of a relatively *unknown* fact, a fact, however, which is none the less recognized or postulated as existing." Nadel and Wilson, in treating most ritual symbols as signs, must ignore or regard as irrelevant some of the crucial properties of such symbols.

## *Field Setting and Structural Perspective*

How, then, can a social anthropologist justify his claim to be able to interpret a society's ritual symbols more deeply and comprehensively than the actors themselves? In the first place, the anthropologist, by the use of his special techniques and concepts, is able to view the performance of a given kind of ritual as "occurring in, and being interpenetrated by, a totality of coexisting social entities such as various kinds of groups, sub-groups, categories, or personalities, and also barriers between them, and modes of interconnexion" (Lewin 1949, 200). In other words, he can place this ritual in its significant field setting and describe the structure and properties of that field. On the other hand, each participant in the ritual views it from his own particular corner of observation. He has what Lupton has called his own "structural perspective." His vision is circumscribed by his occupancy of a particular position, or even of a set of situationally conflicting positions, both in the persisting structure of his society, and also in the rôle structure of the given ritual. Moreover, the participant is likely to be governed in his actions by a number of interests, purposes, and sentiments, dependent upon his specific position, which impair his understanding of the total situation. An even more serious obstacle against his achieving objectivity is the fact that he tends to regard as axiomatic and primary the ideals, values, and norms that are overtly expressed or symbolized in the ritual. Thus, in the *Nkang'a* ritual, each person or group in successive contexts of action, sees the milk tree only as representing her or their own specific interests and values at those times. However, the anthropologist who has previously made a structural analysis of Ndembu society, isolating its organizational principles, and distinguishing its groups and relationships, has no particular bias and can observe the real interconnections and conflicts between groups and persons, in so far as these receive ritual representation. What is meaningless for an actor playing a specific role may well be highly significant for an observer and analyst of the total system.

On these grounds, therefore, I consider it legitimate to include within the total meaning of a dominant ritual symbol, aspects of behavior associated with it which the actors themselves are unable to interpret, and indeed of which they may be unaware, if they are asked to interpret the symbol outside its activity context. Nevertheless, there still remains for us the problem of the contradiction between the expressed meanings of the milk tree symbol and the meaning of the stereotyped forms of behavior closely associated with it. Indigenous interpretations of the milk tree symbolism in the abstract appear to indicate that there is no incompatibility or conflict between the persons and groups to which it refers. Yet, as we have seen, it is between just such groups that conflict is mimed at the milk tree site.

## *Three Properties of Ritual Symbols*

Before we can interpret, we must further classify our descriptive data, collected by the methods described above. Such a classification will enable us to state some of the properties of ritual symbols. The simplest property is that of *condensation*. Many things and actions are represented in a single formation. Secondly, a dominant symbol is a *unification of disparate significata*. The disparate *significata* are interconnected by virtue of their common possession of analogous qualities or by association in fact or thought. Such qualities or links of association may in themselves be quite trivial or random or widely distributed over a range of phenomena. Their very generality enables them to bracket together the most diverse ideas and phenomena. Thus, as we have seen, the milk tree stands for, *inter alia,* women's breasts, motherhood, a novice at *Nkang'a,* the principle of matriliny, a specific matrilineage, learning, and the unity and persistence of Ndembu society. The themes of nourishment and dependence run through all these diverse *significata*.

The third important property of dominant ritual symbols is *polarization of meaning*. Not only the milk tree but all other dominant Ndembu symbols possess two clearly distinguishable poles of meaning. At one pole is found a cluster of *significata* that refer to components of the moral and social orders of Ndembu society, to principles of social organization, to kinds of corporate grouping, and to the norms and values inherent in structural relationships. At the other pole, the *significata* are usually natural and physiological phenomena and processes. Let us call the first of these the "ideological pole," and the second the "sensory pole." At the sensory pole, the meaning content is closely related to the outward form of the symbol. Thus one meaning of the milk tree—breast milk—is closely related to the exudation of milky latex from the tree. One sensory meaning of another dominant symbol, the *mukula* tree, is blood; this tree secretes a dusky red gum.

At the sensory pole are concentrated those *significata* that may be expected to arouse desires and feelings; at the ideological pole one finds an arrangement of norms and values that guide and control persons as members of social groups and categories. The sensory, emotional *significata* tend to be "gross" in a double sense. In the first place, they are gross in a general way, taking no account of detail or the precise qualities of emotion. It cannot be sufficiently stressed that such symbols are social facts, "collective representations," even though their appeal is to the lowest common denominator of human feeling. The second sense of "gross" is "frankly, even flagrantly, physiological." Thus, the milk tree has the gross meanings of breast milk, breasts, and the process of breast feeding. These are also gross in the sense that they represent items of universal Ndembu experience. Other Ndembu symbols, at their sensory poles of meaning, represent such themes as blood, male and female genitalia, semen, urine, and feces. The same symbols, at their ideological poles of meaning, represent the unity and continuity of social groups, primary and associational, domestic, and political.

## *Reference and Condensation*

It has long been recognized in anthropological literature that ritual symbols are stimuli of emotion. Perhaps the most striking statement of this position is that made by Edward Sapir in the *Encyclopaedia of the Social Sciences* (XIV, 492–493). Sapir distinguishes, in a way which recalls Jung's distinction, between two principal classes of symbols. The first he calls "referential" symbols. These include such forms as oral speech, writing, national flags, flag signaling, and other organizations of symbols which are agreed upon as economical devices for purposes of reference. Like Jung's "sign," the referential symbol is predominantly cognitive and refers to known facts. The second class, which includes most ritual symbols, consist of "condensation" symbols, which Sapir defines as "highly condensed forms of substitutive behavior for direct expression, allowing for the ready release of emotional tension in conscious or unconscious form." The condensation symbol is "saturated with emotional quality." The chief difference in development between these types of symbolism, in Sapir's view, is that "while referential symbolism grows with formal elaboration in the conscious, condensation symbolism strikes deeper and deeper roots in the unconscious, and diffuses its emotional quality to types of behavior and situations apparently far removed from the original meaning of the symbol."

Sapir's formulation is most illuminating. He lays explicit stress on four main attributes of ritual symbols: (1) the condensation of many meanings in a single form; (2) economy of reference; (3) predominance of emotional or orectic quality; (4) associational linkages with regions of the unconscious. Nevertheless, he tends to underestimate the importance of what I have called the ideological (or, I would add, normative) pole of meaning. Ritual symbols are at one and the same time referential and condensation symbols, though each symbol is multireferential rather than unireferential. Their essential quality consists in their juxtaposition of the grossly physical and the structurally normative, of the organic and the social. Such symbols are coincidences of opposite qualities, unions of "high" and "low." We do not need a detailed acquaintance with any of the current depth psychologies to suspect that this juxtaposition, and even interpenetration, of opposites in the symbol is connected with its social function. Durkheim was fascinated by the problem of why many social norms and imperatives were felt to be at the same time "obligatory" and "desirable." Ritual, scholars are coming to see, is precisely a mechanism that periodically converts the obligatory into the desirable. The basic unit of ritual, the dominant symbol, encapsulates the major properties of the total ritual process which brings about this transmutation. Within its framework of meanings, the dominant symbol brings the ethical and jural norms of society into close contact with strong emotional stimuli. In the action situation of ritual, with its social excitement and directly physiological stimuli, such as music, singing, dancing, alcohol, incense, and bizarre modes of dress, the ritual symbol, we may perhaps say, effects an interchange of qualities between its poles of meaning. Norms and values, on the one hand, become saturated with emotion, while the gross and basic emotions become ennobled through contact with social values. The irksomeness of moral constraint is transformed into the "love of virtue."

Before proceeding any further with our analysis, it might be as well to restate the major empirical properties of dominant symbols derived from our classification of the relevant descriptive data: (1) condensation; (2) unification of disparate meanings in a single symbolic formation; (3) polarization of meaning.

## *Dominant and Instrumental Symbols*

Certain ritual symbols, as I have said, are regarded by Ndembu as dominant. In rituals performed to propitiate ancestor spirits who are believed to have afflicted their living kin with reproductive disorders, illness, or bad luck at hunting, there are two main classes of dominant symbols. The first class is represented by the first tree or plant in a series of trees or plants from which portions of leaves, bark, or roots are collected by practitioners or adepts in the curative cult. The subjects of ritual are marked with these portions mixed with water, or given them, mixed in a potion, to drink. The first tree so treated is called the "place of greeting" (*ishikenu*), or the "elder" (*mukulumpi*). The adepts encircle it several times to sacralize it. Then the senior practitioner prays at its base, which he sprinkles with powdered white clay. Prayer is made either to the named spirit, believed to be afflicting the principal subject of ritual, or to the tree itself, which is in some way identified with the afflicting spirit. Each *ishikenu* can be allotted several meanings by adepts. The second class of dominant symbols in curative rituals consists of shrines where the subjects of such rituals sit while the practitioners wash them with vegetable substances mixed with water and perform actions on their behalf of a symbolic or ritualistic nature. Such shrines are often composite, consisting of several objects in configuration. Both classes of dominant symbols are closely associated with nonempirical beings. Some are regarded as their repositories; others, as being identified with them; others again, as representing them. In life-crisis rituals, on the other hand, dominant symbols seem to represent not beings but nonempirical powers or kinds of efficacy. For example, in the boys' circumcision ritual, the dominant symbol for the whole ritual is a "medicine" (*yitumbu*), called *"nfunda,"* which is compounded from many ingredients, e.g., the ash of the burnt lodge which means "death," and the urine of an apprentice circumciser which means "virility." Each of these and other ingredients have many other meanings. The dominant symbol at the camp where the novices' parents assemble and prepare food for the boys is the *chikoli* tree, which represents, among other things, an erect phallus, adult masculinity, strength, hunting prowess, and health continuing into old age. The dominant symbol during the process of circumcision is the milk tree, beneath which novices are circumcised. The dominant symbol in the immediate post-circumcision phase is the red *mukula* tree, on which the novices sit until their wounds stop bleeding. Other symbols are dominant at various phases of seclusion. Each of these symbols is described as *"mukulumpi"* (elder, senior). Dominant symbols appear in many different ritual contexts, sometimes presiding over the whole procedure, sometimes over particular phases. The meaning-content of certain dominant symbols possesses a high degree of constancy and consistency throughout the total symbolic system, exemplifying Radcliffe-Brown's proposition that a symbol recurring in a cycle of rituals is likely to have the same significance in each. Such symbols also possess considerable autonomy with regard to the aims of the rituals in which they appear. Precisely because of these properties, dominant symbols are readily analyzable in a cultural framework of reference. They may be regarded for this purpose as what Whitehead would have called "eternal objects." [2] They are the relatively fixed points

[2] I.e., objects not of indefinite duration but to which the category of time is not applicable.

in both the social and cultural structures, and indeed constitute points of junction between these two kinds of structure. They may be regarded irrespective of their order of appearance in a given ritual as ends in themselves, as representative of the axiomatic values of the widest Ndembu society. This does not mean that they cannot also be studied, as we have indeed studied them, as factors of social action, in an action frame of reference, but their social properties make them more appropriate objects of morphological study than the class of symbols we will now consider.

These symbols may be termed "instrumental symbols." An instrumental symbol must be seen in terms of its wider context, i.e., in terms of the total system of symbols which makes up a given kind of ritual. Each kind of ritual has its specific mode of interrelating symbols. This mode is often dependent upon the ostensible purposes of that kind of ritual. In other words, each ritual has its own teleology. It has its explicitly expressed goals, and instrumental symbols may be regarded as means of attaining those goals. For example, in rituals performed for the overt purpose of making women fruitful, among the instrumental symbols used are portions of fruit-bearing trees or of trees that possess innumerable rootlets. These fruits and rootlets are said by Ndembu to represent children. They are also thought of as having efficacy to make the woman fruitful. They are means to the main end of the ritual. Perhaps such symbols could be regarded as mere signs or referential symbols, were it not for the fact that the meanings of each are associated with powerful conscious and unconscious emotions and wishes. At the psychological level of analysis, I suspect that these symbols too would approximate to the condition of condensation symbols, but here we touch upon the present limits of competence of anthropological explanation, a problem we will now discuss more fully.

## *The Limits of Anthropological Interpretation*

We now come to the most difficult aspect of the scientific study of ritual symbolism: analysis. How far can we interpret these enigmatic formations by the use of anthropological concepts? At what points do we reach the frontiers of our explanatory competence? Let us first consider the case of dominant symbols. I have suggested that these have two poles of meaning, a sensory and an ideological pole. I have also suggested that dominant symbols have the property of unifying disparate *significata*. I would go so far as to say that at both poles of meaning are clustered disparate and even contradictory *significata.* In the course of its historical development, anthropology has acquired techniques and concepts that enable it to handle fairly adequately the kind of data we have classified as falling around the ideological pole. Such data, as we have seen, include components of social structure and cultural phenomena, both ideological and technological. I believe that study of these data in terms of the concepts of three major subdivisions of anthropology—cultural anthropology, structuralist theory, and social dynamics—would be extremely rewarding. I shall shortly outline how I think such analyses might be done and how the three frameworks might be interrelated, but first we must ask how far and in what respects is it relevant to submit the sensory pole of meaning to intensive analysis, and, more importantly, how far are we, as anthropologists, qualified to do so? It is evident, as Sapir has stated, that ritual symbols, like all condensation symbols, "strike deeper and deeper roots in the unconscious." Even a brief acquaintance with depth psychology is enough to show the investigator that ritual symbols, with regard to their outward form, to their behavioral context, and to several of the indigenous interpretations set upon them, are partially shaped under the influence of unconscious motivations and ideas. The interchange of clothes between mother and daughter at the *Nkang'a* ritual; the belief that a novice would go mad if she saw the milk tree on the day of her separation ritual; the belief that if a novice lifts up the blanket with which she is covered during seclusion and sees her village her mother would die; all these are items of symbolic behavior for which the Ndembu themselves can give no satisfactory interpretation. For these beliefs suggest an element of mutual hostility in the mother-daughter relationship which runs counter to orthodox interpretations of the milk tree symbolism, in so far as it refers to the mother-daughter relationship. One of the main characteristics of ideological interpretations is that they tend to stress the harmonious and cohesive aspect of social relationships. The exegetic idiom feigns that persons and groups always act in accordance with the ideal norms of Ndembu society.

## *Depth Psychology and Ritual Symbolism*

When psychoanalysts like Theodore Reik, Ernest Jones, or Bruno Bettelheim analyze the ritual symbolism of primitive and ancient society, they tend to regard as irrelevant the ideological pole of meaning and to focus their attention on the outward form and sensory meanings of the symbols. They regard most indigenous interpretations of symbols, which form the main component of the ideological pole, almost as though they were identical with the rationalizations by which neurotics explain and justify their aberrant behavior. Furthermore, they tend to look upon ritual symbols as identical with neurotic and psychotic symptoms or as though they had the same properties as the dream symbols of Western European individuals. In effect, their procedure is the exact reverse of that of the social anthropologists who share the views of Nadel and Wilson. This school of anthropologists, it will be remembered, considers that only conscious, verbalized, indigenous interpretations of symbols are sociologically relevant. The method of the psychoanalysts, on the other hand, is to examine the form, content, and mode of interconnection of the symbolic acts and objects described by ethnographers, and to interpret these by means of concepts formulated in Western European clinical practice. Such psychoanalysts claim to recognize, in the structure and action context of ritual symbols material derived from what they consider to be the universal experiences of human infancy in the family situation. For example, Fenichel (1946, 302) states that two contrary psychic tendencies exist universally in the father-son relationship, namely submission and rebellion, and that both derive from the Oedipus complex. He then goes on to argue that

> since most patriarchal religions also veer between submission to a paternal figure, and rebellion (both submission and rebellion being sexualised), and every god, like a compulsive super-ego, promises protection on condition of submission, there are many similarities in the manifest picture of compulsive ceremonials and religious rituals, due to the similarity of the underlying conflicts.

As against this point of view, we have already shown how the successive symbolic acts of many Ndembu rituals are given order and structure by the explicitly stated purposes of those rituals. We do not need to invoke the nation of underlying conflicts to account for their conspicuous regularity. Psychoanalysts might argue that in patriarchal societies ritual might exhibit a greater rigidity and compulsive quality than among the Ndembu, who are matrilineal. In other words, the formal pattern might be "over-determined" by the unconscious father-son conflict. Ethnographic comparison would seem to refute this view, for the most rigid formalism known to students of comparative religion is found among the Pueblo Indians, who are more strongly matrilineal than the Ndembu, while the Nigerian Nupe, a strongly patrilineal society, possess rituals with a "fluid" and "not over-strict" form (Nadel 1954, 101).[3]

Other psychoanalysts profess to find in symbolic forms traces of orally aggressive, orally dependent, anal-sadistic, and masochistic ideas and drives. Indeed, several anthropologists, after reading psychoanalytical literature, have been tempted to explain ritual phenomena in this way.

Perhaps the most spectacular recent attempt to make a comprehensive interpretation of ritual symbolism by using psychoanalytical concepts is Bruno Bettelheim's book *Symbolic Wounds*. Bettelheim, after observing the behavior of four schizoid adolescent children who formed a secret society, considered that in this behavior lay the clue to an understanding of many features of primitive initiation ritual. From his schizoids, he inferred that one of the (unconscious) purposes of male initiation rites may be to assert that men too can bear children and that "through such operations as subincision men may try to acquire sexual apparatus and functions equal to women's" (1954, 105-123). Womb-envy and an unconscious infantile identification with the mother, in Bettelheim's opinion, were powerful formative factors, both in the *ad hoc* ritual of his four schizoids and in male circumcision rituals all over the world.

Bettelheim's viewpoint is in important respects opposed to that of many orthodox Freudians, who hold that the symbolic events comprising these rituals result principally from the fathers' jealousy of their sons and that their purpose is to create sexual (castration) anxiety and to make the incest taboo secure. Where psychoanalysts disagree, by what criterion can the hapless social anthropologist judge between their interpretations, in a field of inquiry in which he has neither received systematic training nor obtained thorough practical experience?

## *Provinces of Explanation*

I consider that if we conceptualize a dominant symbol as having two poles of meaning, we can more exactly demarcate the limits within which anthropological analysis may be fruitfully applied. Psychoanalysts, in treating most indigenous interpretations of symbols as irrelevant, are guilty of a naïve and one-sided approach. For those

[3] Nadel writes: "We might call the very fluidity of the formalism part of the typical form of Nupe ritual."

interpretations that show how a dominant symbol expresses important components of the social and moral orders are by no means equivalent to the "rationalizations," and the "secondary elaborations" of material deriving from endopsychic conflicts. They refer to social facts that have an empirical reality exterior to the psyches of individuals. On the other hand, those anthropologists who regard only indigenous interpretations as relevant, are being equally one-sided. This is because they tend to examine symbols within two analytical frameworks only, the cultural and the structural. This approach is essentially a static one, and it does not deal with processes involving temporal changes in social relations.

Nevertheless, the crucial properties of a ritual symbol involve these dynamic developments. Symbols instigate social action. In a field context they may even be described as "forces," in that they are determinable influences inclining persons and groups to action. It is in a field context, moreover, that the properties we have described, namely, polarization of meanings, transference of affectual quality, discrepancy between meanings, and condensations of meanings, become most significant. The symbol as a unit of action, possessing these properties, becomes an object of study both for anthropology and for psychology. Both disciplines, in so far as they are concerned with human actions must conceptualize the ritual symbol in the same way.

The techniques and concepts of the anthropologist enable him to analyze competently the interrelations between the data associated with the ideological pole of meaning. They also enable him to analyze the social behavior directed upon the total dominant symbol. He cannot, however, with his present skills, discriminate between the precise sources of unconscious feeling and wishing, which shape much of the outward form of the symbol; select some natural objects rather than others to serve as symbols; and account for certain aspects of the behavior associated with symbols. For him, it is enough that the symbol should evoke emotion. He is interested in the fact that emotion is evoked and not in the specific qualities of its constituents. He may indeed find it situationally relevant for his analysis to distinguish whether the emotion evoked by a specific symbol possesses the gross character, say, of aggression, fear, friendliness, anxiety, or sexual pleasure, but he need go no further than this. For him the ritual symbol is primarily a factor in group dynamics, and, as such, its references to the groups, relationships, values, norms, and beliefs of a society are his principal items of study. In other words, the anthropologist treats the sensory pole of meaning as a constant, and the social and ideological aspects as variables whose interdependencies he seeks to explain.

The psychoanalyst, on the other hand, must, I think, attach greater significance than he now does to social factors in the analysis of ritual symbolism. He must cease to regard interpretations, beliefs, and dogmas as mere rationalizations when, often enough, these refer to social and natural realities. For, as Durkheim wrote (1954, 2–3), "primitive religions hold to reality and express it. One must learn to go underneath the symbol to the reality which it represents and which gives it its meaning. No religions are false, all answer, though in different ways, to the given conditions of human existence." Among those given conditions, the arrangement of society into structured groupings, discrepancies between the principles that organize these groupings, economic collaboration and competition, schism within groups and opposition between groups—in short, all those things with which the social aspect of ritual symbolism is concerned—are surely of at least equal importance with biopsychical drives and early conditioning in the elementary family. After all, the ritual symbol has, in common with the dream symbol, the characteristic, discovered by Freud, of being a compromise formation between two main opposing tendencies. It is a compromise between the need for social control, and certain innate and universal human drives whose complete gratification would result in a breakdown of that control. Ritual symbols refer to what is normative, general, and characteristic of unique individuals. Thus, Ndembu symbols refer among other things, to the basic needs of social existence (hunting, agriculture, female fertility, favourable climatic conditions, and so forth), and to shared values on which communal life depends (generosity, comradeship, respect for elders, the importance of kinship, hospitality, and the like). In distinguishing between ritual symbols and individual psychic symbols, we may perhaps say that while ritual symbols are gross means of handling social and natural reality, psychic symbols are dominantly fashioned under the influence of inner drives. In analyzing the former, attention must mainly be paid to relations between data external to the pysche; in analyzing the latter, to endopsychic data.

For this reason, the study of ritual symbolism falls more within the province of the social anthropologist than that of the psychologist or psychoanalyst, although the latter can assist the anthropologist by examining the nature and interconnections of the data clustered at the sensory pole of ritual symbolism. He can also, I believe, illuminate certain aspects of the stereotyped behavior associated with symbols in field contexts, which the actors themselves are unable to explain. For, as we have seen, much of this behavior is suggestive of attitudes that differ radically from those deemed appropriate in terms of traditional exegesis. Indeed, certain conflicts would appear to be so basic that they totally block exegesis.

## *The Interpretation of Observed Emotions*

Can we really say that behavior portraying conflict between persons and groups, who are represented by the symbols themselves as being in harmony, is in the full Freudian sense unconscious behavior? The Ndembu themselves in many situations outside *Nkang'a,* both secular and ritual, are perfectly aware of and ready to speak about hostility in the relationships between particular mothers and daughters, between particular sublineages, and between particular young girls and the adult women in their villages. It is rather as though there existed in certain precisely defined public situations, usually of a ritual or ceremonial type, a norm obstructing the verbal statement of conflicts in any way connected with the principle and rules celebrated or dramatized in those situations. Evidences of human passion and frailty are just not spoken about when the occasion is given up to the public commemoration and reanimation of norms and values in their abstract purity.

Yet, as we have seen, recurrent kinds of conflict may be acted out in the ritual or ceremonial form. On great ritual occasions, common practice, as well as highest principle, receives its symbolic or stereotyped expression, but practice, which is dominantly under the sway of what all societies consider man's "lower nature," is rife with expressions of conflict. Selfish and factional interests, oath breaking, disloyalty, sins of omission as well as sins of commission, pollute and disfigure those ideal prototypes of behavior which in precept, prayer, formula, and symbol are held up before the ritual assembly for its exclusive attention. In the orthodox interpretation of ritual it is pretended that common practice has no efficacy and that men and women really are as they ideally should be. Yet, as I have argued above, the "energy" required to reanimate the values and norms enshrined in dominant symbols and expressed in various kinds of verbal behavior is "borrowed," to speak metaphorically in lieu at the moment of a more rigorous language, from the miming of well-known and normally mentionable conflicts. The raw energies of conflict are domesticated into the service of social order.

I should say here that I believe it possible, and indeed necessary, to analyze symbols in a context of observed emotions. If the investigator is well acquainted with the common idiom in which a society expresses such emotions as friendship, love, hate, joy, sorrow, contentment, and fear, he cannot fail to observe that these are experienced in ritual situations. Thus, in *Nkang'a* when the women laugh and jeer at the men, tease the novice and her mother, fight one another for the "porridge of *chipwampwilu,*" and so on, the observer can hardly doubt that emotions are really aroused in the actors as well as formally represented by ritual custom. ("What's Hecuba to him or he to Hecuba, that he should weep for her?")

These emotions are portrayed and evoked in close relation to the dominant symbols of tribal cohesion and continuity, often by the performance of instrumentally symbolic behavior. However, since they are often associated with the mimesis of interpersonal and intergroup conflict, such emotions and acts of behavior obtain no place among the official, verbal meanings attributed to such dominant symbols.

### *The Situational Suppression of Conflict from Interpretation*

Emotion and praxis, indeed, give life and coloring to the values and norms, but the connection between the behavioral expression of conflict and the normative components of each kind of ritual, and of its dominant symbols, is seldom explicitly formulated by believing actors. Only if one were to personify a society, regarding it as some kind of supra-individual entity, could one speak of "unconsciousness" here. Each individual participant in the *Nkang'a* ritual is well aware that kin quarrel most bitterly over rights and obligations conferred by the principle of matriliny, but that awareness is situationally held back from verbal expression: the participants must behave as if conflicts generated by matriliny were irrelevant.

This does not mean, as Nadel considers, that what is not verbalized is in fact irrelevant either to the participants or to the anthropologist. On the contrary, in so far as the anthropologist considers problems of social action to fall within his purview, the suppression from speech of what might be termed "the behavioral meaning" of certain dominant symbols is highly relevant. The fact is that any kind of coherent, organized social life would be impossible without the assumption that certain values and norms, imperatives and prohibitions, are axiomatic in character, ultimately binding on everyone. However, for many reasons, the axiomatic quality of these norms is difficult to maintain in practice, since in the endless variety of real situations, norms considered equally valid in abstraction are frequently found to be inconsistent with one another, and even mutually to conflict.

Furthermore, social norms, by their very nature, impose unnatural constraints on those whose biopsychical dispositions impel them to supranormal or abnormal behavior, either fitfully or regularly. Social life in all organized groups appears to exhibit a cycle or oscillation between periods when one set of axiomatic norms is observed and periods dominated by another set. Thus, since different norms govern different aspects or sectors of social behavior, and, more importantly, since the sectors overlap and interpenetrate in reality, causing norm-conflict, the validity of several major norms has to be reaffirmed in isolation from others and outside the contexts in which struggles and conflicts arise in connection with them. This is why one so often finds in ritual that dogmatic and symbolic emphasis is laid on a single norm or on a cluster of closely, and on the whole harmoniously, interrelated norms in a single kind of ritual.

Yet, since at major gatherings of this sort, people assemble not as aggregates of individuals but as social personalities arrayed and organized by many principles and norms of grouping, it is by no means a simple matter to assert the clear situational paramountcy of the norms to be commemorated and extolled. Thus, in the Ndembu boys' circumcision ritual, relationships between social categories, such as men and women, old men and young men, circumcised and uncircumcised, and the norms governing such relationships, are given formal representation, but the members of the ritual assembly come as members of corporate groups, such as villages and lineages, which in secular life are in rivalry with one another. That this rivalry is not mysteriously and wonderfully dispelled by the circumcision ritual becomes abundantly clear from the number of quarrels and fights that can be observed during public dances and beer drinks in the intervals between phases of the ritual proper. Here people quarrel as members of groupings that are not recognized in the formal structure of the ritual.

It may be said that any major ritual that stresses the importance of a single principle of social organization only does so by blocking the expression of other important principles. Sometimes the submerged principles, and the norms and customs through which they become effective, are given veiled and disguised representation in the symbolic pattern of the ritual; sometimes, as in the boys' circumcision ritual, they break through to expression in the spatial and temporal interstices of the procedure. In this essay we are concerned principally with the effects of the suppression on the meaning-structure of dominant symbols.

For example, in the frequently performed *Nkula* ritual, the dominant symbols are a cluster of red objects, notably red clay (*mukundu*) and the *mukula* tree mentioned previously. In the context of *Nkula*, both of these are said to represent menstrual blood and the "blood of birth," which is the blood that accompanies the birth of a child. The ostensible goal of the ritual is to coagulate the patient's menstrual blood, which has been flowing away in menorrhagia, around the fetus in order to nourish it. A series of symbolic acts are performed to attain this end. For example, a young *mukula* tree is cut down by male doctors and part of it is carved into the shape of a baby, which is then inserted into a round calabash medicated with the blood of a sacrificed cock, with red clay, and with a number of other red ingredients. The red medicines here, say the Ndembu, represent desired coagulation of the patient's menstrual blood, and the calabash is a symbolic womb. At the ideological pole of meaning, the *mukula* tree and the medicated calabash both represent (as the milk tree does) the patient's matrilineage and, at a higher level of abstraction, the principle of matriliny itself. This is also consistent with the fact that *ivumu*, the term for "womb," also means "matrilineage." In this symbolism the procreative, rather than the nutritive, aspect of motherhood is stressed. However, Ndembu red symbolism, unlike the white symbolism of which the milk tree symbolism is a species, nearly always has explicit reference to violence, to killing, and, at its most general level of meaning, to breach, both in the social and natural orders. Although informants, when discussing this *Nkula* ritual specifically, tend to stress the positive, feminine aspects of parturition and reproduction, other meanings of the red symbols, stated explicitly in other ritual contexts, can be shown to make their influence felt in *Nkula*. For example, both red clay and the *mukula* tree are dominant symbols in the hunter's cult, where they mean the blood of animals, the red meat of game, the inheritance through either parent of hunting prowess, and the unity of all initiated hunters. It also stands for the hunter's power to kill. The same red symbols, in the context of the

*Wubanji* ritual performed to purify a man who has killed a kinsman or a lion or leopard (animals believed to be reincarnated hunter kin of the living), represent the blood of homicide. Again, in the boys' circumcision ritual, these symbols stand for the blood of circumcised boys. More seriously still, in divination and in antiwitchcraft rituals, they stand for the blood of witches' victims, which is exposed in necrophagous feasts.

Most of these meanings are implicit in *Nkula*. For example, the female patient, dressed in skins like a male hunter and carrying a bow and arrow, at one phase of the ritual performs a special hunter's dance. Moreover, while she does this, she wears in her hair, just above the brow, the red feather of a lourie bird. Only shedders of blood, such as hunters, man-slayers, and circumcisers, are customarily entitled to wear this feather. Again, after the patient has been given the baby figurine in its symbolic womb, she dances with it in a style of dancing peculiar to circumcisers when they brandish aloft the great *nfunda* medicine of the circumcision lodge. Why then is the woman patient identified with male bloodspillers? The field context of these symbolic objects and items of behavior suggests that the Ndembu feel that the woman, in wasting her menstrual blood and in failing to bear children, is actively renouncing her expected role as a mature married female. She is behaving like a male killer, not like a female nourisher. The situation is analogous, though modified by matriliny, to the following pronouncement in the ancient Jewish Code of Qaro: "Every man is bound to marry a wife in order to beget children, and he who fails of this duty is as one who sheds blood."

One does not need to be a psychoanalyst, one only needs sound sociological training, acquaintance with the total Ndembu symbolic system, plus ordinary common sense, to see that one of the aims of the ritual it to make the woman accept her lot in life as a childbearer and rearer of children for her lineage.The symbolism suggests that the patient is unconsciously rejecting her female role, that indeed she is guilty; indeed, "*mbayi*," one term for menstrual blood, is etymologically connected with "*ku-baya*" (to be guilty). I have not time here to present further evidence of symbols and interpretations, both in *Nkula* and in cognate rituals, which reinforce this explanation. In the situation of *Nkula*, the dominant principles celebrated and reanimated are those of matriliny, the mother-child bond, and tribal continuity through matriliny. The norms in which these are expressed are those governing the behavior of mature women, which ascribe to them the role appropriate to their sex. The suppressed or submerged principles and norms, in this situation, concern and control the personal and corporate behavior deemed appropriate for man.

The analysis of *Nkula* symbolism throws into relief another major function of ritual. Ritual adapts and periodically readapts the biopsychical individual to the basic conditions and axiomatic values of human social life. In redressive rituals, the category to which *Nkula* belongs, the eternally rebellious individual is converted for a while into a loyal citizen. In the case of Nkula, a female individual whose behavior is felt to demonstrate her rebellion against, or at least her reluctance to comply with, the biological and social life patterns of her sex, is both induced and coerced by means of precept and symbol to accept her culturally prescribed destiny.

## *Modes of Inference in Interpretation*

Each kind of Ndembu ritual, like *Nkula,* has several meanings and goals that are not made explicit by informants, but must be inferred by the investigator from the symbolic pattern and from behavior. He is able to make these inferences only if he has previously examined the symbolic configurations and the meanings attributed to their component symbols by skilled informants, of many other kinds of ritual in the same total system. In other words, he must examine symbols not only in the context of each specific kind of ritual, but in the context of the total system. He may even find it profitable, where the same symbol is found throughout a wide culture area, to study its changes of meaning in different societies in that area.

There are two main types of contexts, irrespective of size. There is the action-field context, which we have discussed at some length. There is also the cultural context in which symbols are regarded as clusters of abstract meanings. By comparing the different kinds and sizes of contexts in which a dominant symbol occurs, we can often see that the meanings "officially" attributed to it in a particular kind of ritual may be mutually consistent. However, there may be much discrepancy and even contradiction between many of the meanings given by informants, when this dominant symbol is regarded as a unit of the total symbolic system. I do not believe that this descrepancy is the result of mere carelessness and ignorance or variously distributed pieces of insight. I believe that discrepancy between *significata* is a quintessential property of the great symbolic dominants in all religions. Such symbols come in the process of time to absorb into their meaning-content most of the major aspects of human social life, so that, in a sense, they come to represent "human society" itself. In each ritual they assert the situational primacy of a single aspect or of a few aspects only, but by their mere presence they suffuse those aspects with the awe that can only be inspired by the human total. All the contradictions of human social life, between norms, and drives, between different drives and between different norms, between society and the individual, and between groups, are condensed and unified in a single representation, the dominant symbols. It is the task of analysis to break down this amalgam into its primary constituents.

## *The Relativity of "Depth"*

Perhaps this breakdown can best be done within different analytical frameworks. I was formerly in favor of talking about "different levels of analysis," but the term "level" contains an implication of depth which I now find misleading, unless we can agree to take "level" to mean any class of abstraction whatsoever. The question of the relative depth of different ways of interpreting symbols is still very much under dispute. For example, psychoanalysts assert that their interpretations of ritual symbols are "deeper" than those of social anthropologists. On the other hand, anthropologists like Monica Wilson hold that at their "deepest level" rituals reveal values, which are sociocultural facts.

I have suggested in this essay that different aspects of ritual symbolism can be analyzed within the framework of structuralist theory and of cultural anthropology respectively. As I have said, this would be to treat ritual symbols as timeless entities. Many useful conclusions can be arrived at by these methods, but the essential nature, both of dominant symbols and of constellations of instrumental symbols, is that they are dynamic factors. Static analysis would here presuppose a corpse, and, as Jung says, "a symbol is alive." It is alive only in so far as it is "pregnant with meaning" for men and women, who interact by observing, transgressing, and manipulating for private ends the norms and values that the symbol expresses. If the ritual symbol is conceptualized as a force in a field of social action, its critical properties of condensation, polarization, and unification of disparities become intelligible and explicable. On the other hand, conceptualizing the symbol as if it were an object and neglecting its role in action often lead to a stress on only those aspects of symbolism which can be logically and consistently related to one another to form an abstract unitary system.

In a field situation, the unity of a symbol or a symbolic configuration appears as the resultant of many tendencies converging towards one another from different areas of biophysical and social existence. The symbol is an independent force which is itself a product of many opposed forces.

## *Conclusion: The Analysis of Symbols in Social Processes*

Let me outline briefly the way in which I think ritual symbols may fruitfully be analyzed. Performances of ritual are phases in broad social processes, the span and complexity of which are roughly proportional to the size and degree of differentiation of the groups in which they occur. One class of ritual is situated near the apex of a whole hierarchy of redressive and regulative institutions that correct deflections and deviations from customarily prescribed behavior. Another class anticipates deviations and conflicts. This class includes periodic rituals and life-crisis rituals. Each kind of ritual is a patterned process in time, the units of which are symbolic objects and serialized items of symbolic behavior.

The symbolic constituents may themselves be classed into structural elements, or "dominant symbols," which tend to be ends in themselves, and variable elements, or "instrumental symbols," which serve as means to the explicit or implicit goals of the given ritual. In order to give an adequate explanation of the meaning of a particular symbol, it is necessary first to examine the widest action-field context, that, namely, in which the ritual itself is simply a phase. Here one must consider what kinds of circumstances give rise to a performance of ritual, whether these are concerned with natural phenomena, economic and technological processes, human life-crises, or with the breach of crucial social relationships. The circumstances will probably determine what sort of ritual is performed. The goals of the ritual will have overt and implicit reference to the antecedent circumstances and will in turn help to determine the meaning of the symbols. Symbols must now be examined within the context of the specific ritual. It is here that we enlist the aid of indigenous informants. It is here also that we may be able to speak legitimately of "levels" of interpretation, for laymen will give the investigator simple and exoteric meanings, while specialists will give him esoteric explanations and more elaborate texts. Next, behavior directed towards each symbol should be noted, for such behavior is an important component of its total meaning.

We are now in a position to exhibit the ritual as a system of meanings, but this system acquires additional richness and depth if it is regarded as itself constituting a sector of the Ndembu ritual system, as interpreted by informants and as observed in action. It is in comparison with other sectors of the total system, and by reference to the dominant articulating principles of the total system, that we often become aware that the overt and ostensible aims and purposes of a given ritual conceal unavowed, and even "unconscious," wishes and goals. We also become aware that a complex relationship exists between the overt and the submerged, and the manifest and latent patterns of meaning. As social anthropologists we are potentially capable of analyzing the social aspect of this relationship. We can examine, for example, the relations of dependence and independence between the total society and its parts, and the relations between different kinds of parts, and between different parts of the same kind. We can see how the same dominant symbol, which in one kind of ritual stands for one kind of social group or for one principle of organization, in another kind of ritual stands for another kind of group or principle, and in its aggregate of meanings stands for unity and continuity of the widest Ndembu society, embracing its contradictions.

### *The Limits of Contemporary Anthropological Competence*

Our analysis must needs be incomplete when we consider the relationship between the normative elements in social life and the individual. For this relationship, too, finds its way into the meaning of ritual symbols. Here we come to the confines of our present anthropological competence, for we are now dealing with the structure and properties of psyches, a scientific field traditionally studied by other disciplines than ours. At one end of the symbol's spectrum of meanings we encounter the individual psychologist and the social psychologist, and even beyond them (if one may make a friendly tilt at an envied friend), brandishing his Medusa's head, the psychoanalyst, ready to turn to stone the foolhardy interloper into his caverns of terminology.

We shudder back thankfully into the light of social day. Here the significant elements of a symbol's meaning are related to what it does and what is done to it by and for whom. These aspects can only be understood if one takes into account from the beginning, and represents by appropriate theoretical constructs, the total field situation in which the symbol occurs. This situation would include the structure of the group that performs the ritual we observe, its basic organizing principles and perdurable relationships, and, in addition, its extant division into transient alliances and factions on the basis of immediate interest and ambitions, for both abiding structure and recurrent forms of conflict and selfish interest are stereotyped in ritual symbolism. Once we have collected informants' interpretations of a given symbol, our work of analysis has indeed just begun. We must gradually approximate to the action-meaning of our symbol by way of what Lewin calls (1949, 149) "a stepwise increasing specificity" from widest to narrowest significant action context. Informants' "meanings" only beome meaningful as objects of scientific study in the course of this analytical process.

## BIBLIOGRAPHY

Bettelheim, Bruno. 1954. *Symbolic Wounds: Puberty Rites and the Envious Male.* Glencoe, Ill.: Free Press.

Durkheim, E. 1954. *Elementary Forms of the Religious Life.* London: Allen & Unwin.

Fenichel, Otto. 1946. *The Psychoanalytic Theory of Neuroses.* London: Routledge & Kegan Paul.

Jung, Carl G. 1949. *Psychological Types.* London: Routledge & Kegan Paul.

Lewin, K. 1949. *Field Theory in Social Science.* London: Tavistock Publications.

Nadel, S. F. 1954. *Nupe Religion.* London: Routledge & Kegan Paul.

Sapir, E. "Symbols," *Encyclopedia of the Social Sciences,* XIV. New York: Macmillan.

Wilson, M. 1957. *Rituals of Kinship among the Nyakyusa.* London: Oxford University Press, for the International African Institute.

## CHAPTER II

# Ritual Symbolism, Morality, and Social Structure among the Ndembu *

In this paper I wish to discuss the semantic structure and properties of some of the principal symbols found in Ndembu ritual. Each kind of ritual may be regarded as a configuration of symbols, a sort of "score" in which the symbols are the notes. The symbol is the smallest unit of specific structure in Ndembu ritual. The vernacular term for it is *chinjikijilu,* from *ku-jikijila,* "to blaze a trail," by cutting marks on a tree with one's ax or by breaking and bending branches to serve as guides back from the unknown bush to known paths. A symbol, then, is a blaze or landmark, something that connects the unknown with the known. The Ndembu term comes from the vocabulary of hunting and exemplifies the high ritual value attached to this pursuit. Furthermore, in discussing their symbols with Ndembu, one finds them constantly using the term *ku-solola,* "to make visible" or "to reveal," and they associate this term with aspects of the chase. Indeed, in their ritual vocabulary derivatives of this verb are frequent. For example, the temporary shrine erected for ritual to propitiate the spirits of deceased hunter relatives very often consists of a forked branch taken from the *musoli* tree. Ndembu tell me that this tree is used as a symbol in hunters' ritual because its fruit and young shoots are much

* Read at the Third International African Seminar in Salisbury, Rhodesia, Dec. 1960. First published in *African Systems of Thought,* M. Fortes and G. Dieterlen, eds. (London: Oxford University Press, for the International African Institute, 1965).

appreciated by duiker and other woodland animals who emerge from concealment to eat them and may be easily shot by a hidden hunter or caught in his snares. The tree, they say, makes the game "visible." Hence, portions of it are used as medicines (*yitumbu*) in rituals performed to rid hunters of misfortune. It is said that these medicines will "make animals appear quickly to the hunter" when next he goes into the bush. *Musoli* medicines are also used in rituals performed to make barren women fruitful; they will "make children visible," say Ndembu.

Another use of *musoli* is worth mentioning. Ndembu have a ritual called *Ihamba,* the main aim of which is to remove by cupping horns from a patient's body the upper central incisor (also called *ihamba*) of a dead hunter relative which has imbedded itself under the skin. The spirit, materialized as a tooth, is said to "bite" its victim because the latter has forgotten to pour out a libation of blood at its grave after making a kill, or else because there has been quarreling in the victim's village. The victim may not necessarily have been guilty himself of quarrelsome behavior, but may have been selected as a representative of the disordered kin-group. The specialist who supervises the ritual procedure usually insists on those village members who have grudges (*yitela*) against one another or against the patient (*muyeji*) coming forward and making a public confession of their hidden animosities. Only after this, he says, will the *ihamba* consent to being caught in a cupping horn. Now the principal medicine of this ritual, the one at which an invocation to the spirit is made, the one which is collected before all others, consists of the taproot of a *musoli* tree. My informants told me that the root stood for the *ihamba* tooth and that the *musoli* species was used "to make the *ihamba* tooth come out quickly," and "so that people would speak truly (*ku-hosha chalala*) and openly." Here the idea is clearly that relief is brought both to the patient and to the disturbed social group if hidden ill-feeling is brought to light.

Another derivative of *ku-solola* is *"isoli"* or *"chisoli,"* terms that designate "a place of revelation." They refer to specially consecrated sites, used only in the final phases of important rituals, where esoteric rites are performed and secret matters are revealed to the initiated.

Finally, the term *Musolu* stands for a type of ritual performed only by chiefs and senior headmen to bring on or "make visible" delayed rains.

One aspect of the process of ritual symbolization among the

Ndembu is, therefore, to make visible, audible, and tangible beliefs, ideas, values, sentiments, and psychological dispositions that cannot directly be perceived. Associated with this process of revealing the unknown, invisible, or the hidden is the process of making public what is private or making social what is personal. Anything that cannot be shown to be in conformity with the norms or in terms of the values of Ndembu society is potentially dangerous to its cohesion and continuity. Hence the importance of the public confession in the *Ihamba* ritual. By exposing their ill-feeling in a ritual context to beneficial ritual forces, individuals are purged of rebellious wishes and emotions and willingly conform once more to the public mores.

In an Ndembu ritual each symbol makes visible and accessible to purposive public action certain elements of Ndembu culture and society. It also tends to relate these elements to certain natural and physiological regularities. Thus, in various contexts *musoli* relates the value of public confession to the restoration of health and of female fertility. This brings me to another important property of many ritual symbols, their polysemy or multi-vocality. By these terms I mean that a single symbol may stand for many things. This property of individual symbols is true of ritual as a whole. For a few symbols have to represent a whole culture and its material environment. Ritual may be described, in one aspect, as quintessential custom in that it represents a distillate or condensation of many secular customs and natural regularities. Certain dominant or focal symbols conspicuously possess this property of multivocality which allows for the economic representation of key aspects of culture and belief. Each dominant symbol has a "fan" or "spectrum" of referents, which are interlinked by what is usually a simple mode of association, its very simplicity enabling it to interconnect a wide variety of *significata*. For example, the associational link provided by "whiteness" enables white clay (*mpemba*) to stand for a multiplicity of ideas and phenomena, ranging from biological referents as "semen," to abstract ideas such as "ritual purity," "innocence" from witchcraft, and "solidarity with the ancestor spirits."

When we talk about the "meaning" of a symbol, we must be careful to distinguish between at least three levels or fields of meaning. These I propose to call: (1) the level of indigenous interpretation (or, briefly, the exegetical meaning); (2) the operational meaning; and (3) the positional meaning. The exegetical meaning is obtained from questioning indigenous informants about observed ritual behavior. Here again one must distinguish between information given by ritual specialists and information given by laymen, that is, between esoteric and exoteric interpretations. One must also be careful to ascertain whether a given explanation is truly representative of either of these categories or whether it is a uniquely personal view.

On the other hand, much light may be shed on the role of the ritual symbol by equating its meaning with its use, by observing what the Ndembu do with it, and not only what they say about it. This is what I call the operational meaning, and this level has the most bearing on problems of social dynamics. For the observer must consider not only the symbol but the structure and composition of the group that handles it or performs mimetic acts with direct reference to it. He must further note the affective qualities of these acts, whether they are aggressive, sad, penitent, joyful, derisive, and so on. He must also inquire why certain persons and groups are absent on given occasions, and if absent, whether and why they have been ritually excluded from the presence of the symbol.

The positional meaning of a symbol derives from its relationship to other symbols in a totality, a *Gestalt,* whose elements acquire their significance from the system as a whole. This level of meaning is directly related to the important property of ritual symbols mentioned earlier, their polysemy. Such symbols possess many senses, but contextually it may be necessary to stress one or a few of them only. Thus the *mukula* tree viewed in abstraction from any given ritual context may stand for "matriliny," "huntsmanship," "menstrual blood," "the meat of wild animals," and many other concepts and things. The associational link between its various senses is provided by the red gum it secretes, which Ndembu liken to blood. Now in the boys' circumcision ritual (*Mukanda*) the meaning of *mukula* is determined by its symbolic context. A log of this wood is placed near the site where the boys are circumcised. They are circumcised under a *mudyi* tree, which, as we shall see, stands *inter alia* for motherhood and the mother-child relationship. Then they are lifted over a cutting of the *muyombu* tree, which is customarily planted quickset as a shrine to the village ancestor spirits, and placed still bleeding on the *mukula* log. Here the *mukula* log stands mainly for two things. It represents the wish of the elders that the circumcision wounds will heal quickly (from the fact that *mukula* gum quickly coagulates like a scab). It also represents, I was told, masculinity (*wuyala*) and the life of an adult male, who as hunter and warrior has to shed blood. The rite represents (1) the removal of the boy from dependence on his mother (the passage from the *mudyi* tree); (2) his ritual death and subsequent association with the ancestors (the passage over the *muyombu* tree); and (3) his incorporation into the male moral community of tribesmen (the collective setting on the *mukula* tree where the boys are ceremonially fed as though they were infants by the circumcisers and by their fathers. Each boy is given a ball of cassava mush to be eaten directly from the circumciser's knife). In this rite the position of the *mukula* symbol with reference to other symbolic objects and acts is the crucial semantic factor.

The same symbol may be reckoned to have different senses at different phases in a ritual performance, or rather, different senses become paramount at different times. Which sense shall become paramount is determined by the ostensible purpose of the phase of the ritual in which it appears. For a ritual, like a space rocket, is phased, and each phase is directed towards a limited end which itself becomes a means to the ultimate end of the total performance. Thus the act of circumcision is the aim and culmination of a symbol-loaded phase of the *Mukanda* ritual, but itself becomes a means to the final end of turning a boy into a tribesman. There is a consistent relationship between the end or aim of each phase in a ritual, the kind of symbolic configuration employed in that phase, and the senses that become paramount in multivocal symbols in that configuration.

I should now like to consider the exegetical meaning of one of the principal Ndembu ritual symbols, the *mudyi* tree. This symbol is found in more than half a dozen different kinds of ritual, but its *locus classicus* is in the girls' puberty ritual (*Nkang'a*). The novice is laid, wrapped in a blanket, at the foot of a slender young *mudyi* sapling. Ndembu say that its pliancy stands for the youth of the girl. The sapling has been previously consecrated by the novice's ritual instructress (*nkong'u*) and her mother. They have trampled down the grass in a circle around the tree, thus making it sacred—"set apart" (*chakumbadyi*) or "forbidden" (*chakujila*). The site, like that of circumcision for the boys, is called *ifwilu* or "the place of dying." Both sites are also known as *ihung'u,* "the place of suffering" or "ordeal." *Ihung'u* is also applied to a hut where a woman is in labor. It is a "place of suffering" because the novice must not move her limbs until nearly nightfall on penalty of being pinched all over by the older women; nor may she eat or speak all day. The association of the *mudyi* tree with suffering and dying should be borne in mind as an aspect of its positional meaning.

Ndembu begin the exposition of *mudyi's* meaning by pointing out that if its bark is scratched, beads of milky latex are promptly secreted. For this reason they say that *mudyi* or "milk tree" is a symbol (*chinjikijilu*) for "breasts" and "breast milk"—both called in Chindembu *mayeli*. They go on from there to say that *mudyi* means "a mother and her child," a social relationship. They further extend this sense to signify a matrilineage (*ivumu*, literally "a womb or stomach"). A text which I collected well expresses this view:

*Mudyi diku kwakaminiyi nkakulula hakumutembwisha ni ankukulula*
The milk tree is the place where slept the (founding) ancestress, where they initiated her and another ancestress

*mukwawu nimukwawu ni kudi nkaka ni kudi mama ninetu anyana;*
and (then) another down to the grandmother and the mother and ourselves the children;

*diku kumuchidi wetu kutwatachikili ni amayala nawa chochu hamu.*
It is the place where our tribe (or tribal custom—literally "kind") began, and also the men in just the same way.

My informant then added the following comments: "The milk tree is the place of all mothers; it is the ancestress of men and women. *Kutembwisha*, "to initiate a girl," means to dance round and round the milk tree where the novice lies. The milk tree is the place where our ancestors slept, to be initiated there means to become ritually pure or white. An uninitiated girl, a menstruating woman, or an uncircumcised boy is called "one who lacks whiteness (*wunabulakutooka*)."

Contextually, a particular novice's milk tree may be termed "her matrilineage." At one phase of the ritual, the leaves of this tree are said to represent "the novice's children"—a sense that is concerned with a future wished-for state of affairs rather than with the past or present.

In other phases of the *Nkang'a* ritual the milk tree is said to stand for "the women" and for "womanhood." It also has the situational sense of "married womanhood."

Finally, the milk tree stands for the process of learning (*kudiza*), especially for learning "women's sense" or "wisdom" (*mana yawambanda*). An informant said that "*mudyi*" is like going to school; "the girl drinks sense as a baby drinks milk."

The semantic structure of *mudyi* may itself be likened to a tree. At the root is the primary sense of "breast milk" and from this proceeds by logical steps series of further senses. The general direction is from the concrete to the increasingly abstract, but there are several different branches along which abstraction proceeds. One line develops as follows: breast, mother-child relationship, matriliny, the Ndembu tribe or tribal custom of which matriliny is the most representative principle. Another line runs: development of the breasts, womanhood, married womanhood, childbearing. Yet another goes from suckling to learning the tasks, rights, and duties of womanhood. As with many other Ndembu symbols, derivative senses themselves become symbols pointing to ideas and phenomena beyond themselves. Thus "matriliny," a derivative sense from "the mother-child" relationship, and "breast-milk," by the principle of *pars pro toto,* itself becomes a symbol for Ndembu culture in its totality.

However, despite this multiplicity of senses, Ndembu speak and think about the milk tree as a unity, almost as a unitary power. They can break down the concept "milk tree" cognitively into many attributes, but in ritual practice they view it as a single entity. For them it is something like Goethe's "eternal womanly," a female or maternal principle pervading society and nature. It must not be forgotten that ritual symbols are not merely signs representing known things; they are felt to possess ritual efficacy, to be charged with power from unknown sources, and to be capable of acting on persons and groups coming in contact with them in such a way as to change them for the better or in a desired direction. Symbols, in short, have an orectic as well as a cognitive function. They elicit emotion and express and mobilize desire.

Indeed, it is possible further to conceptualize the exegetic meaning of dominant symbols in polar terms. At one pole cluster a set of referents of a grossly physiological character, relating to general human experience of an emotional kind. At the other pole cluster a set of referents to moral norms and principles governing the social structure. If we call these semantic poles respectively the "orectic" and the "normative" pole, and consider Ndembu ritual symbols in terms of this model, we find that the milk tree stands at one and the same time for the physiological aspect of breast feeding with its associated affectual patterns, and for the normative order governed by matriliny. In brief, a single symbol represents both the obligatory and the desirable. Here we have an intimate union of the moral and the material. An exchange of qualities may take place in the psyches of the participants under the stimulating circumstances of the ritual performance, between orectic and normative poles; the former, through its association with the latter, becomes purged of its infantile and regressive character, while the normative pole becomes charged with the pleasurable effect associated with the breast-feeding situation. In one aspect, the tie of milk, under matriliny, develops into the primary structural tie, but in another aspect, and here the polar model is apposite, the former stands opposed to and resists the formation of the latter.

Other important Ndembu symbols have a similar polar structure. *Mukula,* for example, in the context of *Nkula,* a ritual performed to cure menstrual disorders, represents at its orectic pole the "blood of birth," while at the normative pole, it represents matriliny and also the historical connection between the Ndembu and the empire of Mwantiyanvwa in the Congo, whose first incumbent, a female chief called Luweji Ankonde, suffered from menorrhagia. The tough *chikoli* thorn tree, which plays an important role in the boys' circumcision ritual, is said to stand for "masculinity" in the moral and social sense. It is said to stand for courage (*wulobu*), skill at hunting, and for "speaking well in legal cases," but *chikoli* also has its physiological pole. To quote one informant: "*Chikoli* is a very strong tree, its wood is very hard. One name for it is *chikang' anjamba,* from *ku-kang'anya,* to fail, and *njamba,* the elephant. The elephant fails to break it. Neither wind nor rain can break it, and white ants cannot eat it. It stands upright like the male organ or a man's strong body. That is why we say it represents strength (*wukolu*). "*Chikoli,* like *wukolu,* is derived from *ku kola,* "to be strong or potent." I could cite many other Ndembu examples of this polarity, which I consider to be a universal feature of ritual symbols of any semantic complexity.

However, let us return to the *mudyi* tree, this time to observe what takes place near and around it on the day of the novice's ordeal, the phase of *Kwing'ija,* or "putting in," with which the girl's puberty ritual (*Nkang'a*) begins. For now we are going to consider the operational meaning of the milk tree. Immediately we are confronted with a problem. Whereas it can be argued that on the exegetic level of meaning, the structural referents of the milk tree are concerned with the harmonious and solidary aspects of groups and relationships organized by matriliny or femininity, it is immediately obvious that much of the behavior observable in connection with it represents a mimesis of conflict within those very groups and relationships.

For example, in the early hours of the morning only the senior women of the novice's own village may dance around the *mudyi* tree. Later on, only women and no men may dance there, and the women attack the men in jeering and lampooning songs. Moreover, for a long time the girl's mother may not approach the *mudyi* tree, and when she eventually does so, she is mocked by the senior women. I might also mention an episode in which all the senior women compete to be first to snatch a spoon of cassava mush and beans, called "the porridge of *chipwampwilu,*" from the ritual instructress. This porridge represents fertility and in particular, the novice's fertility. If a woman from a distant village grabs the spoon first, this is thought to mean that the novice will bear her children far away from her mother's place of residence. This episode represents competition between the principles of matriliny and virilocality. Other episodes in *Nkang'a* also signify this conflict, though most of them do not have direct reference to the milk tree.

Thus, during different episodes, the value attached to the solidarity of women is contradicted in practice by the conflict between the novice's mother and the adult women who are ritually incorporating her daughter into their married ranks and removing her from her mother's knee. It is further contradicted by the separation of the novice's village members from the other women, and by the rivalry, on a village basis, between the women for the novice's fertility, and between individual women for fertility. The unity of the tribe is contradicted by the mobilization of the women around the milk tree in jeering opposition to the men. The novice's ordeal, with the threat of punishment if she moves, represents one aspect of the conflict between senior women and girls.

What is interesting is that indigenous informants do not relate these conflicts, stereotyped though they be, to their orthodox interpretations of the symbolism of the milk tree. Yet these mimed conflicts have to take place at the *ifwilu,* the novice's "dying-place," which is located next to the milk tree. A psychoanalyst of the Kleinian school might be tempted perhaps to relate the contrast between the exegetic and operational levels of meaning, between the emphasis on harmony and the emphasis on discord, to the infant's ambivalent attitude to the mother's breast, which both soothes him and arouses hostility by its apparently capricious absences. He might regard the lack of interpretation of the conflict behavior as due to the psychological "splitting" mechanism which separates the hostile from the loving attitude to the breast and thrusts this hostility into the unconscious psyche, but it is theoretically inadmissible to explain social facts, such as ritual symbols, by the concepts of depth psychology. A sociological hypothesis to account for the contradiction between these levels of meaning might be advanced to the effect that on the exegetic level, the principle of matriliny is abstracted from its social context and appears in its ideal purity. The conflicts within groups and relationships articulated by matriliny which are exhibited at the operational level are not due to the structural inadequacies of matriliny or to human frailty with regard to keeping rules, but rather result from other principles of social organization which constantly and consistently interfere with the harmonious working of matriliny. Age and sex differences cut across matrilineal affiliation. Virilocal marriage strikes into the cohesion of a local matrilineage. The matricentric family makes rival demands on the loyalty of members of a matrilineage. Type-conflicts of these kinds are acted out before the milk tree, the archsymbol of matrilineal continuity, and of the ultimate dependence of Ndembu society on the mother's breast. The puberty ritual asserts that though matriliny may regularly be challenged by other principles and trends, yet it persists and triumphs.

In conclusion, I would like to draw attention to the relationship between the milk tree symbolism and the symbolic principle of "whiteness" (*wutooka*) on the exegetic level of interpretation. At the apex of the total symbolic system of the Ndembu is the color triad, white—red—black. At certain esoteric episodes in the boys' circumcision ritual and in the initial ritual of the men's and women's funerary associations of *Mung'ong'i* and *Chiwila,* the meanings of these three colors are taught to young Ndembu. Whiteness is most commonly represented by powdered white clay (*mpemba* or *mpezu*), redness by powdered red clay (*mukundu, ng'ula,* or *mukung'u*), and blackness by charcoal (*makala*). These substances are not so much symbols as tokens of three vital principles, akin to the Hindu "strands of life" mentioned in the Bhagavad-Gita. I have collected many texts and made many observations of the use of these colors in ritual and may therefore state briefly that whiteness stands, *inter alia,* for "goodness (*ku-waha*), health (*ku-koleka*), ritual purity (*ku-tooka*), freedom from misfortune (*ku-bula ku-halwa*), for political authority (*wanta*), and for assembling with the spirits (*kudibomba niakishi*). To sum up, it represents the entire moral order plus the fruits of virtue; health, strength, fertility, the respect of one's fellows, and the blessing of one's ancestors. Whiteness differs from redness in that it stresses harmony, cohesion, and continuity, while redness, associated with bloodspilling as well as with blood kinship, tends to denote discontinuity, strength acquired through breach of certain rules, and male aggressiveness (as in hunting, which is represented in many rituals by red clay and red symbols).

There are many symbols that Ndembu themselves class as "white things" and which they believe to be pervaded by the moral attributes of whiteness. The milk tree, representing matriliny, is one of these. For Ndembu, matriliny is what Professor Fortes has called (1949, 344), though in a rather different connection, an "irreducible principle" of social organization, through which the moral order, with all its prescription and prohibitions, is mediated to the individual. Matriliny is the framework of those aspects of Ndembu morality which the people regard as changeless and as harmoniously interrelated nodal points. It would be possible to show that the norms and values controlling those relationships derived from the tie of milk form the "matrix" of the moral order and have ideally what Ndembu would regard as a "white" quality. Matriliny gives a specific form and stamp to a morality which would otherwise be imprecise and general.

## BIBLIOGRAPHY

Fortes, Meyer. 1949. *The Web of Kinship among the Tallensi*. London: Oxford University Press.

CHAPTER III

# Color Classification in Ndembu Ritual: A Problem in Primitive Classification *

THERE has recently been a marked revival of interest in what Durkheim (1963) called "primitive forms of classification," a revival in which the names of Lévi-Strauss, Leach, Needham, and Evans-Pritchard have been prominent. Much attention has been focused on dichotomous classification in kinship and religious systems or on other kinds of isometrical arrangement such as quaternary and octadic divisions. Needham's resuscitation of Robert Hertz's work (1960) and Needham (1960) and Beidelman's recent studies (1961) in the symbolism of laterality, of the opposition of right and left and its sociological implications, represent this interest. During my own investigations of Ndembu ritual symbolism I came across many instances of lateral symbolism and indeed of other forms of dual classification with which the opposition of right and left might or might not be correlated. Since one of my major lines of inquiry was into the problem of social conflict and its resolution, I was sensitive at the time to the symbolization and formalization of such conflict. Many disputes involved opposition between the principles of matriliny and virilocality, and it seemed, therefore, reasonable to suppose that the opposition between the sexes would secure ritual and symbolic representation. I found

* Read at a meeting of the Association of Social Anthropologists of the Commonwealth in Cambridge, July 1963. First published in *Anthropological Approaches to the Study of Religion,* A. S. A. Monograph No. 3 (London: Tavistock Publications, 1965).

that this was indeed the case, but I was not long in discovering that not only the dualism of the sexes but indeed every form of dualism was contained in a wider, tripartite mode of classification.

### *Color Classification in African Ritual*

This tripartite classification relates to the colors white, red, and black. These are the only colors for which Ndembu possess primary terms. Terms for other colors are either derivatives from these—as in the case of *chitookoloka,* "gray," which is derived from *tooka,* "white" —or consist of descriptive and metaphorical phrases, as in the case of "green," *meji amatamba,* which means "water of sweet potato leaves." Very frequently, colors that we would distinguish from white, red, and black are by Ndembu linguistically identified with them. Blue cloth, for example, is described as "black" cloth, and yellow or orange objects are lumped together as "red." Sometimes a yellow object may be described as *neyi nsela,* "like beeswax," but yellow is often regarded as ritually equivalent to red.

When I first observed Ndembu rites I was impressed by the frequent use of white and red clay as ritual decoration. I assumed that only these two colors were ritually significant and that I had to deal with a dual classification. There was, indeed, a certain amount of support for such a view in the anthropological literature on the West Central Bantu. For example, Baumann, writing of the Chokwe of eastern Angola, had asserted that for these people: "White is the color of life, of health, of moonlight and of women. Red, on the other hand, has connections with sickness, the sun, and men" (1935, 40–41). He then attempted to equate the opposition between the colors with that between right and left, associating red with the right and white with the left. Baumann also admitted that white clay "figures as a life-principle" and is consequently forced by the logic of his dual scheme to regard red as the color of "death." Yet when he discusses the red decoration of novices in the circumcision ceremony he writes: "It seems as though the red color were in itself not only the color of illness, but also the color of averting illness." Other authorities on the West Central Bantu are by no means in agreement with Baumann's interpretation. C. M. N. White, for example, holds that "red is symbolic of life and blood in various Luvale contexts" (1961, 15), and the Chokwe and Luvale are culturally very similar. White also writes that various red fruits and trees are "constantly associated with fertility and life."

My own field observations among the Ndembu tended to confirm White's interpretation rather than Baumann's, although it is true that there are a number of ritual contexts in which red is associated with masculinity, as in the red ritual decorations of war chiefs (*tumbanji*), circumcisers, and hunters, and white with femininity, as in the case of the *mudyi* tree which secretes a white latex and is the supreme symbol of femininity and motherhood. On the other hand, I came upon at least an equal number of ritual occasions where white represented masculinity and red femininity. For example, in the *Nkula* rite, performed to rid a woman of menstrual disorder, red clay and other red symbols represent menstrual blood, "the blood of parturition," and matriliny—all feminine things. In the *Wubwang'u* rite, performed for a mother of twins or for a woman expected to bear twins, powdered white clay, kept in a phallus-shaped container and blown over the patient as she stands on a log near a stream source, is explicitly likened to "semen." On the other hand, powdered red clay, kept in the shell of a river mollusk and blown over the patient after the white powder, is said to represent "the blood of the mother." The white clay is applied by a male and the red clay by a female doctor. There is no fixed correlation between the colors and the sexes. Color symbolism is not consistently sex-linked, although red and white may be situationally specified to represent the opposition of the sexes.

It is clear that Baumann's attempt to polarize the symbolic values of white and red is artificial and constrained. This would suggest that we are dealing here with something wider than a dual classification. White and red are certainly opposed in some situations, but the fact that each can stand for the same object—in other words, they participate in one another's meaning—suggests that more than a pair of opposites has to be taken into account. As a matter of fact, as I have already indicated, there is a third factor or term. This is the color black, in some ways the most interesting of the three.

## *Color Classification in Ndembu Life-Crisis Ritual*

Let us now examine some contexts in which the three colors appear together before we look at them singly or in contrasted pairs. Ndembu assure me that the relationship between the colors "begins with the mystery (or riddle, *mpang'u*) of the three rivers: the rivers of whiteness, redness, and blackness (or darkness)." This cryptic utterance refers to part of the secret teaching of the lodge during the circumcision rites (*Mukanda*) and during the phase of seclusion at the rites of the funerary associations of *Chiwila* and *Mung'ong'i*. It is said that girls were also, until recently, taught this mystery (*mpang'u*) during their puberty rites (*Nkang'a*), but I found no evidence of this.

I have not personally observed the instruction of novices in this mystery of the three rivers, but I have recorded several accounts from reliable informants. The first of these is from a member of the *Chiwila* society, which performs elaborate initiation rites for young people at the death of its female cult members. *Chiwila* is no longer held in present day Zambia, but my informant had been initiated as a young girl among the Ndembu of Angola. She described to me how the novices were taught the mystery of one of the "rivers" (*tulong'a*), in this case "the river of blood" (*kalong'a kamashi*) or "the river of redness" (*kachinana*). The prefix *ka-* sometimes signifies that the term it qualifies is a liquid, usually water. Thus *ku-chinana* means "to be red (or yellow)," *chinana* is the radical, and *ka-chinana* means "red fluid" or "red river," and *keyila,* the "black river."

My informant told me that the novices, boys as well as girls, were taken to a long, roofed but unwalled shelter called *izembi*. The senior celebrant, entitled *Samazembi* ("father of *mazembi*"), then took a hoe and dug a trench inside the hut. It was shaped "like a cross" (*neyi mwambu*), but could also be made in the form of an Ndembu axe (*chizemba*) or a hoe (*itemwa*). Next he took sharp reeds, such as are used for making mats, and planted them along both sides of the trench. This was followed by the planting of many small antelope horns, containing pounded leaf medicine (*nsompu*), in lines on either side of the trench. He then filled the trench with water; *Samazembi's* next task was to behead (the term *ku-ketula,* "to cut" is always used for this) a fowl and pour its blood into the "river" to tinge it with red. Not content with this, he added other red coloring matter such as powdered red clay (*mukundu* or *ng'ula*) and powdered gum from the *mukula* tree. *Samazembi* then washed his body with medicine made from root scrapings soaked in water and contained in his personal calabash. What was left after washing he threw into the "river of redness." Next he took some powdered white clay (*mpemba* or *mpeza*), addressed the spirits of "those who had passed through *Chiwila* long ago," anointed himself by the orbits and on the temple with *mpemba,* anointed the novices, and then harangued them as follows:

Pay attention! This river is blood. It is very important (literally, "heavy"). It is very dangerous. You must not speak of it in the village when you return. Beware! This is no ordinary river. God (*Nzambi*) made it long, long ago. It is the river of God (*kalong'a kaNzambi*). You must not eat salt for many days, nor anything salty or sweet (*-towala* means both). Do not speak of these matters in public, in the village; that is bad.

When he had finished, each novice bent down and took one of the small horns by the teeth, without using hands. They all went outside and tried to perform the difficult feat of bending over backwards and tossing the horn up in such a way as to be caught by adepts standing just behind them without spilling the medicine.

*Samazembi* collected all these horns and secreted them in his medicine hut (*katunda*). The medicine was called *nfunda,* a name also applied to the lodge medicine of the *Mukanda* or boys' circumcision rites. In addition to other ingredients it contained ashes from the burnt hut of the deceased. *Nfunda* is never thrown away but the portion left over at the end of each performance of *Chiwila* or *Mung'ong'i* is used at the next performance, where it is mixed with fresh medicine. The *nfunda* used at the circumcision rites, though not in the *Chiwila* rites, contains ashes and powdered charcoal from the seclusion lodge, which is burnt at the end of the seclusion period, and ashes and charcoal from various sacred fires extinguished at the conclusion of the rites. These are held to be "black" symbols. It is interesting to learn from Baumann (1935, 137) that among the Chokwe, *ufunda* stands for "interment" and is derived from the verb *ku-funda,* "to bury." The term *funda,* which seems to be the cognate of *nfunda,* according to Baumann, stands for "a bundle" and "appears to be connected with the idea of the bundled corpse laced on to the carrying-pole." *Nfunda,* as used at *Mukanda, Mung'ong'i,* and *Chiwila,* rites of the Ndembu, is certainly a medicine bundle; but the possible etymological connection with death is suggestive in view of its connection with funerary rites, the destruction of sacred edifices, and black symbols.

My informant on *Chiwila* customs was unable or unwilling to venture much in the way of their interpretation. Other informants on *Mukanda* and *Mung'ong'i* ritual supplied further exegesis. At these rites, they told me, there are "three rivers." "The river of blood," usually made in the shape of an ax, represents "a man with a woman" (*iyala namumbanda*), or "copulation" (*kudisunda*). The man is represented by the axhead with its tang and the woman by the wooden shaft.[1]

[1] It is interesting to note that the art of ironworking is an exclusively masculine occupation and the use of the ax in bush-clearing is restricted to males. On the other hand, by far the greatest number of woodcarvings are of the female body.

The main "river" or "trough," the "elder" one as Ndembu put it, is the "river of whiteness" (*katooka*). This "runs in a straight line to the *izembi* shelter." "The river of red water is junior, and this is followed by the river of black water. The red river is a woman and her husband." The crossing of the mother's and father's blood means a child, a new life (*kabubu kawumi—kabubu* stands for a small organism, such as an insect; it also stands for the umbilical cord; *wumi* signifies generic life rather than the personal life-principle—thus an infant before it is weaned is thought to have *wumi* but not a *mwevulu,* a "shadow-soul" which after death becomes an ancestor spirit of *mukishi*). One informant told me that the *katooka* is whitened with powdered white clay (*mpemba*), "stands for *wumi,*" and is "the trunk to which the red and black rivers are attached like branches." The black river (*keyila*), darkened with charcoal (*makala*) represents "death" (*kufwa*).

During *Mung'ong'i* the novices are asked a number of riddles (*jipang'u*). One of them is, "What is the white water restless by night (*katooka kusaloka*)." The correct answer is "semen" (*matekela*). Thus one of the senses of the "white river" is masculine generative power. This river, too, is described as "a river of God."

In *Mung'ong'i,* and also formerly in *Mukanda,* the novices are taught to chant a song, or rather incantation, full of archaic and bizarre terms. I record the text but cannot translate several of the words:

*Katooki meji kansalu kelung'i chimbungu chelung'a belang' ante-e*
White river water the little grass mat of the country, cannibal monster (or hyena) of the country . . .
*Mukayande-e he-e kateti kasemena mwikindu mwini kumwalula hinyi?*
In suffering (?) the little reed of begetting in the medicine basket (?), the owner who may find him?
*Apika kapumbi mujintiki samazadi ye-e* (meaning unknown)

"The little reed of begetting" is probably the penis; "*mwini,*" the owner, may refer to the name of a territorial spirit or demigod propitiated in the *Musolu* rite for bringing on belated rains and is perhaps connected with the water motif. Incidentally, Ndembu describe semen as "blood whitened (or purified) by water." The verb "to urinate" has the same radical *-tekela* as the noun *matekela,* "semen." Moreover, the urine of an apprentice circumciser is one of the ingredients of the *nfunda* medicine. It is clearly implied that the river of whiteness is untainted, while the river of blood contains impurities. This difference will emerge more sharply when I present informants' interpretations of the individual colors.

While I was discussing the "white river" with one informant he treated me to a short disquisition on the Ndembu theory of procreation, referring it directly to the initiation mysteries. "A child," he said, "means good luck (*wutooka,* which also means "whiteness"). For a child gives things in the first place to his father who first begat him. The mother is like a pot only, the body and soul of a child come from the father. But it is *Nzambi,* God, who gives life (*wumi*) to the child." I asked him why it was, then, that Ndembu traced descent through the mother. He replied, "A man begets children, but they are the mother's because it is she who suckles and nurses them. A mother feeds a child with her breast; without it the child would die." Then he cited the proverb: "The cock begets, but the chickens are the hen's (*kusema kwandemba nyana yachali*)." He went on to point out that breast milk (*mayeli*) is "white" too, a "white stream," and that the *mudyi* tree, dominant symbol of the girls' puberty rites, is a white symbol because it exudes white latex. Indeed, the primary sense of *mudyi* is breast milk. Thus the *katooka* or "white river" is bisexual in significance, representing both semen and milk. White symbols may then stand for both masculine and feminine objects, according to the context or situation and are not reserved, as in Baumann's account of the Chokwe, for feminine objects.

Finally, at *Mung'ong'i* there is a long song, chanted by novices, the refrain of which runs: *"Yaleyi Nyameya lupemba lufunda antu wafunda nimumi nimayili,"* which means literally, "You the man Nyameya, the big *mpemba* which draws lines on people, you draw lines on the living and those who went (i.e. the dead)." *Yaleyi* is a somewhat familiar term of address which may be applied to a person of either sex, like the South African English word "man." *Nyameya* means literally "the mother of whiteness" in the Luvale language, but the prefix *nya-*, "mother of," may be used honorifically of important men, such as chiefs or great hunters, with the flavor of "one who nourishes." *Lupemba* is *mpemba* or *pemba* with the additional prefix *lu-* which often denotes size. Nouns in the *lu-* class are commonly inanimate and include many long articles. Here, however, I am inclined to think that the "greatness" of *mpemba,* and of the "whiteness" it represents, is being stressed. *Ku-funda,* in the Lunda language, means to "draw lines" with white clay, red clay, or charcoal.

When the father or mother of children dies, a line is drawn in white clay from the middle of the chest down to the naval, as a sign that the deceased is desired as a giver of names to his or her descendants. To give someone one's name, for Ndembu, implies a kind of partial reincarnation of certain traits of character or body. When a sterile person dies, however, a line of black is drawn with a stick of charcoal from the navel of the dead person downwards, between the legs and around to the sacrum. This is a sign to the dead not to visit the world of the living again, "to die forever," as Ndembu say.

The living, too, in many rites are marked with white clay. To take one example, when Ndembu address the spirits of their ancestors at special quickset shrine trees planted in their honor in the villages, they take white clay, mark the tree with white, then draw one, three, or four lines on the ground from the base of the tree towards them, and finally anoint themselves with this *mpemba* beside the orbits, on the temple, and above the navel. The *mpemba* is said to represent a state of good will or good feeling between living and dead. There are held to be "no secret grudges" (*yitela*) between them, to "blacken" (*kwiyilisha*) their livers (*nyichima*), the seat of the feelings.

## *Color Classification in Ngonde Life-Crisis Ritual*

Other accounts of initiation rites in Central Africa mention many of the elements just described. For example, Lyndon Harries (1944) records several texts among the Ngonde of southern Tanganyika which discuss the meaning of the color triad in both male and female initiation. He asked native informants to interpret for him some of the cryptic songs of the seclusion lodge. One explanation ran as follows: "A woman conceives through the semen of a man. If the man has black semen there will be no bearing of a child. But if he has white semen he will have a child" (p. 19). The esoteric teaching given to the novices includes the displaying by an elder of "three things symbolic of sexual purity, sexual disease through impurity, and menstruation." These symbols are white flour, black charcoal, and red *inumbati* medicine respectively. "The boys are taught by means of these symbols" (p. 23). Incidentally, red *inumbati* medicine is used for "anointing a newborn child," and the novices' song "I want *inumbati* medicine" Harries takes to mean "I want to bear a child." *Inumbati* medicine is made from the powdered gum or bark of a Pterocarpus tree; the species *Pterocarpus angolensis* plays a major role in Ndembu ritual where it figures as a red symbol. Again, we hear that the boys smear themselves with black clay (*cikupi*) so that "they may not be seen by passers-by in the bush" (p. 16). Blackness, among the Ndembu, is also connected with concealment and darkness. It stands not only for actual but also for symbolic or ritual death among the Ndembu, and it may well have this significance in the Ngonde practice just mentioned.

At girls' puberty rites among the Ngonde, newly initiated girls "are taken by an older initiated girl to the well. Whenever they come to a cross-path, this older girl stoops down and draws three lines on the path, one red one with ochre to represent menses, one black one with a piece of charcoal to represent sexual impurity, and one white one with cassava flour for sexual purity" (p. 39). Here once more we have a relationship between water, the cross motif, and the color triad.

Dr. Audrey Richards, in *Chisungu* (1956), describes how among the Bemba color symbolism plays an important role in the girls' puberty rites. Thus the *mbusa* pottery emblems used to instruct the novices in ritual esoterica are "usually painted with white, black and red" (p. 59). Larger models of unfired clay are decorated with beans, soot, chalk, and red camwood dye (p. 60). The red camwood powder "is the blood," Dr. Richards was informed (p. 66). It is rubbed on those who have passed through danger, such as lion killers or those who have successfully undergone the poison ordeal. Red camwood powder, in some situations, is clearly a male symbol, as when the bridegroom's sisters, stained red, simulate bridegrooms (p. 73). Again, the *mulombwa,* the hardwood tree that exudes a red juice, "represents the male, the lion, and in some cases the chief" (p. 94). Red among the Bemba, as among the Ndembu, also has feminine connotations, for it represents menstrual blood in many ritual contexts. Among the Bemba, white represents the washing away of the menstrual blood (p. 81). All three colors are brought together in the cleansing rite of *ukuya ku mpemba* ("going to whitewash") where the novice is washed and cleansed and her body is covered with whitewash. At the same time, a lump of black mud is put cross-shaped on her head, and this is decorated with pumpkin seeds and red dye. Meanwhile the following song is sung: "We make the girls white (like egrets). We make them beautiful . . . they are white now from the stain of blood . . . it is finished now the thing that was red." This rite marks a definite stage in the puberty ritual (pp. 88–90). In another episode, white beads stand for fertility (as indeed they do among the Ndembu) (p. 72).

In his book *Les Rites Secrets des Primitifs de l'Oubangui* (1936), A. M. Vergiat discusses color symbolism he recorded at the circumcision rites of the Manja (or Mandja) in the following terms (p. 92):

> Black (in the form of powdered charcoal) is devoted to death. Warriors smear themselves with soot when they leave for war. People in mourning stay dirty, they do not wash any more. Black is a symbol of impurity. The color white is that of rebirth. It protects from illness. At the end of the rites the initiated boys paint themselves white. These are new men. At the ceremony of the mourning gathering, the relatives of the dead do the same. White purifies. Red is a symbol of life, joy and health. The natives rub themselves with red for dancing and those who are sick pass it frequently over their bodies.

## *Color Classification and the High God in Central Africa*

It is needless to multiply such citations; they are there in the literature on African initiation rites for all to read. It is perhaps worth mentioning that Baumann (1935, 12) came across a ritual shelter (*izembi*)—called by him "*zemba*"—of the *Mung'ong'i* cult in a Chokwe village north of the upper Kasai and was told that two large fires burning in it "are called *Kalunga* (that means God); they reach 'up to the sky.' " Thus we find the three colors fairly widely associated with initiations and life-crisis rites, and among the Ndembu and Chokwe, at any rate, with the High God. Of the three, white seems to be dominant and unitary, red ambivalent, for it is both fecund and "dangerous," while black is, as it were, the silent partner, the "shadowy third," in a sense opposed to both white and red, since it represents "death," "sterility," and "impurity." Yet we shall see that in its full significance black shares certain senses with both white and red, and it is not felt to be wholly malignant. The colors are conceived as rivers of power flowing from a common source in God and permeating the whole world of sensory phenomena with their specific qualities. More than this, they are thought to tinge the moral and social life of mankind with their peculiar efficacies, so that it said, for example, "this is a good man for he has a white liver," or "he is evil; his liver is black," when in physical fact a liver is dark red. Although the Ndembu, like many other simple societies, may be said to have an otiose God, nevertheless that God may be considered active in so far as from him stream unceasingly the three principles of being that are symbolized and given visible form in the white-red-black triad. Evidences of these principles or powers are held by Ndembu to be scattered throughout nature in objects of those colors, such as trees with red or white gum, bark, or roots, others with white or black fruit, white kaolin clay or red oxidized earth, black alluvial mud, charcoal, the white sun and moon, the black night, the redness of blood, the whiteness of milk, the dark color of feces. Animals and birds acquire ritual significance because their feathers or hides are of these hues. Even human beings, Negroes though they are, are classified as "white" or "black" in terms of nuances of pigmentation. There is here an implied moral difference and most people object to being classified as "black."

## *Ndembu Interpretation of the Color Triad*

What, then, are the novices taught about the meaning of the triad? I have collected a considerable number of texts from my Ndembu informants on color symbolism, recording what they have learnt, at initiation and in the course of their participation in rites of many kinds, about the significance of the colors. Let me begin by citing the basic senses of each.

### WHITE

Informants agree that white clay (*mpemba* or *mpeza*) and other "white things" (*yuma yitooka*) stand for "whiteness" (*wutooka*) which is:

1. goodness (*ku-waha*);
2. making strong or healthy (*ku-koleka* or *ku-kolisha*);
3. purity (*ku-tooka*) [this merely signifies "to be white" but is contextually recognizable as "purity"];
4. to lack (or be without) bad luck or misfortune (*ku-bula ku-halwa*);
5. to have power (*kwikala nang'ovu*) [literally, "to be with power"];
6. to be without death (*ku-bula ku-fwa*) [i.e., not to have death in one's kin-group];
7. to be without tears (*ku-bula madilu*) [as above];
8. chieftainship or authority (*wanta*);
9. when people meet together with ancestor spirits (*adibomba niakishi*);
10. life (*wumi*);
11. health (*ku-handa*);
12. begetting or bringing forth young (*lusemu*);

13. huntsmanship (*wubinda*);
14. giving or generosity (*kwinka*);
15. to remember (*kwanuka*) [i.e., one's ancestors with gifts and offerings at their *muyombu* shrines];
16. to laugh (*ku-seha*) [the mark of friendly sociability];
17. to eat (*ku-dya*) [Ndembu remark that both mother's milk and cassava meal, the main food, are white in color];
18. to multiply (*ku-seng'uka*) [in the sense of the fertility of humans, animals, and crops];
19. to make visible or reveal (*ku-solola*);
20. to become mature or an elder (*ku-kula*) [Ndembu comment here on the fact that elders have white hair—it is their "whiteness" becoming "visible"];
21. to sweep clean (*ku-komba*) [i.e., to rid of impurities];
22. to wash oneself (*ku-wela*) [as above];
23. to be free from ridicule—"people do not laugh at you because you have done something wrong or foolish."

### RED

"Red things (*yuma yachinana*)," say informants, "are of blood (*mashi*) or of red clay (*ng'ula*)." There are different categories (*nyichidi*) of blood. These are:

1. the blood of animals (*mashi atunyama* or *mashi anyama*) [this stands for huntsmanship (*wubinda* or *wuyang'a*), also for meat (*mbiji*)];
2. the blood of parturition, of mothers (*mashi alusemu amama*);
3. the blood of all women (*mashi awambanda ejima*) [i.e., menstrual blood (*mbayi* or *kanyanda*)];
4. the blood of murder or stabbing or killing (*mashi awubanji hela kutapana*) [the blood shed at circumcision comes under this heading as does the red decoration in the rites to purify a homicide or the slayer of a lion, leopard, or buffalo];
5. the blood of witchcraft or sorcery (*mashi awuloji*) [for Ndembu witchcraft or sorcery is necrophagous and in antiwitchcraft rites red stands for the blood exposed in such feasts].

"Red things belong to two categories; they act both for good and ill; (these) are combined (*Yuma yachinana yakundama kuyedi, yela nikuwaha nukutama, yadibomba*)." This statement well expresses the ambivalence of the red symbolism.

6. "Red things have power (*yikweti ng'ovu*); blood is power, for a

man, an animal, an insect, or a bird must have blood, or it will die. Wooden figurines (*nkishi*) have no blood and hence cannot breathe, speak, sing, laugh, or chat together—they are only carvings in wood. But if the figurines used by sorcerers (*aloji*) are given blood, they can move about and kill people."

7. "Semen (*matekela*) is white (lucky, pure) good blood (*mashi atooka amawahi*). If it is red (or) black, there is no begetting (*neyi achinana eyila kusema nehi*). Red semen is ineffective or impotent (*azeka*), it cannot penetrate fully (*ku-dita*)."

### BLACK

Black things include charcoal (*makala*), river mud (*malowa*), dye from the *mupuchi* and *musamba* trees (*wulombu,* the word now used for 'ink'), and the black fruits of the *muneku* tree. Blackness (*wuyila*) is:

1. badness or evil (*ku-tama*), bad things (*yuma yatama*);
2. to lack luck, purity, or whiteness (*ku-bula ku tooka*);
3. to have suffering (*yihung'u*) or misfortune (*malwa*);
4. to have diseases (*yikweti yikatu*);
5. witchcraft or sorcery (*wuloji*) [if your liver is black, you can kill a person, you are bad (*muchima neyi wuneyili wukutwesa ku-jaha muntu, wunatami dehi*); on the other hand, if your liver is white, you are good, you laugh with your friends, you are strong together, you prop one another up when you would have failed alone];
6. death (*ku-fwa*);
7. sexual desire (*wuvumbi*);
8. night (*wufuku*) or darkness (*mwidima*).

### COMMENTARY ON THE BLACK SYMBOLISM

The inventory of black attributes I have recorded here would inevitably give a false impression of how Ndembu regard this color were I to omit all reference to the concept of mystical or ritual death and to the related concept of the death of passion and hostility. The Ndembu concept *ku-fwa* (death) does not have the note of finality that, despite Christianity, death seems to possess in Western civilization. For the Ndembu, "to die" often means to reach the end of a particular stage of development, to reach the terminus of a cycle of growth. When a person dies he is still active, either as an ancestor spirit who keeps watch over the behavior of his living kin and manifests himself to them in various modes of affliction, or as partially reincarnated in a kinsman in the sense of reproducing in the latter some of his mental and physical characteristics. Such a person has undergone not merely a change in social status but also a change in mode of existence; here there is no question of annihilation. The term *ku-fwa* also stands for "fainting," and, indeed, on many occasions Ndembu have told me that they had "died" and recovered after treatment by a doctor (*chimbuki*). An English idiom that perhaps hits off the Ndembu sense best is "to have a black-out." Death is a black-out, a period of powerlessness and passivity between two living states. There is also a connection between the concepts "death" and "maturation" (*ku-kula*) among the Ndembu. One tends to grow up by definite stages, each of which is the death of the previous stage, by a series of "deaths and entrances." Thus when a girl first menstruates Ndembu say "*wunakuli dehi*," "she has matured," and the same remark is made at her first pregnancy rites and when she bears her first child. The connection between *ku-fwa* and *ku-kula* is strikingly illustrated also at the circumcision rites where the site of the operation is termed *ifwilu*, "the place of dying," while the place where the boys sit bleeding while they recover from the operation is a long *mukula* log, a red gum tree whose name is derived from *ku-kula*, "to mature." "Through death to maturity" might well be the motto of *Mukanda*, the circumcision rites. The site where a girl lies motionless, covered with a blanket, for a twelve-hour ordeal on the first day of her puberty rites (*Nkang'a*) is also *ifwilu* or *chilung'u*, the place of suffering (see Black Symbolism, item 3,) and the aim of these rites is to endow the novice with sexual maturity.

Black symbolism plays an important, though unobtrusive part, in the boys' circumcision rites. I have already mentioned how certain black symbolic articles constitute important ingredients of *nfunda* medicine. Again, when the novices are returned to their mothers after seclusion, they beat two sticks over their heads while they are carried by their ritual guardians (*yilombola*). These sticks are striped by alternate bands of white and black which, according to informants, stand for "life and death." Black symbolism sometimes appears also on the face masks of the *makishi* maskers, who are believed by the boys to emerge from under the ground at the *ifwilu* site. There one sees three horizontal rectangular bands, rather like a small flag. One is white, one red, and one black, white being uppermost and black underneath. These are described as "very important." In explanation I was referred to a song of the *Nkula* rites, performed *inter alia* to cure a woman of the frigidity that is preventing her, so Ndembu think, from conceiving a child, and that is associated with such menstrual disorders as menorrhagia and dysmenorrhea. The song runs:

> You destroy lines (stripes) mongoose, that is your habit which makes you refuse men, you destroy lines.
> (*Wakisa nyilenji nkala chaku chey'ochu chiwalekelang'a amayala, wakisa nyilenji.*)

It was then explained that the *nkala* species of mongoose has "red, white, and black stripes down its back." The song means that "the woman patient is a bad, useless woman, she has no power (*hawaheta ng'ovuku*)—you are destroying yourself woman; you ought to have babies, you are unworthy (*hawatelelaku*), guilty. You are a frigid woman (*wafwa mwitala,* literally, dead in the hut). The mongoose has stripes, but this woman, although she has been given her privy parts, has kept them useless." Incidentally, the stub of wood carried at all times during their seclusion by the novices at *Mukanda* and representing their *membrum virile* is also called *nkala,* "mongoose," and this animal is one of the tabooed foods of the lodge. It would seem to be a bisexual symbol for generative power and to represent the simultaneous action of all three color principles. What does black mean in their combination if it does not there mean evil or unlucky things?

There is undoubtedly a connection between the color black and sexual passion (*wuvumbi*). For example, during seclusion older women take the sooty black bark of certain trees, such as the *mudyi* tree, and blacken the novice's vulva. This is thought to enhance her sexual attractiveness. Women with very black skins are said by Ndembu men to be very desirable as mistresses, though not as wives. Sexual passion is associated with darkness and secrecy also. Hence black represents that which is hidden (*chakusweka, chakujinda*) and is not only hidden, but an object of longing. The Wagnerian notion of a love-death, as exemplified in *Tristan und Isolde,* springs to mind here.

Black is also connected with licit love and in several contexts represents marriage. For example, just after the girl's puberty rites are over, the novice spends the night with her bridegroom (known as *kalemba*). The couple have frequent intercourse, and if the bride considers herself satisfied she makes a secret sign of affirmation to her ritual instructress (*nkong'u*), who visits her early in the morning. The latter tiptoes away to collect some *malowa,* black alluvial mud, which she has fetched from a stream the previous evening at sundown and "kept hidden away from the eyes of men." Then she scatters a little *malowa* on the threshold of every hut in the village. This was explained to me as follows by an Ndembu informant: "The *malowa* is a symbol (*chinjikijilu*) of love (*nkeng'i*). For a young girl and her husband now love one another. But everyone in the village must connect with that same love. *Malowa* is used also because it is cold from the river. Their marriage must then be peaceful. *Malowa,* though it is black, does not stand for bad luck here, but marital peace or happiness (*wuluwi*)." Here blackness plus coldness appear to represent the cessation of hostility between two intermarrying groups, a hostility previously mimed in the rites. Black can, therefore, sometimes represent the "death" of an inauspicious or undesirable condition.

## *The White-Black Contrast*

A brief survey of the senses attributed by informants to "white" and "black" respectively indicates that these can mostly be arrayed in a series of antithetical pairs, as for example: goodness/badness; purity/lacking purity; lacking bad luck/lacking luck; lacking misfortune/misfortune; to be without death/death; life/death; health/disease; laughing with one's friends/witchcraft; to make visible/darkness, and so forth.

This mode of arrangement reveals clearly that when the colors are considered in abstraction from social and ritual contexts, Ndembu think of white and black as the supreme antitheses in their scheme of reality. Yet, as we shall see, in rite after rite white and red appear in conjunction and black is seldom directly expressed. In abstraction from actual situations, red seems to share the qualities of both white and black; but in action contexts red is regularly paired with white.

### THE CHARACTERISTICS OF THE COLORS WHITE AND RED

(1) Whiteness. Although each of the ritual colors has a wide fan of referents, nevertheless each has its own distinctive quality, which can be briefly expressed by saying that whiteness is positive, redness ambivalent, and blackness negative. To be "white" is to be in right relation to the living and the dead. To be in right relation to these is to be whole and hale in oneself. One neither incurs the wrath or envy of others, nor does one feel animosity towards them. Hence

one does not fear witchcraft or sorcery, nor is one inwardly tainted by the temptation to practice it. Such a one is admirably equipped to exercise authority (*wanta*), for he will not abuse his power. He will be generous with gifts and hospitality, and magnanimous. He will sweep away "evil things" from the village or chiefdom in his charge, just as he piously sweeps away dust and impurities from the base of the *muyombu* tree where he makes libation to the spirits of his ancestors (with the white maize or bullrush millet beer) and invokes their aid on behalf of his people. He will provide food for his people and nourish them with wisdom. For white is, *inter alia,* the symbol of nurture. This quality is "made visible," as Ndembu say, in such material forms as breast milk, semen, and cassava meal. It represents smooth continuity from generation to generation, and is associated with the pleasures of eating, begetting, and suckling. Begetting and feeding are, indeed, processes that are often identified by Ndembu. For example, after a woman is known to be pregnant her husband continues to have intercourse with her for some time "in order to feed the child" with his semen. The same term *ivumu* is used both for "stomach" and "womb," and a woman undergoing a long and difficult labor is often given food "to strengthen the child."

Another aspect of the white symbolism is the nature of the relationship between persons it represents. This is a relationship of feeder and fed. Dominance and subordination are certainly implied by it, mastery and submissiveness, but it is a benevolent dominance and a mild mastery. The senior partner in the relationship gives nourishment and knowledge to the junior. Whiteness expresses the generosity of the dominant partner and, at the same time, the gratitude of the subordinate. The situation of ancestor veneration brings out these features. The living bring wood, drink, and symbolic food in the form of *mpemba,* the white symbol par excellence, to the ancestor spirits at their shrine trees, which possess a white wood. Thus, at this phase of the proceedings the dead are dependent upon the living. On the other hand, the living are dependent upon the dead for long-term health, happiness, fertility, and good luck in hunting, for the ancestors are believed to have power to withhold these blessings and "to tie up" (*ku-kasila*) the fertility and huntsmanship (*wubinda*) of their living kin, if the latter neglect to make offerings to them. Furthermore, to get a hearing from the ancestors, the whole congregation, the core of which consists of the matrilineal kin of the ancestors, should by rights be at peace and in agreement with one another. This harmony between living and dead and among the living is represented by white marks on the *muyombu* tree, white lines between tree and invoker, white marks on the invoker and finally on the other members of the congregation. Once the circuit of whiteness is established, as it were, material nourishment and benefits and invisible virtues are believed to flow through the whole group including its deceased members.

Whiteness not only has the note of social cohesion and continuity, but also stands for that which can be seen by the eye, what is open, and unconcealed. Ndembu morality is essentially corporate; the private is the suspect, probably the dangerous, possibly the deadly. Persons who eat or work alone, such as certain chiefs and great hunters, are always suspected of possessing sorcery powers. In a society living at bare subsistence level, all must be seen to pull their weight, to share goods and services fairly. Persistent selfishness may actually imperil the survival of the group and must therefore be condemned. It is recognized that a person may live most of his life in full public view and yet have secret reservations about assisting his fellows. He may cherish grudges and nurse ambitions. Such a person, as I have shown in a paper on Ndembu divination (Turner 1961, 61–62), if exposed by divination, is regarded as a sorcerer. Whiteness is thus the light of public knowledge, of open recognition. In fact, it represents daylight, and both sun and moon are said to be its "symbols" (*yijikijilu*), contrary to what Baumann records of the Chokwe who, he says, regard white as "the color of moonlight" and red as "having connections with the sun" (1935, 40). Sun and moon are also regarded as symbols of God (*Nzambi*) and once more we come back to the notion that whiteness, more than any other color, represents the divinity as essence and source, as well as sustentation. Whiteness as light streaming forth from the divinity has, in the sense we are considering here, a quality of trustworthiness and veracity, for Ndembu believe that what is clearly seen can be accepted as a valid ground of knowledge.

White is also the unsullied and unpolluted. This quality of freedom from defilement may have either a moral or a ritual character. Thus I have heard an African storekeeper expostulate, when he was accused by his employer of embezzlement, "My liver is white," much as an Englishman would say, "My conscience is clear." On the other hand, there are certain ritually polluting states or statuses. An uncircumcised boy is known as *wunabulakutooka*, "one who lacks purity or whiteness," and he may not eat food cooked in the same pot as an adult man's meal. If he did so, it is believed that the various mystical powers acquired by a man as a result of having undergone many rites, such as the power to slaughter game, would lose their efficacy. It is believed that the "dirt under the foreskin" (*wanza,* regularly used as a term of abuse) of an uncircumcised boy is defiling in the extreme, regardless of his moral qualities as an individual. Water is regarded as "white" because it cleanses the body from dirt, but more especially because washing symbolizes the removal of impurities inherent in a biological condition or social status which one is now leaving behind. For example, novices at both boys' and girls' initiations are thoroughly washed just before they return to society after the period of seclusion. At the end of the funerary rites a widow or widower is washed, anointed with oil, shaved around the hair line, given a new white cloth, and adorned with white beads, a series of acts that illustrate the close connection between washing and white symbolism. What is being washed off in these life-crisis rites is the state of ritual death, the liminal condition between two periods of active social life. Whiteness or "purity" is hence in some respects identical with the legitimate incumbency of a socially recognized status. To behave in a way that transgresses the norms of that status, however innocuous that behavior might be for the incumbent of another status, constitutes impurity. It is particularly impure to behave regressively, that is, in terms of the norms of a status occupied earlier in the individual life-cycle. This is because the successive stages of life are felt to represent an ascent from the impurity of the uncircumcised to the purity of the aged in the case of men, and from the impurity of a menstruating maiden, through the increasing purity of the mother of many children, to the postmenopausal status of *kashinakaji,* the venerable leader of the village women. Ancestorhood is purer still and albinos are regarded as peculiarly propitious beings because they have "the whiteness of ancestor spirits" (*wutooka wawakishi*).

Behind the symbolism of whiteness, then, lie the notions of harmony, continuity, purity, the manifest, the public, the appropriate, and the legitimate.

(2) Redness. What are we to make of the red symbolism which, in its archetypal form in the initiation rites, is represented by the intersection of two "rivers of blood"? This duality, this ambivalence, this simultaneous possession of two contrary values or qualities, is quite characteristic of redness in the Ndembu view. As they say: "Redness acts both for good and ill." Thus, while it is good to combine the blood of the mother with that of the father, it is bad to practice necropha-

gous witchcraft. Both the blood of childbirth and the blood relished by witches are represented by red oxidized clay or earth (*mukundu, ng'ula*). Red is peculiarly the color of blood or flesh, the carnal color. Hence it is redolent of the aggressiveness and pangs of carnality. It stands for the killing and cutting up of animals and for the pains of labor. There is something impure, too, about redness. A homicide has to be purified from the stain of the blood he has shed, though he is entitled to wear the red feather of Livingstone's lourie (*nduwa*) after the purification rites on subsequent ritual occasions. Red stands also for the menstruation of women in such rites as, for example, *Nkula,* a term that is sometimes used as a synonym for menstruation. The common term for menstrual discharge is *mbayi,* which may be connected with *ku-baya,* "to be guilty," though *kanyanda* is often employed. *Kasheta* represents a menstrual period, but the circumlocution *ku-kiluka kwitala dikwawu,* "to jump to the other hut," is quite commonly heard. For until recently, each village had at least one grass hut near the edge of the bush in which women stayed during their periods. Here they prepared their own food. They were forbidden to cook for their husbands and children or eat food with them during this time. Another woman of the village would undertake these offices for them during their absence. The blood of menstruation and murder is, therefore, "bad" blood and is connected by Ndembu with blackness.[2] However, the blood shed by a hunter and offered at the graves and shrines of hunter ancestors is reckoned to be "good" blood and is associated ritually with white symbolism. Most rites of the hunters' cult are characterized by conjunction of white and red symbols.

There appears to be some correlation of the male role with the taking of life and of the female role with the giving of life, though both activities remain under the rubric of redness. Man kills, woman gives birth, and both processes are associated with the symbolism of blood.

Semen, as we have noted above, is blood "purified by water." The father's contribution to the child is, therefore, free from the impurity that invests female blood. Since whiteness is particularly closely associated with the ancestor spirits and with *Nzambi,* the High God, it might be said that the "father's blood" is more "spiritual" and less "carnal" than the mother's blood. This greater purity is probably linked with the universal Ndembu belief that father-and-child is the

[2] Witches' familiars, called *tuyebela, andumba,* or *tushipa,* are commonly supposed to be kept in the menstruation hut.

one relationship completely free from the taint of witchcraft or sorcery. Mother-and-child, on the contrary, is far from free from this taint, and witches are thought to kill their own infants to provide "meat" for the coven. Again, while a person has a strong jural bond to his maternal kin, he is considered by Ndembu to owe to his father and his father's kin important elements of his personality. For it is his father who has recourse to divination to find a name for him shortly after his birth, and it is from his father's deceased kin that he usually obtains it. It is believed that certain traits of character and physique of the name-giving spirit are reincarnated in the child. Again, the father plays an important role at *Mukanda,* the boys' circumcision rites, in providing care, instruction, and protection (against the carelessness of circumcisers) for his son during seclusion, while the mother is excluded from the lodge altogether. I mention these practices and beliefs to stress the "pure" nature of the father-child tie. It is well known among Ndembu that relationships between matrilineal kin are often strained, since competition is likely to develop between them over matters of inheritance and succession. Competition in kinship relations in African tribal society tends in the long run to give rise to accusations of sorcery and witchcraft, and sorcerers and witches, in Ndembu theory, are people "with black livers" who lust after "red human flesh" and harbor "grudges" (*yitela*) which are classed among "black things." Thus, while harmony lies on the "white" father's side, competition lies on the "red" mother's side (cf. Beidelman 1961, 253–254)—at least on the level of values if not of facts.

## WHITE AND RED AS A BINARY SYSTEM

This discussion of the sex-linking of white and red in the Ndembu theory of procreation leads inevitably to a consideration of these colors as a pair, as a binary system. For black is very often the neglected member of the triad. There are a number of reasons for this. In the first place, Ndembu regard symbols as articles or actions that "make visible" or bring into play the powers inhering in the objects they signify.[3] Thus, to employ a black symbol would be to evoke death, sterility, and witchcraft. Those contexts in which black is displayed openly, for instance the black and white striped sticks in *Mukanda* and the black band on the *ikishi* mask, usually refer to ritual death and are closely connected with the opposite notion of regeneration.

[3] A point I have discussed at length elsewhere, e.g., in *Ndembu Divination* (1961), 4.

When black symbols are used, as in the case of *malowa,* the black alluvial earth, they tend to be swiftly buried or hidden from view. *Malowa,* for example, is in several kinds of rites (*Kayong'u, Chihamba, Wubwang'u*) to propitiate ancestor spirits either plastered round the base of ritual objects, such as tree shrines, or buried under symbols of illness, "to make them cool," i.e., to bring about the death of the "hot" and hence mystically dangerous aspects of the affliction. It is alleged that sorcerers make use of materials considered "black" and "impure" such as the feces of their intended victims, cindered foreskins stolen from circumcisers, and the like, as ingredients of death-dealing "medicine" (*wang'a*). This very allegation illustrates how closely black symbolism is connected with socially undesirable behavior or with the privation of life and goodness. It is the extinction, whether willed or otherwise, of everything that moves, breathes, and has self-determination.

White and red, on the contrary, are associated with activity. Both are considered "to have power." Blood, the main denotation of "redness," is even identified with "power." White, too, stands for life fluids; it represents milk and semen. Black, on the contrary, stands for body leavings, body dirt, and the fluids of putrefaction, and for the products of catabolism. There is, however, an important difference between white and red, for the former represents the preservation and continuance of life, whereas the latter may represent the taking of life, and even where, as in the case of certain red symbols, such as the *mukula* tree, it represents continuity through parturition, it still has a note of danger and discontinuity. Killing is an activity of the living, giving birth is also such an activity. Hence, red, like white, falls under the general rubric of "life." When it is associated with purity, we may think of red as blood shed for the communal good. Red may be tinctured with white in Ndembu thinking, as in the case of normal semen, "blood whitened by water," or with black, as in the case of an impotent man's semen, "dead semen." Where a twofold classification of things as 'white' or 'red' develops, with black either absent or hidden, it sometimes happens that red acquires many of the negative and undesirable attributes of blackness, without retaining its better ones. It is, of course, of the essence of polarity that contrary qualities are assigned to the poles. Therefore, when the threefold color classification yields to a twofold classification, we find red becoming, not only the complement, but also in some contexts, the antithesis of white. It might be apposite here to cite A. B. Kempe, the symbolic logician, who wrote: "It is characteristically human to think in terms of dyadic relations: we habitually break up a triadic relation into a pair of dyads. In fact so ingrained is this disposition that some will object that a triadic relation is a pair of dyads. It would be exactly as logical to maintain that all dyadic relations are triads with a null member" (1890). In cases where white and red are regarded as complementary, rather than as antithetical pairs, we may very probably be dealing with a triadic relation of which black is the "null member." Since it is difficult, owing to Ndembu ideas about the nature of representation, to represent black visibly without evoking its inauspicious power, its absence from view may not necessarily mean its absence from thought. Indeed, its very absence may be significant since it is the true emblem of the hidden, the secret, the dark, the unknown—and perhaps also of potentiality as opposed to actuality. White and red, paired under the various aspects of male and female, peace and war, milk and flesh, semen and blood, are jointly "life" (*wumi*); both are opposed to black as death and negativity.

## *Some Comparative Data*

Since I have had little opportunity to comb through the literature systematically, what follows must necessarily be somewhat haphazard. I begin this comparative survey with ethnographic data on contemporary primitives, grouping them in broad regions.

### AFRICA

M. Griaule (1950, 58–81) describes the relationship among the Dogon of West Africa between a cosmological myth, masks, statuettes, ritual, rupestral painting, and the color rubrics, white, red, and black. Here black is associated with pollution, red with the menstrual blood of the Earth Mother who committed incest with her first-born, the Jackal, and white with purity. A large wooden image of a serpent, representing death and rebirth, is consecrated by blood sacrifices and decorated with these colors. Young male initiands wear masks colored with white, black, and red. Wall paintings used in the rites are renewed with pigments of these hues. Red is also associated with the sun and fire.

Arthur Leib (1946, 128–133) summarizes what he calls "the mythical significance" of colors among the peoples of Madagascar as follows: "With *black,* words like the following are associated: inferior, unpleasant, evil, suspicious, disagreeable, undesirable. With *white:* light, hope, joy, purity. With *red:* power, might, wealth."

I have mentioned the ambivalence of black symbolism among the Ndembu. Black alluvial clay (*malowa*) is a symbol of fertility and marital love. Now, in many African societies black has auspicious connotations. Among the Shona of Southern Rhodesia black represents *inter alia* the rain-bearing clouds which usher in the wet season, and sacrifices to spirit-guardians who send rain are made in black cattle, goats, or fowl while the spirit-mediums or priests wear black cloth. Thus in contiguous Bantu societies, black may represent sterility in one and fertility in the other. According to Huntingford (1953a, 52) a black bullock is slaughtered over the grave of a rainmaker among the Kuku of Bari stock, while at the rainmaking ceremonies of the Lokoya, a black goat is killed and the contents of its stomach smeared on the stones at the grave of the rainmaker's father. It is Huntingford, too, who informs us that among the Sandawe of Tanganyika "priests (or diviners) are also rainmakers and offer sacrifices of black oxen, goats and sheep to bring rain" (1953b, 138).

The Sandawe have often been alleged to have affinities with the Bushmen. It is therefore interesting to find that among the latter, according to Bleek and Lloyd (1911), a lustrous black powder made of pounded specularite (specular iron) and known as *//hara* by the Cape Bushmen, was used as body decoration and hair dressing and appears to have been attributed with magical qualities. Thus, to quote one of Bleek's texts:

> They anoint their heads with *//hara* very nicely, while they wish that their head's hair may descend (i.e., grow long). And it becomes abundant because of *//hara;* because they have anointed their heads, wishing that the hair may grow downwards, that their heads may become black with blackness . . . *//hara* sparkles; therefore our heads shimmer on account of it. . . . Therefore, the Bushmen are wont to say . . . "That man, he is a handsome young man, on account of his head, which is surpassingly beautiful with the *//hara's* blackness" (p. 375, p. 377).

It is worth noting, in anticipation, that specularite was apparently "an often sought after medium for paint in the Later Stone Age in the Cape, judging by the pieces that are found in the occupation sites" (Clark 1959, 244). My own hypothesis is that black tends to become an auspicious color in regions where water is short, for the black clouds bring fertility and growth (apparently of hair, as well as plants!). In regions where water is plentiful and food more or less abundant, black may well be inauspicious. Thus it is not only among the Forest Bantu and Malagasy peoples that we find black to be inauspicious. For example, in a recent article Joan Wescott (1962, 346) writes: "Black is associated (by the Yoruba) with the night and the night is associated . . . with evil. It is at night that sorcery and witchcraft are abroad and men are most vulnerable. Some Yoruba say simply that Elegba (the Trickster deity) is painted black because of his wickedness."

### MALAY PENINSULA

The Bushmen employ all three colors ritually. So also do the Semang, Sakai, and Jakun of the Malay Peninsula. Like the Bushman these peoples are hunters and gatherers. Skeat and Blagden (1906, 31) write that the Sakai paint their bodies in "black, white, red, and occasionally yellow, which last two appear to be of equivalent value from a magical point of view"—incidentally, just as they are among the Ndembu. When children are born among the Sakai the midwife applies stripes of pigment from the eyebrows to the tip of the nose, black in the case of girls, red in that of boys (p. 48). The black nose line is said to be for the protection of women against "the Blood Demon" (*Hantu Darah*) which stops a woman's courses, and so prevents her bringing healthy children into the world. White is generally an auspicious color, among the Sakai and other Malay peoples.

### AUSTRALIA

Charles P. Mountford (1962, 215) mentions that all three colors are used in the cave art of the Australian aborigines—black in the form of manganese oxide or one of the ferruginous ores, white from pipe-clay or kaolin deposits, and red ochre which may be secured by mining and trade—indeed, men will travel a hundred miles or more to collect these ochres from special localities (such as Wilgamia in West Australia and Blinman in the North Flinders Ranges of South Australia) (p. 210).

Mountford describes how white and red pigments are used in the cave paintings of the Wandjinas—tall mouthless figures with a halo-like design around their faces; sometimes these may be eighteen feet high. The face is always in white and surrounded by one, sometimes two, horseshoe-shaped bows which, in some examples, have lines radiating from them. These are usually in red. "The aborigines believe," says Mountford, "that the paintings are filled with the essence of both water and blood; the water, so necessary for all living things, is symbolized by the white face and the blood, which makes men and animals strong, by the red ochre bows." Note once more the close affinity with Ndembu exegesis of white and red. Water is "white" for Ndembu and blood, of course, is "red."

### NORTH AMERICAN INDIAN

My last example from ethnographic sources is drawn from the New World, from Mooney's *Sacred Formulas of the Cherokees* (quoted by Lewis Spence in his article on the Cherokees in *Hastings Encyclopaedia of Religion and Ethics*). Mooney shows how, among the Cherokees, white represents peace, happiness, and the south; red is equated with success, triumph, and the north; black with death and the west; and blue with defeat, trouble, and the east. These senses probably indicate that, as in parts of Africa, blue is felt to have affinities with black. Certain Cherokee divinities and spirits correspond in color to the characteristics imputed to them. White and red spirits when combined were usually regarded as those from whom emanated the blessings of peace and health. The black spirits were invoked to slay an enemy. It is interesting to recall here how white and red in Ndembu ritual are used to betoken powers that may be combined for the benefit of the subject of the rites (e.g., in hunting and gynecological ritual), while black is the color of sorcery or witchcraft.

### THE ANCIENT WORLD

Perhaps the most sophisticated exegesis of the color triad and the most elaborate working out of its implications is to be found in the Chhāndogya Upanishad of ancient Hinduism and in the commentary by Śri Śankārachārya, the great eighth-century philosopher. Swami Nikhilinanda has recently translated the Upanishads and supplied notes based on Śankārachārya's explanations. I shall quote a few passages from the Chhāndogya Upanishad (VI, iv, 1) and follow the first text with Nikhilinanda's commentary:

The red colour of (gross) fire is the colour of (the original fire); the white colour of (gross) fire is the colour of (the original) water [remember here the Ndembu and Aboriginal usages]; the black colour of (gross) fire is the colour of (the original earth). Thus vanishes from fire what is commonly called fire, the modification being only a name, arising from speech, while the three colours (forms) alone are true.

Commentary:

The three colours, or forms, constitute the visible fire. When these three colours are explained as belonging to the original fire, water, and earth, fire as it is commonly known disappears, and also the word "fire." For fire has no existence apart from a word and the idea denoted by that word. Therefore what the ignorant denote by the word "fire" is false, *the only truth being the three colours* [my italics].

The whole world is tripartite. Therefore, as in the case of fire (or in the cases of sun, moon, lightning, etc.) the only truth about the world is the three colours. Earth being only an effect of water, the only truth is water; earth is a mere name. So, too, water, being an effect of fire, is a mere name, the only truth being fire. Fire, too, being an effect of *Sat* or Pure Being, is a mere name, the only truth being Pure Being.

In this Upanishad the colors are sometimes known as "deities." Examples are given of the way in which they manifest themselves in phenomena. Thus, "food when eaten becomes threefold. What is coarsest in it (the black part) becomes feces, what is medium (the red part) becomes flesh, and what is subtlest (the white part) becomes mind" (VI, v. 1).

Also, "water when drunk becomes threefold. What is coarsest in it (or black) becomes urine, what is medium (or red), becomes blood and what is subtlest (or white) becomes *prana* (= the vital breath which sustains life in a physical body or the primal energy or force, of which other forces are manifestations)."

The three colors appear to be identical with the *gunas* or "strands" of existence (a metaphor from weaving) found in the Samkya-Karika, a work attributed to the sage Kapila. These are described by R. C. Zaehner (1962, 91) as "permeating every corner of Nature's being (*praktri*)." These three are called *sattva, rajas,* and *tamas* which can be literally translated as "the quality of being, energy, and darkness." *Sattva* is the quality of purity and tranquility (and may be equated with white); *rajas* is the active principle which initiates *karma* (and may be equated with red), while *tamas* is "constrictive, obstructive, and conducive to lethargic apathy (and may be equated with black)." Zaehner quotes from Book 4, Chapter 5 of the great epic of the Mahabharata some verses that throw further light on the relationship between the *gunas* and the colors:

With the one unborn Female, white, red, and black ["symbolizing the three *gunas,*" as Zaehner writes] who produces many creatures like herself.

Lies the one unborn Male, taking his delight: another unborn Male leaves her when she has had her pleasure of him.

It would seem probable that the notion of the colors is an inheritance from a remote (perhaps pre-Indo-European) past and that the Upanishadic texts are the speculations of a later philosophy on this primordial deposit.

It is again worth recalling at this point that the three colors or forms, in ancient Hinduism, are ultimately reducible to a single nature or being, to *Sat* or *Praktri,* for the Ndembu notion that the "three rivers" of color flow from Deity is not dissimilar. We find again in both cultures the notion that white is connected with purity and peace and is the "subtlest" or most "spiritual" of the colors.

Much the same range of senses seems to be possessed by white in Semitic religions, for Robertson Smith records of the Arabs (1912, 590, 583) that when a man disgraces himself by a breach of traditional custom or etiquette his face becomes black, whereas when he restores the omission, or makes up a quarrel, it again becomes white. There are also similarities between the senses of red in Hindu and Semitic cultures. The common Hebrew word for passion (*quin'ah*) is derived from a verbal root that means primarily "to be crimson"; *rajas,* the second, "red" "strand" is often translated as "passion" by English and American scholars. Maurice Farbridge (*Hastings Encyclopaedia*) writes that for the Old Testament Hebrews, "red, as the colour of blood, represented bloodshed, war & guilt."

## *The Three Colors in Archaeological Literature*

In Africa many finds from the Stone Age from widely separated parts of Africa attest to the use of white, red, and black in ritual contexts. To pick a few at random: Roger Summers (1958, 295) excavated a shelter at Chitura Rocks in Inyanga District on the eastern border of Southern Rhodesia and found in association with Stillbay artifacts of the Middle Stone Age at the back of the shelter numerous small lumps of red ochre mixed with similar sized pieces of charcoal. Leakey (1931, 109) discovered in Gamble's Cave II at Elmenteita in Kenya several skeletons buried in the ultracontracted position, males lying on the right side, females on the left, and all were freely sprinkled with red ochre. These skeletons resembled the

Oldoway skeleton discovered in 1913 in northern Tanganyika. Men of this type have been found in association with Chellean and even pre-Chelles-Acheul cultures with pebble choppers and flake tools.

Van Riet Lowe (quoted by Desmond Clark 1959, 249) describes Later Stone Age Bushman burials at Smithfield in the Orange Free State in the following terms: "An inverted half of an ostrich eggshell lay beneath the arms of the flexed skeleton, coated internally with (black) specularite [which, you will recall, is still used by Bushmen as a hair decoration] and externally with red ochre." At Wilton in the Southern Region, Clark mentions that there were almost invariably a number of gravestones, some of which were grindstones, some covered in ochre or even painted. The body was "liberally covered with red ochre as were some of the grave goods."

White, too, is used in early African rupestral art. For example, C. K. Cooke, writing of the prehistoric artist's materials and techniques in Southern Matabeleland, Rhodesia (in Clark 1957, 284), describes how bird droppings (still called *mpemba,* "white clay," by Ndembu), vegetable substances, and kaolin are used in the manufacture of white pigments for cave and rock paintings.

I cannot here discuss the rich literature on burial practices and cave art in the European Palaeolithic, but it again seems clear that the color triad white-red-black is always prominent, though other colors, such as yellows and browns are also used. Archaeologists are still undecided as to the significance of the colors. Their views may perhaps be typified by Annette Laming's (1959, 112) comments on the Lascaux cave paintings:

> The colours vary from group to group: sometimes one colour seems to have been more in favour than another. These preferences may have been due to the need for an economical use of some raw material which was particularly prized and difficult to obtain; or they may have been inspired by religious faith—by the belief in the greater efficacy of a certain red, or a particularly intense black, for example; or they may have been merely the result of a change in aesthetic taste.

The hypothesis I am putting forward here is that magico-religious ideas of a certain kind were responsible for the selection of the basic color triad and for the assiduity with which its constituent colors were sought or prepared. It is not the rarity of the pigments that makes them prized but the fact that they are prized for magico-religious reasons that make men overcome all kinds of difficulties to obtain or manufacture them. I could cite much evidence to demonstrate the quite extraordinary lengths to which some societies will go to get red or black or white pigments. Sometimes to prepare a pure color many ingredients are used, some of them probably with ritual intent. Thus, to make white paint for Dogon masks, limestone powder is mixed with cooked rice and the excrement of lizards or large snakes; the masks are used in rites connected with a mythical serpent. Among the Luluba, a Northern Nilo-Hamitic people, there is a big trade in a red ochreous substance made from biotite gneiss, which is powdered, buried for two months, and then after several processes roasted, when it can be mixed with simsim oil. Even black pigment may involve some degree of complexity in manufacture, as among the Dogon where it is obtained from the burnt seeds of *Vitex pachyphylla,* the ashes being mixed with a tannin decoction. There are frequent records, both in prehistoric and in contemporary preindustrial societies, of long trading expeditions being made to obtain red ochres.

## *The Significance of the Basic Color Triad*

In ethnographic literature, it is noteworthy that among societies that make ritual use of all three colors, the critical situation in which these appear together is initiation. Each may appear separately as a sign of the general character of a rite; thus red may be a persistent motif in hunting rites among the Ndembu and white in rites dealing with lactation or village ancestral shades. At the initiation of juniors into the rights and duties and values of seniors, all three colors receive equal emphasis. In my view this is because they epitomize the main kinds of universal human organic experience. In many societies these colors have explicit reference to certain fluids, secretions or waste products of the human body. Red is universally a symbol of blood, white is frequently a symbol of breast milk and semen (and sometimes of pus), while, as we have seen, the Chhāndogya Upanishad relates the black color with feces and urine (though other cultures connect urine with semen and both with whiteness). Each of the colors in all societies is multivocal, having a wide fan of connotations, but nevertheless the human physiological component is seldom absent wherever reliable native exegesis is available. Initiation rites often draw their symbolism from the situation of parturition and first lactation, where, in nature, blood, water, feces, and milk are present.

I am going to throw caution to the winds for the sake of stimulating controversy and state boldly that:

1. Among the earliest symbols produced by man are the three colors representing products of the human body whose emission,

spilling, or production is associated with a heightening of emotion. In other words, culture, the superorganic, has an intimate connection with the organic in its early stages, with the awareness of powerful physical experiences.

2. These heightened bodily experiences are felt to be informed with a power in excess of that normally possessed by the individual; its source may be located in the cosmos or in society; analogues of physical experience may then be found wherever the same colors occur in nature; or else experience of social relations in heightened emotional circumstances may be classified under a color rubric.

3. The colors represent heightened physical experience transcending the experiencer's normal condition; they are therefore conceived as deities (Hindu) or mystical powers, as the sacred over against the profane.

4. The physical experiences associated with the three colors are also experiences of social relationships: white = semen is linked to mating between man and woman; white = milk is linked to the mother-child tie; red = maternal blood is linked to the mother-child tie and also the processes of group recruitment and social placement; red = bloodshed is connected with war, feud, conflict, social discontinuities; red = obtaining and preparation of animal food = status of hunter or herder, male productive role in the sexual division of labor, etc.; red = transmission of blood from generation to generation = an index of membership in a corporate group; black = excreta or bodily dissolution = transition from one social status to another viewed as mystical death; black = rain clouds or fertile earth = unity of widest recognized group sharing same life values.

5. While it is possible to find many references to body fluids in white and red symbolism, few societies specifically connect black with processes and products of catabolism and decay, for example, with decayed or clotted blood. It is possible that black which, as we have seen, often means "death," a "fainting fit," "sleep," or "darkness" primarily represents falling into unconsciousness, the experience of a "black-out." Among Ndembu, and in many other societies, both white and red may stand for life. When they are paired in ritual, white may stand for one alleged polarity of life, such as masculinity or vegetable food, while red may represent its opposite, such as femininity or meat. On the other hand, white may represent "peace" and red "war"; both are conscious activities as distinct from black which stands for inactivity and the cessation of consciousness.

6. Not only do the three colors stand for basic human experiences

of the body (associated with the gratification of libido, hunger, aggressive and excretory drives, and with fear, anxiety, and submissiveness), they also provide a kind of primordial classification of reality. This view is in contrast to Durkheim's notion that the social relations of mankind are not based on the logical relations of things but have served as the prototypes of the latter. Nor has society, Durkheim argues, been merely the model on which the classifying thought has wrought: the framework of society has been the very framework of the system of things. Men were themselves first grouped. For that reason they could think under the form of groups. The center of the earliest system of nature is not the individual: it is the society. Against this I would postulate that the human organism and its crucial experiences are the *fons et origo* of all classifications. Human biology demands certain intense experiences of relationship. If men and women are to beget and bear, suckle, and dispose of physical wastes they must enter into relationships—relationships which are suffused with the affective glow of the experiences. These are the very processes the Ndembu call "rivers"—they stream from man's inner nature. The color triad white-red-black represents the archetypal man as a pleasure-pain process. The perception of these colors and of triadic and dyadic relations in the cosmos and in society, either directly or metaphorically, is a derivative of primordial psychobiological experience—experience that can be fully attained only in human mutuality. It needs two to copulate, two to suckle and wean, two to fight and kill, and three to form a family. The multitude of interlaced classifications that make up ideological systems controlling social relationships are derivatives, divested of affectual accompaniments, of these primordial twos and threes. The basic three are sacred because they have the power "to carry the man away," to overthrow his normal powers of resistance. Though immanent in his body, they appear to transcend his consciousness. By representing these "forces" or "strands of life" by color symbols in a ritual context, men may have felt that they could domesticate or control these forces for social ends, but the forces and the symbols for them are biologically, psychologically, and logically prior to social classifications by moieties, clans, sex totems, and all the rest. Since the experiences the three colors represent are common to all mankind, we do not have to invoke diffusion to explain their wide distribution. We do have to invoke diffusion to explain why other colors, such as yellow, saffron, gold, blue, green, purple, etc., are ritually important in certain cultures. We must also look to processes of culture contact to explain differences in the senses attributed to the basic colors in different regions. The point I am trying to make here is that the three colors white-red-black for the simpler societies are not merely differences in the visual perception of parts of the spectrum: they are abridgments or condensations of whole realms of psychobiological experience involving reason and all the senses and concerned with primary group relationships. It is only by subsequent abstraction from these configurations that the other modes of social classification employed by mankind arose.

## BIBLIOGRAPHY

Baumann, H. 1935. *Lunda: Bei Bauern und Jägern in Inner Angola.* Berlin: Würfel-Verlag.

Beidelman, T. 1961. "Right and Left Hand among the Kaguru," *Africa*, XXXI, No. 3.

Bleek, W. H. I., and Lloyd, L. C. 1911. *Specimens of Bushman Folklore.* London: George Allen.

Clark, J. D. 1959. *The Prehistory of Southern Africa.* Harmondsworth: Penguin Books.

Cooke, C. K. 1957. In J. Desmond Clark, ed., *Prehistory* (Third Pan African Congress, 1955). London: Chatto & Windus.

Durkheim, E., and Mauss, M. 1963. In R. Needham, ed., *Primitive Classification.* London: Cohen & West; Chicago: University of Chicago Press.

Fairbridge, Maurice. 1922. Article on "Symbolism (Semitic)," *Hastings Encyclopaedia of Religion and Ethics,* XII, 150. Edinburgh: T. & T. Clark.

Griaule, M. 1950. *Arts of the African Native.* London: Thames & Hudson.

Harries, Lyndon. 1944. "The Initiation Rites of the Makonde Tribe," *Communications from the Rhodes-Livingstone Institute,* No. 3.

Hertz, Robert. 1960. *Death and the Right Hand.* London: Cohen & West.

Huntingford, G. W. B. 1953a. *The Northern Nilo-Hamites.* "Ethnographic Survey of Africa, East-Central Africa," Part 6. London: International African Institute.

—— 1953b. *The Southern Nilo-Hamites.* "Ethnographic Survey of Africa, East-Central Africa," Part 8. London: International African Institute.

Kempe, A. B. 1890. "On the Relation between the Logical Theory of

Classes and the Geometrical Theory of Points," *Proceedings of the London Mathematical Society*, XXI.

Laming, Annette. 1959. *Lascaux*. Harmondsworth: Penguin Books.

Leakey, L. S. B. 1931. *The Stone Age Cultures of Kenya Colony*. London: Oxford University Press.

Leib, Arthur. 1946. *Folklore*, LVII, 128–133.

Mountford, Charles P. 1962. *Oceania and Australia* (Art of the World Series, VIII). London: Methuen.

Needham, Rodney. 1960. "The Left Hand of the Mugwe," *Africa*, XXX, No. 1.

Nikhilinananda, Swami, trans. 1963. *Upanishads*. New York: Harper, Row.

Richards, A. I. 1956. *Chisungu*. London: Faber & Faber.

Skeat, W. W., and Blagden, C. O. 1906. *Pagan Races of the Malay Peninsula*. London: Macmillan.

Smith, Robertson W. 1912. "A Journey in the Hedjaz." In J. S. Black and G. Crystal, eds., *Lectures and Essays*. London: A. & C. Black.

Spence, Lewis. 1911. Article on "Cherokees," *Hastings Encyclopaedia of Religion and Ethics*, III, 506–507.

Summers, Roger. 1958. *Inyanga*. London: Cambridge University Press.

Turner, Victor W. 1961. *Ndembu Divination: Its Symbolism and Techniques* (Rhodes-Livingstone Paper 31). Manchester University Press.

Vergiat, A. M. 1936. *Les Rites Secrets des Primitifs de l'Oubangui*. Paris: Payot.

Wescott, Joan. 1962. "The Sculpture and Myths of Eshu-Elegba, The Yoruba Trickster," *Africa*, XXXII, No. 4.

White, C. M. N. 1961. *Elements in Luvale Beliefs and Rituals* (Rhodes-Livingstone Institute Paper 32). Manchester University Press.

Zaehner, R. C. 1962. *Hinduism*. London: Oxford University Press.

## CHAPTER IV

# Betwixt and Between: The Liminal Period in *Rites de Passage**

IN this paper, I wish to consider some of the sociocultural properties of the "liminal period" in that class of rituals which Arnold van Gennep has definitively characterized as "*rites de passage.*" If our basic model of society is that of a "structure of positions," we must regard the period of margin or "liminality" as an interstructural situation. I shall consider, notably in the case of initiation rites, some of the main features of instruction among the simpler societies. I shall also take note of certain symbolic themes that concretely express indigenous concepts about the nature of "interstructural" human beings.

*Rites de passage* are found in all societies but tend to reach their maximal expression in small-scale, relatively stable and cyclical societies, where change is bound up with biological and meteorological rhythms and recurrences rather than with technological innovations. Such rites indicate and constitute transitions between states. By "state" I mean here "a relatively fixed or stable condition" and would include in its meaning such social constancies as legal status, profession, office or calling, rank or degree. I hold it to designate also the condition of a person as determined by his culturally recognized degree of maturation as when one speaks of "the married or single state" or the "state of infancy." The term "state" may also be applied

* Read at the Annual Meeting of the American Ethnological Society in Pittsburgh, March 1964. First published in *The Proceedings of the American Ethnological Society* (1964).

to ecological conditions, or to the physical, mental or emotional condition in which a person or group may be found at a particular time. A man may thus be in a state of good or bad health; a society in a state of war or peace or a state of famine or of plenty. State, in short, is a more inclusive concept than status or office and refers to any type of stable or recurrent condition that is culturally recognized. One may, I suppose, also talk about "a state of transition," since J. S. Mill has, after all, written of "a state of progressive movement," but I prefer to regard transition as a process, a becoming, and in the case of *rites de passage* even a transformation—here an apt analogy would be water in process of being heated to boiling point, or a pupa changing from grub to moth. In any case, a transition has different cultural properties from those of a state, as I hope to show presently.

Van Gennep himself defined "*rites de passage*" as "rites which accompany every change of place, state, social position and age." To point up the contrast between "state" and "transition," I employ "state" to include all his other terms. Van Gennep has shown that all rites of transition are marked by three phases: separation, margin (or *limen*), and aggregation. The first phase of separation comprises symbolic behavior signifying the detachment of the individual or group either from an earlier fixed point in the social structure or a set of cultural conditions (a "state"); during the intervening liminal period, the state of the ritual subject (the "passenger") is ambiguous; he passes through a realm that has few or none of the attributes of the past or coming state; in the third phase the passage is consummated. The ritual subject, individual or corporate, is in a stable state once more and, by virtue of this, has rights and obligations of a clearly defined and "structural" type, and is expected to behave in accordance with certain customary norms and ethical standards. The most prominent type of *rites de passage* tends to accompany what Lloyd Warner (1959, 303) has called "the movement of a man through his lifetime, from a fixed placental placement within his mother's womb to his death and ultimate fixed point of his tombstone and final containment in his grave as a dead organism—punctuated by a number of critical moments of transition which all societies ritualize and publicly mark with suitable observances to impress the significance of the individual and the group on living members of the community. These are the important times of birth, puberty, marriage, and death." However, as van Gennep, Henri Junod, and others have shown, *rites de passage* are not confined to culturally defined life-crises but may accompany any change from one state to another, as when a whole tribe goes to war, or when it attests to the passage from scarcity to plenty by performing a first-fruits or a harvest festival. *Rites de passage,* too, are not restricted, sociologically speaking, to movements between ascribed statuses. They also concern entry into a new achieved status, whether this be a political office or membership of an exclusive club or secret society. They may admit persons into membership of a religious group where such a group does not include the whole society, or qualify them for the official duties of the cult, sometimes in a graded series of rites.

Since the main problem of this study is the nature and characteristics of transition in relatively stable societies, I shall focus attention on *rites de passage* that tend to have well-developed liminal periods. On the whole, initiation rites, whether into social maturity or cult membership, best exemplify transition, since they have well-marked and protracted marginal or liminal phases. I shall pay only brief heed here to rites of separation and aggregation, since these are more closely implicated in social structure than rites of liminality. Liminality during initiation is, therefore, the primary datum of this study, though I will draw on other aspects of passage ritual where the argument demands this. I may state here, partly as an aside, that I consider the term "ritual" to be more fittingly applied to forms of religious behavior associated with social transitions, while the term "ceremony" has a closer bearing on religious behavior associated with social states, where politico-legal institutions also have greater importance. Ritual is transformative, ceremony confirmatory.

The subject of passage ritual is, in the liminal period, structurally, if not physically, "invisible." As members of society, most of us see only what we expect to see, and what we expect to see is what we are conditioned to see when we have learned the definitions and classifications of our culture. A society's secular definitions do not allow for the existence of a not-boy-not-man, which is what a novice in a male puberty rite is (if he can be said to be anything). A set of essentially religious definitions co-exist with these which do set out to define the structurally indefinable "transitional-being." The transitional-being or "liminal *persona*" is defined by a name and by a set of symbols. The same name is very frequently employed to designate those who are being initiated into very different states of life. For example, among the Ndembu of Zambia the name *mwadi* may mean various things: it may stand for "a boy novice in circumcision rites," or "a chief-designate undergoing his installation rites," or, yet again, "the first or ritual wife" who has important ritual duties in the domestic family. Our own terms "initiate" and "neophyte" have a similar breadth of reference. It would seem from this that emphasis tends to be laid on the transition itself, rather than on the particular states between which it is taking place.

The symbolism attached to and surrounding the liminal *persona* is complex and bizarre. Much of it is modeled on human biological processes, which are conceived to be what Levi-Strauss might call "isomorphic" with structural and cultural processes. They give an outward and visible form to an inward and conceptual process. The structural "invisibility" of liminal *personae* has a twofold character. They are at once no longer classified and not yet classified. In so far as they are no longer classified, the symbols that represent them are, in many societies, drawn from the biology of death, decomposition, catabolism, and other physical processes that have a negative tinge, such as menstruation (frequently regarded as the absence or loss of a fetus). Thus, in some boys' initiations, newly circumcised boys are explicitly likened to menstruating women. In so far as a neophyte is structurally "dead," he or she may be treated, for a long or short period, as a corpse is customarily treated in his or her society. (See Stobaeus' quotation, probably from a lost work of Plutarch, "initiation and death correspond word for word and thing for thing." [James 1961, 132]) The neophyte may be buried, forced to lie motionless in the posture and direction of customary burial, may be stained black, or may be forced to live for a while in the company of masked and monstrous mummers representing, *inter alia*, the dead, or worse still, the un-dead. The metaphor of dissolution is often applied to neophytes; they are allowed to go filthy and identified with the earth, the generalized matter into which every specific individual is rendered down. Particular form here becomes general matter; often their very names are taken from them and each is called solely by the generic term for "neophyte" or "initiand." (This useful neologism is employed by many modern anthropologists).

The other aspect, that they are not yet classified, is often expressed in symbols modeled on processes of gestation and parturition. The neophytes are likened to or treated as embryos, newborn infants, or sucklings by symbolic means which vary from culture to culture. I shall return to this theme presently.

The essential feature of these symbolizations is that the neophytes are neither living nor dead from one aspect, and both living and dead from another. Their condition is one of ambiguity and paradox, a confusion of all the customary categories. Jakob Boehme, the German mystic whose obscure writings gave Hegel his celebrated dialectical "triad," liked to say that "In Yea and Nay all things consist." Liminality may perhaps be regarded as the Nay to all positive structural assertions, but as in some sense the source of them all, and, more than that, as a realm of pure possibility whence novel configurations of ideas and relations may arise. I will not pursue this point here but, after all, Plato, a speculative philosopher, if there ever was one, did acknowledge his philosophical debt to the teachings of the Eleusinian and Orphic initiations of Attica. We have no way of knowing whether primitive initiations merely conserved lore. Perhaps they also generated new thought and new custom.

Dr. Mary Douglas, of University College, London, has recently advanced (in a magnificent book *Purity and Danger* [1966]) the very interesting and illuminating view that the concept of pollution "is a reaction to protect cherished principles and categories from contradiction." She holds that, in effect, what is unclear and contradictory (from the perspective of social definition) tends to be regarded as (ritually) unclean. The unclear is the unclean: e.g., she examines the prohibitions on eating certain animals and crustaceans in Leviticus in the light of this hypothesis (these being creatures that cannot be unambiguously classified in terms of traditional criteria). From this standpoint, one would expect to find that transitional beings are particularly polluting, since they are neither one thing nor another; or may be both; or neither here nor there; or may even be nowhere (in terms of any recognized cultural topography), and are at the very least "betwixt and between" all the recognized fixed points in space-time of structural classification. In fact, in confirmation of Dr. Douglas's hypothesis, liminal *personae* nearly always and everywhere are regarded as polluting to those who have never been, so to speak, "inoculated" against them, through having been themselves initiated into the same state. I think that we may perhaps usefully discriminate here between the statics and dynamics of pollution situations. In other words, we may have to distinguish between pollution notions which concern states that have been ambiguously or contradictorily defined, and those which derive from ritualized transitions between states. In the first case, we are dealing with what has been defectively defined or ordered, in the second with what cannot be defined in static terms. We are not dealing with structural contradictions when we discuss liminality, but with the essentially unstructured (which is at once destructured and prestructured) and often the people themselves see this in terms of bringing neophytes into close connection with deity or with superhuman power, with what is, in fact, often regarded as the unbounded, the infinite, the limitless. Since neophytes are not only structurally "invisible" (though physically visible) and ritually polluting, they are very commonly secluded, partially or completely, from the realm of culturally defined and ordered states and statuses. Often the indigenous term for the liminal period is, as among Ndembu, the locative form of a noun meaning "seclusion site" (*kunkunka, kung'ula*). The neophytes are sometimes said to "be in another place." They have physical but not social "reality," hence they have to be hidden, since it is a paradox, a scandal, to see what ought not to be there! Where they are not removed to a sacred place of concealment they are often disguised, in masks or grotesque costumes or striped with white, red, or black clay, and the like.

In societies dominantly structured by kinship institutions, sex distinctions have great structural importance. Patrilineal and matrilineal moieties and clans, rules of exogamy, and the like, rest and are built up on these distinctions. It is consistent with this to find that in liminal situations (in kinship-dominated societies) neophytes are sometimes treated or symbolically represented as being neither male nor female. Alternatively, they may be symbolically assigned characteristics of both sexes, irrespective of their biological sex. (Bruno Bettelheim [1954] has collected much illustrative material on this point from initiation rites.) They are symbolically either sexless or bisexual and may be regarded as a kind of human *prima materia*—as undifferentiated raw material. It was perhaps from the rites of the Hellenic mystery religions that Plato derived his notion expressed in his *Symposium* that the first humans were androgynes. If the liminal period is seen as an interstructural phase in social dynamics, the symbolism both of androgyny and sexlessness immediately becomes intelligible in sociological terms without the need to import psychological (and especially depth-psychological) explanations. Since sex distinctions are important components of structural status, in a structureless realm they do not apply.

A further structurally negative characteristic of transitional beings is that they *have* nothing. They have no status, property, insignia, secular clothing, rank, kinship position, nothing to demarcate them structurally from their fellows. Their condition is indeed the very prototype of sacred poverty. Rights over property, goods, and services inhere in positions in the politico-jural structure. Since they do not occupy such positions, neophytes exercise no such rights. In the words of King Lear they represent "naked unaccommodated man."

I have no time to analyze other symbolic themes that express these attributes of "structural invisibility," ambiguity and neutrality. I want now to draw attention to certain positive aspects of liminality. Already we have noted how certain liminal processes are regarded as analogous to those of gestation, parturition, and suckling. Undoing, dissolution, decomposition are accompanied by processes of growth, transformation, and the reformulation of old elements in new patterns. It is interesting to note how, by the principle of the economy (or parsimony) of symbolic reference, logically antithetical processes of death and growth may be represented by the same tokens, for example, by huts and tunnels that are at once tombs and wombs, by lunar symbolism (for the same moon waxes and wanes), by snake symbolism (for the snake appears to die, but only to shed its old skin and appear in a new one), by bear symbolism (for the bear "dies" in autumn and is "reborn" in spring), by nakedness (which is at once the mark of a newborn infant and a corpse prepared for burial), and by innumerable other symbolic formations and actions. This coincidence of opposite processes and notions in a single representation characterizes the peculiar unity of the liminal: that which is neither this nor that, and yet is both.

I have spoken of the interstructural character of the liminal. However, between neophytes and their instructors (where these exist), and in connecting neophytes with one another, there exists a set of relations that compose a "social structure" of highly specific type. It is a structure of a very simple kind: between instructors and neophytes there is often complete authority and complete submission; among neophytes there is often complete equality. Between incumbents of positions in secular politico-jural systems there exist intricate and situationally shifting networks of rights and duties proportioned to their rank, status, and corporate affiliation. There are many different kinds of privileges and obligations, many degrees of superordination and subordination. In the liminal period such distinctions and gradations tend to be eliminated. Nevertheless, it must be understood that the authority of the elders over the neophytes is not based on legal sanctions; it is in a sense the personification of the self-evident authority of tradition. The authority of the elders is absolute, because it represents the absolute, the axiomatic values of society in which are expressed the "common good" and the common interest. The essence of the complete obedience of the neophytes is to submit to the elders but only in so far as they are in charge, so to speak, of the common good and represent in their persons the total community. That the authority in question is really quintessential tradition emerges clearly in societies where initiations are not collective but individual and where there are no instructors or *gurus*. For example, Omaha boys, like other North American Indians, go alone into the wilderness to fast and pray (Hocart 1952, 160). This solitude is liminal between boyhood and manhood. If they dream that they receive a woman's burden-strap, they feel compelled to dress and live henceforth in every way as women. Such men are known as *mixuga*. The authority of such a dream in such a situation is absolute. Alice Cummingham Fletcher tells of one Omaha who had been forced in this way to live as a woman, but whose natural inclinations led him to rear a family and to go on the warpath. Here the *mixuga* was not an invert but a man bound by the authority of tribal beliefs and values. Among many Plains Indians, boys on their lonely Vision Quest inflicted ordeals and tests on themselves that amounted to tortures. These again were not basically self-tortures inflicted by a masochistic temperament but due to obedience to the authority of tradition in the liminal situation—a type of situation in which there is no room for secular compromise, evasion, manipulation, casuistry, and maneuver in the field of custom, rule, and norm. Here again a cultural explanation seems preferable to a psychological one. A normal man acts abnormally because he is obedient to tribal tradition, not out of disobedience to it. He does not evade but fulfills his duties as a citizen.

If complete obedience characterizes the relationship of neophyte to elder, complete equality usually characterizes the relationship of neophyte to neophyte, where the rites are collective. This comradeship must be distinguished from brotherhood or sibling relationship, since in the latter there is always the inequality of older and younger, which often achieves linguistic representation and may be maintained by legal sanctions. The liminal group is a community or comity of comrades and not a structure of hierarchically arrayed positions. This comradeship transcends distinctions of rank, age, kinship position, and, in some kinds of cultic group, even of sex. Much of the behavior recorded by ethnographers in seclusion situations falls under the principle: "Each for all, and all for each." Among the Ndembu of Zambia, for example, all food brought for novices in circumcision seclusion by their mothers is shared out equally among them. No special favors are bestowed on the sons of chiefs or headmen. Any food acquired by novices in the bush is taken by the elders and apportioned among the group. Deep friendships between novices are encouraged, and they sleep around lodge fires in clusters of four or five particular comrades. However, all are supposed to be linked by special ties which persist after the rites are over, even into old age. This friendship, known as *wubwambu* (from a term meaning "breast") or *wulunda,* enables a man to claim privileges of hospitality of a far-reaching kind. I have no need here to dwell on the lifelong ties that are held to bind in close friendship those initiated into the same age-set in East African Nilo-Hamitic and Bantu societies, into the same fraternity or sorority on an American campus, or into the same class in a Naval or Military Academy in Western Europe.

This comradeship, with its familiarity, ease and, I would add, mutual outspokenness, is once more the product of interstructural liminality, with its scarcity of jurally sanctioned relationships and its emphasis on axiomatic values expressive of the common weal. People can "be themselves," it is frequently said, when they are not acting institutionalized roles. Roles, too, carry responsibilities and in the liminal situation the main burden of responsibility is borne by the elders, leaving the neophytes free to develop interpersonal relationships as they will. They confront one another, as it were, integrally and not in compartmentalized fashion as actors of roles.

The passivity of neophytes to their instructors, their malleability, which is increased by submission to ordeal, their reduction to a uniform condition, are signs of the process whereby they are ground down to be fashioned anew and endowed with additional powers to cope with their new station in life. Dr. Richards, in her superb study of Bemba girls' puberty rites, *Chisungu,* has told us that Bemba speak of "growing a girl" when they mean initiating her (1956, 121). This term "to grow" well expresses how many peoples think of transition rites. We are inclined, as sociologists, to reify our abstractions (it is indeed a device which helps us to understand many kinds of social interconnection) and to talk about persons "moving through structural positions in a hierarchical frame" and the like. Not so the Bemba and the Shilluk of the Sudan who see the status or condition embodied or incarnate, if you like, *in* the person. To "grow" a girl into a woman is to effect an ontological transformation; it is not merely to convey an unchanging substance from one position to another by a quasi-mechanical force. Howitt saw Kuringals in Australia and I have seen Ndembu in Africa drive away grown-up men before a circumcision ceremony because they had not been initiated. Among Ndembu, men were also chased off because they had only been circumcised at the Mission Hospital and had not undergone the full bush seclusion according to the orthodox Ndembu rite. These biologically mature men had not been "made men" by the proper ritual procedures. It is the ritual and the esoteric teaching which grows girls and makes men. It is the ritual, too, which among Shilluk makes a prince into a king, or, among Luvale, a cultivator into a hunter. The arcane knowledge or *"gnosis"* obtained in the liminal period is felt to change the inmost nature of the neophyte, impressing him, as a seal impresses wax, with the characteristics of his new state. It is not a mere acquisition of knowledge, but a change in being. His apparent passivity is revealed as an absorption of powers which will become active after his social status has been redefined in the aggregation rites.

The structural simplicity of the liminal situation in many initiations in offset by its cultural complexity. I can touch on only one aspect of this vast subject matter here and raise three problems in connection with it. This aspect is the vital one of the communication of the *sacra,* the heart of the liminal matter.

Jane Harrison has shown that in the Greek Eleusinian and Orphic mysteries this communication of the *sacra* has three main components (1903, 144–160). By and large, this threefold classification holds good for initiation rites all over the world. *Sacra* may be communicated as: (1) exhibitions, "what is shown"; (2) actions, "what is done"; and (3) instructions, "what is said."

"Exhibitions" would include evocatory instruments or sacred articles, such as relics of deities, heroes or ancestors, aboriginal *churingas,* sacred drums or other musical instruments, the contents of Amerindian medicine bundles, and the fan, cist and tympanum of Greek and Near Eastern mystery cults. In the Lesser Eleusinian Mysteries of Athens, *sacra* consisted of a bone, top, ball, tambourine, apples, mirror, fan, and woolly fleece. Other *sacra* include masks, images, figurines, and effigies; the pottery emblems (*mbusa*) of the Bemba would belong to this class. In some kinds of initiation, as for example the initiation into the shaman-diviner's profession among the Saora of Middle India, described by Verrier Elwyn (1955), pictures and icons representing the journeys of the dead or the adventures of supernatural beings may be shown to the initiands. A striking feature of such sacred articles is often their formal simplicity. It is their interpretation which is complex, not their outward form.

Among the "instructions" received by neophytes may be reckoned such matters as the revelation of the real, but secularly secret, names of the deities or spirits believed to preside over the rites—a very frequent procedure in African cultic or secret associations (Turner 1962a, 36). They are also taught the main outlines of the theogony, cosmogony, and mythical history of their societies or cults, usually with reference to the *sacra* exhibited. Great importance is attached to keeping secret the nature of the *sacra,* the formulas chanted and instructions given about them. These constitute the crux of liminality, for while instruction is also given in ethical and social obligations, in law and in kinship rules, and in technology to fit neophytes for the duties of future office, no interdiction is placed on knowledge thus imparted since it tends to be current among uninitiated persons also.

I want to take up three problems in considering the communication of *sacra.* The first concerns their frequent disproportion, the second their monstrousness, and the third their mystery.

When one examines the masks, costumes, figurines, and such displayed in initiation situations, one is often struck, as I have been when observing Ndembu masks in circumcision and funerary rites, by the way in which certain natural and cultural features are represented as disproportionately large or small. A head, nose, or phallus, a hoe, bow, or meal mortar are represented as huge or tiny by comparison with other features of their context which retain their normal size. (For a good example of this, see "The Man Without Arms" in *Chisungu* [Richards 1956, 211], a figurine of a lazy man with an enormous penis but no arms.) Sometimes things retain their customary shapes but are portrayed in unusual colors. What is the point of this exaggeration amounting sometimes to caricature? It seems to me that to enlarge or diminish or discolor in this way is a primordial mode of abstraction. The outstandingly exaggerated feature is made into an object of reflection. Usually it is not a univocal symbol that is thus represented but a multivocal one, a semantic molecule with many components. One example is the Bemba pottery emblem *Coshi wa ng'oma,* "The Nursing Mother," described by Audrey Richards in *Chisungu.* This is a clay figurine, nine inches high, of an exaggeratedly pregnant mother shown carrying four babies at the same time, one at her breast and three at her back. To this figurine is attached a riddling song:

> My mother deceived me!
> *Coshi wa ng'oma*!
> So you have deceived me;
> I have become pregnant again.

Bemba women interpreted this to Richards as follows:

> *Coshi wa ng'oma* was a midwife of legendary fame and is merely addressed in this song. The girl complains because her mother told her to wean her first child too soon so that it died; or alternatively told her that she would take the first child if her daughter had a second one. But she was tricking her and now the girl has two babies to look after. The moral stressed is the duty of refusing intercourse with the husband before the baby is weaned, i.e., at the second or third year. This is a common Bemba practice (1956, 209–210).

In the figurine the exaggerated features are the number of children carried at once by the woman and her enormously distended belly. Coupled with the song, it encourages the novice to ponder upon two relationships vital to her, those with her mother and her husband. Unless the novice observes the Bemba weaning custom, her mother's desire for grandchildren to increase her matrilineage and her husband's desire for renewed sexual intercourse will between them actually destroy and not increase her offspring. Underlying this is the deeper moral that to abide by tribal custom and not to sin against it either by excess or defect is to live satisfactorily. Even to please those one loves may be to invite calamity, if such compliance defies the immemorial wisdom of the elders embodied in the *mbusa*. This wisdom is vouched for by the mythical and archetypal midwife *Coshi wa ng'oma*.

If the exaggeration of single features is not irrational but thought-provoking, the same may also be said about the representation of monsters. Earlier writers—such as J. A. McCulloch (1913) in his article on "Monsters" in *Hastings Encyclopaedia of Religion and Ethics*—are inclined to regard bizarre and monstrous masks and figures, such as frequently appear in the liminal period of initiations, as the product of "hallucinations, night-terrors and dreams." McCulloch goes on to argue that "as man drew little distinction (in primitive society) between himself and animals, as he thought that transformation from one to the other was possible, so he easily ran human and animal together. This in part accounts for animal-headed gods or animal-gods with human heads." My own view is the opposite one: that monsters are manufactured precisely to teach neophytes to distinguish clearly between the different factors of reality, as it is conceived in their culture. Here, I think, William James's so-called "law of dissociation" may help us to clarify the problem of monsters. It may be stated as follows: when *a* and *b* occurred together as parts of the same total object, without being discriminated, the occurrence of one of these, *a*, in a new combination *ax*, favors the discrimination of *a, b,* and *x* from one another. As James himself put it, "What is associated now with one thing and now with another, tends to become dissociated from either, and to grow into an object of abstract contemplation by the mind. One might call this the law of dissociation by varying concomitants" (1918, 506).

From this standpoint, much of the grotesqueness and monstrosity of liminal *sacra* may be seen to be aimed not so much at terrorizing or bemusing neophytes into submission or out of their wits as at making them vividly and rapidly aware of what may be called the "factors" of their culture. I have myself seen Ndembu and Luvale masks that combine features of both sexes, have both animal and human attributes, and unite in a single representation human characteristics with those of the natural landscape. One *ikishi* mask is partly human and partly represents a grassy plain. Elements are withdrawn from their usual settings and combined with one another in a totally unique configuration, the monster or dragon. Monsters startle neophytes into thinking about objects, persons, relationships, and features of their environment they have hitherto taken for granted.

In discussing the structural aspect of liminality, I mentioned how neophytes are withdrawn from their structural positions and consequently from the values, norms, sentiments, and techniques associated with those positions. They are also divested of their previous habits of thought, feeling, and action. During the liminal period, neophytes are alternately forced and encouraged to think about their society, their cosmos, and the powers that generate and sustain them. Liminality may be partly described as a stage of reflection. In it those ideas, sentiments, and facts that had been hitherto for the neophytes bound up in configurations and accepted unthinkingly are, as it were, resolved into their constituents. These constituents are isolated and made into objects of reflection for the neophytes by such processes as componental exaggeration and dissociation by varying concomitants.

The communication of *sacra* and other forms of esoteric instruction really involves three processes, though these should not be regarded as in series but as in parallel. The first is the reduction of culture into recognized components or factors; the second is their recombination in fantastic or monstrous patterns and shapes; and the third is their recombination in ways that make sense with regard to the new state and status that the neophytes will enter.

The second process, monster- or fantasy-making, focuses attention on the components of the masks and effigies, which are so radically ill-assorted that they stand out and can be thought about. The monstrosity of the configuration throws its elements into relief. Put a man's head on a lion's body and you think about the human head in the abstract. Perhaps it becomes for you, as a member of a given culture and with the appropriate guidance, an emblem of chieftainship; or it may be explained as representing the soul as against the body; or intellect as contrasted with brute force, or innumerable other things. There could be less encouragement to reflect on heads and headship if that same head were firmly ensconced on its familiar, its all too familiar, human body. The man-lion monster also encourages the observer to think about lions, their habits, qualities, metaphorical properties, religious significance, and so on. More important than these, the relation between man and lion, empirical and metaphorical, may be speculated upon, and new ideas developed on this topic. Liminality here breaks, as it were, the cake of custom and enfranchises speculation. That is why I earlier mentioned Plato's self-confessed debt to the Greek mysteries. Liminality is the realm of primitive hypothesis, where there is a certain freedom to juggle with the factors of existence. As in the works of Rabelais, there is a promiscuous intermingling and juxtaposing of the categories of event, experience, and knowledge, with a pedagogic intention.

But this liberty has fairly narrow limits. The neophytes return to secular society with more alert faculties perhaps and enhanced knowledge of how things work, but they have to become once more subject to custom and law. Like the Bemba girl I mentioned earlier, they are shown that ways of acting and thinking alternative to those laid down by the deities or ancestors are ultimately unworkable and may have disastrous consequences.

Moreover, in initiation, there are usually held to be certain axiomatic principles of construction, and certain basic building blocks that make up the cosmos and into whose nature no neophyte may inquire.

Certain *sacra,* usually exhibited in the most arcane episodes of the liminal period, represent or may be interpreted in terms of these axiomatic principles and primordial constituents. Perhaps we may call these *sacerrima,* "most sacred things." Sometimes they are interpreted by a myth about the world-making activities of supernatural beings "at the beginning of things." Myths may be completely absent, however, as in the case of the Ndembu "mystery of the three rivers" (which I have described, pp. 61–65). This mystery (*mpang'u*) is exhibited at circumcision and funerary cult association rites. Three trenches are dug in a consecrated site and filled respectively with white, red, and black water. These "rivers" are said to "flow from Nzambi," the High God. The instructors tell the neophytes, partly in riddling songs and partly in direct terms, what each river signifies. Each "river" is a multivocal symbol with a fan of referents ranging from life values, ethical ideas, and social norms, to grossly physiological processes and phenomena. They seem to be regarded as powers which, in varying combination, underlie or even constitute what Ndembu conceive to be reality. In no other context is the interpretation of whiteness, redness, and blackness so full; and nowhere else is such a close analogy drawn, even identity made, between these rivers and bodily fluids and emissions: whiteness = semen, milk; redness = menstrual blood, the blood of birth, blood shed by a weapon, etc.; blackness = feces, certain products of bodily decay, etc. This use of an aspect of human physiology as a model for social, cosmic, and religious ideas and processes is a variant of a widely distributed initiation theme: that the human body is a microcosm of the universe. The body may be pictured as androgynous, as male or female, or in terms of one or other of its developmental stages, as child, mature adult, and elder. On the other hand, as in the Ndembu case, certain of its properties may be abstracted. Whatever the mode of representation, the body is regarded as a sort of symbolic template for the communication of *gnosis,* mystical knowledge about the nature of things and how they came to be what they are. The cosmos may in some cases be regarded as a vast human body; in other belief systems, visible parts of the body may be taken to portray invisible faculties such as reason, passion, wisdom and so on; in others again, the different parts of the social order are arrayed in terms of a human anatomical paradigm.

Whatever the precise mode of explaining reality by the body's attributes, *sacra* which illustrates this are always regarded as absolutely sacrosanct, as ultimate mysteries. We are here in the realm of what Warner (1959, 3–4) would call "nonrational or nonlogical symbols" which

> arise out of the basic individual and cultural assumptions, more often unconscious than not, from which most social action springs. They supply the solid core of mental and emotional life of each individual and group. This does not mean that they are irrational or maladaptive, or that man cannot often think in a reasonable way about them, but rather that they do not have their source in his rational processes. When they come into play, such factors as data, evidence, proof, and the facts and procedures of rational thought in action are apt to be secondary or unimportant.

The central cluster of nonlogical *sacra* is then the symbolic template of the whole system of beliefs and values in a given culture, its archetypal paradigm and ultimate measure. Neophytes shown these are often told that they are in the presence of forms established from the beginning of things. (See Cicero's comment [De Leg. II. 14] on the Eleusinian Mysteries: "They are rightly called initiations [beginnings] because we have thus learned the first principles of life.") I have used the metaphor of a seal or stamp in connection with the ontological character ascribed in many initiations to arcane knowledge. The term "archetype" denotes in Greek a master stamp or impress, and these *sacra,* presented with a numinous simplicity, stamp into the neophytes the basic assumptions of their culture. The neophytes are told also that they are being filled with mystical power by what they see and what they are told about it. According to the purpose of the initiation, this power confers on them capacities to undertake successfully the tasks of their new office, in this world or the next.

Thus, the communication of *sacra* both teaches the neophytes how to think with some degree of abstraction about their cultural milieu and gives them ultimate standards of reference. At the same time, it is believed to change their nature, transform them from one kind of human being into another. It intimately unites man and office. But for a variable while, there was an uncommitted man, an individual rather than a social *persona,* in a sacred community of individuals.

It is not only in the liminal period of initiations that the nakedness and vulnerability of the ritual subject receive symbolic stress. Let me quote from Hilda Kuper's description of the seclusion of the Swazi chief during the great *Incwala* ceremony (1961, 197–225). The *Incwala* is a national First-Fruits ritual, performed in the height of summer when the early crops ripen. The regiments of the Swazi nation assemble at the capital to celebrate its rites, "whereby the nation receives strength for the new year." The *Incwala* is at the same time "a play of kingship." The king's well-being is identified with that of the nation. Both require periodic ritual strengthening. Lunar symbolism is prominent in the rites, as we shall see, and the king, personifying the nation, during his seclusion represents the moon in transition between phases, neither waning nor waxing. Dr. Kuper, Professor Gluckman (1954), and Professor Wilson (1961) have discussed the structural aspects of the *Incwala* which are clearly present in its rites of separation and aggregation. What we are about to examine are the interstructural aspects.

During his night and day of seclusion, the king, painted black, remains, says Dr. Kuper, "painted in blackness" and "in darkness"; he is unapproachable, dangerous to himself and others. He must cohabit that night with his first ritual wife (in a kind of "mystical marriage"—this ritual wife is, as it were, consecrated for such liminal situations).

> The entire population is also temporarily in a state of taboo and seclusion. Ordinary activities and behavior are suspended; sexual intercourse is prohibited, no one may sleep late the following morning, and when they get up they are not allowed to touch each other, to wash the body, to sit on mats, to poke anything into the ground, or even to scratch their hair. The children are scolded if they play and make merry. The sound of songs that has stirred the capital for nearly a month is abruptly stilled; it is the day of *bacisa* (cause to *hide*). The king remains secluded; . . . all day he sits naked on a lion skin in the ritual hut of the harem or in the sacred enclosure in the royal cattle byre. Men of his inner circle see that he breaks none of the taboos . . . on this day the identification of the people with the king is very marked. The spies (who see to it that the people respect the taboos) do not say, "You are sleeping late" or "You are scratching," but "You cause the king to sleep," "You scratch him (the king)"; etc. (Kuper 1947, 219–220).

Other symbolic acts are performed which exemplify the "darkness" and "waxing and waning moon" themes, for example, the slaughtering of a black ox, the painting of the queen mother with a black mixture—she is compared again to a half-moon, while the king is a full moon, and both are in eclipse until the paint is washed off finally with doctored water, and the ritual subject "comes once again into lightness and normality."

In this short passage we have an embarrassment of symbolic riches. I will mention only a few themes that bear on the argument of this paper. Let us look at the king's position first. He is symbolically invisible, "black," a moon between phases. He is also under obedience to traditional rules, and "men of his inner circle" see that he keeps them. He is also "naked," divested of the trappings of his office. He remains apart from the scenes of his political action in a sanctuary or ritual hut. He is also, it would seem, identified with the earth which the people are forbidden to stab, lest the king be affected. He is "hidden." The king, in short, has been divested of all the outward attributes, the "accidents," of his kingship and is reduced to its substance, the "earth" and "darkness" from which the normal, structured order of the Swazi kingdom will be regenerated "in lightness."

In this betwixt-and-between period, in this fruitful darkness, king and people are closely identified. There is a mystical solidarity between them, which contrasts sharply with the hierarchical rank-dominated structure of ordinary Swazi life. It is only in darkness, silence, celibacy, in the absence of merriment and movement that the king and people can thus be one. For every normal action is involved in the rights and obligations of a structure that defines status and establishes social distance between men. Only in their Trappist sabbath of transition may the Swazi regenerate the social tissues torn by conflicts arising from distinctions of status and discrepant structural norms.

I end this study with an invitation to investigators of ritual to focus their attention on the phenomena and processes of mid-transition. It is these, I hold, that paradoxically expose the basic building blocks of culture just when we pass out of and before we re-enter the structural realm. In *sacerrima* and their interpretations we have categories of data that may usefully be handled by the new sophisticated techniques of cross-cultural comparison.

## BIBLIOGRAPHY

Bettelheim, B. 1954. *Symbolic Wounds*. Glencoe: Free Press.

Cicero, M. Tullius. 1959. *De Legibus*. Ed. by de Plinval. Paris: Les Belles Lettres.

Douglas, Mary. 1966. *Purity and Danger*. London: Routledge & Kegan Paul.

Elwin, Verrier. 1955. *The Religion of an Indian Tribe*. London: Geoffrey Cumberlege.

Gennep, A. van. 1960. *The Rites of Passage*. London: Routledge & Kegan Paul.

Gluckman, Max. 1954. *Rituals of Rebellion in South-East Africa.* Manchester University Press.

Harrison, Jane E. 1903. *Prolegomena to the Study of Greek Religion.* London: Cambridge University Press.

Hocart, A. M. 1952. *The Life-Giving Myth.* London: Methuen.

James, E. O. 1961. *Comparative Religion.* London: Methuen.

James, William. 1918. *Principles of Psychology.* Vol. 1. New York: H. Holt.

Kuper, Hilda. 1947. *An African Aristocracy.* London: Oxford University Press, for International African Institute.

McCulloch, J. A. 1913. "Monsters," in *Hastings Encyclopaedia of Religion and Ethics.* Edinburgh: T. & T. Clark.

Richards, A. I. 1956. *Chisungu.* London: Faber & Faber.

Turner, V. W. 1962. *Chihamba, the White Spirit* (Rhodes-Livingstone Paper 33). Manchester University Press.

Warner, W. L. 1959. *The Living and the Dead.* New Haven: Yale University Press.

Wilson, Monica. 1959. *Divine Kings and the Breath of Men.* London: Cambridge University Press.

# CHAPTER V

# Witchcraft and Sorcery: Taxonomy versus Dynamics*

It is greatly to the credit of the editors of *Witchcraft and Sorcery in East Africa* (Middleton and Winter, 1963) that they have made generally available ten systematic accounts of witch beliefs in East and Central African societies. All teachers of anthropology must surely be grateful to them on this account alone. Moreover, the book is spiced with many insights into sociocultural problems connected with the main theme. A permissive editorial policy has stimulated a rich diversity of viewpoints and presentations, but one is left with the feeling that Monica Wilson's plea for the comparative analysis of these "standardized nightmares"—a plea that forms the book's motto—as one of the "keys to the understanding of society" has not met here with a wholly satisfactory response.

The fault—if fault it is—does not lie with the highly competent contributors but with the declining adequacy of the theoretical frames employed. These are the structural frame of reference and "cultural analysis" with which the editors (p. 9) hope to "develop explanatory formulations which can subsume the facts from more than one society." However, "the facts" have changed within the last decade and theory must change with them. Anthropologists are still vitally concerned to exhibit "structures" of social relations, ideas, and values, but they now tend to see these in relation to processes of which they are both the products and regulators. Process-theory involves a "becom-

* First published in *Africa*, XXXIV, No. 4 (October, 1964).

ing" as well as a "being" vocabulary, admits of plurality, disparity, conflicts of groups, roles, ideals, and ideas, and, since it is concerned with human beings, considers such variables as "goal," "motivation," "intention," "rationality," and "meaning." Furthermore, it lays stress on human biology, on the individual life cycle, and on public health and pathology. It takes into theoretic account ecological and economic processes both repetitive and changing. It has to estimate the effects on local subsystems of large-scale political processes in wider systems. These developments have taken place as a result of the increased use of the extended case method which studies the vicissitudes of given social systems over time in a series of case studies, each of which deals with a major crisis in the selected system or in its parts. Data provided by this method enable us to apprehend not only the structural principles of that system but also processes of various kinds, including those of structural change. Such case material must, of course, be analyzed in constant and close association with social "structure," both in its institutionalized and statistically normative senses. The new "facts" do not oust but complete the old.

In African social systems, witch beliefs and witchcraft accusations are classes of data that demand a dynamic theoretical treatment. The editors of *Witchcraft and Sorcery in East Africa* have pointed out (p. 18) that "in the cycle of development of a lineage or of a family, accusations of wizardry may be made between different categories of persons at different stages of the cycle, and these accusations point to the areas of sharpest tension." Yet no essay in the book explores the possibilities of this approach which demands the extended case method for its full exploitation. This is all the more surprising since one of the editors, Professor Middleton, made exemplary use of this method in his recent book (1960).

On the other hand, preoccupation with a group's developmental cycle—which is a process of internal structural adjustment—sometimes tends to deflect attention from other types of process. Among these may be listed processes of adaptation to the social environment and to the natural environment. It is not sufficiently recognized how closely witch beliefs are associated with the high rates of morbidity and mortality that afflict most tribal societies. Morbidity, like rainfall, often has a strongly localized distribution. Analyses of witchcraft ought in future to include local statistics of disease and death. For surely it is the sudden and unpredictable onset of severe illness which partly accounts for the random and motivelessly malignant character ascribed to many aspects and types of witchcraft? I mention this seemingly obvious matter as a corrective to the optimism of what Douglas, in a perceptive essay in *Witchcraft and Sorcery in East Africa,* has called the "obstetric view." This view, based too narrowly on a study of Central African cycles of village development, has been expounded most persuasively by Professor Max Marwick (1952, 120–135, 215–233) who writes that when Cewa social relations become intolerably strained, witch beliefs help to "dissolve relations that have become redundant"; they "blast down the dilapidated parts of the social structure, and clear the rubble in preparation for new ones." (What kind of structure, one is prompted to ask, is this: forced abstract or reinforced concrete?) Douglas, from whose essay the quotation from Marwick is taken, for good measure throws in his comment that witchcraft accusations "maintain the virility of the indigenous social structure" by allowing "periodic redistributions of structural forces" (Middleton and Winter, 1963, 233).

Against this "obstetric" view she asserts that for the Lele of Kasai witchcraft is "an aggravator of all hostilities and fears, an obstacle to peaceful co-operation." This statement holds good for all disease-ridden societies where most deaths are attributed to witchcraft. Illness strikes indiscriminately at groups in every stage of their developmental cycle, at villages full of tension and at harmoniously integrated communities. Indeed, a few sudden deaths in a happy village may provoke severer anger and sharper witchcraft accusations among its members than death in an already quarrelsome group where, so to speak, mystically harmful action is anticipated. A major feature of witch beliefs, as Evans-Pritchard (1937) has so memorably demonstrated, is that they are attempts to explain the inexplicable and control the uncontrollable by societies with only limited technological capacity to cope with a hostile environment. If witch beliefs were solely the products of social tensions and conflicts, they would betray their origins by possessing a more markedly rational form and content. Constant exposure to ugly illness and sudden death, and the need to adapt to them swiftly, have surely contributed to the formation of these ugly and irrational beliefs. Once formed, the beliefs feed back into the social process, generating tensions as often as "reflecting" them.

Nevertheless, it is perfectly legitimate to connect with the later and more tension-ridden stages of a group's growth cycle those rumors and accusations of witchcraft that arise with reference to relatively minor occasions of illness yet are pressed home with venom and assiduity. Here one will often find a group on the point of fission, radically cleft into competing factions. In such cases, internal adjustment rather than adaptation to biotic or social environments would appear to be the dominant process.

In brief, each instance or set of accusations has to be examined within a total context of social action which includes the operation of biotic, ecological, and intergroup processes, as well as intragroup developments. A considerable time-depth is necessary to make adequately comprehensible the patterning and motivation of accusations in a given area of social life. These specifications can be met only by the extended case study. In *Witchcraft and Sorcery in East Africa* several authors (notably Beattie, Beidelman, and La Fontaine) have documented their essays with case material, but of the 299 pages of the book only 49 are taken up by cases and their analysis. Most cases are appended without comment as illustrations of some "structural" feature or other. Quitc commonly, attention is concentrated on distinguishing the categories of kin, affines, neighbors, and the like, between whom accusations are "most frequent." Marwick, who has used this approach, has at least documented it with meticulously collected and presented numerical data. Figures are few and hard to find in this symposium, and to my mind, the approach itself is a misleading one. The significant point about a given instance of accusation is not that it is made by someone against a specific type of relative, but that is is made in a given field situation. This situation would include not only the structure of the group and subgroups to which the accuser and accused belong, but also their extant division into transient alliances and factions on the basis of immediate interests, ambitions, moral aspirations, and the like. It would also include as much of the history of these groups, subgroups, alliances, and factions as would be considered relevant to the understanding of the accusation by leading actors in the field situation. It would further include, wherever possible, demographic data about subgroup and factional fluctuations over the relevant time period, together with information about the biological and sociological factors bearing on these, such as epidemics, rise and fall in the death and birth rates, labor migration, wars, and feuds. The fact that A accused B would finally appear not as an instance of the "tension that exists between agnates of the same generation" or between "male uterine kin of adjacent generations" but as the product of a complex interplay of processes and forces, among which the norms governing behavior between members of a single kinship category constitute only a single (and possibly minor) class. Kinship status may only be "phenotypical" here: "genotypical" may be membership in opposed factions in the local community in struggles for land, authority, prestige, or movable wealth, membership in opposed religious cult groups, the likes and dislikes of leading actors, or combinations of all or any of these, or a variety of other, locally significant factors. What the significant variables are in particular situations and how they are combined will yield to the probing of the extended case method coupled with the collection of numerical data on the basis of the clues it provides. In situations of radical change, where "structure" is breaking down, traditional kinship norms can give little guidance. Even in repetitive, "cyclical" systems it is only after we characterize the total action-field context that we shall be able to say with some assurance why A accused one "mother's brother" B and yet found among his staunchest supporters "mother's brothers" C, D, and E.

In their essays on the Kaguru and Mandari, Dr. Beidelman and Dr. Buxton have indeed presented the kind of detailed case material that would make this method of analysis possible, but since many variables have to be isolated and then considered in their independence and interdependence, each extended case study ought to be preceded by the setting up of a construct of its action-field. Such a construct must admittedly display the inadequacies of all models. As Max Black has pointed out (1962, 223), citing Duhem and Braithwaite, the employment of models has been regarded by some philosophers as no more than "a prop for feeble minds" or a convenient short cut to the consideration of deductive systems. There may be some practical utility in using the "field" (of social action) as an analogue-model, a species which, according to Black, who does not deny it all theoretical value, "shares with its original not a set of features or an identical proportionality of magnitudes but, more abstractly, the same structure or pattern of relationships." Since structural analogy is compatible with a wide variety of content there are indeed the attendant risks, which Black notes, of "fallacious inference from inevitable irrelevances and distortions in the model." Analogue models furnish "plausible hypotheses, not proofs." But our action-field construct is not, strictly speaking, a theoretical model, only an attempt to reproduce as carefully as possible the structure or "web of relations" in the observable data. For this a certain amount of recourse to "visual aids" is a prerequisite. Thus, in Beidelman's excellently detailed case of

Kaguru subchief Isaak (p. 81), our understanding of the events would have been further enhanced by a diagram bringing out the main structural properties of the subchiefdom he rules. In the narrative of the case, for example we learn that in subchiefdoms there are "dominant clans," and that Isaak "owes his political power to his father's clan" (and this fact alone raises interesting problems in a matrilineal society). Such a diagram might therefore have included the distribution of the members of the dominant clan throughout the villages of Isaak's subchiefdom and in neighboring subchiefdoms. For another important "property" of the action-field in question is that "a Kaguru feels that he can rely upon his own [matri-]clan above all kinsmen." Next we require a village genealogy, presented so as to bring out the relationships between the main actors in the case. We learn that Isaak is a village headman as well as a subchief and therefore occupies leading positions in two sets of structural relations. The major intersections of these sets or "subsystems" might have been shown schematically. In Isaak's village there are two factions, one headed by Isaak and the other by an unmarried elderly woman. Both heads, and many of their followers, are "members of the same [matri-] clan." No genealogy is given to make completely clear to us in visual terms precisely how the faction heads are related to one another and to their followers. Isaak's matrikin seek favors from him in his capacities both as subchief and as headman. Some of them practice illegal activities that embarrass Isaak. Mention of a division of the village into "hamlets" underlines the need for a hut plan bringing out the spatial distribution of the main actors. Finally, a diagram might have been devised to bring out the overlapping and interpenetrating of political and kinship networks of alliance and factional cleavage in the sociospatial field constituted by subchiefdom, village, and hamlet.

Beidelman's case demonstrates that the "kinship category" approach to witchcraft accusations is unsatisfactory. For he shows that Kaguru believed that children in the village became ill and died "from exposure to the cross-fire of witchcraft" from Isaak and two female heads of the rival faction. Accusers, accused, and victims in the instances he cites are all kin or affines of one another of much the same categories. The question "who accuses whom?" is partially answered by the roles they play in the factional struggle.

Although he goes further than most writers on witchcraft in placing accusations in a case-method setting, Beidelman does not, in my view, go quite far enough. The extended case method, which his rich data would probably have allowed him to use, would have placed his "Isaak" case in a longer time-series and perhaps in a wider and more complex field setting. We would have been able by it perhaps to account for the genesis of the factional struggle in Isaak's village, and in studying rumors and accusations of witchcraft over protracted periods of time, would have gained an extensive knowledge of the phenomenon in its Kaguru variety. For the method I am advocating does not exclude cultural facts, such as beliefs, symbols, values, moral rules, and legal concepts, from its theoretical purview, in so far as these constitute determinable influences inclining persons and groups to action in the field context.

This brings me to the crux of this critique. For it may well be asked, What bearing has a method of sociological analysis on the study of witch beliefs? The reply would be first that the editors have themselves found sociological significance in the cultural distinction between "witchcraft" and "sorcery," and secondly, that by its very nature the extended case method uses a finer mesh to catch nuances of belief (as these are invoked by the actors in social crises) than does the questioning of even the most gifted of informants away from the field of social action. For cases that involve witchcraft beliefs are dramas that include in their phases of development recourse to diviners to determine guilt and establish innocence. The observation of diviners at work and the study of their apparatus reveal that in African societies beliefs may include a multiplicity of types of mystical evildoers, who practice a wide variety of ways of causing mystical harm. This variety in beliefs is generated in some measure by the variety of concrete circumstances where misfortune is mystically "explained." The tendency to multiply beliefs is, of course, accelerated under present conditions of social change when members of many hitherto isolated tribes are meeting and mingling. Wider fields of social action are in process of formation, and they tend to contain beliefs drawn from many quarters and, in addition, syncretisms and totally new formulations. Witch beliefs can no longer—if they ever could—be usefully grouped into two contrasting categories, witchcraft (in its narrow sense) and sorcery.

When Evans-Pritchard first made this distinction he clearly intended to confine it to Zande culture (1937, 21): "Azande believe that some people are witches and can injure them in virtue of an inherent quality. A witch performs no rite, utters no spell and possesses no medicines. An act of witchcraft is a psychic act. They believe also that sorcerers may do them ill by performing magic rites with bad medicines." He further stated that the Zande witch has an inherent power to work evil, perhaps unknown even to himself. This power derives from the presence in a witch's body of an inherited organ or substance called *mangu,* the presence or absence of which can be determined by autopsy. Witchcraft, in short, may be unconscious and involuntary, though it is often intentional, inherited, and inherent. Sorcery is always conscious and voluntary, and is taught and often bought. Witchcraft operates directly and sorcery indirectly through spells, rites, and medicines. This dichotomy, verbalized and explicit among the Azande, is not made in many societies. Rather, these possess a wide range of beliefs about types of persons who seek to harm their fellows by nonempirical means. A brief survey of some of the recent literature dealing with such beliefs will make this clear.

In a well-documented study of a recent spate of "witchcraft cases" brought before the courts in Barotseland, Zambia, Barrie Reynolds, Keeper of Ethnography of the National Museums of Zambia, has made a thorough survey (1963, 14–47) of evidence cited in the courts and of the available ethnographic literature bearing on witchcraft in Central Africa. He found that in Barotseland the single term *muloi* was used for all evil practitioners, whatever the means of doing harm they were believed to employ. Some were thought to kill by means of "familiars" [1] in human shape ("zombies" or figurines), by animal and nonhuman familiars (in the shape of monstrous crabs, snakes, or by magically created elephants, hippopotami, etc.), by *siposo,* the projection of magic in the form of an invisible missile, by "the introduction or attempted introduction of any poisonous or supposedly poisonous powder or similar substance into the stomach, lungs, or flesh of the victim with the object of causing his death or illness," by burying charms in a path frequented by the intended victim or under his threshold, by sucking the victim's "breath or spirit" from his body through a hollow reed, and by many other devices. Since these are real or imaginary *techniques,* which the people say can be taught or sold, they might all be classified as "sorcery," in terms of the Zande prototype. However, the question of inheritance arises over certain familiars, known as *tuyebela* or *vandumba* among the Luvale, Luchazi, and Lunda peoples in the Protectorate. These are supposed to resemble miniature men and to be inherited matrilineally by women.

[1] Defined by Reynolds as "agents or animated weapons capable of seeking out the victim and of carrying out the task assigned by the master."

This raises the issue of what is meant by "inheritance." Certainly, among the Mwinilunga Lunda I found that when a *muloji* (cognate with *muloi*) dies, her familiars are said to seek out a close matrilineal kinswoman, who happens at the time to be residing near by, and attach themselves to her, forcing her in the end to let them kill one of her junior matrikin. Lunda say that when a woman reputed to be a *muloji* dies, her female matrikin flee her neighborhood in case they are adopted by her *tuyebela*. Now this is "inheritance" in a different sense from the inheritance of witchcraft substance among the Azande. The Lunda or Luvale witch is not born a witch but has witchcraft "thrust upon her," usually late in life. In tribal belief, too, she is thought to be quite aware of what has happened but for fear of her own life cannot resist the lethal demands of her familiars against her kin. The Zande witch, on the other hand, may be quite unaware of his mystical power until another person's divination discloses that he possesses it. After that he may be tempted, so Azande think, to use it. Yet, among the Lunda and related West Central Bantu tribes, it would be improper to distinguish women with *tuyebela* familiars as "witches" from other evildoers who are believed either to "grow" familiars from "medicines" or to carve and animate hominoid figurines. For these deliberately produced or acquired familiars also make irresistible demands on their owners and force them to kill their close kin. Thus intention, awareness, and possession of familiars are common to both male and female *baloi*. To call men "sorcerers" and women "witches" would be to miss the point of Evans-Pritchard's distinction. What is crucial is not whether witchcraft is "inherent" or "inherited" (two different attributes, by the way, since a person may be innately malicious or musical or friendly without having inherited these capacities from either parent) but that witchcraft acts directly by nonempirical means whereas sorcery operates mediately through spells, rites, and noxious substances. Even this qualification would not meet the Barotseland case. For while it is believed that male *baloi* create their familiars by medicine, once created such familiars as *ilomba,* the invisible snake, and *nkala,* the crab-monster, have an independent existence (they are thought of, too, as containers of their owners' life-principle, so that if the familiar is injured or slain, its owner also sickens or dies). They kill for their owners in ways that can only be described as "nonempirical" or "mystical," that is, without the intervention of medicines.

Let us now examine how the contributors to *Witchcraft and Sorcery in East Africa* employ the terms embodied in the book's title and how the editors have used the distinction in comparative sociological analysis. Beattie, in proposing to translate the Nyoro word *burogo* as "sorcery," adds the cautionary comment that "here . . . translation involves some degree of misrepresentation" (p. 29). "*Burogo* . . . is a technique; people do it because they so choose and it is learnt, not inborn" (p. 29). Nyoro also mention "people called *basezi,* who disinter and eat corpses, dance naked in the fields at night, and cause death to those who see them . . . some Nyoro say . . . they are born that way; others say that like *burogo, busezi* can be learnt" (p. 30). Nyoro have little practical concern with *basezi,* since diviners never attribute illness or misfortune to them. Nyoro have, therefore, no unconscious, involuntary witches who injure people "in virtue of an inherent quality." Their practitioners of evil magic learn how to use it, "know what they are doing and . . . do it on purpose" (p. 30). Beattie calls them "sorcerers." To illustrate the current inconclusiveness about terminology, Beidelman uses the term "witches" for persons who are "fully aware of their own witchcraft acts" (p. 64), who kill by intention "out of revenge, ill will, jealousy, or desire for power." These *wahai* "have various plant and animal substances which are said to produce witchcraft" (p. 65). "The simplest way to become a witch is to purchase *uhai* from a reputed witch" (p. 67). Such "witchcraft" is not then inherited, nor is it innate, since to make it really active its owner must "commit incest and/or murder and devour a human, sometimes even a kinsman" (p. 67). As among the Nyoro, the Kaguru recognize exceptionally terrible witches (*wakindi*), who, like their interlacustrine counterparts, are believed "to dance naked in the clearing before a victims' house and are necrophagous." These "work their powers merely by exerting their ill-wills," but acquire and do not inherit them. Like the Nyoro *basezi* these "night-dancing witches" differ from others only in degree and not in kind.

It might seem at first glance that Mandari "witches," described by Buxton, do correspond to the Zande paradigm. They work "with a hereditary power" (p. 101), and those who harm through the Evil Eye act directly on their victims. However, it is clear from Buxton's text (pp. 100, 106) that witches are believed by Mandari both to will and to know what they are doing. Moreover, we learn (p. 102) that "sorcery can be used by witches" in the form of imprecations and *materia medica.* Witches are said to train their children in night dancing (p. 100).

Douglas, in her book on the Lele (1963, 220–258) and in her article, employs the term "sorcerers" throughout for persons alleged to strike their fellows with illness and misfortune. "Sorcery required materials, actions and a formula of words . . . had to be bought, and used with the consent of the vendor" (*The Lele,* p. 220). It is thus consciously and voluntarily acquired and used. Like the *baloi* of Barotseland, Lele sorcerers are thought to use many means of harming victims, including the use of familiars, various medicines, the calling up of lightning and sandstorms. Like Kaguru and Mandari "witches," Lele "sorcerers" are necrophagous.

Professor Gray writes that among the Mbugwe of Tanganyika "witches are believed to be constitutionally different from other people, but the difference is an acquired rather than a genetic trait. The art is normally transmitted in a secret initiation rite from parents who are themselves witches to their children. . . . In theory, a person accepts initiation into witchcraft voluntarily. . . . Mbugwe witches are supposed to be fully conscious in carrying out their malicious acts, and are therefore held responsible for any . . . injury they may cause" (*Witchcraft and Sorcery in East Africa,* 161). In terms of Evans-Pritchard's definition, Mbugwe "witches" are clearly "sorcerers." Nevertheless, as regards certain modes of operation employed by them, such as harming through the Evil Eye, Mbugwe "witches" fall within the Azande definition.

As we proceed from author to author, the difficulties attendant on keeping the Zande witch-sorcerer model "pure" increase. For we have just seen how among the Mbugwe, witchlike means of doing harm are socially, not biologically, inherited. Parents are thought to teach their children how to be witches. It seems that what would be sorcery —in terms of the Zande distinction—as well as witchcraft can be "inherited" in kinship groups.

In his article on Nandi witchcraft, Huntingford is forthright in his condemnation of "an artificial distinction of terms, like 'witch' or 'sorcerer' " (p. 175). Nandi use only the one name for those who have the power to kill or injure people by means of spells. This term *ponik,* which he translates as "witches," is derived from *pan,* a verb meaning "to cast a spell." "Witchcraft" is "worked either through direct speech or through indirect speech accompanied by the use of material objects.

However, it soon becomes apparent that Nandi also recognize, in the possession of the Evil Eye, something that is very like Zande "witchcraft," since it has "an innate quality which causes its possessor to harm others merely by looking at them, even though they may have no wish or intent to hurt" (p. 175). Since what Huntingford has called "witchcraft" is similar to Zande "sorcery," it seems that we are by no means out of the terminological wood (or jungle) yet.

La Fontaine, in her essay on the Gisu of Mount Elgon in Uganda, very sensibly decides to refer to "all supernatural attacks as witchcraft," confining "sorcery" to "the powerful spells in the possession of the specialists in magic" (p. 192). Indeed, there is no warrant in the European tradition for restricting witchcraft to innate and inherited mystical power to work harm. Witches were generally thought to become such by entering into a compact with the Devil and to perform rites and utter spells to "conjure" others. Their association with toads and black cats, which were supposed to embody their "familiar" demons, derived from the compact into which they entered voluntarily and were not inherited from kin.

The Gusii of southwestern Kenya, according to LeVine, distinguish between the "witch" (*omorogi*) and the "sorcerer" (*omonyamosira*) as follows. The witch is "a person with an incorrigible, conscious tendency to kill or disable others by magical means" (p. 225). It is "an acquired art, and though it is handed down from parent to child, others can learn it as well" (p. 228). Witches operate by means of "the magical use of poisons, parts of corpses taken from graves, and the exuviae of the victims" (pp. 226–227). The witch practices in secret but the sorcerer is invariably a known practitioner whose tasks are "to kill magically the particular witch who is harming his client and to protect the client and his family from further witchcraft" (p. 234). Whereas witches tend to be women, sorcerers are invariably men, but there is "a dangerously thin line" between professional sorcery and witchcraft (p. 236). It is not only witches that sorcerers are believed to kill but also innocent persons who have incurred their wrath or jealousy. LeVine's use of the terms "witch" and "sorcerer" resembles La Fontaine's and has much to recommend it. Witches are all who are believed to harm others by mystical means, directly or indirectly, through magical techniques or innate power, with or without the aid of familiars. Sorcerers are professional witch-fighters. Since they are believed to kill other persons, it is largely a matter of structural perspective whether they are also regarded as "witches" or not—the victims' close kin would so dub them at any rate. Sorcerers are not "witch doctors," since they do not perform public rites or conduct witch-finding seances, nor do they wear regalia. They act in private at the behest of particular clients.

It would seem, therefore, from the various usages I have discussed [2] that there is little general agreement on the criteria that distinguish sorcery from witchcraft. In his essay in *Witchcraft and Sorcery in East Africa,* Professor Middleton finds among the Lugbara of Uganda something approaching the Zande model. "Witches have an inherent power which can harm others, whereas sorcerers use medicines which they acquire from other people." However, we learn from *Lugbara Religion* (1960) that "the ability, and the wish, to poison people by sorcery may be inherited, especially from the mother" (p. 245). In other words, sorcery is inherited among the Lugbara, apparently genetically. It also seems to be inherent, since Professor Middleton was told of a certain woman, said to be a sorcerer, that "her heart does not stay with others, it is bad." On the other hand, Professor Middleton does not tell us if and how witchcraft is inherited. Indeed, Lugbara themselves find it difficult to distinguish between deaths brought about by witchcraft and by "ghost invocation" by elders against habitually disobedient juniors. Both are said to be motivated by the sentiment Lugbara call *ole* (1963, 38; 1960, 239). In a witchcraft context *ole* may be translated as "jealousy" (an unrighteous sentiment) and in a ghost-invocation setting as "righteous indignation." Middleton's rich case material shows that the same death may be interpreted by different factions as one or the other, again according to the structural perspective of the interpreters. The fact, too, that both "witches" and "sorcerers," in Middleton's usage (1960: 245), may be called *oleu* (a derivative of *ole*) makes it clear that what is regarded as ideologically important by the Lugbara is belief in the existence of a broad class of persons who can injure others by mystical means irrespective of motive. It is only in the action-field context that allegations of the use of this or that specific means are made by interested parties. Almost every society recognizes such a wide variety of mystically harmful techniques that it may be positively misleading to impose upon them a

[2] Also others in the literature since the publication of *Witchcraft, Oracles and Magic among the Azande;* e.g. Dr. Kuper's definition of witchcraft among the Swazi (*An African Aristocracy* [1947], 173) involves the "inoculation" of a witch's child with "the special medicines of witchcraft," followed by deliberate "training" in witchcraft matters.

dichotomous classification. Their name is legion, their form is protean, for the very reason that individual spite is capricious, the ultimate corrosive of structure and rationality. That is why I am not altogether happy about the term "inversion" employed by Middleton and Winter as a fundamental characteristic of the behavior of witches. The behavior of witches in most societies is not altogether, as Winter argues (1963, 292), "the exact reverse" of that of other people. It has certainly some "inverted" features, but others are rather caricatures of normal behavior. The world of witchcraft, as it appears in tribal beliefs, is not the "structural" world upside down or in mirror image. It is a world of decay, where all that is normal, healthy, and ordered is reduced to chaos and "primordial slime." It is "anti"-structure, not inverted structure.

Professor Winter, in his essay on the Amba of western Uganda, feels justified in analyzing their witch beliefs in terms that approximate the Zande model. There is not a complete correspondence, since we find him classing as "witches" not only those who are born but also those who "have been initiated into the secret community of witches" (p. 280). Winter departs further from the Zande model when he states that Amba sorcerers and witches are differently motivated: sorcerers have intelligible motives for harming others, "such as envy, jealousy, and hatred," while witches are motivelessly malignant or kill merely to satisfy "their abnormal desire for human flesh" (p. 281). Zande witches, on the other hand, are believed to kill out of envy and hatred—sentiments that activate the witchcraft substance within them.

Winter and Middleton, the editors, are perhaps more deeply committed than the other contributors to establishing a sharply dichotomous cleavage between "witchcraft" and "sorcery," since they have attempted to make a rather ambitious comparative structural analysis with this distinction as a major conceptual tool. We have seen, mainly on the basis of data quoted from the symposium itself, how traits assigned by one writer to "witchcraft" are assigned by another to "sorcery"—in short, how there is as yet no standard usage of these terms.

Our editors, however, unperturbed by this major difficulty, gallantly "stick their necks out" and hypothesize that between societies that utilize either "witchcraft" or "sorcery" beliefs in making specific accusations, but not both, there are certain significant structural differences. "Witchcraft beliefs are thus utilized in societies in which unilineal kinship principles are employed in the formation of local residential groups, larger than the domestic household, while sorcery beliefs tend to be similarly utilized when unilineal principles are not so used" (p. 12). The Lugbara and the Nyoro are cited as illustrations of these respective differences, but two swallows do not make a summer, and two examples do not confirm a generalization. In any case, it is not at all clear that Lugbara accuse one another only of witchcraft, since in *Lugbara Religion* (pp. 163, 175, 178) certain persons, e.g., Okavu and Olimani, are suspected at times (if not openly accused) of being sorcerers (in terms of Middleton's definition).

Middleton and Winter are on firmer ground when they examine the conditions under which specific accusations of "wizardry" [3] are made against women and conclude that these "tend to occur only in those patrilineal societies characterized by the presence of the house property complex" (p. 15). Here they have based their conclusion on a wide range of good ethnographic studies and have felt no need to rely on an arbitrary and artificial terminological distinction.

One is forced to the conclusion that a holistic or "labelling" approach to the definitional problems discussed in this article is likely to sidetrack investigation from the study of actual behavior in a social field context to an obsession with the proper pigeonholing of beliefs and practices as either "witchcraft" or "sorcery." Antisocial magical beliefs and practices have a multitude of "components" or "attributes" and operate on a number of sociocultural "levels," as our authors have shown. An approach that is fully recognizant of the componential character of these phenomena is likely to be better adapted than the traditional one to the study of African societies as time sequences, in which persons and groups divide and combine in terms of situationally changing interests, values, and issues. Many African societies recognize the same range of components: "innate," "acquired," "learned," "inherited" skills to harm and kill; power to kill immediately and power created by medicines; the use of familiars, visible and invisible; the magical introjection of objects into enemies; nocturnal and diurnal hostile magic; invocation of ghosts by a curse; and so on. However, as between societies, and often in different situations in a single society, these components are varyingly clustered and separated.

[3] The term they propose to use for both "witchcraft" and "sorcery." Since in British folklore a wizard is commonly regarded as a male witch, it does sound a little odd to talk about "female wizards."

Clues to their clusterings and segregations may be found if societies are analyzed in terms of process-theory. Componential analysis at the cultural level is the natural counterpart of social dynamics.

## BIBLIOGRAPHY

Black, Max. 1962. "Models and Archetypes," in *Models and Metaphors.* Ithaca: Cornell University Press.

Douglas, Mary. 1963. *The Lele of the Kasai.* London: Oxford University Press, for International African Institute.

Evans-Pritchard, E. 1937. *Witchcraft, Oracles and Magic among the Azande.* London: Oxford University Press.

Kuper, Hilda. 1947. *An African Aristocracy.* London: Oxford University Press, for International African Institute.

Marwick, Max. 1952. "The Social Context of Cewa Witch Beliefs," *Africa,* XXII, Nos. 2 and 3.

Middleton, John. 1960. *Lugbara Religion.* London: Oxford University Press, for International African Institute.

Middleton, John, and Winter, E. H., eds. 1963. *Witchcraft and Sorcery in East Africa.* London: Routledge & Kegan Paul.

Reynolds, Barrie. 1963. *Magic, Divination and Witchcraft among the Barotse of Northern Rhodesia* (Robins Series, Rhodes-Livingstone Museum). London: Chatto and Windus.

# PART II

CHAPTER VI

# Muchona the Hornet, Interpreter of Religion*

I FIRST became aware of Muchona on a dusty motor road of packed red clay towards the end of a Northern Rhodesian dry season. In one direction the road ran to harsh, colorful Angola, in the other to the distant Copperbelt town of Chingola. Along it passed an occasional truck, mail van, or missionary's car, and many tough black feet, most of them going east to European mines and towns. On this day the road was almost empty in the hot late afternoon. Kasonda, my African assistant, and I had walked a few miles from our home village to a cluster of villages where we had collected census material. Now we were returning, gay with the millet beer and gossip that usually rounded off our more serious sessions. To make the miles go faster we played a game popular among Ndembu children: each of us tried to be the first to spot the budding *kapembi* shrubs with their frail red presentiment of the rains. Even Ndembu find it hard to distinguish this species from three others. Kasonda, of course, soon had a higher total than myself, for like all Ndembu he prided himself on his knowledge of the mystical and practical properties of the herbs and trees that flourish in this area.

We were so absorbed in our rivalry that we failed to notice a swart elderly gnome who was padding perkily beside us. He was evidently keenly observant, for he joined in our sport and soon took the lead. Kasonda told me he was a *chimbuki,* a "doctor," in several kinds of

* First published in *In the Company of Man,* J. Casagrande, ed. (New York: Harper Bros., 1959).

curative ritual, and "knew many medicines." I pricked up my ears, for ritual symbolism was my major interest. Each plant used in ritual stood for some aspect of Ndembu social life or belief. In my opinion a full interpretation of these symbols would lead me to the heart of Ndembu wisdom. Consequently, I seized the opportunity of asking the little man, whose name was Muchona, the meaning of some of the medicines I had seen doctors handle.

Muchona replied readily and at length, with the bright glance of the true enthusiast. He had a high-pitched voice, authoritative as a schoolteacher's when conveying information, expressive as a comedian's when telling a tale. Kasonda found his manner and mannerisms both funny and irritating, as he tried to show me by giggling conspiratorially behind his hand whenever Muchona had his back to us. I did not respond, for I liked the doctor's warmth, and thus began Kasonda's bitter jealousy of Muchona. Kasonda was worldly, and a shade spiteful, *au fait* with the seamier side of Ndembu (and indeed human) nature. He took a rancorous zest in the struggles for headmanship, prestige, and money that were the bane of village life. Muchona, for all his battling against witchcraft and the moody, punitive dead, had a curious innocence of character and objectivity of outlook. I was to find that in the balance mankind came off well for Muchona. Between these men lay the gap that has at all times divided the true philosopher from the politician.

Muchona showed me his quality that first day when he pointed to a parasitic growth on a *mukula* tree (a red hardwood). "That plant is called *mutuntamu,*" he said. "Do you know why it has that name?" Before I could confess my ignorance he rattled on:

> Well, it is from *ku-tuntama,* "to sit on somebody or something." Now, hunters have a drum [a ritual] called *Ntambu,* an old word for "lion." In *Ntambu,* a hunter who has been unlucky and has failed to kill animals for many days, goes into the bush and finds a big *mukula* tree like this one. The *mukula* tree has red gum, which we call "*mukula's* blood." It is a very important tree for hunters, and also for women. For hunters it means "the blood of animals." They want to see this blood when they go hunting. Now this unlucky hunter puts his bow over his right shoulder and his axe into his right hand—for the right side is for men and the left side for women, who carry their babies on their left arm—and he climbs up the *mukula* bearing bow and ax. When he is high up, he stands with one foot on one branch and one foot on another. Then he shoots an arrow at a *mutuntamu* plant. His arrow goes in strongly. Then he cries, "I have shot at an animal." Then he says, "I have shot you, *Ntambu* spirit. Please bring

me quickly to animals." After that he roars like a lion. Then he puts his strung bow over the *mutuntamu* branches and breaks them with the strength of the bowstring. He throws the broken twigs on the ground. They will later be mixed with other medicines for washing his body and his hunting gear. Just as the *mutuntamu* "sits on" the tree of blood, so must the spirit come and sit on the animal and blind it, in order that the hunter may kill it easily. He shoots *Ntambu* to show the spirit that he has found him out. He now wants *Ntambu* to help him, and not to trouble him any longer.

Now I had heard many other Ndembu interpret plant symbols before, but never so clearly and cogently as this. I was to become familiar with this mode of exposition, the swift-running commentary on unsolicited details, the parenthetical explanations, the vivid mimicry of ritual speech, and above all, the depth of psychological insight: "What hurts you, when discovered and propitiated, helps you."

Kasonda was whispering to me, "He is just lying." I could not heed him, for Muchona had already pointed out another tree and had begun to explain its ritual use and significance in a way that also compelled belief. I felt that a new dimension of study was opening up to me. Sympathy was quickly growing between us and when we parted we arranged to meet again in a few days.

Muchona did not come. Perhaps he hesitated to visit me, for my camp was in Kasonda's village, and it is probable that Kasonda had already hinted that he would be unwelcome there. Perhaps he had been performing curative rituals in distant villages. He was a restless man, seldom at home anywhere for long, like many another Ndembu doctor. Soon afterwards I also had to go away—to Lusaka, for a conference of anthropologists. For one reason or another I did not see him again for two months.

Meanwhile, I learned many details of Muchona's life which were common knowledge in his neighborhood. He did not live in the traditional circular village, but with his two wives occupied a couple of low huts near the motor road. He had seven children, the eldest of whom was a clerk at the government township, a well-educated youth by Ndembu standards. Kasonda insinuated that this tall son of a meager father was the by-blow of a youthful affair of Muchona's senior wife. The remark was pure malice. The alert intellect of the father was unmistakably reproduced in his son; and the son's achievement was reflected in his father's pride in him.

Muchona came from Nyamwana chiefdom, just across the Congo

border. His mother had been a slave, taken by the Ndembu before British rule was firmly established. His maternal kin were widely scattered over Mwinilunga District and adjacent areas in Angola and the Belgian Congo. The nuclear group of a Ndembu village is a small matrilineage; and no such nucleus had been formed by Muchona's kin. Later he was to complain to me that his two sisters in distant villages had ten children between them and that if they had come to live with him he could have founded a real village. He ignored the fact that Ndembu women customarily reside with their husbands after marriage and that, indeed, his own wives had left their brothers' villages to live with him. Poor Muchona had been doomed to rootless wandering from early boyhood. First of all he had lived in the village of his mother's captors. That village had split, and Muchona and his mother went with the dissident group. His mother was then transferred as a debt slave to yet another group where she was married to one of her owners. It seems that when he was a young man, Muchona bought his freedom and lived in the villages of several successive wives. However, he was never able to achieve a high secular status or an established position in a single village. These vicissitudes were both his curse and the source of his great ability to compare and generalize. Living as he had done on the margins of many structured groups and not being a member of any particular group, his loyalties could not be narrowly partisan, and his sympathies were broader than those of the majority of his fellow tribesmen. His experience had been richer and more varied than that of most Ndembu, though all Ndembu, being hunters and seminomadic cassava cultivators, travel considerable distances during their lives.

When I returned from Lusaka, I decided to pursue my inquiries into ritual esoterica very much further than before. In this quest I was assisted by the senior teacher at the local Mission Out-School, Windson Kashinakaji by name, Ndembu by tribe. Windson was a man of independent mind, obsequious to no European, arrogant to no villager. He was a keen but by no means uncritical student of the Bible. We often discussed religion together, and he became as eager as myself to learn the hidden meanings of Ndembu beliefs and practices. Most of his boyhood had been spent at a Mission Station behind a sort of spiritual *cordon sanitaire* against "paganism."

"I know the very man to talk about these hidden matters with you," he said after my return, "Kapaku. He has very many brains." Next day he brought Kapaku—none other than Muchona! Muchona, as fluid and evasive in his movements as wood smoke, had many names and Kapaku was one of them. It turned out that Muchona and Windson were neighbors, the one inhabiting a big house of sun-dried "Kimberley" brick, the other his pole-and-daub hut. Thus began an association that was to last eight months. Eight months of exhilarating, quick-fire talk among the three of us, mainly about Ndembu ritual. Sporadically, our colloquy would be interrupted by Muchona's doctoring trips, but most evenings after school Windson would stroll over to my grass hut and Muchona would rustle on its still green door for admittance. Then we would spend an hour or so running through the gamut of Ndembu rituals and ceremonies. Many I had seen performed, others I had heard about, and still others were now no more than old men's memories. Sometimes, under Windson's prompting, we would turn to the Old Testament and compare Hebrew and Ndembu observances. Muchona was especially fascinated by the fact that the symbolism of blood was a major theme in both systems. My method was to take a Ndembu ritual that I had observed and go through it, detail by detail, asking Muchona for his comments. He would take a symbol, say the *mudyi* tree which is the pivotal symbol of the girl's puberty ritual, and give me a whole spectrum of meanings for it.

*Mudyi* has white gum [latex]. We say that this is mother's milk. So *mudyi* is the tree of motherhood. Its leaves represent children. So when the women seize *mudyi* leaves and thrust them into the hut where the novice's bridegroom is sleeping, this means that she should bear many live and lovely children in the marriage. But the *mudyi* is also the matrilineage. For our ancestress lay under the *mudyi* tree during her puberty ritual; and women danced round her daughter, our grandmother, when she lay in that place of death or suffering. And our mother who bore us lay there. And the *mudyi* also means learning. It is like going to school today, for it stands for the instruction the girl receives in her seclusion hut.

Later, Muchona would relate the whiteness of the *mudyi* to the white beads that are draped on a miniature bow and placed in the apex of the novice's seclusion hut. "These beads stand for her capacity to reproduce, her *lusemu*—from *ku-sema,* 'to bear children or beget.' When the girl comes out of seclusion and dances publicly her instructress hides these beads in a pack of red clay on her head. No man but her husband may see these beads. She reveals them to him on her nuptial bed." Then he would discuss the meaning of the quality of whiteness which many symbols possess. "It means good luck, health, strength, purity, friendship towards other people, respect for the elders and for the ancestors; it means revealing what is hidden."

At other times, I would ask Muchona to describe a ritual from the beginning, whether I had seen it or not. Sometimes I would mention to him what other Ndembu specialists had said about its symbols. His accounts and glosses were always fuller and internally more consistent than theirs. He had evidently pondered long on the mysteries of his profession, critically comparing the explanations given him by those who had instructed him in the various cults in which he was an adept.

Windson's comments were usually to the point. His father had been a famous councilor in the court of a former subchief and from him as well as from the Mission School, Windson has acquired a flair for elucidating knotty questions. Although he was a product of modern change, he had never lost his deep respect for the now passing traditional order and its "reverend signors." At the time I knew him, he was, like other converts to Christianity, beginning to look askance at the privileged lives of certain of the white missionaries and to wonder whether the religion of his loved father was really such a farrago of deviltries as he had been led to believe. His major value for me lay in his ability to slow down Muchona's word-spates into digestible sentences and intelligible texts. For, as I have indicated, Muchona was an enthusiast, not only in talk, but, as I have seen him, in professional action as well—brisk, agile, full of prescience and *élan*. Windson spanned the cultural distance between Muchona and myself, transforming the little doctor's technical jargon and salty village argot into a prose I could better grasp. When taking a text I made him repeat slowly word by word Muchona's staccato speech so as not to water down its vividness. After a while, the three of us settled down into a sort of daily seminar on religion. I had the impression that Muchona had found a home of some kind at last.

I also came to know a few of Muchona's peccadilloes. For example, his knock would now and then be ragged; he would totter into the hut, his greeting an octave higher than usual, and slump down on a stool. He would then boast that his real name was "Chief Hornet" (*Mwanta Iyanvu*). This was his weak pun on the title of the mighty Lunda potentate in the Belgian Congo from whose realm the Ndembu had come some centuries previously. This title, Mwantiyanvwa, was the most important name the Ndembu knew. Iyanvu was Muchona's "beer-drinking name" (*ijina dakunwa walwa*), and when he used it he had come from drinking warm honey beer, a heady brew bobbing with bees. "Like a hornet or a bee," he would say, "I stay near the beer calabashes, talking loudly, and stinging those who annoy me." Hereupon Windson would fix him with a stern look, relieved by a twinkle of amusement, and tell him to go away and stay away until he had become "Mwanta Muchona" again. So the mighty "Chief Hornet," bedraggled with beer, would creep out of the hut.

This was the Muchona at whom men might scoff—at whom some did scoff, although others who had been treated by him for illness took a different view. Along with other motives less altruistic perhaps, Muchona had a genuine desire to cure the ailing and help the unlucky by his magical therapy. For instance, he would often say when describing how he first came to learn some curative technique, "I dearly wanted to cure well by means of *Kaneng'a* [or *Kayong'u* or some other ritual]." *Kaneng'a* doctors are often feared, as well as invoked, for they are the authentic "witch-doctors" who fight off the attacks of those given to the use of black art against their kin and neighbors. There is an implicit threat in the very knowledge the *Kaneng'a* doctors possess about the ways of witches and sorcerers. Muchona himself practiced a modified form of *Kaneng'a,* exempt from most of its terrifying elements. Thus, while most *Kaneng'a* practitioners collected medicines from the interior of graves, and some would even brandish human thighbones while they danced, Muchona merely took grass from the surface of graves and leaves and barkscrapings from trees growing in a circle around them. It is difficult to deduce attitudes from the behavior of members of another culture, but I once attended a *Kaneng'a* of Muchona's in company with a South African artist from Natal who had seen Zulu doctors at work. Muchona was treating an unfortunate woman who was suffering from delusions as the result of puerperal fever. My friend was impressed by what he considered the "compassionateness" of Muchona's demeanor. Gone was the rather uneasy pertness and comicality of his usual manner; in its stead was an almost maternal air—kind, capable hands washing with medicine, a face full of grave concern. My friend commented on the "heroism" with which Muchona, at one phase of the ritual, ventured out alone into the ghost-ridden graveyard, far from the firelight, to exorcise the agencies of evil that were making the poor victim writhe and babble nonsense. He subdued his fear to his curative vocation.

The compassionate side of Muchona's nature also emerged in the form of comments he made from time to time during our sessions on the luckless spirits whom Ndembu call *ayikodjikodji*, "mischief-makers." These are the spirits of persons inimical to society for one reason or other: through their greed and selfishness, because they were sterile, because they loved to stir up trouble, and so on. At many rituals gifts of food and beer are offered to the ancestors and always a small portion is set aside for the *ayikodjikodji*, usually at the margin of the sacred site and far from the person being treated. Instead of emphasizing the outcast position of these entities, Muchona invariably called attention to the fact that despite their delinquencies in life these spirits were still entitled to be fed. "For were they not human beings once, men and women like ourselves? Wickedness is in the heart [literally "liver"] and few can change the hearts they are born with. We do not want the *ayikodjikodji* to harm the living, but once they lived in the villages, were our kin." Other Ndembu brought out the propitiatory character of this rite in their interpretations; Muchona had mercy on the disreputable dead. Could it have been because he himself had to wander around the margins of respectable society that he felt fellowship with the despised and the rejected?

In our "seminars," Muchona seldom betrayed the emotional bases of his calling. A new and exhilarating intellectual dimension had opened up to him as well as to myself in our discussions of symbolism. At such times he had the bright hard eye of some raptor, hawk or kite, as he poised over a definitive explanation. Watching him, I sometimes used to fancy that he would have been truly at home scoring debating points on a don's dais, gowned or perhaps in a habit. He delighted in making explicit what he had known subliminally about his own religion. A curious quirk of fate had brought him an audience and fellow enthusiasts of a kind he could never have encountered in the villages. In this situation, he was respected for his knowledge in its own right. What has become of him since? Can he ever be again the man he was before he experienced the quenchless thirst for objective knowledge?

For Muchona, the homeless, was peculiarly susceptible to nostalgia. He had a recurrent dream which I translate literally to keep the smack of his speech. "I dream of the country of Nyamwana where I was born and used to live. I am where my mother died. I dream of the village which is surrounded by a palisade, for bad people raided for slaves. Streams which were there I see once more. It is as though I were walking there now. I talk, I chat, I dance. Does my shadow [*mwevulu*—the personal life-principle] go there in sleep?" Here the rational side of Muchona came uppermost, for he went on: "I find that place the same as it was long ago. But if I had really visited it, the trees would have grown big, grass perhaps would have covered it. Would there have been a stockade? No, it is just a memory." He shook his head lugubriously and said, lingering on each syllable, "Ākā" (meaning "alas," with a flavor of "Eheu fugaces!").

Muchona appears to have had an exceptionally close relationship with his mother, even for an Ndembu. This emerges in three ways from the history of his inductions into many kinds of ritual. First, it is apparent in the fact that Muchona was initiated into the preliminary grades of certain cults along with his mother, who held the position of senior novice or patient—in Ndembu ritual one must suffer before one is entitled to learn how to cure. Secondly, one finds that after Muchona's mother died she became for him an agent of supernatural affliction in at least one ritual context. The spirits of one's kin in Ndembu society punish one for a number of reasons, but through punishment, bane may become blessing, for the conduct of a ritual to mollify the spirit gives the patient the right of entry into a tribal cult. Affliction may thus well be a blessing in disguise. Thirdly, Muchona's attachment to his mother appears obliquely in that dead male relatives on her side plagued him into the acquirement of *expertise* in a number of rituals from which women are debarred, such as hunting cults.

My relationship with Muchona was at a professional rather than a personal level; we maintained towards one another a certain reserve about our intimate affairs. I did not ask him direct questions about his past, especially where the delicate question of his slave origin was concerned, but I learned much about it indirectly from his long spoken reveries on rituals in which he had taken part. Now and then, to be sure, he would suddenly take Windson and myself into his confidence about some matter that was currently troubling him. In the main, however, the pattern of his personality, like that of a poet in his poems, expressed itself in his accounts and interpretations of ritual, and in the nuances of gesture, expression, and phrase with which he embellished them. In a sense, therefore, Muchona's ritual history is his inner biography, for in ritual he found his deepest satisfactions.

Muchona's mother had been an adept in many kinds of ritual, for among the Ndembu slavery does not debar a person from ritual eminence. She also encouraged her children to acquire ritual skills.

Muchona had been initiated into three women's cults concerned with curing reproductive disorders. One of these, *Nkula,* is performed principally to cure menstrual disorders, but also to remove frigidity and barrenness. Its dominant medicine is the red *mukula* tree, which Muchona had mentioned to me at our first encounter. Here the tree symbolizes the blood of birth or motherhood, and the aim of the ritual is to placate an ancestress who is causing the patient's maternal blood to drain away and not to coagulate around the "seed of life" implanted by her husband. At the esoteric phase of *Nkula,* a *mukula* tree is ceremonially cut down and then carved into figurines of infants which are medicated with red substances and put into small round calabashes, representing wombs. These amulets are then given to the patients to carry on strings adorned with red feathers until they bear "live and lovely children."

Muchona was inducted into the *Nkula* cult when he was about seven years old. His mother was principal patient. At her request he was given the role of *Chaka Chankula,* usually taken by the patient's husband or uterine brother, although sometimes a classificatory "brother" or "son" may be chosen. The idea behind these choices is that a male who occupies a social position in which he might be called upon to support the patient jurally and economically should enact a role symbolizing the protective and responsible aspects of the male-female relationship. In practice, however, it is indeed very seldom that a patient's own son becomes *Chaka.*

A *Chaka's* main task is to squat behind the patient, after she has been washed with medicines by the doctor, and then to lead her backwards, while she rolls her head round and round under the doctor's flat collecting basket, to a small hut built for the afflicting spirit behind her own marital hut. Then the *Chaka* pulls her into the hut, both of them with their backs to the entrance. Later they emerge in the same fashion and return to the ritual fire. Muchona displayed his interest in "etymological" interpretations—an interest, incidentally, very common among Ndembu—when he told me that *Chaka* was derived from *kwaka,* "to deliver a child," or, more accurately, "to catch it as it drops."

Only a circumcised male can perform the role of *Chaka* since uncircumcised persons are reckoned ritually impure. An uncircumcised boy, like a menstruating woman, is *wunabulakutooka,* "one who lacks whiteness," and hence purity, good luck, and other qualities possessed by "whiteness." Again, an uncircumcised boy represents social immaturity, and a barren woman is also regarded as in some sense immature. As Muchona explained, "*Mukula* and *Nkula* both come from *ku-kula,* 'to grow up or become mature.' When a girl has her first menstruation she has grown up a little. When she has her first child she has grown up still more. Both of these occasions have to do with blood. After a boy is circumcised he sits, with others who have been cut, on a long log of *mukula,* the tree of blood. He has also grown up a little."

Another curious feature of *Nkula* should be noted here, for it may well have influenced Muchona's development as a doctor. In the role of *Chaka* a man is regarded as a midwife, in Muchona's case his own mother's, in contradiction to the strict Ndembu norm that only a woman may deliver another woman in childbirth. Since many *Yaka* (plural of *Chaka*) become *Nkula* specialists, and since such specialists are thought to cure reproductive disorders, the implication is that they are spiritual midwives. In addition, the *Nkula* patient is thought of as being ritually reborn into fruitful maturity, reborn that she too may bear. Muchona's desire to help the unfortunate by the only means known to Ndembu, leechcraft and ritual, may have found its first channel in this early indoctrination in his mother's *Nkula.*

Without being markedly effeminate in his deportment, Muchona always seemed more at ease among women than men. In my mind's eye I can still see him pleasantly gossiping with Kasonda's sister, both of them clucking their tongues at the misdeeds of their little world. This gay, full-blown woman had scant time for her scheming brother, whom she often scolded for his meanness to her. Muchona, to his credit, or perhaps through timidity, never to my knowledge said a word out of place about Kasonda, who himself had no hesitation in slandering Muchona behind his back. I fancy that Kasonda's sister more than once, in her imperious way, defended the tiny doctor against Kasonda's insinuations. Certainly, she called him in to perform the *Kayong'u* ritual for her, a ritual I shall shortly describe, for Muchona's first induction into it was a critical point in his development. Muchona might be described as a Tiresias figure, in that he had considerable insight into feminine as well as masculine psychology, especially in the fields of sex and reproduction. It seems certain that he identified himself closely with his mother, even to the extent of speaking in an alto voice. A young man I knew in Kasonda's village used to speak in a similar way, copying his mother, until he went away to work in a European township. When he came back he possessed a rich baritone, but had acquired a stutter in the process of masculinization. Muchona never lost his shrill pitch.

He resembled Tiresias in another important respect, for he was a diviner as well as a doctor. Here again the secret influence of his mother can be seen at work. During her lifetime she had caused Muchona to be initiated into no less than four kinds of ritual. After her death Muchona believed that she came as a spirit to afflict him "in the mode of *Kayong'u*," and thus to make a diviner of him. *Kayong'u* is the name of a specific set of symptoms, of the spirit that inflicts them, and also of the ritual to cure the victim. It has two variant forms, one to cure the illness and the other to prepare the patient to be a diviner as well as to cure him. Women may suffer from *Kayong'u* and may be treated by the curative ritual, but they cannot become diviners. They may, however, carry out minor ritual tasks during subsequent performances of *Kayong'u*, if they have been cured. Muchona's mother had been, in this sense, a *Kayong'u* doctor.

Muchona's initiation into *Kayong'u*, and the events leading up to it, stood out in his memory with harsh clarity. He was in his early thirties at the time and was living with his recently acquired wife, Masonde, among his stepfather's kin on the Angolan border. Apparently it was just about this time that he emancipated himself from slavery. One pictures him then as a minuscule fellow with a needle-sharp and pin-bright mind. He must have already developed a streak of buffoonery to curry the favor of the bigger and better-born. He must already have been something of an intellectual prodigy for his society, half derided and half grudgingly admired—and entirely unable to belong.

He told me that for a long time he had intermittent attacks of "being caught by a very heavy sickness in my body; I found it hard to breathe, it was like being pricked by needles in my chest, and sometimes my chest felt as though it has been blown up by a bicycle pump." A diviner was consulted, and he diagnosed that Muchona was suffering from the sickness of *Kayong'u*. Furthermore, not one but three spirits had come out of the grave to catch him, two full brothers of his mother, and his father. He himself had dreamed of one of his uncles and of his father while he was ill. Both these spirits, he said, were urging him to become a diviner, for they had practiced that profession. He had also dreamed of his mother, significantly enough. "She came too," he told me, "but she was so weak that the diviner did not recognize her." It is typical of Muchona that he felt compelled to stress the novelty of his personal lot in religious matters. A whole battery of spirits, not merely a single ancestor, had singled him out for this arduous and dangerous profession.

The values and attitudes expressed and inculcated in Ndembu ritual leave their stamp on its subjects. Personality is shaped at the forge of ritual, especially where the ritual deals with life-crisis, serious illness or, as I believe in Muchona's case, with a severe psychosomatic disorder. Thus, an account of one phase of Muchona's *Kayong'u* and his interpretations of it may reveal something of the man.

Let us go back thirty years or so to the flaring ritual fire of green wood outside Muchona's hut in the dull dawn. All night he has been washed with medicine, shuddering convulsively to the *Kayong'u* drum rhythm, a plaything of the savage spirits within him. At the first faint light, the senior officiant, a hunter-diviner, who was Muchona's father's brother-in-law, brings a red cock to the sacred site and holds it up before the patient by its beak and legs. *Kayong'u* like *Nkula* and the hunting cults is a "red" ritual, full of red symbolism standing for killing, punishment, witchcraft, and in general, for violent breach in the natural and social orders. Muchona, in a sudden spasm, leaps on the cock and bites through its neck, severing the head. Blood spouts out and Muchona "beats the bloody head on his heart to quieten his mind." Then the big doctor orders a goat to be beheaded. Its blood pours on the ground and Mucona laps it up where it puddles. The cock's head is placed on a pole called *muneng'a,* newly cut from the same species of tree from which ancestor shrines of quickset saplings are made, symbolizing ritual death and contact with spirits. The sun now rises and the doctor takes a hoe, a cupful of goat's blood, the hearts of the cock and goat, various "sharp" objects, and leads a procession of the doctors from the village into the bush. They go to a fork in the path and keep straight on instead of following either path. They find the principal medicine tree of the ritual, a *kapwipu* tree, which stands in this context for initial misfortune followed by success —a meaning it also possesses in hunting cults. They pray to the afflicting spirits and then heap up a mound of earth at the foot of the tree roughly in the shape of a crocodile, with legs and a tail. Next they conceal the various small objects, such as a knife, a razor, needles, a bracelet, and a string of beads under the mound, at the head, tail, and sides. Before concealing the razor and needle, the big doctor pricks the cock's and goat's hearts with them. Then they bring the drums and beat out the *Kayong'u* rhythm.

Now Muchona is led out of the village to the crocodile image and seated on its "neck" facing forward. The doctors question him on why he has come to *Kayong'u* and he gives the stereotyped responses regarded as appropriate. Next he has to divine where each of the objects has been concealed. He told me jubilantly that he was completely successful in this, that he seemed to know just where everything was hidden. Each time he answered correctly, he said, the women who had accompanied him to the sacred site trilled their praises aloud, "making me very happy." Suddenly, two doctors dart off to the village to hide something there. Muchona is led home where he begins searching and snuffling about to find what has been concealed. At length he says, "You have kept something here for the name of a dead man." He approaches the *muneng'a* pole, he claws up the earth near it. He shouts aloud, "The name of the dead man is *Nkayi* ["duiker"], for you have hidden a duiker horn here." Someone called *Nkayi*, he said, had recently died in the village. Then he explains to the doctors, showing off a little, one suspects, "A duiker-antelope is an animal of the bush. An animal lives in the bush, but a man lives in the village." He explained this to me by saying that while hunters seek out hidden animals in the bush, diviners hunt out the secret affairs of men in villages. At any rate, according to Muchona, the big doctor is highly impressed and calls out, "This man will make a true diviner." All gather round Muchona and praise him, but he had to pay the doctors many yards of cloth, he added rather ruefully. Nevertheless, he had been cured of his malady. It had gone immediately. The spirits that had afflicted him henceforth helped him to divine and protected him from evil. Shortly after the performance, he apprenticed himself to a famous diviner and learned the difficult manipulative and interpretative techniques of that profession, many of which he went on to describe in a series of sessions.

Muchona's interpretation of the symbolism of *Kayong'u* was compounded of both traditional beliefs and his own deeper insights: "The cock represents the awakening of people from sleep; at dawn the cock begins to crow and rouses them. The goat too stands for waking up, for at dawn it begins to bleat when it runs after she-goats and it disturbs people with its sound. The *Kayong'u* spirit too awakens people it has caught. It makes them emit a hoarse breathing, like a cock or a goat." I have myself heard Muchona and other diviners make a deep asthmatic wheezing noise in the course of ordinary conversation. This is supposed to be the voice of the *Kayong'u* spirit inside them. The *Kayong'u* then endows its possessor with special alertness, with the power of the first light that follows the secretive night, full of witches and mysteries.

Muchona continued: "It is the power of the *Kayong'u* spirit that makes a man kill the cock with his teeth. It makes a person a little mad. When he is shuddering he feels as though he were drunk or epileptic. He feels as though he were struck suddenly in his liver, as if by lightning, as if he were being beaten by a hoe-handle, as if his ears were completely closed, as if he could not breathe. He is stopped up. But he is opened when he kills the cock. From the killed animals he gets wakefulness, alertness, for he must be wide awake to become a diviner and seek out hidden things." The orifices of various senses—ears, nostrils, eyes—are stopped up during his ritual seizure; then the novice experiences a release, an access of heightened sensitivity. Again the curious parallel with Tiresias springs to mind for the Greek soothsayer was smitten with blindness before he attained insight.

Muchona said of the fork in the path:

When people come to a fork, they must then choose exactly where they want to go. It is the place of choice. Usually they have foreknowledge of the way to go. Everyone has such knowledge. But the diviner goes between the paths to a secret place. He knows more than other people. He has secret knowledge.

When the doctor pricks the hearts with needle and razor, he is representing the patient's pain. The patient must not feel it again because it has already been done in the hearts of the cock and goat. But if he becomes a diviner, he will again feel that pricking inside him—while he is divining. It is the thing which tells him to look at the *tuponya* [the symbolic objects shaken up in a basket whose combinations tell the diviner the cause of his client's illness or bad luck or how someone's death was brought about by a witch or sorcerer]. The diviner must be sharp like the needle, cutting like the knife. His teeth must be sharp to bite off the cock's head with one bite. He goes straight to the point in hidden matters. The crocodile in *Kayong'u* stands for divination because it has many sharp teeth, like needles.

A diviner can catch witches by *Kayong'u,* by its sharpness, and also by his divining basket. These help one another. A person who has *Kayong'u* is safe from witchcraft. Thus if someone tries to bewitch me, my three *Tuyong'u* [plural of *Kayong'u*] would kill that witch. For they are terrible spirits.

I have tried to sketch some of the factors that may have been responsible for making Muchona a "marginal man" in Ndembu society. His slave origin, his unimpressive appearance, his frail health, the fact that as a child he trailed after his mother through several villages, even his mental brilliance, combined to make him in some measure abnormal. His special abilities could not overcome the handicaps of his social marginality and psychical maladjustment. But he found some kind of integration through initiation into curative ritual and especially into divinatory status. For these, his outsider characteristics were positive qualifications. In a ritual context he could set himself apart from the battles for prestige and power that bedevil kinship and village relationships in Ndembu society. Ndembu ritual, like ritual everywhere, tends to assert the higher unifying values of the widest effective congregation. The doctor-diviner heals or judges by reference to commonly held beliefs and values which transcend the laws and customs of everyday secular society. Thus Muchona's very weakness and vulnerability in village life were transmuted into virtues where the maintenance of the total society was concerned.

The rich symbolism of oral aggression in *Kayong'u* points up a very different aspect of the diviner's role, and since Muchona set so much store by his occupancy of such a role it must have modeled many of his attitudes. In the past, a diviner had to ply a dangerous trade. I have been told of diviners who were shot or speared by the relatives of those they had declared to be witches or sorcerers. Moreover, they had to overcome by aggressive means much fear and guilt in themselves to reach decisions that might result in the death by burning of their fellow men. At its mildest, their profession entailed the probability of declaring in public that someone was a witch. No one but a diviner would do this, for as in all societies, the polite fiction prevails among Ndembu that social intercourse is governed by amity and mutual consideration. Only the diviner, fortified by ritual and protected by ferocious spirits that torment him while they endow him with insight, can pubicly expose the hates that simmer beneath the outward semblance of social peace.

One feels, therefore, that there is an aspect of unconscious revenge against the social order in divination. In Muchona's case, one may speculate that beneath his jester's mask, and under his apparent timidity, he may have cherished hatred against those more securely placed in the ordered groupings of society. Such hatred may itself have given him a certain clairvoyance into tense relationships in the kinship and political systems. Forever outside the village circle, he could see the villagers' weak spots and foibles more clearly than most. His very objectivity could further his general revenge. Nevertheless, he may himself have felt unconscious fear that those he disliked plotted counter-retribution against him. This fear made him at once meek and comical in his daily doings. By playing the timorous fool he belittled his own powers and thus defended himself. Moreover, his fear may have had something to do with the fact that he invariably rationalized his ritual tasks as being for the good of society. The flower of altruism sometimes has twisted roots.

It was an undoubted fact that Muchona, popular with most elderly women, was disliked by many men. For example, when his junior wife's baby died, a child who he admitted to everyone was not his, men from a number of villages took pleasure in telling me that they suspected he had bewitched it to death. To discredit these damaging views, communicated to Muchona by innuendo, he took the trouble to make a wearisome journey of several score miles to his parents-in-law to report the details of the baby's illness and the remedial measures he had taken. He told me wryly on his return that they had taken fifteen shillings—a considerable sum for a villager—from him as compensation for the child's loss to their lineage. Muchona, as the husband, was held responsible for the child's welfare. He said that they had taken no account of the money he had already paid a diviner to ascertain the cause of death, nor of the cost of treatment by a herbalist, also borne by Muchona himself. The diviner had declared him innocent of the child's death in the presence of his wife's kin, had indeed nominated as the sorcerer an important headman belonging to her lineage. If Muchona had been a tougher personality in secular affairs, he might have refused to pay compensation for an illicit child and have gotten away with it. As it was, he felt constrained to ingratiate established authority whenever he met it—or else to run away and build his hut in a different area.

There is another instance of Muchona's tendency to capitulate without a struggle to public pressure. One day, after he had been working with me for about three months, he strutted in wearing a suit of white ducks, paid for out of my cash gifts. He had informed everyone with some pride, I was told later, that his son Fanuel Muchona had given him the suit. Indeed, poor Muchona often tried to give the impression that Fanuel was more solicitously filial than he really was. It was soon discovered that Fanuel had only put his father in touch with the vendor, not given him the money for the suit. After our session, schoolmaster Windson said to me sadly, "That fine suit will make everyone jealous, for people will realize that you have been paying him well, and we Ndembu are a very jealous people."

Sure enough, a few days later Muchona came to us in his usual khaki rags, looking utterly woebegone. "What on earth's the matter?" I asked. He replied, "This is the last time we can speak about customs together. Can't you hear the people talking angrily in the village shelter? When I passed it on my way here, they were saying loudly, so that I could hear, that I was giving away our [tribal] secrets, and that I was teaching you witchcraft matters." I was distressed and a little hurt to hear this, for my relations with the villagers had always seemed extremely friendly. I said as much to Muchona, who went on, "No, it is not the people of this village, at least only a few of them, who are talking like this, but others who come to hear a case discussed in the village shelter. But the people of this village, especially one man—I name no names—say that I am telling you only lies. Before I came, they say, you heard only true things about our ceremonies, but now you just hear nonsense. But one thing I found wonderful. The village people call me a liar, the strangers say I am betraying secrets. Their reasons [for disliking me] don't agree, but they agree with each other!" I knew that it was Kasonda who called Muchona a liar, for he had hinted as much to my wife often enough, but Muchona was too polite or too diplomatic to say so, for everyone knew that Kasonda and I had been friends of long standing.

When Windson heard this sorry tale, his expression grew bleak and precipitous, as I suspect it must often have done when he dealt with refractory schoolchildren. "I must have a word with some of these people," he said. "Most of them have children at my school." He turned to Muchona, "Don't take any notice of these troublemakers. They won't say another word." Nor did they. For Windson was not only deeply respected as a man of integrity, but he also had effective sanctions at his command. As village schoolmaster, he could recommend or fail to recommend children for Middle School education at the distant Mission Station. Village Africans in Zambia are well aware that a good education is a vital means to such upward social mobility as is available to black people. If the schoolmaster were to become unduly aware of acts of naughtiness on the part of certain borderline cases for promotion, he might well send in an adverse report. I don't think Windson would have done this, for he was a gentle, earnest, and not unkindly man, but a hint in the proper quarters that Muchona was not to be bothered again had a wonderfully sobering effect.

Windson had become uncommonly fond of Muchona in the course

of our discussions. At first, he had tended to display a certain coolness, bordering on disparagement, towards Muchona's "paganism," but in a very short time he grew to admire the little man's intellect and his appreciation of the complexity of existence. Later still, Windson came to take positive pride in the richness and sonority of the symbolic system Muchona expounded to us. He would chuckle affectionately at Muchona's occasional flashes of dry wit.

One of those flashes came after we had spent a long session on a painful subject, the *ihamba*. In its material expression, an upper front incisor tooth of a dead hunter imbeds itself in the body of a person who has incurred the hunter's displeasure. The tooth is removed by means of a ritual procedure which includes confession by the patient and by his village relatives of their mutual grudges, and the expression of penitence by the living for having forgotten the hunter-ancestor in their hearts. Only after "the grudge has been found" will the tooth cease "to bite" its victim and allow itself to be caught in one or another of a number of cupping horns affixed to the patient's back by the doctor's principal assistant. After about a couple of hours, Muchona became very restive on his hardwood stool. Full of the zest of inquiry, I had become thoughtless and had forgotten to give him his usual cushion. Eventually he burst out, "You have been asking me where an *ihamba* goes. Well, just now I have an *ihamba* in the buttocks." I silently passed him his cushion. However, this was not all. We used to punctuate our deliberations pleasantly enough with an occasional cigarette. Today I had forgotten even to pass around the yellow pack of "Belgas." So Muchona said, "I have another *ihamba*." "What's that one?" "The angriest *ihamba* of all, the *ihamba* of drinking [i.e., smoking] tobacco." Like a true professional, Muchona could make innocuous quips about his craft.

Muchona normally took *ihamba* beliefs very seriously. He had been treated no less than eight times, he said, to gain relief from an *ihamba* that made his joints sore. Either because the doctors were charlatans —one tried to deceive him with a monkey's tooth—or more often because "the grudge was unknown," the *ihamba* remained to vex him. Several divinations had established to his satisfaction that the *ihamba* came from a mother's brother who had been taken while still a boy by Luba slave raiders many years ago. Later, his mother had learned that her brother had become a famous hunter and a wealthy man in Lubaland, having purchased his freedom there, but she never saw him again. Muchona believed that he held an undying grudge against his maternal kin, perhaps because he had not been captured but had been sold into slavery by them—who could tell so long afterwards? Muchona was being afflicted on account of this grudge. Since no one could now find out what it was, he felt he could never be cured of the biting, creeping *ihamba*. May we not see in this a projection of Muchona's own state? Did he bear an unconscious grudge against his mother—displaced on to her unknown brother—for saddling her son with slavery? Did he not have the fantasy that even a slave could become great, as his uncle was reputed to have done? At any rate, in Muchona's phrasing of *ihamba* beliefs, he seemed to feel that he was in the grip of some irremediable affliction, that indeed his sickness was himself. Although suffering made him a doctor in many curative cults, he never became an *ihamba* specialist. One fancies that this one incurable trouble represented for him the deathless gnawing of his chagrin at being of slave origin and at not really "belonging" in any snug little village community.

No man can do justice to another's human total. I have suggested that in Muchona there was a deep well of unconscious bitterness and a desire for revenge against a society that had no secular place for him compatible with his abilities. Yet the small man had a big mind. He was only too sensitively aware of the undertone of derision and resentment with which many men regarded him. Although he was paramountly intellectual rather than warm-hearted, he tried on the whole to speak and act civilly and charitably; and he treated his patients with compassion. In our long collaboration he achieved an amazing degree of objectivity about the sacred values of his own society. Whether his outlook was radically altered by our threefold discussions I was not to know. All I do know is that shortly before I left his land, probably forever, he came to see me, and we had an outwardly cheerful drink together. Presently, he grew quiet, then said, "When your motor car sets out in the early morning do not expect to see me nearby. When someone dies we Ndembu do not rejoice, we have a mourning ceremony." Knowing Muchona as I did, I could not help feeling that he was not simply feeling sorry at the loss of a friend. What grieved him was that he could no longer communicate his ideas to anyone who would understand them. The philosophy don would have to return to a world that could only make a "witchdoctor" of him. Had not some kind of death occurred?

# CHAPTER VII

# *Mukanda*: The Rite of Circumcision

Several good accounts exist of circumcision rites in the West Central Bantu culture area. White's "Notes on the Circumcision Rites of the Balovale Tribes" (1953), provides data from the Balovale, Kabompo, and Mwinilunga districts of Northern Rhodesia, and deals with circumcision among the Lunda, Luvale, Chokwe, and Luchazi. Gluckman's "The Role of the Sexes in Wiko Circumcision Ceremonies" (1949) is based on observations in Barotseland, mainly on Luvale immigrants. Data on the Chokwe in Angola and the Belgian Congo is provided by: Baumann (1932), Borgonjon (1945), Delille (1944), Holdgredge and Kimball Young (1927). Delille also published an account of Lunda and Luvale circumcision in the Belgian Congo (1930). Tucker (1949) published some notes on Lwimbi circumcision in Angola, while Hambly has written on "Tribal Initiation of Boys in Angola" (1935).

The Ndembu circumcision rites, called *Mukanda* like those of the Chokwe, Luvale, and Luchazi, provide an interesting variation on the general pattern. I present an account, based on personal observation and informants' description, of the Ndembu rites, partly to add to the general store of ethnographic information about such rites, and, more importantly to provide data for the kind of analyses I am undertaking here. With the latter aim in mind, I present *Mukanda* as a set of successive episodes, based primarily on my own observations of a particular performance, with interpolated comments and exegesis of symbolism by Ndembu informants.

White summarizes major aims and common features of circumcision rites among the Balovale tribes in his article (1953). He considers that these rites cannot be associated with Islamic influences and that there is no general tradition to explain the source of the practice of circumcision among these tribes, although "they all have a common origin in their dispersion from the southwest Congo basin from Mwantiyanvwa's empire, and no doubt brought circumcision with them when they entered Northern Rhodesia."

The normal age of circumcision in the past was higher than it is to-day, and was usually coincident with puberty or just after. The novices remained in seclusion for as long as a year. To-day the rites take place during the cold weather as being the most hygenic period of the year but the novices remain in seclusion for only three or four months. The novices of to-day are commonly about 8–10 years old and rarely over 14–15. This lowered age and shortened period of seclusion is largely due to such modern influences as the need for school attendance and the pressure of a modern economy which requires a young man to earn money.

The rites are typical *rites de passage* in which the novices are reborn as men after a symbolic death. During this period the novices are secluded and finally emerge with new adult names. An uncircumcised person remains a child and eats alone or with women, since he cannot join grown and circumcised men in their meals. No woman in the past would have sexual relations with him, although to-day the women of these tribes have relaxed this latter taboo, as a result of contacts with uncircumcised tribes, and may now have sexual relations in some cases with uncircumcised men. In the past a circumcised man would not have his food cooked on a fire used to cook food for uncircumcised persons. Combined with the attainment of full manhood, the rites stress the sexual maturity of the participants. As befits one who has attained to manhood, the novice ensures by the rites that he will be fully capable in sexual capacity.

Although White believes that there is no general tradition of origin for circumcision among the Balovale tribes, he mentions that "some say that a woman left her child playing on the grass in her garden and it was accidentally circumcised by a sharp grass; when the result was seen, people decided to adopt it for general use." Among the Mwinilunga Ndembu, I collected several foundation myths that contained the elements: mother, child, and grass. The fullest, as ever, was Muchona's which I translate:

Once there was a woman and her son. They went together to collect some grass for burning into salt. The child tried to follow his mother along the way she was going, collecting the salt grass (*matahu amung'wa*). By accident, a piece of *kaleng'ang'ombi* grass cut round his penis. The boy fell down crying. The woman rushed to him to see why he was crying. She felt very sorry; she took the boy to his village. There some men said; "The boy must be taken somewhere (away) from his own mother and from the other women." There they brought a razor (*ntewulu*, the same kind of razor that is used for shaving around the hair-line to mark the end of seclusion at funerary ritual, at girl's puberty, and in several kinds of curative cults) and cut the penis round properly, removing the foreskin completely. The father was responsible for his own child. Medicine was put on the penis. After some weeks the boy recovered, became well again. Men were very pleased to see how the cut healed up, so they tried other boys. Just the same thing happened—after some weeks the boys were healed again. So the people began to understand that it was better for all to be circumcised. So men of full growth were circumcised also. They danced and drank beer (to celebrate) the cutting of penes well and how nice they looked. That is how they began [*Mukanda*].

Muchona added here that *Mukanda* is to heal, not to make fertile. It is "to cure (a novice) that he may be strong, that he may catch power (*kumuuka akoli akwati ng'ovu*)." Later we shall see that the avoidance of salt by the parents of a novice between his circumcision and the healing of his scars is an important feature of the Ndembu rites.

Other accounts mention boys, adult males, and grass, but not the mother-child relationship. For example, Headman Sampasa, one of the circumcisers in the rites I observed, told me that

once upon a time some young boys were playing near a river. They were accidentally circumcised (*kwalama*) by some *kalembankwaji* grass (said to have sharp triangular blades). When they returned to the village, the elders said, "This is very bad. What bad person has cut the children like this?" But afterwards those boys who had been cut seemed stronger than other lads. So the elders decided to do like the grass, and circumcise the boys with razors.

Sampasa's structural perspective as a circumciser may have led him to emphasize the physical operation itself and not the social relationships involved. The latter are very important in *Mukanda*. For as Gluckman writes (1949, 145), "the boys are ritually separated from their mothers to be identified with their fathers."

A circumcised person is forbidden to eat food from a fire used to cook food for uncircumcised persons. This prohibition is still observed in many parts of Ndembu territory today. An uncircumcised boy is described as *wunabulakutooka*, "one who lacks whiteness or purity."

The same term is applied to a menstruating woman. An uncircumcised man is permanently polluting, a woman only during her periods. If either eats those portions of a hunter's kill reserved to members of the hunters' cult the hunter is believed to lose his luck at the chase, while his medicines lose their efficacy.[1] Similarly, neither may approach a hunter's village shrine. The man is believed to run the risk of bleeding to death when he is circumcised and the woman of suffering from an unnaturally long menstrual period. Circumcised men "can eat from one plate and from one fire (*hejiku dima*)." An uncircumcised man is polluting because of the dirt beneath his foreskin (the term "*wanza*" means just this and is used to revile someone). This "dirt" is due to the retention of urine and accumulation of sebaceous secretion from the *glandulae odoriferae* known as *smegma praeputii*. After the circumciser has cut off a section of the prepuce, he rolls back the rest to reveal the glans. This act is known as *ku-solola,* "making visible." Similarly, when a new *muyombu* is planted to the ancestors, the bark and some of the wood are removed at the top, leaving a peg of bright white wood, which is compared to a circumcised penis. A circumcised man is "white" (*watooka*) or "pure." What was hidden (and unclean) is now visible. The dryness of the glans is also commended.

I observed only one complete performance of *Mukanda,* (though I collected many accounts of the rites from informants), but I was able to obtain much information about the social background of this performance. I recorded genealogies in all but one of the villages that sent novices to the circumcision lodge or provided officiants. I made hut diagrams of these villages, noted some of the more important social characteristics of the main performers, and gradually uncovered political ties and cleavages between the groups and subgroups taking part. This sociological information helped me to understand better the interrelations of the performers, and even to interpret breaches of ritual custom. In order to give the reader a picture of the sort of social matrix within which Ndembu rituals are performed, I propose to sketch in the structural outlines of the social field made visible by this performance of *Mukanda.*

[1] My Ndembu informants, Sakutoha and Kasonda, formulated the prohibition in the following terms: "It is because of the ancestor spirits (*akishi*). A man who has many spirits can become ill if he eats with uncircumcised boys. An uncircumcised person is unclean, and so the spirits feel angry."

With regard to the actual performance, I recorded its ritual details as accurately as I could, took photographs of important episodes and sites, and enlisted the aid of officiants on the spot to interpret symbols. Accounts of how *Mukanda* should be performed were given me by Chief Ikelenge, Kasonda, Sandombu, Kenson, and, best of all, by Muchona (a character study of Muchona is given at pp. 131–150). Besides these, I collected items of information and exegesis from many men and women in the course of pursuing other inquiries, as one always does in fieldwork.

Description and indigenous interpretation of the ritual customs in episodic order must follow an analysis of the social field in which they are set. The most prominent social unit taking part in any circumcision ritual is the vicinage, or cluster of neighboring villages. A vicinage consists of a number of villages—anything from two to more than a dozen—separated from one another by distances varying from fifty yards to a couple of miles. Few of these villages are interlinked by matrilineal ties, that is, by the dominant principle of descent. Most of them have only short histories of local settlement and have migrated from other vicinages or chiefdoms in the recent past. Such villages soon become interlinked by a complex network of marriages, and affinity assumes a political significance. Since marriage is virilocal, and since many marriages occur within the vicinage, most villages rear as their seminal "children" the junior matrilineal members of neighboring villages. I mention this because it is an important feature of *Mukanda* that fathers protect and tend their sons during circumcision and seclusion. The father-son link which is crucial for the integration of the vicinage is also stressed in ritual custom.

In *Schism and Continuity in an African Society: A Study of Ndembu Village Life* (1957), I have shown that vicinages are unstable groupings, for villages frequently split up through time and wander over a wide territory. The split-off section or migrant village often changes its vicinage affiliation. Such instability and transience render virtually impossible the clear-cut political dominance of one headman over the others. As in other sets of Ndembu social relations, we find rather the coexistence and situational competition of several criteria that confer prestige but not control. In each vicinage there are usually at least two villages that claim moral pre-eminence over the others. I shall now describe in detail the pattern of conflict prevailing in the vicinage where I observed a whole performance of *Mukanda*.

## *The Vicinage of Mukanda*

A Ndembu vicinage, then, is a cluster of villages, of changeable territorial span, and fluid and unstable in social composition. It has no recognized internal organization that endures beyond the changes in the identity of the villages making it up, but it is not just a neighborhood round any village. The vicinage becomes visible as a discrete social entity in several critical situations, including *Mukanda*, and a particular headman within it on such occasions exercises moral and ritual leadership. Since the crucial occasions on which such leadership may be asserted are relatively infrequent, and since a vicinage is always changing in group and numerical composition, an important ritual like *Mukanda* becomes a trial of strength between former leaders and aspirants to leadership. In the course of such a struggle, various criteria are appealed to by the contestants. Both the people themselves and, after a time, the anthropologist become aware of the relative importance in terms of these criteria of the persons and groups engaged.

First of all, I must enumerate the social groups participating in the *Mukanda* situation. Diagram 1 is a schematic representation of the approximate spatial arrangement of residential units in the vicinage. Six of these units, Nyaluhana, Machamba, Wadyang'amafu, Sawiyembi, Sampasa, and Kafumbu are villages entered on the Government Tax Register. The other units, Nyampasa, Mukoma, Wukengi, Robert, Kafumbu Kamu, Towel, Simon, and Kutona, are known by Ndembu as *mafwami*, from the English term "farm" (a term said to be borrowed from African tribes living near the Copperbelt who possess similar units) and have not yet been so entered. Farms pay their tax through the headman of a registered village. They have recently split off from registered villages and continue to pay a tax as members of it, or they may have come from a distance and attached themselves to a registered village near their new site. The term "farm," however, conceals two clearly distinguishable types of residential grouping. One type represents the first stage in the life cycle of the traditional Ndembu village: it has the form of a circle of pole-and-mud huts, and is occupied by a nucleus of matrilineal kin of the headman, male kin preponderating over female as the result of virilocal marriage. In *Schism and Continuity in an African Society,* I called such units "unregistered villages." A large unregistered village is structurally identical with a registered village. The other type de-

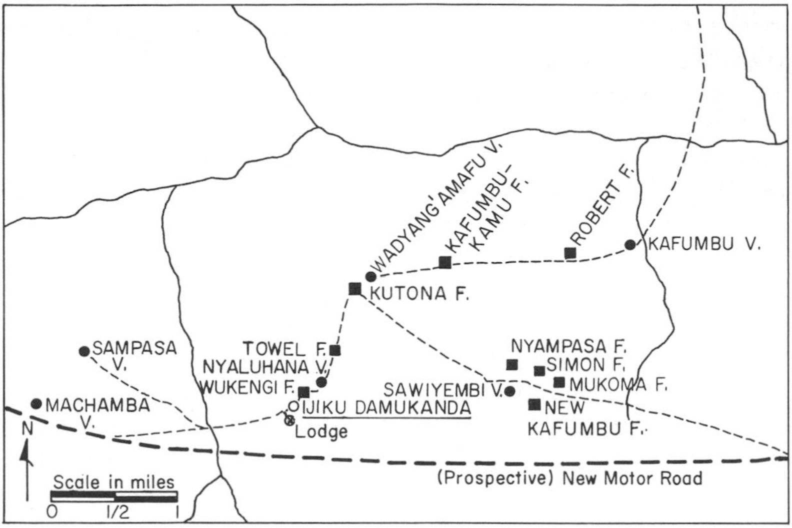


*Diagram 1.* Nyaluhana vicinage

serves to be described as a "farm" and possesses certain features of hut arrangement and social composition unknown to the pre-European Ndembu social organization. It is no longer a circular grouping of huts but consists of one or more buildings of sun-dried (Kimberley) brick, much larger than the average hut, flanked on either side by a few small pole-and-mud huts and kitchens. The typical farm head is a man who has earned money, often on the line-of-rail, and who intends to earn more locally. He may be a petty trader, a tailor with his own sewing machine, a "tearoom" proprietor, or a peasant producer growing crops for sale. For all these purposes, access to administrative or trading centers is advantageous. There were few true "farms," in the modern sense, in the vicinage we are considering, for although most of its villages were situated within a few miles from the "Boma" or administrative headquarters, access to it was by footpath only. To reach the Boma, the direct path was across the Mudyanyama River which became a rushing torrent in the rains. However, during the period of *Mukanda* a new motor road was in process of construction from the Boma to the village of Nyachiu, just beyond the vicinage, and this road passed through the vicinage. The new road avoided a wide bend in the old road and put most of the vicinage on the direct labor migration route to the Copperbelt from Senior Chief Kanongesha's capital, where there is a large concentration of population, and from Angola. In anticipation of the effects of this road, several of the more astute members of the vicinage, such as Towel and Simon, had built farms set off from their villages of origin, intending to sell food, beer, and other products of their industry to travelers. The basic unit in a farm is the elementary or polygynous family rather than the matrilineage. The farm head builds separately from his matrilineal kin to assert his economic and jural independence from them. He is struggling towards emancipation from traditional norms, in order to participate more fully in the modern cash economy.

Farms and the road, then, in this vicinage were pointers to future developments. The road especially was a feature of the cultural landscape that influenced some of the events I shall describe, but due to the partial isolation of the vicinage, traditional norms and values continued to play the dominant part in shaping what went on during *Mukanda*. Most of the so-called "farms" were in reality "unregistered villages" in form and composition. People tended in fact to speak of Nyampasa, Mukoma, and even Kafumbu Kamu as villages" (*nvikala*), rather than as "farms." Wukengi, too, was making a bid for village rating, although outsiders to the vicinage still looked on it as part of Nyaluhana Village. Kutona, like Wukengi, was considered by most people a part of its parent village. Robert was reckoned a "farm." Its head, and most of its other members, were of the Luvale tribe, and like most Luvale in Mwinilunga District, engaged in trade, raising crops for sale (mainly to the Boma residential area), and selling beer. Robert, Towel, and Simon were the only true "farms" in the vicinage.

There were, then, six registered villages, five unregistered villages, and three farms in the vicinage. In addition to these, a section of Machamba Village began to build separately but near to the parent village just about the time *Mukanda* began, but this division did not appear to influence *Mukanda* significantly. Throughout, Machamba Village exhibited a high degree of unity vis-à-vis other groupings. For Machamba sought to raise its prestige in *Mukanda*, and this common purpose transcended for a time incipient cleavages within the village. This was not always the case. There was, indeed, far more of a general tendency for seceding groups after the fission of a village to seek allies among that village's external opponents. In this case, both the main sections of Machamba stood to gain more by alliance than by division.

There were two major contenders for the right to sponsor this *Mukanda* and to perform its leading roles. One was Headman Machamba, the other, Headman Nyaluhana. Each had his factional following in the vicinage during the *Mukanda* situation. Generally speaking, factions were multiples of village memberships, but as we have noted, internal quarrels in villages sometimes resulted in dissident groups and individuals supporting, sometimes openly but more often clandestinely, the faction opposed to their headman's. On the face of it, Nyaluhana was supported by Wukengi, whose head was Nyaluhana's classificatory sister's son, by Wadyang'amafu, by Kafumbu, by Nyampasa, and by Mukoma. Machamba, on the other hand, was supported by Sampasa, and by Sawiyembi. It would seem that Nyaluhana's claim was the more strongly backed up, but it must be mentioned that much of Nyaluhana's following had closer links with Wukengi than with himself, and that Nyaluhana and Wukengi were by no means on the best of terms. The outcome of their rivalry was by no means a foregone conclusion when it was first suggested that *Mukanda* should be performed.

Nevertheless, Nyaluhana's claims to sponsor *Mukanda* and allocate its key roles were formidable. His village was "a village of the chieftainship" (*mukala wawanta*), and men belonging to its matrilineal nucleus may become candidates for the Kanongesha senior chieftainship, or rather for the Chibwika chieftainship, whose incumbent is Kanongesha's heir apparent. Indeed, the current Kanongesha, Ndembi, belonged to the Nyaluhana matrilineage; but for this very reason, it was unlikely that the next Chibwika would be nominated from Nyaluhana Village, for it is the Ndembu convention for each new Chibwika to be appointed from a different village belonging to the chiefly maternal descent group. Nyaluhana claimed that his lineage was descended from Nkeng'i, the uterine sister of the founder of the Kanongesha chieftainship, supposedly a son of the great Lunda emperor Mwantiyanvwa, whose homeland lay around the Lulua River in the Congo. The village itself had been established by a later Kanongesha, Nkomesha, for his sister Nyaluhana Chikuya, allegedly a woman of forceful character. This event must have taken place between about 1870 and 1880. My genealogies of Ndembu villages record several female village heads in the nineteenth century, and indeed there was a woman village head, Nyampasa, in the vicinage when I made my study of this *Mukanda*. The present Kanongesha's mother's mother was an older sister of the first Nyaluhana. Kanongesha Ndembi had married Wukengi's sister's daughter when this woman, Mulosu by name, had been a member of Nyaluhana's village, that is, before Wukengi had split from Nyaluhana Village. By her Kanongesha had a son, a most intelligent little hunchback, whom he had sent to be circumcised at this *Mukanda*. Nyaluhana Village, like the other villages in the vicinage, lay within Kanongesha's own area. Kanongesha thus held a twofold authority over the vicinage. He was Senior Chief and Native Authority of all Ndembu and was also the local territorial chief. Since he was a matrilineal kinsman of Nyaluhana, and had clearly indicated that he favored Nyaluhana's claims by sending his son to the latter's village, it seemed long odds at the time when I first heard that *Mukanda* would be performed in the vicinage, that Nyaluhana would control the most important ritual roles.

Nyaluhana himself had been Senior Circumciser (*Mbimbi wamukulumpi* or *Mbimbi weneni*) at no less than three previous performances of *Mukanda*. The first occasion had been in 1928, shortly after Nyaluhana had succeeded to the headmanship of his village. The novices' seclusion lodge had been erected near his village (which was then situated beside the Kanjimu River, a mile or two from its location in 1953). Nyaluhana had again been Senior Circumciser in 1941, when a *Mukanda* was held at Katong'i Farm, an offshoot of Nyaluhana Village. The third time was in 1943, at Nyaluhana Village itself, when the village was not far from its present site, near the Kachibamba River. Thus, there were abundant precedents for Nyaluhana's continuing to fill the senior role.

In theory, *Mukanda* provides three roles of almost equal importance. The first is Senior Circumciser, a post that ought to go to the most skillful with the circumcising knife and the most adept in the magical and medicinal lore connected with the operation. In practice, this role often goes to a reasonably skilled operator who, in addition, enjoys high prestige by other criteria, such as: headmanship of a large and long-established or traditionally renowned village; connection with a chiefly family; reputation as a specialist in several kinds of ritual; wealth in cash or kind. Almost equal in importance is the role of *Chijika Mukanda*, "he who stops up *Mukanda*," an official whom I will call the Establisher (see also White 1953). His main task is to preside over ritual and circumcision activities in a cleared site between the lodge and his village, for it is usually his village that is nearest the lodge. He is commonly a middle-aged man who has at least three sons to be circumcised. He need not necessarily be a headman, but should stand a good chance of succeeding to the headmanship of an important village in the not so distant future. The third ritual role is that of *Mfumwa Tubwiku* or *Mfumwa Wanyadi* (literally, "husband of the novices"), the Senior Instructor in the seclusion lodge (*ng'ula*). This man may also have several sons in the lodge as novices or acts as their "guardian" (*ayilombola*, sing. *chilombola;* or *ayilombweji*, sing. *chilombweji*). The role of Lodge Instructor carries rather less prestige than the other roles mentioned, but is nevertheless highly coveted. In principle, the Establisher is the initiator or "setter-up" [2] of *Mukanda*, and he is often called "The Owner of *Mukanda*" (*Mwenimukanda*). However, since he is often below the age thought appropriate for headmanship, in practice the real sponsor of *Mukanda* is the headman of his village. The man who prays first at the village ancestral shrine at dusk on the eve of the circumcision rite is generally reckoned to be the sponsor. If the headman of the Establisher's village is also a renowned circumciser, it is almost certain that he will be regarded as the sponsor or "true" (*walala* or *wachikupu*) owner of *Mukanda*. In the three previous performances mentioned, Nyaluhana had prayed first at the ancestral shrine, even when *Mukanda* had been held from a farm that had split off from his village. Thus, he had maintained a paramount position in each ritual situation. He had been Senior Circumciser, and each time the Establisher had been one of his junior kinsmen.

In 1953 Nyaluhana was an old man. He had many jealous rivals in the vicinage and some within his own matrilineal kin group, all of whom would have rejoiced to see him humbled. Most of the younger men regarded him as old-fashioned and well behind the times—which were times of wage labor, labor migration, Mission and Government schools. His unyielding pride, indeed arrogance, angered the independent spirits of his near-contemporaries. How had he come to be what he was?

At first, I found considerable difficulty in getting Nyaluhana to talk about himself, or about anything else, for that matter. When I arrived at his village in the early June of 1953, I saw Nyaluhana, an extremely black ancient, horny-eyed like a tortoise, sitting in a deck chair with goatskin instead of canvas for support. Unlike all other Ndembu headmen I had known, he did not rise to greet me, nor would he shake hands. After a while he thawed out a little, especially when some of his own relatives, whom I had known for a long time,

[2] C. M. N. Whites' term.

spoke up on my behalf. Suddenly he said, with a half-smile, that he had distrusted all Europeans ever since the days of "Yekisoni." "Yekisoni" or "Jackisoni" (as Ndembu call him to this day) was one of the early Native Commissioners sent by the British South African Company to administer the Mwinilunga Lunda. His real name was McGregor and he was discharged from the Service for his excessive cruelty to the Lunda. Yekisoni used to come to Ndembu villages, said Nyaluhana, and confiscate goats, sheep, and chickens. He used to "sleep with our daughters and catch our young men by the saddle." He "beat men, women, and children for no reason at all." Later I learnt that Nyaluhana had fled with the rest of his village (and indeed half the population of the District fled from Yekisoni to the Belgian Congo or Angola), to Mushimba in Angola. There he had remained for over fifteen years with his mother's brother, Headman Nswanamumi, son of the founding woman head of Nyaluhana Village. Nyaluhana then told me that other Europeans he had known after Yekisoni were better, but not much better. I had seldom met so blunt a headman.

The purpose of my visit had been to find out when the first phase of the *Mukanda* ritual, the so-called *Kwing'ija* or "bringing-in" phase, would take place. Actually, I had previously been informed by an old acquaintance from Kafumbu Village that *Mukanda* would begin the following day. This man, Kayineha, had told me that large quantities of beer had been brewed for it and would not keep for more than a few days. Nevertheless, I thought it mere courtesy to ask Nyaluhana for permission to attend, as I had heard that it was "his *Mukanda.*" I asked him whether he had sent a messenger, as was customary, to Kanongesha, informing him that *Mukanda* would take place on a given date. The local chief or senior headman is asked to bless the forthcoming rites and to make invocation for the novices. This is known as *kwokola kesi* ("to take an ember from the fire") or *kutambula kesi* ("to receive fire"). The chief does not in fact send an ember, but provides white clay with which the sponsoring headman prays to his remote ancestors on the eve of circumcision.

At that time, I was unaware of the rivalries behind the scenes, so I thought that Nyaluhana was being evasive when he said that he had not yet sent a messenger to Kanongesha and did not know when *Mukanda* would begin. That was the affair of his sister's son Wukengi, he said, who was to be Establisher. "Carry on down the path," he went on, "and ask Wukengi. He knows everything." What I did not know then was that Wukengi had little love for Nyaluhana, although he stood in some awe of him. Wukengi had recently built his own farm, or rather unregistered village, about a quarter of a mile from Nyaluhana. I was told later by Kafumbu people—Wukengi's wife was a Kafumbu woman—that Wukengi feared Nyaluhana's alleged powers of sorcery. I am convinced that Wukengi, like many others in the vicinage, dreaded Nyaluhana's sinister arts, but a glance at the Nyaluhana Village genealogy (Diagram 2) will show that Wukengi was senior male of a group of uterine siblings and was thus a likely man to lead a seceding section from a village. I have shown in *Schism and Continuity* that the most common unit of secession is just such a group. Most middle-aged men in this position in Ndembu society like to found their own villages, where they and their uterine siblings, and occasionally their parallel cousins, may lord it as the dominant generation. However, if the headman of their village is a just and generous man who had built up a large village, such a uterine sibling group may well think it worth while to remain in the village until the headman dies, for their oldest brother may then succeed him. In many things he said and did in my presence, Nyaluhana showed that he resented Wukengi's bid for social and spatial independence from him. Similarly, Wukengi gave every indication that Nyaluhana's overweening manner irritated him immensely, and it was undoubtedly one reason for his secession.

Indeed, I found out later that Wukengi had secretly connived at the sending of a messenger from Machamba Village, Chikwamu by name, to Kanongesha. Now, as we have seen, Machamba Village had had pretentions to sponsor *Mukanda*, or at least to weaken Nyaluhana's role in it. I will shortly discuss the kinds of claim Machamba people were making. The point of major interest for us here is that Wukengi had deliberately kept Nyaluhana in the dark about the last-minute arrangements for the *Kwing'ija* rites. More than that, he had tried to win over the traditional rivals of the Nyaluhana lineage (to which Wukengi himself belonged) by allowing them to make the formal announcement to the chief of the commencing date of *Mukanda*.

When Nyaluhana told me to ask Wukengi when *Mukanda* would begin, I felt with some disappointment that he was being evasive. If he had previously been blunt about his attitude towards Europeans, he now seemed to be not altogether open with one particular European, but in fact, as I realized later, he actually did not know the

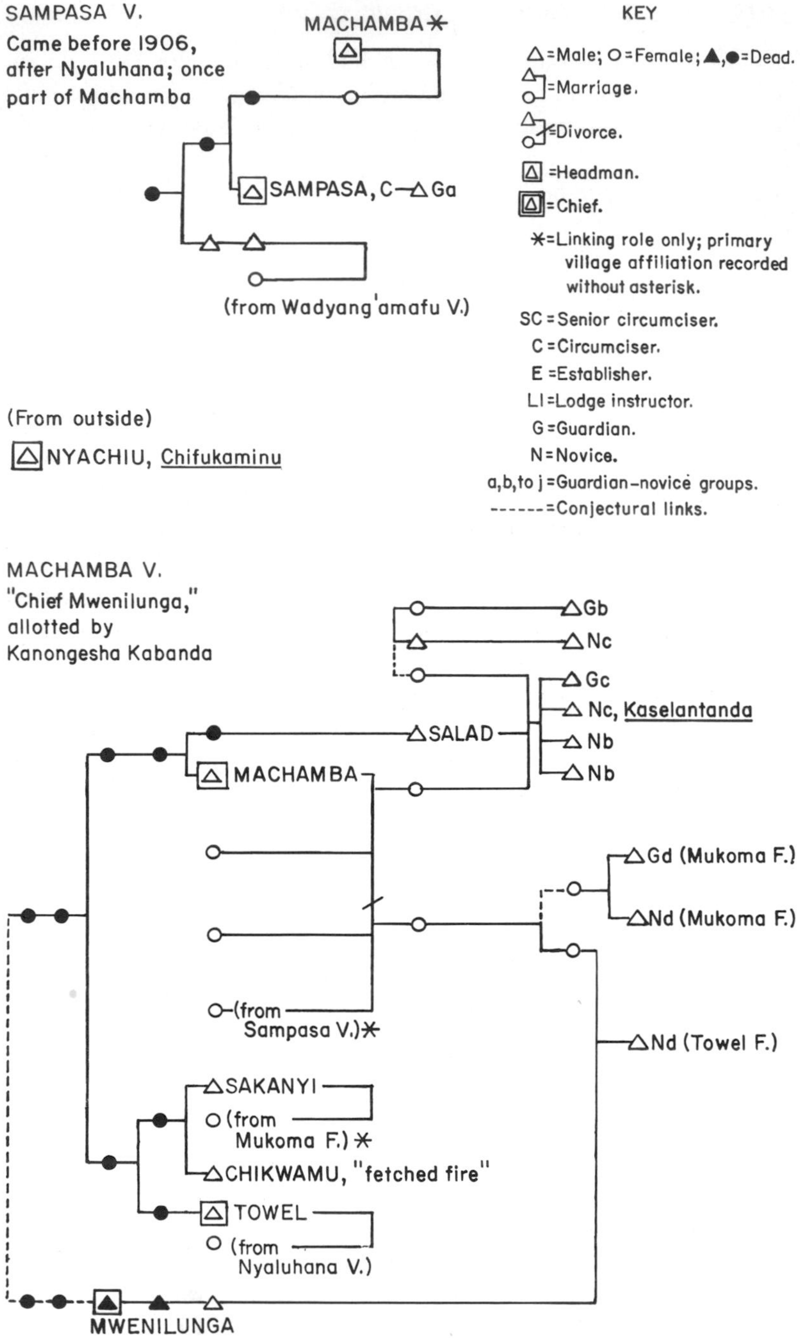


*Diagram* 2. Vicinage of Nyaluhana: Skeleton genealogies illustrating *Mukanda*

NYALUHANA V. and WUKENGI F.
Founded by Kanongesha Nkomesha
in the 19th century

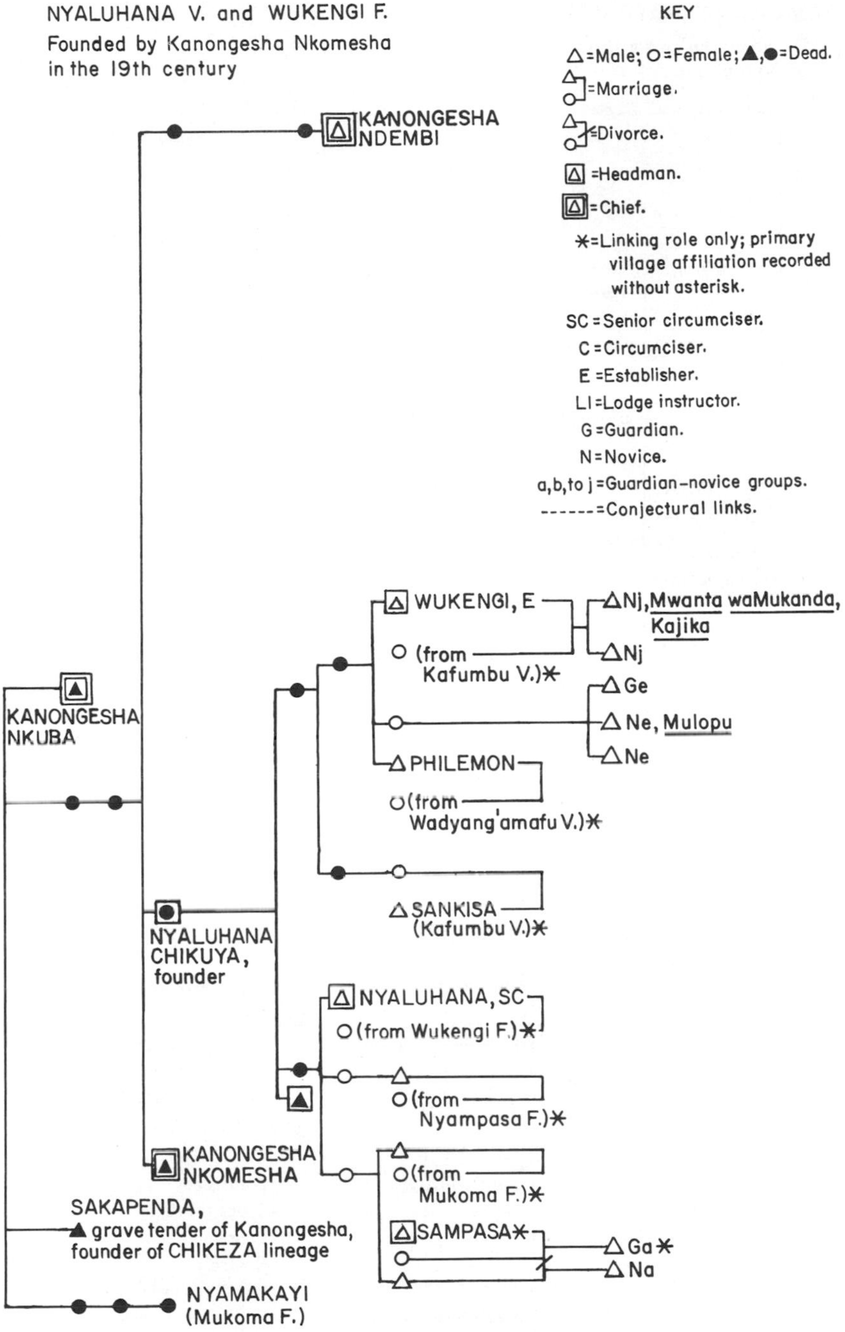

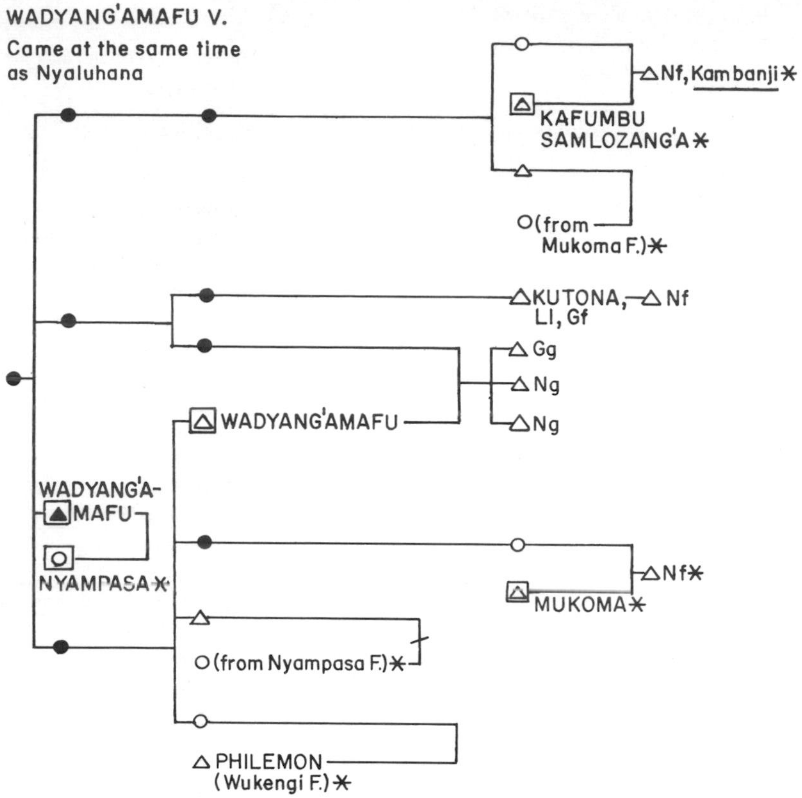


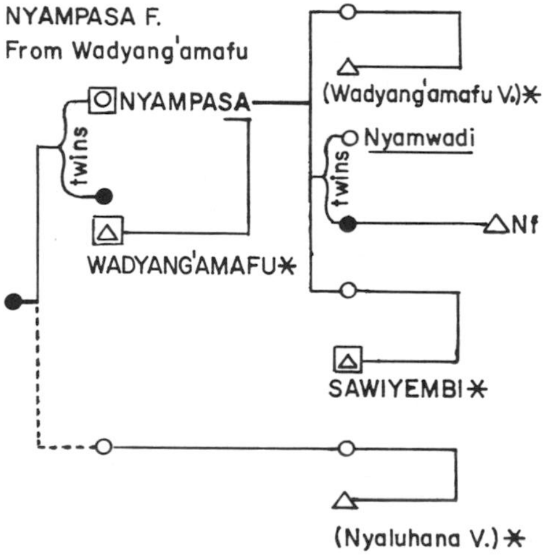


KEY

△ = Male; ○ = Female; ▲, ● = Dead.
= Marriage.
= Divorce.
= Headman.
= Chief.
* = Linking role only; primary village affiliation recorded without asterisk.
SC = Senior circumciser.
C = Circumciser.
E = Establisher.
LI = Lodge instructor.
G = Guardian.
N = Novice.
a, b, to j = Guardian–novice groups.
------ = Conjectural links.

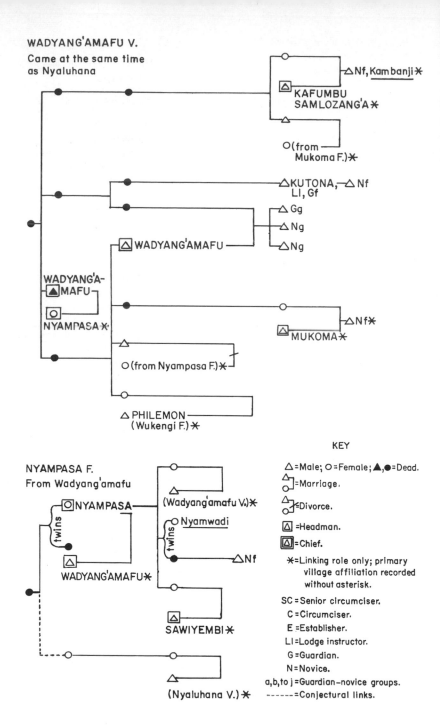

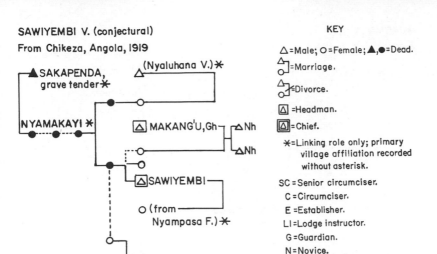

SAWIYEMBI V. (conjectural)
From Chikeza, Angola, 1919

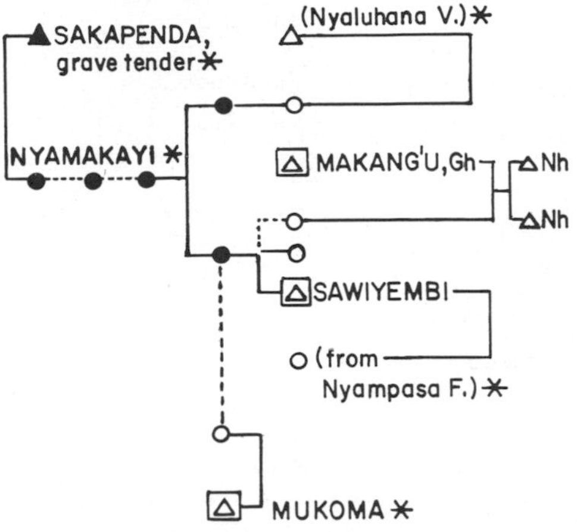


KEY

△ = Male; ○ = Female; ▲, ● = Dead.
= Marriage.
= Divorce.
= Headman.
= Chief.
✱ = Linking role only; primary village affiliation recorded without asterisk.
SC = Senior circumciser.
C = Circumciser.
E = Establisher.
LI = Lodge instructor.
G = Guardian.
N = Novice.
a, b, to j = Guardian-novice groups.
------ = Conjectural links.

KAFUMBU V.
From Mukanza, 1931

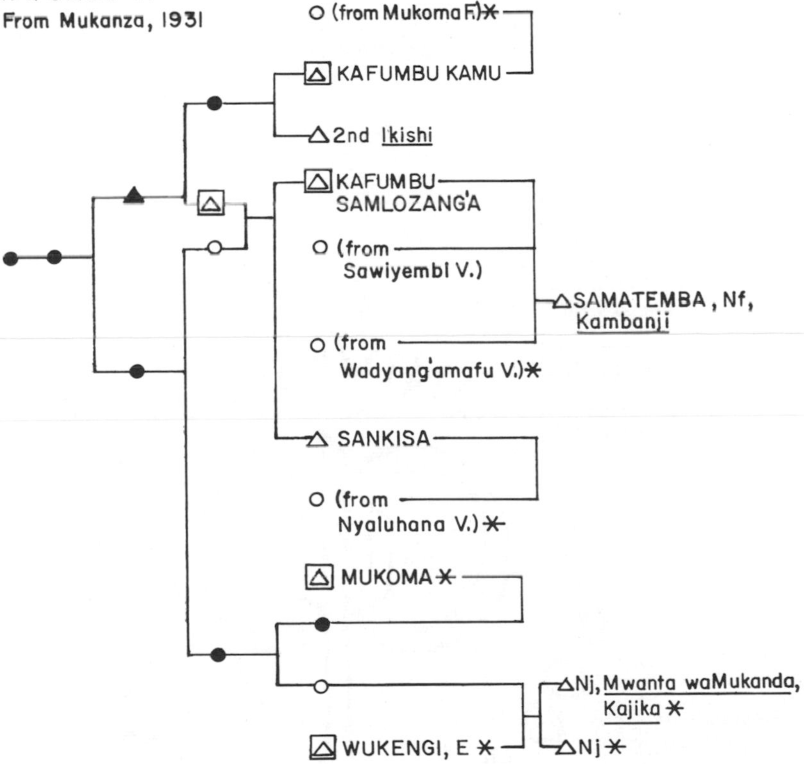

MUKOMA F.
From Sawiyembi, 1949

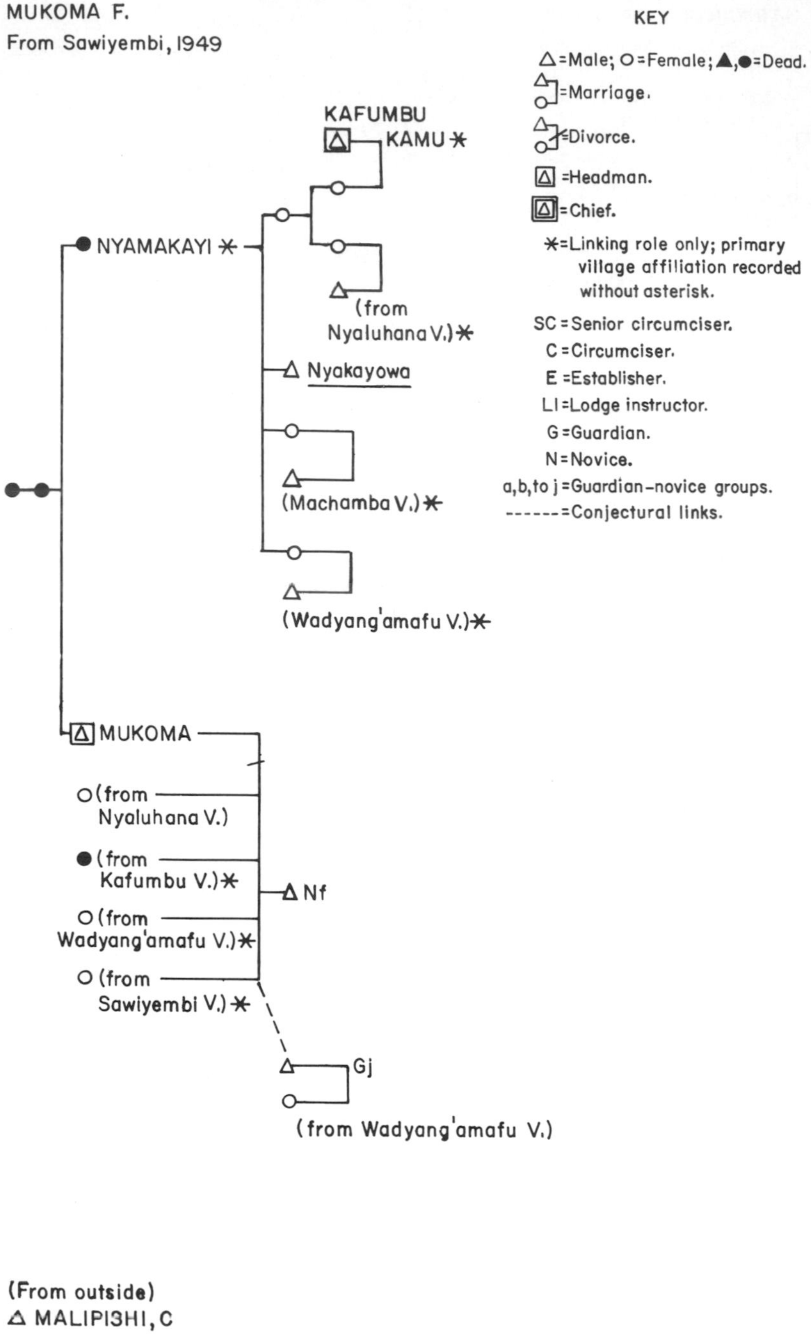
KEY
Δ=Male; ○=Female; ▲,●=Dead.
=Marriage.
=Divorce.
=Headman.
=Chief.
*=Linking role only; primary village affiliation recorded without asterisk.
SC = Senior circumciser.
C = Circumciser.
E = Establisher.
LI = Lodge instructor.
G = Guardian.
N = Novice.
a, b, to j = Guardian-novice groups.
------ = Conjectural links.
KAFUMBU
KAMU *
NYAMAKAYI *
(from Nyaluhana V.) *
Nyakayowa
(Machamba V.) *
(Wadyang'amafu V.) *
MUKOMA
(from Nyaluhana V.)
(from Kafumbu V.) *
Nf
(from Wadyang'amafu V.) *
(from Sawiyembi V.) *
Gj
(from Wadyang'amafu V.)
(From outside)
Δ MALIPISHI, C

salient details. His ignorance was a function of the structural cleavage between his sublineage and that of Wukengi. For some time afterwards, I must confess I felt a certain prejudice against Nyaluhana, but that was because my companions were often his rivals and opponents.

We left Nyaluhana and proceeded to Wukengi's new-made "farm." Just outside we had a fleeting glimpse of Wukengi, whom I had visited a month earlier with a substantial gift, in full retreat into the bush. When we reached the village shelter (*chota*), Wukengi's wife told us that he had gone to visit a relative and was not expected back for some hours. My henchman Kasonda (many of whose deeds are recorded in *Schism and Continuity*) was of the opinion that Wukengi was afraid I might disapprove of "a full African *Mukanda*." The missionaries at Kalene Mission Station performed the operation quickly and hygienically without the "pagan" ritual accompaniments, which they condemned. Wukengi might well have felt that I wanted to attend only in order to condemn. Even at the time, this explanation seemed unlikely. I had already been present at and openly approved many performances of Ndembu ritual, and this was familiar knowledge throughout the District. On reflection, it seems more probable that Wukengi, who may have had advance information of my talk with Nyaluhana from one of the inquisitive small boys who bear tales from village to village in Central Africa, felt ashamed or afraid on account of his reticence towards his uncle and simply escaped from an embarrassing situation.

On the way back, we were met by Nyaluhana who gave us a red hen and some potatoes as a present. Kasonda, who was connected by affinal ties with Wukengi, made out that these gifts "came tardy off" and were of poor quality and ambiguous meaning. For "red" objects can mean hostility in certain contexts. Another Ndembu friend, however, pointed out that "redness" could also stand for *Mukanda*—later, we shall see an abundance of red symbols in the rites—and that therefore Nyaluhana was "giving me a *Mukanda*," that is, letting me know that he approved of my attending. Either interpretation could be correct, and it could be that Nyaluhana had a quiet chuckle to himself over that matter. Nyaluhana told us that he would send messages both to Kanongesha and myself when he knew for certain the day *Mukanda* would begin.

Further along the path, which led to the Boma, we met Philemon, Wukengi's younger brother. Philemon owned a sewing machine and was allowed on payment of a small rental to run a private tailoring business on the veranda of one of the European-owned stores in the commercial area of the Boma township. During the rains he had lived at the Boma, but in this dry season he preferred to live at his brother's farm, where he had built a hut for each of his two wives. Philemon had been a labor migrant and knew the big world better than his brother did. He assured us that, whatever Nyaluhana might have said to the contrary, *Mukanda* would begin next day. He had seen the beer brewed with his own eyes. Anyway, *Mukanda* had to begin on a Saturday for that was everyone's day off at the Boma, and it was expected that many Boma workers and clerks would come out in hopes of a drink, a sweetheart, or a dance. Philemon too promised to send us a message on the morrow if *Mukanda* was "on." His cronies at the Boma would be angry if there was no *Mukanda,* of that we could be sure; not to speak of the laborers on the new road the P.W.D. (Public Works Department) was making to Nyachiu. Philemon brought us a whiff of the modern, of the "townee," the man committed to the cash economy, but he was still a Kandembu and loved ritual. I was to see him dancing many a traditional dance in the next few months.

These episodes revealed the cleavage between Nyaluhana and Wukengi. Further comments by Kayineha of Kafumbu Village, who had accompanied Kasonda and me to Wukengi, made clear that Kafumbu and Wukengi were on most friendly terms. For Kayineha declared that he would visit Wukengi that very night and vehemently persuade him that I would cause no trouble, if I attended *Mukanda.* He was in a position to influence Wukengi, he went on, since Wukengi had married his sister's daughter. Indeed, the two sons Wukengi had put into *Mukanda* belonged to the Kafumbu matrilineage. On the other hand, Sankisa of Kafumbu Village, Kayineha's sister's son, had married Wukengi's mother's sister's daughter. The villages were more than friendly, they were structurally allied by marital interchange. It became increasingly clear to me that few found Wukengi's ritual eminence obnoxious, but many were jealous of Nyaluhana and the number of his friends was small. This *Mukanda* was a major crisis in his long life. If he had been forced into accepting anything less that the leading role in it, he would have become a nobody, an old man on his way to "second childishness and mere oblivion," like so many Ndembu old men who have lost effective control in political and ritual matters. His main hope was to prop his chances on his traditional status, on the precedents created by his past dominance in *Mukanda* rituals, and especially on his customary ascendancy over Wukengi, the titular sponsor of this current *Mukanda.* He was Wukengi's classificatory mother's brother, and sisters' sons in Ndembu society must respect their maternal uncles. Until recently he had been Wukengi's village headman. For most of Wukengi's adult life, namely, for twenty-four years, Nyaluhana had exerted authority over him as headman, and Nyaluhana, I gathered, had never been the hospitable, tolerant type, but rather the autocrat—perhaps because he had himself been once in the running for the Chibwikaship. Even now, Wukengi Farm had no independent existence in the Government Tax Register, and its inhabitants were recorded as belonging to Nyaluhana Village. To my mind at least, the fact that Wukengi had built his farm so close to Nyaluhana's village was a sign of the psychological primacy the older man still exerted over the younger. Wukengi personally lacked Nyaluhana's incisive forcefulness; he was inclined to waver when he should have taken command at crucial phases of the ritual. However, he was well liked, whereas Nyaluhana was feared.

Now let us consider Nyaluhana's main "external" rival, Machamba. Machamba's objection to Nyaluhana's commandeering the senior role was based on corporate and not on personal grounds. He himself had no specialized ritual skills, he was no circumciser, and he did not possess the exceptional knowledge of lodge esoterica that might have given him the role of *Mfumwa Tubwiku*; nor did he have any sons to be circumcised. However, a member of his village, named Salad, another former labor migrant, had four uncircumcised sons whom he wished to send to *Mukanda.* Salad was Machamba's own sister's son and had married Machamba's daughter, his primary cross-cousin. He was generally reckoned to be Machamba's successor as village headman and was the main driving force against Nyaluhana. One of the qualifications necessary for the role of Establisher (*Chijika Mukanda*) is to have two or more boys in the lodge. Wukengi had only two sons of the right age to be circumcised, although there were two others from his farm and one from Nyaluhana Village. Salad claimed that he should be Establisher, because he had more eligible children than any other father in the vicinage, but it was pointed out to him, or so my informants told me, that Machamba Village was located several miles from most villages in the vicinage and would be a most inconvenient venue for the ritual. Salad and Machamba had to accept this view, and henceforward they strove energetically to get qualified claimants from villages in their own faction. Their main aim was to keep Nyaluhana out. This aim coincided with that of Wukengi, but the motives of Salad and Machamba were different from those of Wukengi. Wukengi's title to a central ritual role depended on the fame of Nyaluhana himself. He now wished to oust Nyaluhana from the leadership of the lineage, not to discount the value of that lineage. Wukengi and Nyaluhana were united in defending the honor of the lineage; they were divided over its leadership. Wukengi's waverings during *Mukanda* may be partially explained by his conflicting interests and loyalties. At one time he appeared to support Nyaluhana's position, at another Machamba's.

Machamba's opposition to Nyaluhana was based on the values governing vicinage structure, rather than on personal rivalry, and as usually happens when corporate groups dispute, each party invoked the authority of history to back its claims. History is such a tangle of success and failure, and of deeds of dubious interpretation, that almost any group can find some favorable precedent for its present demands and some circumstance to invalidate those of its rivals. In every Ndembu vicinage, one village claims to have been settled there longest. Such a village calls itself *mwenimbu*. The primary sense of *mwenimbu* is a person who lives at a village and has his domicile there. Thus, a child is a *mwenimbu* at his own village. The antonym of *mwenimbu* is *ngeji*, which like the Latin *hospes* means both "stranger" and "guest." I am no Bantu etymologist, but I consider it reasonable to suppose that *mwenimbu* is connected both with *mweni*, which means "owner" or "the one with most rights *in personam* and/or *in rem* over a specified person or thing," and with *kwimba*, "to dig." A *mwenimbu* village is reckoned to be that which has most abandoned "diggings," residential sites, gardens, and graves in a vicinage. In the course of time, a village leaves many such signs of past occupancy on the cultural landscape. It has the right to deny newcomers access to its abandoned gardening and residential sites and the right to let them cultivate or dwell in them. The spirits of its dead are believed to haunt its graveyards and old villages (*mahembi*). It has the closest jural, economic, and mystical associations with the land and the bush. A *mwenimbu* village headman therefore has strong claims to be regarded as the moral leader of the vicinage. As we have seen, moral leadership is signally expressed in the right to sponsor a *Mukanda* and perform its leading roles.

Machamba Village asserted that it was *mwenimbu* of the vicinage, on the following grounds. The nuclear matrilineage of Machamba Village came from Mwenilunga Village, after which the present Administrative District is named. A large tract of bush adjoining the present Boma, mostly in the fork of the Lunga and Mudyanyama Rivers, had been allocated to the first Mwenilunga by the first Ndembu Senior Chief, Kanongesha Nkuba, who came from Mwantiyanvwa's empire more than two centuries ago. Mwenilunga was thus a Lunda invader, not one of the autochthonous Kawiku people who were connected with the Mbwela of Angola and of the Balovale and Kabompo Districts of Zambia. His village had been situated on the ridge of land overlooking the Lunga River where the Boma now stands. When the British South Africa Company decided to establish its headquarters by the Lunga, Mwenilunga Village was driven from its site, some say after a show of resistance. At any rate, Mwenilunga was never recognized by the British as a subchief. In time, Mwenilunga Village dwindled into half a dozen huts outside its original vicinage. It is worth mentioning that while Mwenilunga Village was in decline, Nyaluhana Village flourished, at one time containing more than twenty huts (or about twice the Ndembu average). The Mwenilunga lineage increased in importance once again when Machamba, one of its senior members, collected together a number of his scattered matrilineal kin and built a new village in the vicinage of Nyaluhana, formerly that of Mwenilunga. For a while, Machamba and some of his kin lived in Sampasa Village in the same vicinage. At that time they resided about a mile from the contemporary site of Nyaluhana Village, but when Machamba founded his own village he placed over three miles between his group and Nyaluhana's.

By virtue of Machamba's origin in Mwenilunga Village he claimed the honorific of *mwenimbu* of the vicinage. I was to hear this claim made repeatedly during *Mukanda* by members of Machamba's faction, notably by Salad. The fact that the balance of power was against them in the vicinage, and that it would have been impracticable to hold *Mukanda* near Machamba, did little to dispel the fantasy of "how pleasant it would have been if Salad had been *Chijika Mukanda,* the Establisher, if Machamba had prayed to the ancestors to bless the proceedings, and if Sampasa had been Senior Circumciser." For Headman Sampasa, whose sister's daughter was a wife of Machamba, was a famous circumciser. Many Machamba people had once resided in his village. There were not enough boys of suitable age in his village at that time for him to try to sponsor a *Mukanda.* Besides it is doubtful whether he would ever have been able to take the initiative in this respect, for his matrilineal ancestors were not Ndembu but had come from the Lunda-Kosa chiefdom of Musokantanda across the Lunga River. He could never hope to be recognized as *mwenimbu* in Ndembu territory as long as his Kosa origins were remembered.

Even when Machamba and Salad had given up the idea of holding *Mukanda* near their village, they continued to urge that Sampasa, not Nyaluhana, should be given the role of Senior Circumciser. Actually, there were only two "great circumcisers" in the vicinage, that is to say, circumcisers who possessed *nfunda,* the medicine that conferred mystical protection on the lodge during the rites. One of them was Nyaluhana, the other Sampasa. I heard that during the rainy season before *Mukanda,* hot debates went on throughout the vicinage about which of them should be Senior Circumciser. Machamba's faction insisted that Nyaluhana was old and that his hand would most likely be shaky and he would cut the novices deeply. They said that even at the last *Mukanda* in the vicinage, when Nyaluhana was ten years younger, he had "cut" more slowly than other circumcisers, so what would he be like now? His defenders said that if he was slow he was careful and that he had more than forty years experience behind him, twenty-five of them "with *nfunda.*" Nyaluhana himself apparently said little but bided his time.

Nyaluhana was scornful about Machamba's pretensions. He made a point of telling me that Nkuba, the first Kanongesha, who gave Mwenilunga the right to occupy the Lunga bush area, was his matrilineal ancestor. More than this, when Kanongesha Nkomesha made a village for his sister Nyaluhana, that village became the senior village in the vicinage. Again, Nyaluhana himself was a close kinsman of the present Kanongesha. On the other hand, Mwenilunga had fled from the vicinage at the coming of the Europeans. Then Machamba himself was not Mwenilunga, but "just a farm from Sampasa." True, Nyaluhana Village itself had left the area when Yekisoni came, but a few years after the people had returned, he, Nyaluhana, had held a big *Mukanda* from his village and everyone had recognized his right to hold it. Since Nkomesha founded it, Nyaluhana Village had occupied the vicinage territory for a longer time than any other village now within it. He was the real *mwenimbu.*

It will be noted how the rival headmen ransacked the repository of past deeds to justify their current acts and aims. They also sought in the present state of the vicinage field arguments to boost their worth. Thus, Machamba would point out that his village was larger than Nyaluhana's, now that Wukengi had left it in dread of Nyaluhana's sorcery. And Nyaluhana would rebut this by insisting that Wukengi's "farm" was part of Nayaluhana's village according to Government, and that both combined exceeded Machamba in population. Ndembu social life, in fact, contains a medley of discrepant criteria of importance whereby the politically inclined carry on their unending struggles.

What of the other villages and farms in the vicinage? Which villages were involved in the dispute? Which villages remained neutral? Which villages acted as mediators? Machamba and Sampasa, as we have seen, were firm allies on one side, Also reckoned on their side was Sawiyembi, a village that had migrated from Angola in 1919. Its parent village was that of Chikeza, whose headman held the title *Ntete Mwenimajamu* or "he who looks after the nail-parings and graves (of the dead Kanongeshas)." Now, as I pointed out in *Schism and Continuity,* Ndembu tribal territory is roughly bisected by the Angola-Zambia boundary, and in each there is a Kanongesha, recognized by the Portuguese and British administrations respectively. Since the Kanongesha in Angola possesses the most important emblem of chieftainship, the *lukanu* bracelet, he is regarded by Ndembu in both colonies as the legitimate chief. Chikeza is the official who tends the graves of the dead chiefs. Sawiyembi is said by Kafumbu people to have been of slave origin, but his lineage formed the original nucleus of the village in Zambia. In that village was a uterine sibling-group consisting of two sisters and a brother of freeborn origin. On their mother's side they traced their descent from the apical ancestress of the Chikeza lineage. This ancestress resided with her brother, who was the first Kanongesha's younger brother Sakapenda. Sakapenda was passed over for the succession after Kanongesha Nkuba's death and was given the ritual office of Gravetender in compensation; but there lingered a sense of resentment against this ancient slighting of their line among the matrilineal descendants of Sakapenda. Once upon a time, I was told by some Angolan Ndembu, a Kanongesha raided a village where members of Sakapenda's lineage lived and killed several of its inhabitants. This Kanongesha alleged that they had been plotting to overthrow him and re-establish the claims of their lineage to the chiefly

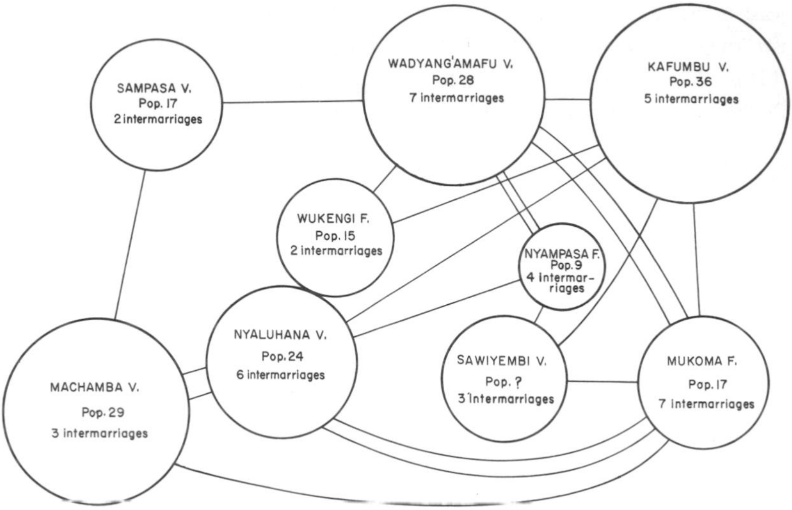


*Diagram* 3. Marriages interlinking the vicinage of Nyaluhana

chair. Perhaps it had been through fear of the Angolan Kanongesha that Sawiyembi and the three Chikeza people had migrated to Zambia. At any rate, one of the Chikeza women had four children, three of them daughters who proved themselves fruitful, and in 1949 this group split off from Sawiyembi Village and founded Mukoma Farm, named after the brother. I believe, but cannot prove it, that the Chikeza group did not come with Sawiyembi when they migrated from Angola but settled at first in Subchief Nyakaseya's capital in the northwestern pedicle of Mwinilunga District. At any rate, their father, Kayombu, was Nyakaseya's second-in-authority (*mulopu*). It is likely that Kayombu's wife lived virilocally, for men seldom reside uxorilocally in Ndembu society, least of all men holding political office.

Both Nyaluhana and Mukoma were descended from sisters of Kanongesha Nkuba. Their residential units were interconnected by marriages past and present (see Diagram 3). One of Nyaluhana's sisters' sons was married at the time of investigation to Mukoma's sister's daughter's daughter, thus linking the two lineages. Sawiyembi Village, of which Mukoma's group had once been a part, had several extant marital ties with Machamba, Nyaluhana's rival, and none with Nyaluhana Village (I was unable to record genealogical data at

Sawiyembi before the rains arrived and made the path to the village impassable). It is interesting to note that the single extant marriage between Mukoma Farm and Machamba Village linked Mukoma's sister's daughter with Machamba's classificatory brother, Sakanya, the head of a segment of the village matrilineage, who started to build his own "farm" shortly before *Mukanda* began—but a mere fifty yards from the parent village. These alliances fall into the pattern previously discussed: schism within a village is associated with the alliance of the dissident group with its rival's external opponents. Whether internal schism changes external alliance or vice versa I cannot say in the present context. Probably both processes coexist. Evidence from studies I have made in other vicinages supports this view. Certainly, in the case of Machamba's classificatory brother, marriage with a Mukoma woman preceded his split from Machamba. I do not mean to imply that all marriages among Ndembu are consciously arranged to further private and sectional "political" aims—to secure residential independence and leadership or to win allies. Some may well have this character, but people tend, without thinking too closely about the matter, to seek friendship and marriage among those in a position to further their material interests and striving for status, or among those who might supply them with a following. The anthropologist who isolates the major relationships and properties of the social field to which they belong is able to determine the nature and strength of the forces that draw some of its members together and drive others apart.

Two villages had close ties of marriage and friendship with Wukengi Farm. These were Wadyang'amafu Village and Kafumbu Village. Wukengi himself was married to a Kafumbu woman, and his two children by her were novices in *Mukanda*. His brother Philemon had a wife from Wadyang'amafu. Headman Kafumbu's wife also came from Wadyang'amafu. A further feature in the set of marital alliances should be mentioned. The younger brother of Headman Kafumbu's wife from Wadyang'amafu was married to a woman from Mukoma Farm, Mukoma's sister's daughter, in fact. Wadyang'amafu had come long ago from Nyamwana chieftainship in the Belgian Congo, whose chief in the past sent tribute independently to Mwantiyanvwa and not through one of the Senior Chiefs of the Southern Lunda Musokantanda and Kanongesha. There are several villages in the modern Mwinilunga District whose nuclear lineages originated in Nyamwana, and these villages claim lineal relationship. There is widespread agreement that these villages are descended from a group of slaves who were either captured by Ndembu in a raid or were paid to Ndembu chiefs as compensation for homicide. Wadyang'amafu claims to have been in the vicinage before the British South Africa Company began to administer the District. It is just possible that its present matrilineal core is descended from slaves of the first female head of Nyaluhana, Kanongesha Nkomesha's sister. At any rate, it seemed to be accepted in the vicinage that Wadyang'amafu Village automatically supported the Nyaluhana lineage. Wadyang'amafu Village was terribly afflicted with leprosy and few of its inhabitants were free from the disease. It is possible that Philemon of Wukengi, who had contracted leprosy, had been infected by his Wadyang'amafu wife. Since leprosy (*mbumba*) is believed to be one of the mystical sanctions for breaking a taboo or revealing a secret of the *Mukanda* lodge, it is likely that if a novice shows signs of leprosy in the future this will be attributed to his having broken a taboo and not to having come into close contact with a member of this unfortunate village. Other members of the Nyamwana community dispersed throughout the District suffered in the same way. One young man I knew quite well when my camp was at Subchief Ikelenge's capital village in the northwestern pedicle was in the horrible last stages of the disease. One of those apparently free from the disease at Wadyang'amafu was Kutona, Senior Lodge Instructor during *Mukanda*. Indeed, the reason he gave me for building a farm about a hundred yards from that village was his fear of infection. Mission doctors who had treated several of the villagers had urged him to build separately. They had also told the lepers, who included the headman and his wife, to live in grass huts (*ankunka*) outside the main village circle. The grass huts were made but seldom occupied, and Wadyang'amafu people mixed freely with the rest of the people at *Mukanda,* some of them even sleeping in the lodge, while the headman's wife as a *Nyamwadyi,* or novice's mother, cooked food for her two sons as part of her ritual role. I mention these circumstances as an example of the way most Ndembu still adhere to mystical beliefs as the explanation of disease. They also illustrate the empirical conditions that maintain those beliefs.

Kafumbu Village entered the vicinage about 1928, having split off from Mukanza Village as described in *Schism and Continuity*. Most of its members are descended from slaves of Mukanza, but, like Mukanza, it is reckoned a "Kawiku" village, that is, a village belonging to the dispersed group of autochthonous people who inhabited the district when the Lunda invaders arrived. Its main importance in *Mukanda* was due to the fact that Wukengi's sons belonged to Kafumbu lineage. The Establisher himself then depended to a considerable extent on the cooperation of Kafumbu people. However, Headman Kafumbu was not on good terms with Nyaluhana and although he was himself a skilled circumciser, he did not offer his services at *Mukanda*, giving the excuse that he had to visit some distant relatives. For much of the seclusion period he was away from the vicinage. I was unable to ascertain the cause of this ill feeling. Kafumbu's senior wife came from Sawiyembi Village, which supported Machamba's claim to be reckoned the most important village in the vicinage, and it is possible that she may have influenced him against Nyaluhana's move to sponsor the ritual. The fact that his former rival for the headmanship of Kafumbu Village, his own father's sister's son, was on relatively good terms with Mukoma people who seceded from Sawiyembi Village, and had married a Mukoma woman, may have been an additional factor. Indeed, his rival had set up a small farm of three huts which he insisted was the "true Kafumbu Village." This unit was called by Ndembu with a humorous turn of mind Kafumbu Kamu, meaning "Kafumbu Once" or "Kafumbu Alone," since its head had no following. Here again, the principle is exemplified that a dissident faction seeks alliance with the external opponents of the group to which it previously belonged. Headman Kafumbu Ndumba Samlozang'a (to give him his full sonorous name) was linked to Wukengi; Farm Head Kafumbu Kamu was attached to Nyaluhana. Thus, Kafumbu villagers were divided between their attachment to Wukengi and their opposition to Nyaluhana. Yet, since Wukengi himself had to placate Nyaluhana and even to rely upon his technical skill, Kafumbu people for his sake had to try to conceal their dislike of the older man. On the other hand, Kafumbu villagers were on fairly good terms with Machamba people. The reason for this will emerge presently.

Near Sawiyembi and Mukoma was another Kawiku residential unit. This was Nyampasa Farm named after its female head. She was the widow of the previous headman of Wadyang'amafu Village, and one of her daughters had married a man from that village. Another daughter was the wife of Nyaluhana's sister's son. Nyampasa was a neutral in the competition between Nyaluhana and Machamba. She had friendly relations with both parties and was connected by marriage with members of both. She was an enormously fat, merry woman, with a considerable reputation as a specialist in curative ritual. She was especially famed for her knowledge of the medicines and techniques of the *Wubwang'u* ritual, on behalf of mothers of twins before or after confinement. Nyampasa was herself a twin and had successfully borne and reared twins. She was a classificatory sister's daughter of the senior Kawiku headman Nsang'anyi (Turner 1957, 210–220). The Kawiku in the vicinage were to some extent in sympathy with Machamba, for the latter was personally friendly with an important Kawiku headman called Nyachiu, whose village was only a mile or two beyond Machamba Village. Nyachiu was not reckoned to be a member of the Nyaluhana vicinage, but only a neighbor, because it was a *mwenimbu* (oldest-established) village in its own small vicinage. I have heard Kawiku and Machamba (Mwenilunga) people in the *Mukanda* situation delightedly agreeing that both their groups were in the area before Nyaluhana Village was founded. Here the value attached to priority in local settlement was stressed as against the Lunda-Kawiku cleavage, for Machamba lineage, like that of Nyaluhana, is descended from the invaders but not from the indigenous inhabitants. In Ndembu culture, as in all other cultures, values abstracted from the social process do not form an orderly system but are rather a medley of disparities. "System" in society emerges in the pursuit of long-term or immediate interests. The fact that values are a medley of disparities gives flexibility to social life, for most kinds of purposive action can be justified by the invocation of some generally accepted criterion. Other criteria can be conveniently ignored if they appear to render the contemplated action invalid. Thus, for the purpose of alliance in pursuit of the specific aim of reducing Nyaluhana's prestige, Machamba and certain Kawiku ransacked their shared repository of values for those that legitimized their ephemeral friendship and discarded others that might at the time have imperiled it. It is easy to imagine altered circumstances—a dispute over marital or funerary payments, for example—in which the value asserting the unity of all Kawiku against all those of Lunda stock would become paramount and historical precedent in old wars would be eagerly cited in support of contemporary animosities. Gluckman and Colson have brought out the importance of crosscutting affiliations for the maintenance of institutionalized groups—persons interlinked in one set of customary relationships are divided from one another in other sets. Here I would add that unprecedented and ephemeral alliances in pursuit of short-term goals are always coming into being in all societies. These are legitimized—made socially acceptable or at least innocuous—by the selection and rejection of those customary values from the unsystematized reservoir of values that have pertinence for the current goals of the alliance. Values are systematized by purposes; their mutual structuring depends on the aims of the participants in given situations. Machamba, then, sought to win Kawiku support or at any rate to reduce the opposition of those Kawiku groups situationally aligned with Nyaluhana, by wooing Nyachiu.

We are now in a position to state the ways in which the main rivals for vicinage prestige would have allocated the ritual offices and roles. Machamba wanted Salad to be Establisher, Sampasa to be Senior Circumciser, and Nyachiu and Nyaluhana to be assistant circumcisers; and he would have liked Kafumbu Samlozang'a to have been a circumciser. As we shall see, however, Nyachiu would probably have refused to circumcise, because he lacked confidence to perform what Ndembu consider a difficult and dangerous task. In that case, Nyachiu would have taken the role of *Chifukaminu* (from *ku-fukamina*, "to kneel"), the official who kneels behind the novice and holds him up to be circumcised. For Lodge Instructor, Machamba favored Headman Makang'u, whose wife came from Sawiyembi Village. Makang'u had left his own village in Kanongesha's area for the period of *Mukanda* in order to have his two sons circumcised, for there was no *Mukanda* in those years in his own vicinage. For the Senior Novice, who is called *Kambanji*, or "war-leader," Machamba would have preferred Makang'u's older son. Makangu's wife, according to members of the Machamba faction, suggested before anyone else did that *Mukanda* should be held. Sampasa told me that her son had in fact come to him at the end of the rains and, according to custom, ritually abused him "for having a blunt knife and being too lazy to use it." This formula officially opens *Mukanda* and establishes both the Senior Circumciser and the Senior Novice. By this time, said Sampasa, the elders of the vicinage, including Machamba, had agreed that Wukengi, who was well liked personally by most people in the vicinage, should be Establisher. Wukengi had then approved of Sampasa's appointment as Senior Circumciser and of Makang'u's son as Senior Novice. Indeed, he had given Sampasa a ceremonial arrow and knife, confirming his choice, but shortly afterwards, under pressure from Nyaluhana, he had changed his mind.

Nyaluhana, as we have noted, had his own views on the allocation of ritual roles. He wanted to be Senior Circumciser himself, a role he had fulfilled three times previously. He was on good terms with Headman Wadyang'amafu, who was a conservative Ndembu like himself. Wadyang'amafu had two sons to be circumcised. The older of them was a burly lad of about sixteen years of age who had been just too young for the operation, according to modern Ndembu notions, when the last *Mukanda* was held in the vicinage ten years previously. Nyaluhana asked Wadyang'amafu to send this lad to him to inaugurate *Mukanda* formally. This was done, and Nyaluhana declared that his boy, and not Makang'u's son, would be *Kambanji.* He then browbeat Wukengi into accepting this position. It would have suited Wukengi's book perfectly well if Sampasa had become Senior Circumciser, for such an appointment would have signalized his further emancipation from Nyaluhana's control. Wukengi, though likable, was not forceful, and, as he often said, he feared Nyaluhana's sorcery. Nevertheless, many people were affronted by Nyaluhana's highhandedness, and it was still an open question whether Nyaluhana or Sampasa would be Senior Circumciser right up to the last moment, as we shall see. Even Wadyang'amafu's son hoped that Sampasa would have the senior role, and the story Salad and Machamba were putting about that Nyaluhana was too old to operate skillfully was having a definite effect. Wukengi himself, I know, believed or affected to believe this story. At any rate, all fathers who had sons in *Mukanda* must have felt extremely worried by it, and Wukengi had two sons for circumcision.

Nyaluhana, if everything were to go according to his wishes, wanted Wukengi to be Establisher, Wukengi's wife to be Senior Mother of the Novices, himself to be Senior Circumciser, Kutona from Wadyang'amafu Village as Lodge Instructor, and Wadyang'amafu's son as Senior Novice. He was prepared to accept Sampasa as one of his colleagues helping with the operation. He also agreed to a general request that Malipishi, a renowned circumciser from Shika Village, outside the vicinage, should be asked to help. Malipishi was a Christian and took no part in the ritual aspect of the *Mukanda* ceremonies he attended, but he was both quick and gentle as an operator and was greatly in demand. Nyaluhana probably approved of this appointment partly because Shika Village, like his own, was a village of the Kanongesha chieftainship. In this way, he may have felt that he would have further support for his supreme ambition to be the *de facto,* and not merely the *de jure,* sponsor of *Mukanda.*

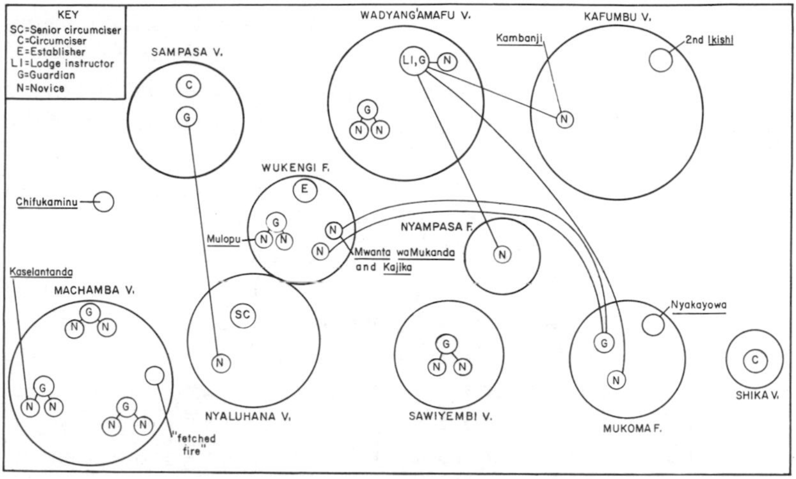


*Diagram 4*. The Nyaluhana villages and the distribution of roles in *Mukanda*

In the end, as we shall see, Nyaluhana had his way in practically all these matters (see Diagram 4), but the reluctance to bring him into the picture right up to the last, the resentment his acts aroused, and the kinds of quarrels that developed during the ritual, all testified to the strength of the various sorts of opposition he encountered. Opposition to Nyaluhana was the resultant of certain properties of the vicinage itself. Among these properties we have noted differences in the size, origins, and extant interests of villages, their internal segmentation, their marital interconnections, the sociospatial distances between them, and other aspects of their interdependence with and independence from one another. Another class of properties comprised customary relationships between categories of persons, and yet another, individual psychological differences. Again, Nyaluhana's greater chronological age, and where genealogical connections could be traced, his structural seniority to most of the other headmen in the vicinage, made him a target for those who wished to obtain the highest status locally in a gerontocratic society.

On the other hand, the same social conditions that explained the existence of rivalry against Nyaluhana also accounted for his continued capacity to enlist support, willing or otherwise, for his aims. These aims were not merely to maintain and extend his personal prestige, but were guided by corporate loyalties to the chieftainship, to his lineage, to his village, and even to the vicinage. Nyaluhana was a representative figure and, as such, could appeal to certain values regarded by Ndembu as having axiomatic force. That he himself believed that what he was doing was right was exemplified by many of his actions and sayings during the *Mukanda* situation. It was the force of his personal conviction of the social value of his authoritarian behavior that compelled many of his rivals to give ground before him at crucial moments in the gradually unfolding ritual. In actual practice, Nyaluhana had the main weight of tradition and precedent behind him, while the arguments of his opponents had more than a little speciousness. Nevertheless, although much of what Nyaluhana said and did could not be refuted in terms of Ndembu tradition, it was generally felt that the social changes going on visibly around the people of the vicinage were rendering all that he stood for obsolescent. At the public dances that punctuated the ritual, many of the attenders were laborers on the new road that was opening up the vicinage to the great world of modern industrial Africa. Boma office clerks and maintenance workers came along to poke surreptitious fun at the customs, including Hehe from Tanganyika, Bemba, Nyasalanders, and men from the far Luapula. Salad and others in the vicinage itself eagerly pressed me to ask the District Commissioner to build a primary school in the vicinage, as it was too difficult in the rainy season for boys to walk to the Boma school. Labor migrants from the Copperbelt kept on arriving throughout the ritual to visit their home villages and bring a breath of urban sophistication. Guitar music from "town" could be heard from their huts, and talk about the Northern Rhodesian African Mineworkers Union could be heard in the village forums. There was a diffuse feeling that while Nyaluhana could certainly justify his role in terms of the old ways, those ways were themselves rapidly passing. However, since they had agreed to hold *Mukanda*, one of the main ritual mechanisms for upholding tribal custom, Nyaluhana's opponents were compelled to accept the tribal values he was able to manipulate so well in the interests of his major group loyalties. His opponents were forced to couch their opposition to Nyaluhana, the real grounds for which resided in modern changes, in terms of traditional criteria where they were at a disadvantage against his stronger claims.

I have now described the vicinage, setting out its principal alignments and struggles in the period immediately preceding *Mukanda*. What remains to be described is *Mukanda* itself, its successive episodes, and the behavior of the participants as determined both by the prescriptions of the ritual and by their positions in the vicinage field.

## Mukanda: *The Rites*

### SEQUENCE OF EPISODES

Formal invitation to Senior Circumciser

#### KWING'IJA: CAUSING TO ENTER

(Preliminary)

Assembling of food and beer at the sponsoring village
Clearing a site for the camp of the novices' parents and kin

(Day before Circumcision)

The collection of *ku-kolisha* strengthening medicine
The sacralization of the camp and sponsoring village
Prayer to the ancestors of the sponsoring village
Sacralization of the *ijiku daMukanda* fire by the Establisher
The setting up of a *chishing'a* pole
Sacralization of the circumcisers' fire
The night dance, in which novices' parents take a leading part

(Day of Circumcision)

Ritual washing
Novices' meal
Procession to the circumcision site
The beating of the guardians
The *mukoleku* gate
Preparation of the circumcision site
The hyena
The circumcision
Ritual washing and feeding of novices

#### KUNG'ULA: SECLUSION

The building of the lodge
The healing-up period (before *Chikula*)
The small *Chikula,* the appearance of *makishi* masked dancers
The training and esoteric teaching of the novices (after *Chikula*)

KWIDISHA: THE RITES OF RETURN
(*First Day, the great* Chikula)

*Katewu kanyanya,* the small shaving place
*Nyakayowa*
The first entry
The *ifwotu*
The second entry
The night dance

(*Second Day*)

The burning of the lodge
The final purification
*Katewu keneni,* the great shaving-place
The making of *nfunda*
The Lodge Instructor's final harangue
The third entry
The *ku-tomboka* war dance
Payment

## *The Rites*

In social reality circumstances rarely go according to plan or norm. Thus, when I set out the ideal order of events in *Mukanda*—the customary "time-table" as it were—it must be remembered that the sorts of pressures and intrigues I have described in the previous section are continually at work to cause omissions and modifications in the order and form of the episodes as they are presented by informants with tidy minds. Nevertheless, the ideal temporal structure of *Mukanda* gives coherence to the succession of events, for the participants as well as for readers of this study.

After the elders of the vicinage have agreed to perform *Mukanda* in the coming dry season and their womenfolk have endorsed their decision, the first ritual step is taken. This is a formal invitation to the Senior Circumciser. The novice who is to become *Kambanji* or "war-leader"—usually the oldest and best-developed—and who is the first to be circumcised, is sent to the Senior Circumciser to revile and disparage him. His usual mode of address is as follows: "Old man *mbimbi* (circumciser), you have become lazy and your knife is now blunt. Nowadays, you are no use at circumcising boys. Why should we call you to circumcise us at *Mukanda*?" The circumciser affects to be angry, then puts a certain medicine on the boy's brow from a galagoskin pouch (called *isaku*) and tells him to inform the future Establisher to get everything ready for the rites. *Kambanji* is then told to notify the chief or senior headman, and the headmen of the vicinage and of adjacent vicinages, that *Mukanda* has officially begun. From this time forth, boys chosen as novices must avoid certain kinds of food.

Circumcisers are preferred whose medicines have not been polluted by death. Kasonda, when discussing his own circumcision with me, said that during the period of seclusion the circumciser's wife and a novice had died, the latter as the result of a snakebite. This was because the circumciser's *nfunda* medicine, which is believed to guard the welfare of all concerned in the rites, had been polluted by contact with a ritually unclean person (*wunabulakutooka*) before *Mukanda* began.

The Senior Circumciser, after notification, puts the names of other circumcisers to the future officials of the Lodge. If these are agreed upon, they are invited to attend and operate. Before they come, each prays at the ancestor-shrines in his village for the assistance of his shades in his responsible task.

After the Senior Circumciser has been notified, the Establisher has the task of organizing supplies of food and beer for the *Kwing'ija* ("causing to go in") or induction phase. Many people, sometimes a thousand or more, attend the public dance on the night before circumcision. A high proportion of these have to be given beer. In the past, it was also the Establisher's responsibility to see that villages whose members were at *Mukanda* were properly guarded against slave raiders or internal enemies.

Ndembu recognize three main phases in *Mukanda*: (1) *kwing'ija*, "causing to enter"; (2) *kung'ula*, "at the circumcision lodge"; and (3) *kwidisha*, "to take outside," a verb that has the additional sense of "to approve publicly." The rites, it may be seen, are orientated towards the lodge and are regarded as preparation to enter it, sojourn within it, and removal from it.

### KWING'IJA: CAUSING TO ENTER

The rites of *kwing'ija* have secular as well as sacred episodes and aspects, and the last of them occur in the bush at the site where the lodge will be built.

I shall begin by describing the collection of *ku-kolisha* medicines, for it was at this point that I arrived at the performance at Wukeng'i Farm. Kasonda and I had set out on foot from Mukanza Village on receiving Philemon's message. Most villages on the way were almost empty except for the very old and very young. At Kafumbu Village we saw a novice, wearing only a strip of cloth around his waist and with a spot of *mpemba* white clay beside each eye. His older relatives were urging him to hurry to *Mukanda,* otherwise he might be chosen as *Kajika kaMukanda,* a title given to the last novice to be dealt with in any of its component rites. *Kajika* is the "late" or "reluctant" one who "closes" *Mukanda.* A novice who is late in coming to the *mukoleku* frame of *mukula* wood, under which the boys are taken on their way to circumcision; the last novice to be circumcised; the boy who cries loudest when being cut; the slowest to answer questions or learn *Mukanda* mysteries and riddles; any or all of these criteria may determine who is to be *Kajika,* the last novice to dance solo in public at the end of the *kwidisha* ("taking outside") rites which complete *Mukanda.*

I was greeted most affably by Headman Nyaluhana at his village. He then escorted me to Wukengi Farm. Wukengi showed me the beer he had collected in his *nkalang'a* grass grain store—thirteen calabashes, a total Kasonda thought most meager. Indeed, in a few days time, we were to attend *Nkula* rites at Shika Village (described in Turner, *The Drums of Affliction*) where twenty-five calabashes of beer were offered.

I was also shown the novices who had so far been mustered. Among them was the *Kambanji*-elect, or warleader," the first to be circumcised, treated with medicine, fed, and so forth. He was a big lad of about sixteen and was a son of Headman Wadyang'amafu. Wukengi told me that nineteen novices were due to be circumcised. One of his own sons would take the role of *Mwanta waMukanda,* or "chief of *Mukanda*" among the novices, for this title was always given to the oldest son of the Establisher. As it happened, both these boys lost their titles as the result of their performance during seclusion. Samatemba, the boy from Kafumbu, became *Kambanji* and Wukengi's boy was relegated to *Kajika!* I mention this to show the keen interest taken by elders in the performance of individual novices.

When we arrived, a group of circumcisers were collecting a medicine known as *ku-kolisha* or "strengthening" medicine. The site for the parents' and relatives' camps had already been roughly cleared of undergrowth and small trees.

The medicine consisted of the leaves and bark scrapings of certain species of trees, collected approximately in a circle around the site of the novices' parents' camp. *Nsompu* medicine for sprinkling and washing was to be made from these ingredients. *Ku-kolisha* medicine is used in several episodes. The circumcisers wash their own faces and chests and those of the novices' mothers with it, just before the boys are circumcised. Later, just before the *chikula chanyanya* ritual, when the masked dancers emerge, marking the official healing of all the novices' circumcision scars, the novices are washed with it. Finally, the novices are given ashes of burnt *ku-kolisha* medicine to eat before they are taken back to their mothers at the final *kwidisha* phase of *Mukanda.*

The *ishikenu* tree, the focal symbol of *ku-kolisha,* was a young *chikoli* thorn tree (*Strychnos spinosa*). It was roughly at the center of the campsite, which had already been cleared of bush growth by members of the sponsoring village under Wukengi's supervision. The circumcisers encircled the *ishikenu* several times. They were led by Headman Sampasa, who then prayed to the tree that the novices should be strong and heal quickly. Then he scraped off some bark with his medicine-ax into the round flat *lwalu* basket he carried. He brought the bark scrapings and some *chikoli* leaves into contact with two phallus-shaped containers of circumcision medicine. The containers, openly compared to male genitalia by Ndembu, were called *tudiwu.*[3] The medicine itself had the same name as the basket in which the *tudiwu* were carried, that is, *nfunda.*

After collecting *chikoli* medicine, the circumcisers took leaves and bark-scrapings from *mudyi* (*Diplorrhyncus condylocarpon*), *chikwata* (*Ziziphus mucronata*), *musoli* (*Vangueriopsis lanciflora*), *museng'u* (*Ochna pulchra*) and *kata Wubwang'u* (Uvaria nyassensis).

When all the ingredients have been collected, the circumcisers returned to the *chikoli* tree. A meal mortar for pounding the leaves and bark scrapings was brought and a pounding-pole, around which was tied a twist of *ileng'i* cane leaves.

Headman Nyaluhana now moved forward and took over the pounding-pole. He proceeded to pound the medicines while the others began to dance around the *chikoli* tree. For a time the *lwalu,* holding the two *tudiwu* containers, was placed in a fork of the *chikoli.* There were three circumcisers and three *yifukaminu* dancing.

[3] These are sometimes called *inzala.* They have stoppers of leaves.

A *chifukaminu* has the task of holding a novice still while the circumciser (*mbimbi*) operates.

The dancers crouched with legs wide apart, arms akimbo, and made sudden menacing uprearings. They took the *lwalu* basket and displayed the *tudiwu* containers in it above their heads as they danced. The circumcisers wore red lourie feathers (see Turner 1962b, 151) in their hair just over the brow. All the dancers were anointed on the brow and by the outer orbits with red clay (*mukundu* or *ng'ula*). They scowled fiercely and sang throatily, periodically making a bubbling sound with their lips.

The words of the song were as follows:

> *Eye yami nkalawanda chidyila hanjila*
> I am the lion who eats on the path
>
> *Wukama kankanta wutaleng'a mwewulu*
> You sleep on your back, you look into the sky
>
> *Chala chankumbi kusemina chiyimbi*
> Nest of the marabout stork where a black kite lays eggs
>
> *Ewina wantoka kusemina chitombu*
> Hole of a mamba where a (harmless) lizard lays eggs
>
> *Inyamwadyi wantukileng'a*
> Novice's mother, you used to revile me
>
> *Leta mwaneyi nikwang'ijekeli*
> Bring me your child that I may mistreat (him)
>
> *Mwaneyi nayi*
> Your child has gone
>
> *Mwana kamwanta wafwana musuka*
> The son of a chief is like a slave.

After preparing *ku-kolisha* medicine, the circumcisers left the mortar beside the *chikoli* and in succession danced and sang as recorded on all the paths leading into Wukengi Farm.

In this episode several categories of persons important in the *Mukanda* rites appear, either directly, like the circumcisers, or indirectly, like the novices and their mothers. It might be as well to say a few things and cite a few texts about these categories.

When one writes about the circumcisers, it is impossible to avoid discussing their *nfunda* medicine, and so they must be considered together.

First let us have a look at the meanings ascribed by informants to the *ku-kolisha* medicine, for this medicine provides a link between the three categories mentioned—circumcisers, novices, and novices' mothers—all of whom wash with it at critical points in the ritual.

Like *chikoli, ku-kolisha* is derived from *ku-kola,* "to be strong, healthy," of which it is the causative form. *Ku-kola* is often applied to the genital organs and especially to the penis. "*Ilomu dakola*" means "a penis capable of strong erections." There is thus a sexual component in the notion of health.

I have asked a wide range of informants about the meanings of *chikoli,* including Headman Mukanza, all the lodge officials at Nyaluhana, also Kasonda, Sandombu, Sakazao, Chikasa and other elders of Mukanza Village, Sakutoha, Muchona, and many more. It is one of the dominant symbols whose meaning most people agree about. Headman Mukanza put it well enough when he said: "*Chikoli* is a very strong tree like *mubang'a* on which the novices urinate when they sleep at the lodge. Its wood is very hard. One of its names is *chikang'a-njamba,* from *ku-kang'anya* (to fail), and *njamba* (the elephant). The elephant fails to break it. Neither wind nor rain can break it, and white ants cannot eat it. It stands upright like an erect penis, or a man's strong body. That is why we say that it means strength (*wu-kolu*)." Other informants agreed that *chikoli* stood for "*wuyala,*" which means both the penis and masculinity in general, including the masculine virtues of courage, skill at hunting, and endurance. It is used in *Kaluwi,* a hunters' cult, as part of a medicine "to strengthen huntsmanship."

The other ingredients are all familiar to us from previous articles, but I mention the meanings stressed by informants when discussing *Mukanda. Mudyi* is used, according to all, because "the first novice is circumcised under a *mudyi* tree and lies on a bed of *mudyi* leaves." Comparisons were made with *Nkang'a,* where the girl novice lies motionless at the foot of a *mudyi* all day.

*Chikwata* is said to have large thorns. "A man's body stays well if he is caught by them. They catch him strongly so that his blood inside him stays strong." Ndembu derive *chikwata* from *ku-kwata,* "to catch." Like *chikoli* it is also said to give a man a hard erection.

*Musoli* and *museng'u* are discussed elsewhere (Turner 1962, 12; and p. 288 below). Both are "hunters' medicines" and both are also symbols of female fertility (*lusemu*). One interesting point is that the general sense of *musoli,* "to reveal the hidden," is connected in *Mukanda* with the act of circumcision, which exposes the *glans penis.*

One of the songs for the masked *ikishi Mvweng'i,* who first appears after the boys' wounds are healed, praises "the dry *glans*" (*Mwembu yawuma*). In discussing the effects of the operation with me, one circumciser said that it "got rid of the dirt under the foreskin" and spoke with distaste of the "wetness" of an uncircumcised penis. Circumcision makes manhood visible. Both *musoli* and *museng'u* are considered appropriate for "strengthening medicine," said Chikasa, "because they are tough and lasting, white ants cannot eat them, and string cannot be made from their bark, to tie up huntsmanship and fertility."

*Kata Wubwang'u* is said to stand for "fertility" (*kusemu*) and also for the "shameless" (*nsonyi kwosi*) cross-sexual joking (*wusensi wa-Wubwang'u*) of the *Wubwang'u* "Twin" Cult, for which it is the dominant symbol. Such joking is said to give the patient "strength" (*wukolu*). *Kata Wubwang'u* stands, in short, for "the joyous struggle between men and women" which Gluckman (1949) considered to be a conspicuous feature of Wiko circumcision ceremonies.

The circumcisers' song contains three main themes. The first relates to the ritual "killing" of the novice by the circumciser. The second betrays the antagonism between the circumciser and the novice's mother. The third stresses major changes in the everyday order of nature and society brought about by *Mukanda.*

The circumciser is compared to a lion (*nkalawanda,* an archaic term; see also Delille 1930, 852) which devours the novice. Muchona said that "*Mbimbi* is like a lion because he will deal with the novices quickly, without delaying. The novice is the one who lies on his back while being circumcised." We shall meet further references to the "lion" theme in *Mukanda;* it is a general symbol for courage, masculinity, huntsmanship, and chiefliness. According to Windson Kashinakaji, the lion "eats on the path, before reaching the exact place, which is the lodge itself."

The circumciser's remark to the mother that formerly she abused him, but now he would give her son rough treatment, indicates that hostility is culturally expected between novices' mothers and those who sever the boys from dependence on them.

*Mukanda* is a complete reversal of the natural order. According Windson, Kasonda, and others, a cowardly creature like the *chitombu* lizard ousts the mamba from its hole. The kite, which hovers high over bush and village, lays its eggs in the nest of the ground-loving stork of the river plains. The status hierarchy of secular society is temporarily in abeyance (see above in "Betwixt and Between," pp. 98–99). The chief's son receives the same treatment as a slave, but the slave does not become a chief's son. In the lodge situation there is reduction to equality not reversal of status.

Muchona interpreted the "egg-laying" part of the song to mean that "the novices who were living comfortably with their mothers will now be in a different—and worse—place." In his interpretation, the timid lizard is the mother, her eggs are her novice sons, and the "mamba's hole" is circumcision and seclusion. Similarly, the young kites will be out of their element in a marabout stork's nest in the swamps.

The whole song is charged with aggressive and minatory feeling and imagery. It seems principally to be an expression of masculine antagonism to mothers in a matrilineal society.

The mimetic movements characteristic of the circumcisers' dance are derived from two sources. In the first place, the alternate crouching and rearing represent a lion's motions in anger. The bubbling noise of the dancers and the hoarseness of their singing are said to simulate the growling and slavering of lions. In the second place, when the dancers open their legs wide as they dance crouching, this is said to mime the posture of a novice during circumcision.

The bubbling sound, made with vibrating tongue between lips, is called "*ku-tatisha*." The same term is applied to the custom whereby men make this sound to their infants and then utter the word "*tata*," meaning "father." The aim of *ku-tatisha* is to make a child say "*tata*" as its first word, and not "*mama*," "mother." Saying "mother" first is reckoned to be most unlucky, and, indeed, many informants insist that in the past a child would have been put to death for it.

My informants told me that if during circumcision a boy cried out for his father, this was all right, but if he appealed to his mother, he was reckoned to be a coward and might be made *Kajika*.

It is not enough for a man to be skillful and dexterous in the use of the circumcision knife; he must also have "caught *nfunda*," if he wishes to become a "great" (*weneni*) or "senior" (*wamukulumpi*) circumciser. *Nfunda* may be more aptly described as a "fetish," in the sense attached to this term by West Africanists, than a medicine, for although limited amounts of it are applied to the novices, it is used principally for the protective influence it exerts over the whole scene of *Mukanda* and especially over the lodge.

*Nfunda* is not prepared for a single specific ritual, but is kept by the circumciser and renewed from time to time as it runs out. It is kept, as mentioned, in a small calabash called *kadiwu*,[4] which in its turn is kept in a basketwork container called *nfunda*. Two arrows are bound together just beneath the barbs. The feathered ends are uppermost and diverge to opposite sides of the basket. One arrow, called *chikeng'i*, is of the type used with arrow-poison (*wulembi*), the other is an ordinary iron-barbed arrow (*nsewu*). A galago skin (*chinyandi*) is wrapped round the receptacle.

When it is not in use, the *nfunda* container is placed in the high fork of a tree behind the circumciser's hut and well outside his village. On no account may women and children, and even young circumcised men, approach it closely, on penalty of contracting smooth leprosy (*mbumba yaluzong'a*), losing their reason, or becoming impotent or sterile.

When a circumciser dies, his *nfunda* is inherited by a man whom he has been training in the technical and ritual skills of his craft. The trainer is called *mama danfunda* ("mother of *nfunda*") and the apprentice *mwana wanfunda* ("child of *nfunda*"). A similar use of the terms "mother" and "child" in connection with the learning of a partly technical, partly ritual set of skills, is found in the hunters' cults, where a great hunter-doctor is known as *mama daWubinda* (or *daWuyang'a* for gun hunters), "mother of huntsmanship," and a candidate for admission to the cult as *mwana waWubinda*, "child of huntsmanship." The metaphorical use of these terms is similar to our own "imbibing of knowledge."

The apprentice is often, but not necessarily, a junior kinsman of the established circumciser. It is recognized by Ndembu that skill is not always inherited—it is a matter of a man's "liver" (*muchima*) or "inherent disposition" (*chisemwa*), what is his own and not from other people. Training consists in graduating from the role of guardian (*chilombola* or *chilombweji*), who carries the novice from the circumcision site to the *ifwilu* or "site of dying," where the novice sits until his wound stops bleeding; through the role of *chifukaminu*, who holds the novice astraddle for the circumciser to operate; to the role of junior, and then senior, *mbimbi* or circumciser. At every *Mukanda* he attends, he is expected to watch the circumciser carefully and to learn his surgical skills. Eventually, he will be given the knife himself and

[4] *Tudiwu* containers are made from a plant called *kankomi* which is obtained from Mwantiyanvwa's kingdom of Luunda in the Belgian Congo, traditional homeland of the Ndembu. The name is derived from *ku-koma*, "to chop" (of trees).

told to circumcise under his instructor's eye. However, until he acquires his own *nfunda* he will never rate as "a great circumciser," whatever his skill. A *nfunda* basket is always inherited from a deceased practitioner; new ones can be made only for persons already possessing *nfunda* by inheritance.

Before an apprentice can hope to become a "full *mbimbi,*" he must take a highly personal part in the preparation of new *nfunda* medicine. I shall describe the preparation of *nfunda* here, although chronologically speaking, it properly belongs to the *kwidisha* phase of *Mukanda.* I shall do this because *nfunda* contains the essence of *Mukanda's* many meanings, and because it presides over the entire ritual from its beginning.

I myself was fortunate to have been given the opportunity, by Headman Nyaluhana, Wukengi, and Sampasa, of observing the preparation of *nfunda.* I had just come back to the lodge site from watching the novices throw the grass skirts they wore during seclusion into a nearby stream. The lodge itself had been set on fire at the rising of the morning star (*ntanda*) at about 4 A.M. It was now about eight o'clock in the morning. The lodge was a black, still smoking ruin. In the *ifwilu* site (where the boys had sat bleeding after being circumcised) sat Headman Sampasa, Headman Nyachiu, and Headman Nyaluhana, all circumcisers, preparing *nfunda* (*adinakupanda nfunda*). The new *nfunda* was to eke out Sampasa's and Nyaluhana's which had been somewhat depleted in the course of *Mukanda,* and to give a *kadiwu* to Nyachiu full of new *nfunda,* "for his own was nearly finished."

A new *kadiwu* container had been cut for Nyachiu and neatly divided in half across the middle. When I arrived, various ingredients were being pounded by Sampasa in a mortar that had remained throughout the seclusion phase in the *ifwilu* site. Sampasa used as a pestle the handle of a small ritual ax used in the collection of lodge medicines, that had been kept in the novices' enclosure on the side of the lodge opposite the *ifwilu.* Nyachiu and Nyaluhana were stirring the pounded ingredients in potsherds (*yizanda*) with long sticks, hitherto used for beating the novices for breach of discipline.

The ingredients used consisted of ashes from a number of sites and objects sacralized for *Mukanda.* These included: ashes [5] from the burned-out lodge (*ng'ula*); ashes from the leaf bed of the first boy to

[5] *Makala,* used also to mean "charcoal."

be circumcised, that is, from the *mudyi* leaves of *Kambanji's* bed; ashes from the long fire in the novices' enclosure; ashes from the "*ijiku daMukanda*," the fire lit at the parents' camp by the Establisher on the eve of *Mukanda*; ashes from a tuft of grass that had been tied into a knot to mark the site where the *mukula* log had been laid (on this log the novices had sat immediately after circumcision); ashes from the burned harnesses of bark string (*musamba*) used to support the boys' penes after circumcision; and ashes from the grass pad or bark string pad (both called *mbung'a*) placed under the boys' circumcised penes to soak up the blood.

To moisten the mixture of ashes, Sampasa used blood from a red fowl that had been beheaded at the moment the lodge had been set ablaze. This fowl had been dedicated to the remote ancestors of Nyaluhana Village. Sacred "white" beer (made from large white millet or maize) had been drunk by lodge officials and some had been poured out as a libation (*kwichila*) to those spirits at that time. Some of the dregs were mixed with the ashes.

Two men who wished "to catch *nfunda*," that is, to become full circumcisers in the near future, were now told to strip completely and enter the burned lodge at the *ifwilu* side, near the three circumcisers. They complained bitterly about the role they were expected to play and demanded *nyishing'u*, payment for the right to see something esoteric, from the onlookers. Modern ideas that nakedness is shameful are becoming entrenched.

The men sat upright in the ashes of the lodge facing one another and worked their way into a favorite Ndembu position for copulation, the legs of one over the other's thighs. Sampasa now squeezed from the complete intestines of the beheaded chicken all the excrement into a clay pot. This pot, already containing the chicken's blood, he then placed under the entwined legs of the men. Next, he laid the intestines on the genitals of the apprentice playing the male role and led them along the legs and around the other's genitals. This apprentice's penis had been tied up against his stomach. Sampasa warned the men not to do anything to break the intestines, otherwise their own legs would break and they would become impotent.

Sampasa then told the first apprentice to urinate into the clay pot. This he did, having previously drunk some of the sacred beer for the purpose. The mixture in the pot was then stirred several times by Sampasa, who afterwards put some of it in one half of the new *kadiwu* container. In the other half of the *kadiwu* he placed the soggy mixture of ashes. Then he suddenly drew his circumcising knife lightly along the genitals of both men. This was the signal for them to get up and hop on one leg right across the smoldering ashes of the lodge. Senior men, aged about forty to fifty, rushed around to meet them with small sticks and lashed at them, driving them back towards the *ifwilu* side. As they entered *ifwilu* they were beaten quite hard. They hopped across the *ifwilu* site to a dry (probably lightning-struck) tree. This belonged to the *musesi wezenzela* species, but my informants told me it was its dryness and hardness that were important, not what kind it was. Each man stamped his leg on the tree, simultaneously slapping his hand on his calf. Then Sampasa made two small incisions with his circumcising knife, one in the small of the back, and one under the navel. After this they returned to their clothes and dressed, swearing good-naturedly at those who had beaten them. Several senior men followed their example by hopping to the dry tree, stamping on it, and getting cicatrized. Then Nyaluhana and Headman Mukanza, who had come specially for the *kwidisha* rites, went apart to another dry tree and cicatrized one another in turn. Both these men were regarded as belonging to a senior generation to all the others who had been cut and therefore had to be cicatrized separately—or so they told me. Both these old men bore the scars of many such incisions, each one representing attendance at a performance of *Mukanda*. The rest of the medicine was shared between Nyaluhana and Sampasa, each replenishing his *tudiwu*. The process of preparing this medicine was called "*ku-pandu kadiwu*." Muchona gave me his version of the preparation of *nfunda*. He had not attended the *Mukanda* at Wukengi Farm and hence was not influenced by what was done there. In the course of his statement he touched on sundry other aspects of the rites which are worth citing here.

*Yaya mukwadika nachu anyana. Dichu ayilombang'a kudi mwanta wampata,*
(It is) the senior or "elder" in the initiation of children. Thus they ask the chief of the country:

*nawu etu tukukeng'a kwadika anyana. Analombi dehi kesi kudi*
"We want you to initiate the children." (After) they have asked for fire from

*mwanta waMukanda hikuya kudi mbimbi nawu eyi mbimbi komana*
the chief of the *Mukanda*[6] they go to the circumciser and say: "You circumciser,

[6] Not to be confused with the title *Mwanta waMukanda* accorded to the second ranked novice, son of the *chijika Mukanda*.

*hiwalaminuku? Twaya wutetesheli anyana twakeng'iji Mukanda.*
did you really not circumcise? Come and get the children cut, we must start *Mukanda.*

*Chaka chamakonu ching'a twing'iji Mukanda chikupu chikupu anyana,*
This present year we must put the children into *Mukanda* most completely,

*tutiyi kuwaha. Anyana ejima ayi kuMukanda mulong'a wena*
that we may feel happy. All the children must go to Mukanda because they

*hiyayidima. Nawu dichu chenochu tunachitiyi dehi etu ambimbi.*
are uncircumcised." They reply, "Just so, we circumcisers are in complete agreement."

*Ndichi nkumininaku Chijika Mukanda nindi ami yami nukujika*
So in the next place the Establisher says; "I am about to hold (literally, erect, get up poles)

*Mukanda wami. Nyanenu ejimu upompeli kuMukanda wami ejima wawu*
my *Mukanda.* All your children must assemble together at my *Mukanda,* all of them."

*Dichu ching'a yenowu mbimbi awani nfunda yakulong'a dehi*
Thus that circumciser must find *nfunda* medicine (which has) already been poured in

*chachiwahi kuna. Hikutiyang'ana nanawa anyanyadi nawu*
well over there. When the novices' mothers have agreed to these things, they say:

*twing'ijenu Mukanda; nimbimbi nindi eng'a mwomwenomu.*
"Let us inaugurate *Mukanda*"; and the circumciser says, "Yes, just so."

*Hikwema walwa asambilang'a kwema walwa hela kuzambika masa hela kabaka hikwema dinu walwa wejima*
For brewing beer, they begin to brew beer by soaking either large white millet or maize, then to brew all kinds of beer.

*Owu awuzambikang'a naluseng'a lwanfunda. Hela nfunda cheng'i*
That beer is soaked with *nfunda* powder. Or *nfunda* also

*hakupanda chayu nikunyaka nikunyakuluka chayu. Ching'a*
is prepared throughout the years from the beginning of time. It must

*kupanda nekabakaba, dayu diyu kankomi kumuketula hamu hakachi*
be prepared with *ikabakaba,* which is (a name for) *kankomi,* it is cut from the middle (of the tree) [7]

[7] This suggests that *kankomi* is a species of gourd.

*mwakupandila yuma hamu yanfunda. Twapandang'a nawuyana makala*
and in it are prepared the ingredients (literally "things") of *nfunda*. We magically prepare (it) with cinders

*amuMukanda nimutondu wuna weshikenu wamwifwilu*
from within the *Mukanda* (site) and the *ishikenu* tree [8] from the place of dying

*watapilang'awu anyadi, nimukula nimuyombu. Dichu neyi awupanda dehi*
where the novices are killed, and the *mukula* [on which the novices sat after circumcision] and the *muyombu* [over which they were passed to the *mukula* tree]. And so when it has already been prepared—

*twapandang'a hana hakwidika anyadi kuMukanda neyi anyana anawudiki dehi,*

we do the preparing when the novices come out of *Mukanda*—when the children have already come out

*ng'ula anochi dehi, kunona makowa awanyana hikushita*
and the lodge has already been burned, they take the (fore)skins of the children and burn them with fire

*shite-e to-o, kuleta manji hikwinkahu nimashi akasumbi*
completely (to ashes), they take oil and add it in and add the blood of a fowl

*kuweja hohana wekombu, kunona mujing'wa hikutandumuna wudi*
therein, of a cock, they take the intestine and extend it from

*naniwu kudi namukwawu. Yenona kunona wuyala kufutula.*
one man to another. The latter takes his penis and puts it up in his belt.

*Kunona ninyitondu nikulala henahana hashakaminuwu anyana*
They take branches and put them one by one in the place where the children sat

*haMukanda hakesi kaMukanda. Waha dehi dinu nikuleta niji*
at *Mukanda* at the fire of the circumcision camp. When they are ready they take these

*nantewula mwadikili nachu anyadi hikupanda dinu kadiwu pande-e to-o.*
and razors by means of which they circumcised the novices and completely prepare the *kadiwu*.

*Hikusala dinu ayilombola niambimbi sale-e to-o dinu. Diku kumanisha.*
Then the guardians and circumcisers make cuts in their bodies and insert (*nfunda*) medicine completely. That is to end (the preparation of *nfunda*).

[8] The *mudyi* tree, beneath which the principal novice is circumcised.

*Yinashali iwu walamaku kindi kanti, iwu walamaku kindi kanti*
The pieces (of prepuce) that are left, one keeps a little piece for himself, another keeps a little piece,

*ejima wawu kakushitila, anyana nakuleketa hela nakuyomona*
all of them (keep little pieces) for burning, in order to put (the cinders) on the children's tongues or to mark them [as with *mpemba*] on the temples, brow, and navel,

*kulonda kumfuntishila mujimba windi. Dichu nawa neyi*
so that (a novice's) body may be returned to him. Thereupon, when

*anapandi dehi tudiwu hikwinka mujinfunda jina jakutung'a.*
they have already medicated the *tudiwu* containers they put them in the *nfunda* baskets that have been made.

*Ndichi nawa nfunda jina jakala kuhang'ana anju. Neyi etu*
Therefore, *nfunda* baskets are hard (or dangerous) to dance with. When we

*ambimbi tudi nakuhang'ana ching'a tunona tudiwu tutenteka*
circumcisers are dancing, we must pick up the *tudiwu* containers and put them

*hacheng'i tukudyika kuna kunyichanka. Kushala nfunda*
in another place; we hang them up on (ritual) forked poles. The baskets remain

*hitukuhang'ana naju jamukunkulwayi.*
and we will dance with them empty (literally, "worthless, without efficacy").

It will have been noted that there are several differences between my observations and information on the spot and Muchona's account. For one thing, I did not mention that cindered foreskins were among the ingredients of *nfunda* medicine. This is because no one said anything about them at the time. It is quite possible that this ingredient had been put in, for I missed the earlier stages of preparation, having accompanied the novices to the stream for their purification rites. On the other hand, I was assured by many Ndembu, including such reliable informants as Chief Ikelenge, Kasonda, and Sakutoha, that foreskins were burnt to put in *nfunda*. Other informants, including men from Nyaluhana Village, insisted that the fathers of novices took the foreskins after they had been removed "and kept them in a secret place." These men expressed horror at the idea of burning them; this would render the boys impotent (*afwa mwitala,* "dead in the hut"), they cried. However, I believe that they were deliberately misleading me, for the others I have mentioned were men of probity whose comments on matters of custom I was able to check by my own observations on numerous occasions. Indeed, Muchona's remark that when the novices were given cindered foreskins to taste they were "being given their bodies back to them" seems to meet the argument about impotence. I was unfortunately unable to see for myself how the foreskins were disposed of during the process of circumcision, for my attention was fully occupied in treating the boys' cuts with disinfectant. Kasonda told me that the circumcisers' assistants put the foreskins in *tudiwu* containers as they were excised.

Again, when the apprentice circumcisers and others were being cicatrized, I did not see any *nfunda* medicine rubbed into the cuts and do not believe that this was done. Nevertheless, since I observed that certain ritual elements I had previously been told were important were omitted at the Nyaluhana performance, I am prepared to believe that the rubbing in of *nfunda* medicine is an authentic traditional practice.

I was not told at Nyaluhana that portions of the *mukula* pole on which the boys sat after the operation, and of the *muyombu* tree over which they were lifted, were used as ingredients; only that ashes of the knotted grass originally marking the site of the pole were employed. Again, I am inclined to believe Muchona's version, for I always found him an honest man.

Muchona interpreted a number of the symbolic acts and objects found in this episode. He said that the urination (*ku-tekela*) of the apprentice "was for hopping (*ku-zandama*)." Hopping, he said, was like the "pounding" (*ku-twa*) of a penis during intercourse. "Sometimes," he said, "a penis may become without strength (*wukolu*). To make urine in the medicine means that power (*ng'ovu*) is added to it, for urine (*masu*) represents the penis (*wuyala*), its strength (*ku-kola*)." The connection between urine and semen is certainly made linguistically by Ndemba, for the term for "semen" is *matekela,* while "to urinate" is *ku-tekela,* though the noun form "urine" is *masu.* According to Ndembu belief, semen is "blood mixed with water."

According to Muchona, to cut oneself above the navel it *kudijanyika,* literally, "to stretch oneself out straight." Here too the sexual implication is obvious. Rubbing in *nfunda* medicine after making such an incision is also undertaken to prevent impotence. "If a man is not marked with *nfunda,* which is very strong, he will become impotent."

One function of *nfunda,* according to Muchona, is to protect the novices from female witches and their familiars. "The lodge is burned to prevent the boys from being killed by *ndumba* (witches' familiars), who collect medicines from the novices' beds in the lodge. If the *akwandumba* (the *ndumba* people) collect medicines from such a bed, that boy who slept in the bed is also collected in order to be killed. For women are jealous of men. They also like their meat." Putting ashes from the lodge in *nfunda,* therefore, means escaping from witches' familiars.

*Nfunda* medicine has been described to me by many informants as "a symbol (*chinjikijilu*) for *Mukanda* itself." Eating it is like incorporating the very nature of *Mukanda.* Each particular lot of *nfunda* putatively contains medicine from performances going back "to the beginning of time," for new *nfunda* is added at each performance. It would not be fanciful, perhaps, to see the "death" of each individual occasion of *Mukanda,* and of the novices "killed" in it, as being a necessary corollary of the immortality of *Ndembu,* and indeed of Lunda society as a whole, including all the groups that "came from Mwantiyanvwa." Ashes (*makala*) stand for "death" (*ku-fwa*) in many ritual contexts, as do the potsherds used in preparing *nfunda,* and the beheading of the chicken whose blood and excrement (also symbolizing death) form a component of the medicine. Although no informant gave me this interpretation, it seems to me that a connection might be established between the ritual death (a concept recognized by Ndembu) of a specific set of novices and the use of death symbolism in the medicine. The verb *ku-fwa* "to die," contains in many contexts of situational usage the implication of "summing up," of marking off a distinct phase or period of time. The meaning of a chain of events is condensed into it. There seems to be a close relationship, in the implicit philosophy of the Ndembu, between the uniqueness of a sequence of events or acts, such as the life of an individual, a court case, or the performance of a ritual, and the notion of death. Death is the punctuation mark that gives the series its idiosyncratic meaning and immortalizes it for thought. However, *nfunda* is immortal since it is an infinite series of such summations. Here we are in deeper waters than Nembu would consciously venture in, but I can at least show that Ndembu are subliminally aware of the relationship between death, individuality, and tribal continuity.

We have noted the tension in the circumcisers' song between them and the novices' mothers, the *anyanyadi*. Since these woman play a most important role in the rites, and since this episode is their first effective entrance upon the scene, a word or two should be said about them here. Many features of their behavior will be discussed below, but a general picture of their role from the Ndembu point of view will be of use. An old Ndembu from the Belgian Congo, Chimwang'a, furnished the following account:

*Ifuku dakwing'ija Mukanda anyanyadi akuleta yuma yejima*
(On) the day of inaugurating *Mukanda*, the novices' mothers bring everything (fish, meat, meal and beer)

*kudi Chijika Mukanda, yena diyi wukwanjang'ana walwa, wukwawu wawambimbi,*
to the Establisher, he is the one who shares out beer, some for the circumcisers,

*wukwawu wawantung'i janyikala, wukwawu wawantu muyasemwakena,*
some for village headmen, and some for people in the kinship group.

*Akuchisha nachu ng'oma yaMukanda hakwila mbiji ninshi niwung'a*
They will stay awake all night to the drums of *Mukanda* but with meat, fish and meal—

*yakutentekela anyadi yawu yakudya mafuku ejima.*
They will set out food for their novices every day.

*Chijika Mukanda watondang'a antu ayedi ambanda hela asatu*
The Establisher appoints three or four womenfolk

*akuteleka kudya kwawanyadi*
who will cook food for the novices.

*Awa ambanda kutwesa kwila wuvumbi nehi hela kuya nakukama*
Those women cannot commit adultery nor go and sleep (with their husbands)

*kumatalawu nehi hela kutelekela anyadi mbiji yambang'ala*
in their huts nor cook for the novices the meat of the guinea fowl

*hela mbiji yanshimba hela mbiji yatulolu hela amaseng'i nehi.*
or the meat of the genet cat or of the small elephant shrews or of the large elephant shrews.

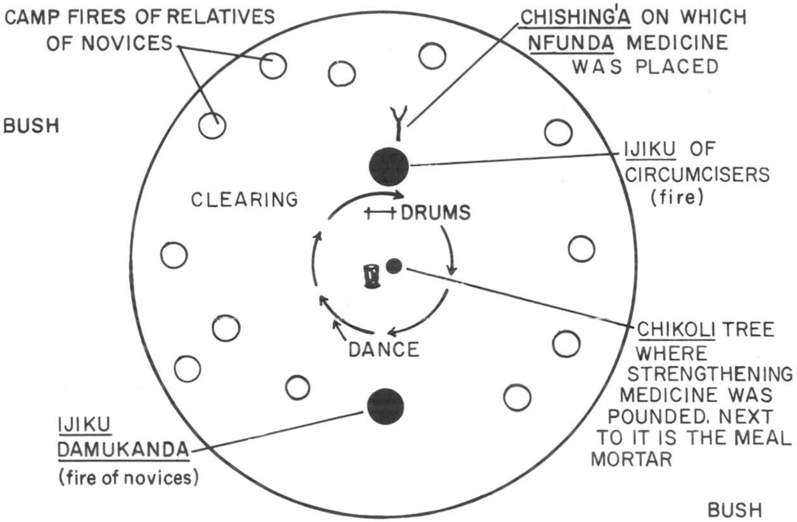


*Diagram 5.* Camp at *Ijiku daMukanda* on the first night

*Awu ambanda akukamang'a hanji hejiku daMukanda. Budidi*
Those women sleep outside by the fire of *Mukanda* [at the novices' parents' camp—see Diagram 5]. Early in the morning

*akubidika nawu kwalamo-o, anayadi kuMukanda akwakula nawu . .*
they shout out "Circumcision!"; the novices at Mukanda answer

*woho-o; hela anyadi anatwesi kutachika nawu kwalamo-o,*
"Woho!"; or the novices can begin by saying "Circumcision,"

*amama jawu akwakula nawu woho-o.*
their mothers will reply "Woho."

*Anyamwadi diwu ahondang'a nshima nakumwinka iyala wumu*
Novices' mothers make cassava mush and give it to a man

*hakutwala nakwimba kamina hohu ninichi chakushikayi*
who takes it away singing only until he has arrived

*kudi anyadi ejima. Namelela akutelekela anyadi yakudya.*
where all the novices are. In the afternoon they will cook food for the novices.

*Chakumanishawu to-o kuteleka akupompa kwijiku nakwimba*
When they have quite finished cooking, they will gather around the fire and sing

*kamina nawu wujilang'a inyamwadi, wujilang'a kudi anshindwa;*
songs, as follows, "A novice's mother is taboo, *nshindwa* fruit [a euphemism for the female genitalia] is forbidden;

*hela kwila yuma yatama yamukunkulwayi mwaneyi hakutwesa*
if (you) do bad, worthless things your son cannot

*kwaluka swayuku hela wukukata musong'u mulong'a*
heal up quickly or he will be sick with an illness because

*munamushimani mwana. Chamba kedishawu Mukanda anyanyadi*
you have behaved unnaturally towards the child. When eventually they perform the *kwidisha* rites, the novices' mothers

*akwakuhonda ayifweteng'a nyishing'a ipeka dawusang'a*
who stirred mush are given (ritual) payment—a necklace of beads,

*hela luvung'a lwehina hela nyibulu hela tunyama*
or four yards of cloth or ankle-rings or portions of meat.

I discussed the concept of *ku-shimana,* "to behave unnaturally" with Windson Kashinakaji, and he gave me a few examples of how it was employed by Ndembu. "If a father were to eat his own child, if a child were to order an elder about, or if an animal were to dress up in clothes, these things would be *ku-shimana.* In the same way, women who break the taboos of *Mukanda* would be said to behave in an unnatural way (*ku-shimana*) towards their sons." He said that the same term would be applied to incest.

Discussion of the food taboos mentioned in this text falls more appropriately into the section on seclusion. I shall consider the role of the novices in that section as well.

While the circumcisers were preparing *ku-kolisha* medicine, novices had been arriving singly and in groups from villages in the vicinage, accompanied by their senior kin. Each had been anointed beside the outer orbits with white clay, betokening that he had been prayed for at the *muyombu* ancestor-shrines in his village of residence. The boys had been anointed by their own fathers or in the absence of the latter by close male matrilineal kin. At about 5:30 P.M. Headman Nyaluhana gathered all the novices into a crouching circle around the *nyiyombu* trees near Wukengi's hut and made a long prayer on their behalf. He called on the spirits of the ancient Kanongeshas, senior chiefs of the Ndembu tribe, some of whom, like Nkomesha, were matrilineal ancestors of Wukengi and himself. He also invoked former village headmen, such as Nswanamumi and the woman head

Nyaluhana for whom the village has been founded by her brother Kanongesha Nkomesha; in these prayers he sought their protection for this *Mukanda* against the harm that might come from sorcery, witchcraft, and from the presence of uncircumcised persons at the dance (such as members of other tribes employed at the Boma who did not circumcise), and of "Europeans" (i.e., myself). He then asked the spirits to help the officiants, naming each of them, their relationship, if any, to himself, and their roles in *Mukanda*. When he had finished he drew three lines in powdered white clay (*mpemba*) (from a stock of *mpemba* sent to Wukengi for this *Mukanda* by the reigning Kanongesha, Ndembi) from the biggest *muyombu* tree towards himself. Then he anointed himself with *mpemba,* first in a short line from his naval upwards, then beside his orbits. Next he anointed the officiants—the Establisher Wukengi, the senior Lodge Instructor, and the circumcisers—in the same fashion. He concluded by anointing all the novices, additionally rubbing *mpemba* on their shoulders "where they would be held during circumcision."

Kasonda and my other companions from Mukanza Village whispered to me that Nyaluhana should have invited Wukengi, the Establisher, to pray after he had done so, and also Sampasa, whom everyone still thought would be Senior Circumciser. The senior Lodge Instructor (*Mfumwa Tubwiku*), they said, should have prayed too, but Nyaluhana monopolized the function, and dismissed everyone when he had anointed the novices.

The mode of prayer differs from the general pattern of Ndembu prayers to ancestral shades in the important respect that ancient chiefs and other remote ancestors were invoked. This can partly be accounted for by the personal factor of Nyaluhana's assertion of authority and prestige—he was publicly stressing the importance of his lineage as against Machamba's. However, I have gathered from accounts of other performances that the invocation of distant ancestors, especially politically significant ones at the tribal level, is a regular feature of prayers made at *Mukanda*. This is because the effective core of participants is much wider than in most rituals of affliction or in the girls' puberty ritual. The novices are drawn from at least one whole vicinage and sometimes from several adjacent vicinages, whereas candidates in a cult of affliction and girls undergoing puberty rites are usually initiated individually. I shall consider the sociological implications of this difference in a later part of this essay.

After the prayer, preparations went on vigorously at the camp for the night dance. Small village groups were laying in stocks of firewood and erecting screens of leafy boughs as sleeping shelters in a wide circle around the sacred *chikoli* tree where the circumcisers had danced. A long fire, at the opposite end of the clearing from the village, was built up and just at sunset was kindled by Wukengi, the Establisher. This was the *ijiku daMukanda,* the sacred "fire of *Mukanda,*" which was to be kept burning night and day until the lodge had been burned, and on which the novices' mothers had to cook all the food eaten by their sons during seclusion. Many people gathered round to see Wukengi light the fire.

When everyone had arrived, I counted twenty-four fires and windscreens around the circumference of the clearing. Each village group had divided into at least two campfire groups. This arrangement was to preserve rules of cross-sexual in-law avoidance, for both sexes were present in each group. After dark, in the glaring firelight, drums were brought into the middle of the clearing. The *ing'ung'u* dance began to thud out its heady rhythm—it was a wilder version of the circumcisers' dance in the afternoon. Immediately, the senior male kin of the novices, fathers or older brothers mainly, lifted the boys on to their shoulders and all proceeded in a cavorting circle round the drums. Not only novices, but other young lads also—those who had attended less than three performances of *Mukanda*—were carried or else they had to climb up trees, anything to avoid touching the earth. In addition, they had to keep their hands over their ears in order not to hear the drums. The mystical sanctions against touching the ground were said to be lifelong incontinence of urine or else bleeding to death from even a trifling cut (hemophilia?). According to my Mukanza friends, who were drinking beer with me at our village leafscreen, "this is because *ing'ung'u* is the dance of the circumcisers with their *nfunda.*"

Suddenly the circumcisers entered in procession, apparently from the bush, carrying their apparatus. The *tudiwu* containers were now newly striped with red and white clay. All the rest of the gathering followed them as they danced crouching, holding up different items of apparatus, and chanting hoarsely. In the firelight and moonlight the dance got wilder and wilder. Two circumcisers or two *yifukaminu* would break into a *pas de deux* from time to time. Holding between them a *nfunda* basket or a knife, they would dance with open legs, sinking ever closer to the ground and approaching ever nearer to one another, performing the circling movements of the lower abdomen typical of one Ndembu mode of sexual intercourse. This behavior is said "to give power" to the apparatus. When they made their spectacular entrance, they carried in a very tall *chishing'a* forked pole of *musoli* wood, similar in form to those used as hunters' shrines. This was taken at Nyaluhana's command to the opposite side of the *chikoli* tree to the "fire of *Mukanda*." There it was solemnly planted in the ground, and Nyaluhana, to "help the *ambimbi*," addressed a brief prayer to the spirit of the circumciser from whom he had inherited his first *nfunda*. A *lwalu* medicine basket was placed in the fork of the *chishing'a* and kept in place by two arrows. One *nfunda* basket and all the *tudiwu* containers of the actual medicine powder (*luseng'a lwa-nfunda*) were placed on it. It was explained to me that if *nfunda* medicine touched the ground it would lose all its efficacy and would even be harmful to those in the lodge. (See Plate 1 for dancing circumcisers.)

After the *chishing'a* had been planted, Sampasa ordered firewood to be piled up near the front of it and he lit it with a brand from the *ijiku daMukanda*. This new fire was known as the *ijiku dawambimbi*, "the circumcisers' fire" (see Diagram 6). There the circumcisers could rest during the night when they were tired from dancing. I noticed that they had no beer, unlike most of the other groups, and mentioned this to Sampasa and Headman Nyachiu. They replied that they were not drinking because they would have to circumcise boys the following day. A drunken man might harm them terribly. Sampasa went away and Nyachiu confessed to me privately that "it was a hard and heavy thing to be a circumciser." In the past, he said, a novice's father would stand with an ax or spear in his hand, at no great distance from a circumciser when he was cutting, and if the circumciser "made a mistake," the father would wound him in the shoulder. As it turned out, Nyachiu eschewed the role next morning and acted as Nyaluhana's *chifukaminu*, on the pretext that "three circumcisers were sufficient."

Meanwhile, the novices had been led to the *ijiku daMukanda*, where they sat in a solemn little line fussed over by their fathers and mothers. Establisher Wukengi and his wife, the senior *nyamwadi*, or novice's mother, sat on the opposite side of the fire to the novices. At intervals during the night, *ing'ung'u* was played and danced again, and the sleepy small boys had to be roused and carried in the harsh male dance. Before the main public dance began, Nyaluhana made a speech, shouting that he wanted no fighting or quarreling, for

1. Circumcisers Sampasa and Nyachiu (who, in the end, did not ply the knife) dance near the *chikoli* tree on the day before the operation, displaying the baskets containing *nfunda* medicine. Note the lourie feather over Sampasa's brow and the two arrows placed point downwards in the baskets.

2. The *mukoleku* "gateway" between "impure" infancy and circumcised masculinity. The gateway is placed at the junction of a well-trodden footpath and a new path leading to the site of circumcision. The discarded clothing of the novices' childhood drapes the "crossbar."

3. The lodge (*ng'ula*) in which the novices live during seclusion.

4. Naked novices confront circumcised adults across the sacred fire in the lodge enclosure a few days after circumcision.

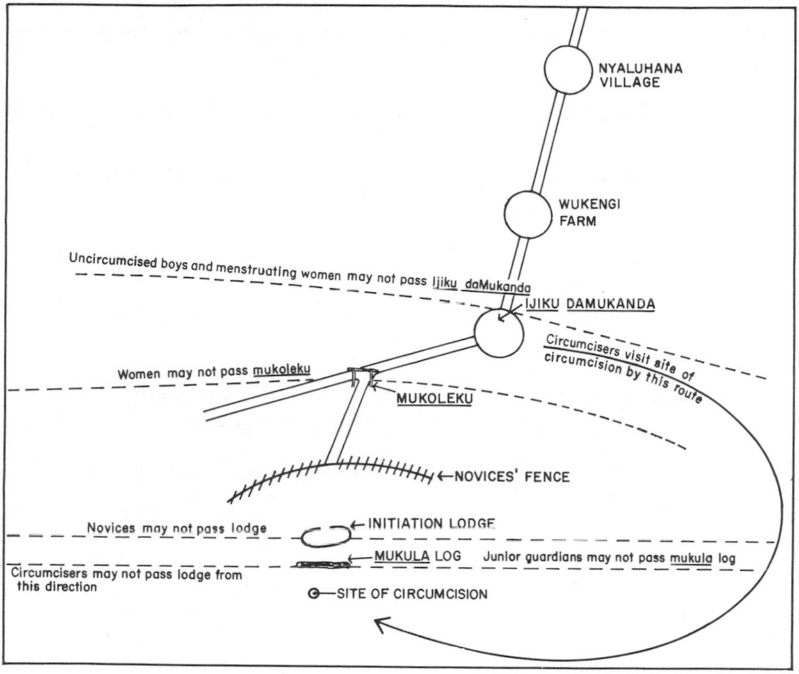


*Diagram 6.* Ritual area of *Mukanda*

angry feelings in the parents would hinder the boys from healing quickly.

On the general taboo against certain objects and persons in certain ritual states touching the ground, I was told by Muchona: "When novices are being circumcised, they lie on the ground. Part of *nfunda* medicine consists of foreskins. *Nfunda* is raised in the air, therefore everything must be in the air, not on the ground where the boys suffered. The ground is where there was suffering and where the novices were killed. It is the place of death. To be high up is to have life and strength."

The role of the circumcisers on the eve of circumcision is well brought out by Chimwang'a:

*Mbimbi wamuneni wukweti nfunda namelela neyi hakwinza.*
The great circumciser has *nfunda* medicine in the afternoon when he comes.

*Akuya nakimukinkilila nanswaha yawalwa nimushing'a. Walwa*
They will go and meet him with a calabash of beer and a ritual present. Beer

*wukunwina kunjila. Chakumanishayi walwa to-o wukwinza ninfunda yindi*
he will drink on the way. When he has finished the beer completely he will come with his *nfunda*

*niambimbi amakwawu akushikena kwaChijika Mukanda akukudika nfunda*
and other circumcisers, they will arrive at the Establisher's place, they will hang their *nfunda*

*yawu kwakwihi nakesi. Yowu muntu wukuhitila kwakwihi namfunda*
near the fire. Any person who will pass close to the *nfunda*

*wukusupa hela kwandala mbumba yalunzong'a. Antu ejima ching'a*
will become an idiot or be smitten with leprosy. All people must

*akuhitila halehi nanfunda yakadiwu.*
keep well away from the *nfunda* (medicine) of the *kadiwu* (container).

*Antu ejima wufuku wejima akachishi nakuhang'ana nakukundisha*
Everybody must stay awake the whole night dancing and making

*anyadi. Neyi hiyakwimba tumina twang'ung'u anyadi ejima*
the novices' dance. When they sing the songs of *ing'ung'u,* all the novices

*akuyeleka neyi anakwimba tumina nakukindisha anyadi akuyisulwisha nakuyikindisha*
are carried, when they sing the songs of *ku-kindisha* they make them come down and dance *ku-kinda* fashion [9]

*nakuyibulila ny'ing'ula* [10] *ninichi chikukucha to-o.*
and make cries of approbation by beating their hands on their lips, praising the novices, until it is full dawn.

White reports a similar nocturnal dance before a Luvale circumcision (1953, 45). The dance is called *kusangisa funda;* the bundle of medicines of *nganga-mukanda* (circumciser) is carried about on a flat

[9] See Turner, *The Drums of Affliction,* 1968, 75. *Ku-kinda* is a special dance performed by novices, I believe in imitation of the circumcisers' dance.

[10] *ku-bula nying'ula* (see also Turner 1962d, 43) is a welcoming noise when people have returned from a long journey through wild bush or when hunters return with a kill.

basket (*lwalo*) and handled by the men participating to ensure that they will enjoy its protection; the women though present do not handle it.[11] This period is marked by great freedom, obscene gestures are freely indulged in, and individuals curse each other without offense. This aspect of the dance has its place in the rites by conveying the protection of the *nfunda*. The novices are also warned at this stage of the need to observe the rules of the lodge; one (Lunda) song sung for this purpose runs: "*Hiwadya nshimba ninkala unadyi, wavwala nshimba, wadikolomwena* (You have eaten genet and mongoose, and are wearing a genet skin, you have brought injury on yourself.)" At the same time their fears are allayed; they are told that there will be nothing uncomfortable in the rites; they will eat off plates, sleep on beds, and only have to jump over a bush of *muvangwa* (*Paropsia brazzeana*).

Besides *ing'ung'u* and *ku-kundisha* (which I did not see), other *Mukanda* dances and *Wubinda* (hunting cult) dances and songs were performed. Meanwhile, calabashes of beer were sent to the shelters of the more important visitors, and gossiping circles formed around the beer providers. A circle for the *Chikinta* (a modern secular dance) also formed up, consisting as usual of the younger people. A number of Boma employees from other parts of central Africa came to my fire and had a drink. Among them was a Hehe from Tanganyika, now a motor mechanic. He was full of scorn because he had heard that Ndembu novices were not blamed if they cried out while they were being circumcised. He said that no women would ever sleep with a Hehe if he acted in such a cowardly fashion. He was delighted that Ndembu women could be married for a trifling marriage payment by Hehe standards. He himself had "three beauties for a few pounds: in Hehe country he would have had to pay many cattle."

Not long before dawn, several young bloods near me began to egg one another on "to take a *nyamwadi* (novice's mother) in the bush and have intercourse with her." It was strictly taboo for either parent of a novice to have intercourse from the beginning of the night dance until the circumcision scars healed up. Naturally, it would have added a spice to their evening if they could have obtained a forbidden pleasure, but the lads soon returned and remarked gloomily that they had had no success. "*Mukanda* is very heavy," [12] they said.

[11] This is also the case at the Ndembu rites. See pp. 187, 194 for taboos against unauthorized persons touching *nfunda*.

[12] That is, a grave matter.

At this time, I was told that parents of novices must also avoid eating salt until the wounds healed and that they had to fast until their son's operation was over.

Just after sunrise, I saw Sampasa wash the senior Lodge Instructor, Kutona, from Wadyang'amafu Village, with *ku-kolisha* medicine from the mortar beside the *chikoli* tree in the middle of the campsite. After that, he washed himself and the other circumcisers, *yifukaminu* assistant circumcisers, and guardians with the medicine, then all the novices' mothers and fathers.

Next a really big meal of fish and cassava meal was given to the novices by their mothers, each mother feeding her son by hand as though he were an infant. After eating, the novices sat trying to look impassive (as Ndembu say "not showing their liver"), while a number of lads who had already been to *Mukanda* stood by them offering encouragement, much as White had described it. The mothers looked grave and subdued. There was a feeling of tense expectation. Wukengi was nowhere to be seen. Someone told me that before dawn he had gone into the bush with the important circumcisers and Lodge Instructor to select the site of the lodge and of the *ifwilu* where the boys would be circumcised. There were various ritual "properties" to get ready—a *muyombu* pole and a *mukula* log, for example. Perhaps Wukengi was helping with these things.

Shortly after the novices' meal, all the circumcisers, looking thoroughly menacing with red clay daubed on brow and temples and each with a red lourie feather in his hair, marched in and proceeded to dance round the *chikoli* tree, holding up their equipment.

Next they started off in procession, led by Sampasa down a village path. After about a hundred yards the old path met a new one made before dawn that very day by the senior officiants and leading to the chosen site of circumcision. At this fork between old and new paths, three drums were set up, the circumcisers' drum rhythm was beaten, and the circumcisers and *yifukaminu* danced again for the last time their "lion" dance. Only those who had been initiated in a traditional Ndembu *Mukanda* were allowed near the new path. Several boys who had been circumcised at the mission station were chased away and jeered at. I noticed that Nyaluhana was carrying a long knife—not a circumcision knife—which he brandished at the mission-circumcised.

The two apprentice-circumcisers mentioned in connection with the preparation of new *nfunda* medicine now held one of the arrows from the *nfunda* basket, then the *lwalu* basket with the *tudiwu* containers, against their genitals. Next the *tudiwu* were removed from the *nfunda* basket by the circumcisers. One of the apprentices took the empty *nfunda* basket, placed it decisively on the ground near the junction of the paths, then carried it back about ten yards towards the village and put it on the ground again near where the Lodge Instructor was standing.

Sampasa now stood at the head of the new path with his feet wide apart right over it. He faced towards the village and held up his penis in both hands. All the other circumcisers, *yifukaminu* and their assistants, then stood with their backs to Sampasa, along the new path, to form a tunnel of legs over it. Each held his penis up. Next all the guardians, the Lodge-Instructor first, began to walk backwards from the spot where the *nfunda* basket was set down, the Instructor carrying the basket. Crouching, they passed under the tunnel of legs. As they emerged from the far end they were soundly whipped by other adult men who used long thin branches for this purpose. Then they hopped quickly on one leg to a *mubang'a* tree near the circumcision site. Their next task was to complete the preparations for the operation proper. The "dragging (*ku-kuka*) of *nfunda*," as it was called, was "to make the guardians' male members strong." Some of the onlookers thought that the beating was too light, but one boy, Kawana, son of Headman Wadyang'amafu, complained bitterly to his father that Philemon of Wukengi Farm had beaten him too severely. The old headman rebuked Philemon, who retorted that Kawana was a cheeky boy who was always swearing at his elders instead of being quiet and obedient. The whole point of the beating, he said, was to chastise such lads.

What should have been done next, but was in fact omitted until circumcision was over, was to erect a frame of *mukula* poles, in the shape of a soccer goal post, over the entrance to the new path. Earlier the officiants had forgotten to cut three poles of *mukula* for the frame, called *mukoleku*, from *ku-kola*, "to be strong." Later, the frame was erected in the precise spot where Sampasa had stood as a living entrance to the tunnel of legs. Through it the novices had to pass on the way to circumcision, and over it were hung the clothes they wore as children and would wear no more as circumcised tribesmen (see Plate 2).

For the preparation of the circumcision site (see Diagram 7) the guardians brought a long log of *mukula* with the branches lopped off

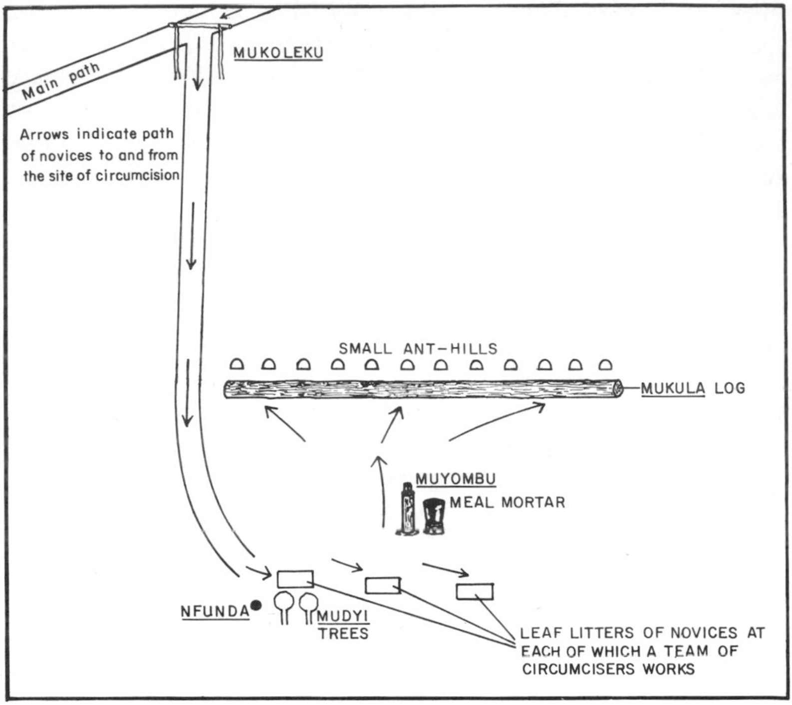


*Diagram 7.* The site of circumcision (*ifwilu danyadi*)

and placed it horizontally on the ground. They then distributed a number of small termites' nests at regular intervals a short distance in front of the log. A shallow cavity was hollowed out on top of each nest. Other guardians manufactured girdles and harnesses of *musamba* bark string to support the boys' penes after the operation and to prevent them from rubbing painfully against their bodies. The Lodge Instructor fetched a calabash of sweet millet beer for the boys to drink when the first bleeding had stopped.

By this time, the circumcisers had arrived, wearing only short waistcloths. They prepared the actual site of the operation. This was located about six or seven yards from the *mukula* log and consisted of three heaps of *mudyi* leaves about a yard apart. The so-called "bed of *kambanji*," on which the principal novice would be circumcised, was placed directly under a small *mudyi* tree. Indeed, this tree provided one of the fixed points in the spatial structure of the lodge situation, the other being a tall *mubang'a* tree near which the lodge entrance would be sited.

About equidistant from the *mudyi* tree and the *mukula* log a small quickset sapling of *muyombu,* the tree usually planted in villages as a living ancestor shrine, was planted. Next to it was placed a meal-mortar full of pounded leaf medicine to apply to the boys' wounds.

After this had been done, Nyaluhana inserted a hard-skinned fruit, called *mukunkampombu* or *kampobela,* cut exactly in half, in a hole in the ground just under the *mudyi* tree and then laid all the *nfunda* kits of the circumcisers on it, on a flat round *lwalu* basket. Next he poured "white" maize beer into the *lwalu* itself and put in a *mudyi* leaf for each circumciser. All the circumcisers scooped up some beer in their leaves and held them suspended in the air while Nyaluhana prayed to the spirit of his father from whom he had inherited his *nfunda.* I was unable to catch everything he said in the general confusion of preparation but heard the following: "My father, you have taught me the things of *nfunda.* All my relatives are here. Give these circumcisers strength. Help the novices who will come. If anyone wishes to kill the novices by sorcery, may it not be here today." While Nyaluhana prayed, Sampasa held up the basket with *nfunda.* When the prayer was finished, all the circumcisers poured beer over the *tudiwu* phallus-shaped containers. Having done this, they went to the mortar and splashed themselves with medicine from it. Then they arranged themselves in teams of three, a circumciser to operate, a *chifukaminu* to hold the boy steady from behind, and an assistant to carry him over the *muyombu* tree to the *mukula* log and to collect the prepuce in a *kadiwu* container.

Back at the village, all the novices were sitting in front of *ijiku daMukanda* when I returned. Their mothers had now separated from them and were standing to their right. *Kambanji* was trying, rather desperately I thought, to look brave.

The drums at the cross paths began to beat very loudly and frantically. Suddenly a novice called "*chimbu*" (the hyena) came to summon the novices and their mothers to the cross paths, where the *mukoleku* gateway should have been set up. The whole group danced around several times on the village side of the new path. The guardians and fathers of the novices rushed furiously down the new path, stripped the novices of all their clothes (should have slung them over the *mukoleku*), and dashed off to the circumciser-site, known now as *ifwilu* or *chifwilu,* "the place of dying" or as *ihung'u* or *chihung'u* "the place of suffering or affliction." The "hyena" chased the mothers back to the "fire of *Mukanda*" in the camp, where they at first wailed as at the announcement of a death. Later, as the novices' mothers told my wife, they "sang softly and cried; they felt sad and afraid, not good at all."

Now drums at the *ifwilu* began to thunder loudly to drown the cries of the novices. *Kambanji* was the first novice to be carried in—by his older brother. The latter tried to take *Kambanji* to Sampasa, for the Senior Circumciser is the one who circumcises the principal novice, but Nyaluhana who had, as of right, taken up position by the *mudyi* tree, beckoned to him and said authoritatively, "To me, Nyaluhana." *Kambanji* looked really alarmed, for he must have heard the current talk that Nyaluhana was shortsighted and shaky-handed. Anyway, he yelled out as Nyachiu, now Nyaluhana's *chifukaminu,* seized him from behind and held him steady for the operation. Most Ndembu circumcisers stretch out the prepuce, make a slight nick on top and another underneath as guides, then cut through the dorsal section with a single movement and follow this by slitting the ventral section, thus removing sufficient of the prepuce to leave the glans well exposed. What is left of the prepuce they roll back. Speed, as well as dexterity, is highly valued among a circumciser's qualifications. It must be said for Nyaluhana that although he only managed to circumcise five boys against seven each by Sampasa and Maripishi of Shika Village (the third circumciser), nevertheless the boys he operated on healed on average rather more quickly than the others. Sampasa circumcised *mwanta waMukanda,* the second novice in order of ritual precedence, and Maripishi circumcised *kaselantanda* ("he of the rising morning star"), the third. Then, as Nyaluhana had not finished cutting *Kambanji,* Sampasa took the fourth novice, *mulopu,* the last titled one other than *Kajika* "the dunce." The performances of the circumcisers were watched with keen interest by the other men and provided the occasion for disputes afterwards.

I was myself too much occupied at the *mukula* site in washing the boys' cuts with antiseptic to observe much of what happened elsewhere, but Kasonda and other Mukanza men gave me the gist of it. After circumcision, each novice was lifted by one of the circumcisers' assistants or by his guardian or by both, over the *muyombu* sapling to the *mukula* log, in no order of precedence but merely where room could be found to sit. There a *musamba* penis-support was fastened round his waist in such a way as to hold the penis upright. A grass pad (*mbung'a*) was at first held under the penis to soak up blood, and afterwards it was allowed to drop on the hollowed-out tops of the termites' nests. A custom omitted here was the practice of leading a ribbon of *musamba* bark over the tops of all the termitaries, setting fire to it, and making the boys keep their penes in the smoke. The smoke, issuing from bark string, is believed to communicate its binding-up properties to the cuts, but I was told that as I had brought European medicine, known to be very powerful, this was unnecessary.

As the boys were passed over the *muyombu* they were splashed all over the body with the medicine in the mortar.

When the first bleeding had stopped, their cuts were washed with a decoction of *kavulawumi* [13] pounded-leaf medicine, then a small piece of *musamba* leaf was placed on the tip of the penis, said to prevent urination through fright. One of the most striking and touching features of this episode was the concern shown by fathers for their sons as the latter sat on the *mukula* log with their backs to the site of circumcision. This concern was expressed in solicitous and encouraging words and gestures. When, after a while, sweet beer and a ritual repast of beans mixed with cassava mush was given to the boys, fathers broke custom by seizing the food and feeding their sons out of turn. Strictly the procedure was this: the Senior Circumciser—here Sampasa took the initiative and occupied the role—divided the mush into three small balls and put them on his circumcising knife (washed in special medicine for the purpose). First he fed the four titled novices in traditional order from *kambanji* to *mulopu*, each boy taking the knife himself and swallowing the food quickly, and then all the others in no set sequence. However, fathers grabbed pieces of mush and fed their sons by hand, growling at Sampasa's slowness.

After circumcising, the *ambimbi* washed their hands with a decoction of the following kinds of bark: *kata Wubwang'u, musesi, mubang'a, kayiza, kabalabala* and *musafwa*. Later, this mixture, in a bark-container, would be placed beside the *mubang'a* tree on which the novices urinated at night.

After the boys had been fed, the men, led by the circumcisers and *yifukaminu*, returned to the "fire of *Mukanda*." The women were still wailing as we returned with the drums. They were now lined up before the fire. As the circumcisers bore down on them, they retreated, miming fear. Then the whole group formed into a dancing circle, men in one half, women in the other. One *chifukaminu* held out the *lwalu* basket, used for carrying the circumcising equipment, for *nyishing'a* presents, and the women threw in pennies, threepenny

[13] Some said that *mupuchi* medicine was used.

bits, and strings of beads. The *kwing'ija* rites concluded with the circumcisers complaining about the meanness of the novices' mothers, after all that they had done for the boys. Sampasa told me that neither circumcisers nor novices would be washed with medicine for the next two days.

I have commented little on the last nine episodes because an analysis of their symbolism has already been published ("Three Symbols of Passage," Turner 1962b, 124–173). These episodes have an urgent dramatic unity; they are packed with symbolism.

Here is Muchona's version of the preparation of the circumcision site:

*Chikukucha hitukwinka tudiwu munfunda jejima, hitukupulisha kakusweka nfunda.*
At dawn we will put the *tudiwu* in all the *nfunda* baskets, and we will take *nfunda*.

*Chikukucha itang'wa tu-u, anyadi hiyakudya nshima de-e.*
When the sun has dawned, the novices eat up all their food completely.

*Hikubusa*[14] *nukubusa mukanda*[15] *nijing'oma nijifunda nilwalu.*
They select a site for *mukanda* with drums and *nfunda* baskets and a *lwalu* flat basket.

*Hikubusa hikuya kushikena, nfunda jejima chipu jiyedi chipu yimu*
When they have selected (a site) they go to get ready (for the novices), they put all the *nfunda* baskets, two or one

*chipu jisatu chipu jiwana hikwinka mulwalu; kuteta iyala*
or three or four in a *lwalu* basket; they cut (figurines) of a man

*namumbanda; hikukobeka kulwalu kunsewu kulwalu; hikukoka*
and a woman; they fix them in the *lwalu*, at the arrow in the *luwalu;* they drag

*manfuntanyima hikukoka ninfunda nilwalu. Anshali ambimbi enda*
backwards and drag the *nfunda* and *lwalu*. The remaining circumcisers will

*atala kwatela kukokela niMukanda kushika. Nawu henahanu dihu*
look for a place suitable for them to be dragged to and arrive at Mukanda. They say "This place

[14] See *Ku-busa isoli* in the *Chihamba* rites.
[15] *Mukanda* here means the lodge and its environs.

*hatela kushikena, henahanu hefwilu himudyi. Neyi dihu Mukanda*
is suitable for arrival, this place is the place of dying, here is a *mudyi.*" If the site of another *Mukanda*

*wekwawu mwatena wamuyombu hikuya nakuteta nikushimika mwenamuna*
is mentioned with a *muyombu* tree, they go and cut it and plant it there

*mwifwilu muna. Hikuya nakukeng'a kampobela nakukakela nakwinka*
in that (new) place of dying. They go to look for a *kampobela* (fruit) for cutting open and put it

*mwifwilu. Kunona iyala namumbanda akumani kwishina dakampobela*
in the place of dying. They take (the figurines) of a man and woman and put them under the *kampobela,*

*kwishina iyala namumbanda hewulu. Kunona nsewu hikushimika*
the man below and the woman above. They take the arrow and insert

*kweniku kumuyombu iku. Kuleta chikomu hikupapa kweniku.*
it upright here at this *muyombu.* They bring a *chikomu* peg and hammer it in here.

*Chikomu chimu ichi chikwawu ichi; chikomu diyu chikang'anjamba*
One *chikomu* is of one kind (of wood), another of another kind: one *chikomu* is of *chikang'anjamba* wood

*chikoli nikaleng'ang'ombi, ona wamung'enji waleteli Mukanda,*
(i.e., *chikoli* wood), another of *kaleng'ang'ombi* wood, it (means) the stranger who brought *Mukanda,*

*nichikwata ona wakwatang'a niyileng'i dina datapana. Didu ifwilu*
or of *chikwata* wood, the one that catches, or of *ileng'i,* the one that cuts or kills. That *ifwilu*

*dinamani tohu. Kanletenu nyana, kambanji wakutachika kutapila*
is completely finished. "Bring the children, *kambanji* is the first to be killed

*mwifwilu nimwanta waMukanda nikaselantanda. Hikutetesha nyana yejima.*
in the place of dying, then *mwanta waMukanda,* then *kaselantanda.*" They get all the children cut.

Muchona told me that "*chikomu* is a sign of strength; it stands very strongly. It may be the horn of an animal or a peg of wood, of the kinds mentioned." He said that "*kaleng'ang'ombi* comes from *kuleng'a,* "to cut into strips," and *ng'ombi,* "a cow." The hide of a cow is cut into long strips. It stands for the sharp grass which circumcised the boys long ago" (see p. 153). *Ileng'i* he also derived from *ku-lenga.*

Chimwang'a also provided an account of the circumcision rites proper:

*Budidi ambimbi akusenda ntewula jawujambuka akuya kwifwilu*
Early in the morning the circumcisers will bring their sharp razors and go to the place of dying

*nakuching'ilila anyadi. Chidikushika itang'wa budidi akutwala*
and await the novices. On arrival, early in the day, they will take away

*mwanta waMukanda, chiyakushika kwakwihi chimbu wukuhukula swayi*
*mwanta waMukanda;* when they arrive nearby the "hyena" will snatch (him) up quickly

*nakumutwala swayi kumukoleku akuna akumuketula mahinindi*
to take him away quickly to the *mukoleku* frame where they will cut his clothes [i.e., remove them]

*nakuyishiya hamukoleku, nakumutwala kudi mbimbi nakumwadika,*
and leave them on the *mukoleku,* in order to take him to the circumciser to be circumcised,

*iku adi nakwimba ng'oma yakuluwang'esha anyadi. Neyi anamwadiki dehi*
where they are playing drums to drown the sound of the novices' crying. When they have already circumcised him

*akuleta kambanji akumwadika. Chikumanayi akuleta kaselantanda.*
they bring *kambanji* and circumcise him. When he is finished they bring *kaselantanda.*

*Chikumanayi nianyadi ejima akuyitambola kudi mbimbi himbimbi*
When he is finished they take all the novices separately to each circumciser

*nakuyalamisha. Yowu mbimbi wanyakala natwesi kwadika natanu nasatu*
to get them circumcised. Any circumciser who hurries can circumcise nine

*hela ikumi. Ilang'a wajijiwila wukwadika atanu hela atanu nawumu.*
or ten. But a slow one will (only) circumcise five or six.

*Yowu mbimbi wajijiwila kwadika akumutukola kudi akweti nyana.*
Any circumciser who is slow to circumcise will be abused by everybody with children.

*Neyi anyadi ejima anamani dehi akuyishakamisha kumutondu wawulehi*
When all the novices are finished already, they will make them sit on a long,

*wututa wamukula. Ayilombola aletang'a yitumbu yakusesa*
freshly-cut *mukula* tree. The guardians bring medicines of the outer bark

*yamafulu amupuchi akwinka muchizanda nakuyikamwina kumawuyala*
and leaves of the *mupuchi* tree, put it in a potsherd and squeeze it on the penes

*awanyadi ejima. Neyi mashi anamani dehi kuhita, ayilombweji*
of all the novices. When the blood has stopped flowing, the guardians

*akuleta yitumbu yikwawu yakulamba nakukasaku njing'amuki*
will bring a different soothing medicine and bind (the penis) around

*nakachilondu kantesha*
with a very small piece of *musamba* bark-cloth.

*Kufuma ifuku dakwadika anyadi, ambimbi kwinza kudi anyadi nehi.*
After the day of circumcising novices, the circumcisers do not come to the novices.

*Hela tata yamwana wumu indi kwiji ayedi kutwesa kwinza nawa cheng'i*
Even if he is the father of one or indeed two children, he cannot come again

*nakutala anyadi nehi, mulong'a neli dehi muntu watama. Anyadi*
to look after the novices, because he has already acted (like) a bad man (towards them). The novices

*chakamonawu mbimbi wumu akutachika kumutukola matuka.*
when they see a circumciser begin to revile him.

*Mbimbi chakutiyayi hiyakumutukola yena hakutemuka kwakulehi jimu.*
When the circumciser hears them abusing him he will run as far away as he can.

*Mbimbi wamuneni wanonang'a makowa akumawuyala, amakwawu nakuyilama,*
The great (or senior) circumciser takes the (fore) skins from the penes, some to keep

*munfunda yindi nakwila nachu yitumbu nakuseng'ula awa anyadi*
in his *nfunda* basket, to make with them medicine to blow (blessing) on the novices

*nikukadiwu.*
and for *kadiwu* (medicine).

It will be noted that in this account *mwanta waMukanda* is circumcised first. According to my own observations—and every other account I have recorded—*kambanji* is circumcised first. This is because "the chief (*mwanta*) sends his war-leader (*kambanji*) before him," as one informant said.

White (1953, 46–47) makes some valuable comments on the circumcision rites proper, which both confirm and extend my own data. He writes:

> At the operation the novice is held by a person skilled in this work, known as *chifukaminu* in Lunda, *chihungu* in the other languages. The fathers normally sit some distance away, lest, it is said, they feel sorry for their children and might strike the circumciser. Among the Lunda, the novices after circumcision are placed sitting on the trunk of a *mukula* tree (*Pterocarpus angolensis*). This tree has reddish glutinous exudations from its bark which in many rites are associated with blood and fertility, hence its name from the root-*kula*, to be mature. . . .
>
> The blood of the novices, as they sit thus, is allowed to drip into a piece of grey ant-hill earth, suitably scooped out to receive it; the foreskins are also placed in it. . . .
>
> The place of circumcision is known as *fwilo* (in Luvale) or a similar derivation in other languages, denoting the place of dying, since it is there that the novices have undergone their symbolic death. In earlier days at least, even after the novices had emerged and were grown men, they avoided passing over this spot which was regarded as a graveyard. Hence the act of circumcision was euphemistically referred to as "killing." The strict terms for it are *adika* (Lunda) and *enga* (other languages). This avoidance of the *fwilo* in the past was rendered easy because the lodge was placed at a considerable distance from the village and villages moved more often than today. The *fwilo* is today no longer avoided so strictly after the novices have emerged, and indeed is often so close to the village, that avoidance would be an impossibility.

Most of these remarks are confirmed either by my observations or by my informants' accounts, but I did not see the boys' foreskins in the termitaries. Indeed, I was told that they are quickly collected by circumcisers, as both Muchona and Chimwang'a state. If they were left in the open, it is said, sorcerers might take them as ingredients for black magic medicines.

Ndembu use both *kwadika* and *kwalama* to mean the act of circumcision. In addition, they contextually specify the general terms *ku-ketula* and *ku-teta* "to cut," as meaning "to circumcise." They derive *mwadi*, "a novice" from *kwadika*. The same term is used for a senior wife. I asked if there was any connection between novices and senior wives and was told by Ndembu informants that the novices were regarded as "married by" the Lodge Instructor, whose Ndembu name *mfumwa tubwiku* or *mfumu wanyadi* means "husband of the novices." In the words of Muchona: "*Mfumwa tubwiku wahoshang'a nindi yami mfumwenu; ami nasumbuli anyadi. Ami mfumwenu nukuyilama nakuyitala* (The lodge instructor says "I am your husband; I have married novices. I am your husband, I will guard you and look after you)."

Although *kwadika* means "to circumcise," I suspect that its original sense is "to initiate," for novices in the *Mung'ong'i* society, which performs its rites at the funerals of its members, are also called *anyadi*. The term *mwadi* is applied to a chief during his installation ritual. In marriage, the original sense of *mwadi* seems to be the first wife married by a man, rather than the senior wife in a polygynous household. If this were so, all the uses of *mwadi* would be consistent. It would mean a person undergoing an experience for the first time.

One explanation offered me was that the novices at circumcision open their legs like women in marital intercourse, but this seems like a *post hoc ergo propter hoc* rationalization. However, it does appear to be compatible with the homosexual element undoubtedly present in the *Mukanda* situation. We have seen how, in the preparation of *nfunda* medicine, the apprentice-circumcisers mime copulation, and how circumcisers act likewise in the *ing'ung'u* dance. At the *kwidisha* rites we shall have further evidence of homosexual behavior in the *Nyakayowa* episode (see below, pp. 254). Moreover, White mentions (1953, 49) that during seclusion "the novices play with the penes of the *vilombola* (Luvale); this is considered to hasten healing. . . . The same is done to visitors in the lodge to help the novices to heal."

Terms used for a circumcised man include: *walama dehi, wamotoka dehi,* literally "one who jumped already," and *waya dehi kuMukanda,* "one who went already to *Mukanda*." An uncircumcised person is called *chidima, chizuzu, izuzu* or *wunabulakutooka,* "one who lacks whiteness, is impure or unlucky."

Like White, I was informed that in the past the lodge was far from the village—"over a mile away" some said.

### KUNG'ULA: SECLUSION

The seclusion phase at the *Mukanda* I witnessed lasted from June 14 until August 8, 1953, or nearly two months. This was about half as long as is usual today. The reason given was that my medicines had caused the boys to heal quickly.

This phase may conveniently be divided up as follows:

(1) The building of the lodge.

(2) The healing-up period (before the *chikula* rites).

(3) The *chikula* rites with the *makishi* masked dancers.

(4) The training of the novices (after *chikula*).

I went back to Mukanza Village after the *kwing'ija* rites, but returned to Wukengi Farm the following morning about 10 A.M. The lodge (*ng'ula*), where the novices and their guardians slept during seclusion, had already been made. Guardians present said that they had built it at dawn that very day, the novices having spent their first night of seclusion in the open. Circumcisers do not take any part in erecting the lodge, I was told. Indeed, they were forbidden to enter it. The nearest they could go was into the *ifwilu dawanyadi*. There they could call out to the boys. If the latter chose to swear at them, the circumcisers were not allowed to reply. After all, they were the ones who had made the novices suffer. However, on the first day after circumcision the circumcisers could shout stereotyped questions at the boys and they would reply in unison. (See Plate 3 for lodge where novices slept.)

The lodge was built immediately in front of the dying-place which it concealed from the view of anyone going along the old path (see Diagram 8). The novices might not enter the "dying-place" on pain of contracting leprosy or becoming idiots. The lodge was a roughly obovate structure of leafy boughs without a roof. The "dying-place" was said to be at the north, the single entrance of the lodge was said to face south, while the bed where *kambanji* slept was at the eastern end and that of *kajika* to the west. *Mwanta waMukanda*'s fire was next to *kambanji*'s and *kaselantanda*'s was next to *kajika*'s.

While I was present, a meal was given to the novices to the left of the lodge entrance. A number of balls of cassava mush cooked on the "fire of *Mukanda*" by the novices' mothers were brought in on baskets, not bowls or plates as is the general modern practice, by some junior guardians. Some duiker meat was also brought in. Two of the large round balls were given to each group of three or four boys, and two equal portions of meat. *Kambanji* was served first, then *mwanta waMukanda, kaselantanda,* and *mulopu,* each in a separate food group, then others in no set order. Each of them was given a single ball and piece of meat apiece. The meat was fed to the boys by hand, by three guardians; they ate the mush themselves, using large flat leaves as plates. They were forbidden to speak while eating, on

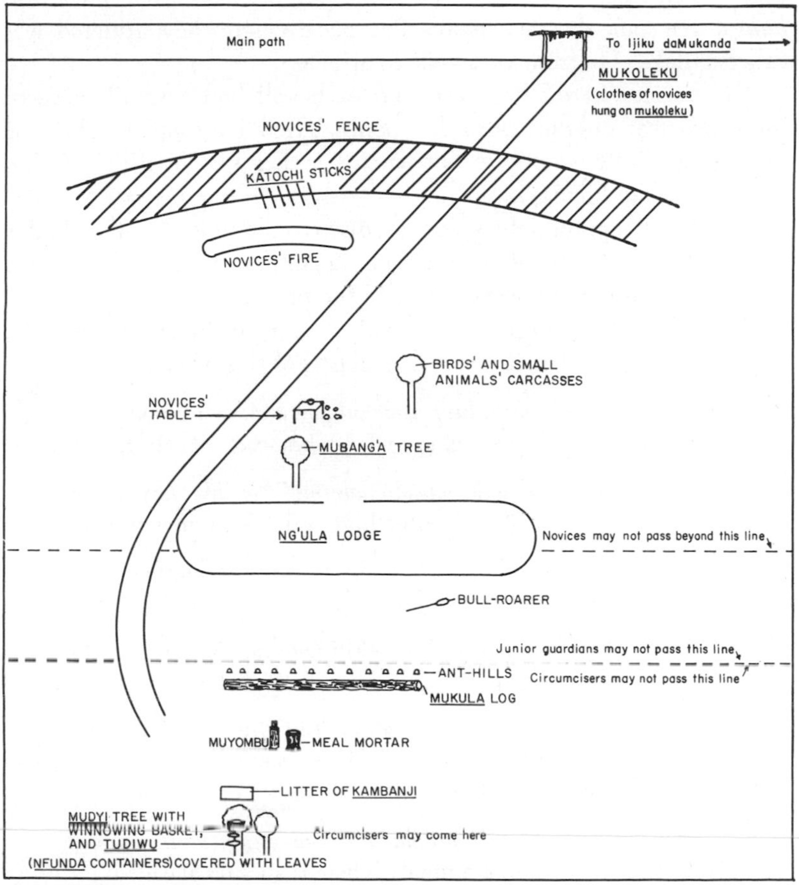


*Diagram 8*. Lodge area

penalty of a beating. A lodge official told me that they would sleep in the lodge in the same groups around the fires. These groups were based on friendship rather then kinship. After eating they all clapped in unison to signify their thanks. Then they all stamped together on thick stubs of *kabalabala* wood, called, in the speech of the lodge, *ankala* (*nkala* means "mongoose"), each picked up his stub in his left hand, and they all hopped on their left legs to the *mubang'a* tree near the entrance to the lodge. I was told that whenever a boy wanted to urinate, he should report it to his personal guardian, who would then lead him, both hopping to a *mubang'a* tree. They would not use the one near the lodge, said Wakengi, "because of the smell," but a *mubang'a* tree some distance away. The place where they urinated was called *chitekelelu* (from *ku-tekela,* to urinate).

The novices were still naked and each still had a small piece of *mubang'a* leaf on the tip of his penis. Their scars appeared to be healing up nicely. I noticed that whenever they sat down they sat on their stubs (see Plate 4).

This is an appropriate place to discuss the role of the Lodge Instructor and the guardians in greater detail than hitherto, since they play an increasingly important part in the proceedings. Regarding the Lodge Instructor, I can do no better than to begin by citing a text by Chimwang'a on the functions and attributes of this official.

*Mfumwa tubwiku diyi mukulumpi wakuhemba anyadi ejima.*
The Lodge Instructor is an elder who takes care of all the novices.

*Neyi mwadi wakata yena wukumutala nakumukwashaku nayitumbu.*
If a novice is sick he will look after him and help him with medicine.

*Neyi chilombola wunasweji kukabisha anyadi, yena wukumwinka*
If a guardian bullies the novices unduly, he will bring a case

*chilombola mulong'a hela mwadi natamishi wukumwinka mulong'a–*
against him or if a novice is naughty he will bring a case against him—

*wakutwala kumukala kudi mama yindi akafuti ifutu. Diyi wukutala*
he will take it to the village to the (novice's) mother that she may pay a fine. He is the one who will maintain

*yijila yang'ula niyatunyama. Kwekala kanyama wumu, ijina dindi*
the taboos of the lodge and of animals. There is an animal called

*nshimba, neyi mwadi wukudya mbiji yanshimba wukuwana mulong'a,*
the genet cat, if a novice should eat its meat he will find a case (i.e., have one made against him),

*wakutwala kudi amvwali jindi, akafuti ifutu. Neyi mwadi*
(the Lodge Instructor) will take it to his parents and they must pay a fine. If a novice

*wukudya imfwa, injina dindi kalolu, wukuwana mulong'a, wakafuta*
eats a kind of mouse called *kalolu* (a small species of elephant shrew), he will find a case, he will pay

*ifutu kudi mama yindi hela tata yindi hela mandumi yindi hela*
a fine. It will be paid on his behalf by his mother, father,

*kawusoku windi wukumufuntila. Kalolu amujilika mulong'a*
mother's brother or (other) relative. The elephant shrew is forbidden to him

*wukweti muvumbu wawulehi neyi mwana weyala*
because it has a long "trunk" (*muvumbu* also means foreskin), like a boy

*chekalang'ayi namuvumbu kuwuyala henonu kanda amwadiki.*
when he has a foreskin on his penis before he is circumcised.

*Dichi nawu bayi kumudaku mulong'a wukweti muvumbu ni iseng'i*
Therefore they (the Lodge Instructors) say "Do not eat it because it has a trunk, nor the large elephant shrew."

*Cheng'i nawu neyi mwadi wukudya kajila ijina dindi mbang'ala*
Again, they say, "If a novice eats a bird called the guinea fowl

*chinjila wukukata musong'u wambumba mulong'a mujimba windi*
(it is taboo) he will catch leprosy because its body

*wamang'alamang'ala neyi mbumba. Nawa cheng'i neyi mwadi*
is covered with spots like leprosy. Yet again, if a novice

*wukudya nkala wukufwa mwitala, mulong'a nkala diyi mutondu*
were to eat the *nkala* species of mongoose, he will die in the hut (i.e., become impotent), because *nkala* is the (name of the) piece of *kabalabala* wood

*wachikunku chakabalabala hakushakama mwadi neyi chitwamu chindi*
on which the novice sits as his chair

*mafuku akumwadikawu. Kuyinata chinjila; ching'a kuyihemba*
in the days after he has been circumcised. It is taboo to throw them away; they must be cared for

*nakuyilemesha mafuku ejima sampu mwadi nediki.*
and honored every day until the novice comes out."

*Mfumwa tubwiku nindi neyi kansi nalawuli kambunji ching'a*
The Lodge Instructor says when a child has snared a *kambunji* mongoose,

*kumusenda hamukambu wakutembuka nakutula, chinjila*
"You must carry it on a carrying pole to put it down, it is taboo

*kumusendela mumakasa hela kukasila hefunda; mama yenona*
to carry it in the hands or tie it up in a bundle; mother over there

*kumukala wakahana ifutu. Yijila yejima yayilejang'awu;*
at the village will pay a fine." All taboos are explained;

*anyadi kuMukanda ching'a kuyihemba nonu hela nuku mukala*
the novices at *Mukanda* must keep them perfectly, even when they are in the village

*ching'a kuyihemba hohu. Neyi mwadi nafumi dehi kuMukanda*
they must keep them perfectly. When the novice has gone away to the lodge

*neyi nakeng'i kudya mbiji yanshimba ching'a kwinza kudi*
if he wants to eat the meat of genet cat he must come to

*mfumwa tubwiku hela kudi mbimbi hela kudi tata hela mandumi*
the Lodge Instructor or to a circumciser or to his father or maternal uncle

*nakumuseng'ula namafu epupa mumbulukutu nihehama. Kanyama*
to have leaves of the *ipupa* tree spat upon his temples and brow. Animal

*hakanyama kakukeng'a kudayi ching'a kumuseng'ula hohu.*
after animal (that are tabooed) he wants to eat he must have medicine spat upon him properly.

*Neyi wukudya chakadi kumuseng'ula wukukata musong'u wambumba*
Were he to eat without being medicated he will fall ill with the disease of leprosy

*hela kuhewuka. Mpang'u jejima jaMukanda kujishimuna kumukala*
or become stupid. It is taboo to explain any of the secrets of *Mukanda* at the village

*kudi ambanda chinjila hela kudi amazuzu. Ambanda ejima*
to women or to uncircumcised men. All women

*akuhosha kudi anyadi nawu tulejenu mpang'u yaMukanda*
who say to the novices "Tell us the secret of *Mukanda*

*akwandala mbumba hela musong'u wacheng'i neyi anyadi anediki*
will catch leprosy or another disease when the novices have come out

*kuMukanda.*
at *Mukanda.*

Muchona added a few words on the economic functions of the Lodge Instructor:

*Nindi wunajahi nimumoni aleti kudi ami atwali kwijiku daMukanda*
He says: "I must see anyone who has made a kill; he must bring (it) to me. It must be taken to the 'fire of *Mukanda*,'

*chili nyama chili inshi chili imfwa, kutota wuchi, ching'a*
whether it be game, fish, or rodents; if honey is collected, you must

*muletang'a kudi ami yinashali nukudya, yinashali yakwijiku daMukanda*
bring me what remains to eat, what is left from the 'fire of *Mukanda*'
*kulonda mudyang'a nachu nshima jeyi. Neyi nshima yinenzi dehi*
that you may eat it with your cassava mush." When cassava mush has already come
*atulilang'a hakaweji. Yena enza nukwinza hakunona menji hakwisuka,*
they put it on the *kaweji* (table of woven twigs). He (the Lodge Instructor) comes, water is brought up, he washes his hands,
*hakwanazang'ana yikanka nimbiji hela anshi hela mafu. Wukwanzang'ana*
he divides the mush (into) portions with meat or fish or leaf relish. He does the dividing
*diyu yena hohu hela hamukwashang'aku kudi kalombola, diyi mwanyikindi*
by himself alone, or he may be helped by a junior guardian—it is his younger brother
*wamukwashang'aku mfumwa tubwiku.*
who helps the Lodge Instructor.

Chimwang'a has something to say about the guardian who brings food to the novices, and about the behavior of the novices in the first period of seclusion:

*Ona ching'a ekali wakadi kwilang'u wuvumbi hela kumotoka*
(The man who brings food) must not be someone who indulges in fornication or who breaks (literally "jumps") all the
*yisela yayidika yejima. Anyanyadi chakuhondawu makumbu anshima,*
ritual customs. When the novices' mothers have made balls of mush,
*ona iyala wukuketula nshima muyikanka hejiku hejiku muyadilang'awu*
that man will divide the mush into portions for each fire where the novices eat.

*Ching'a chakudya nachu chamuchidi wumu hohu hela inshi hanshi hela*
A single kind of relish must be eaten with it only,[16] whether it be fish,
*mbiji hambiji hela mafu hamafu neyi kanda alukuku. Ching'a kudya*
meat, or leaf relish, if they have not yet left (the lodge).[17] It must be eaten
*mwasamuka ni amama jawu kumukala hamu.*
without salt, and their mothers in the village must observe the same rule.

[16] Different kinds of relish must not be eaten at the same meal. Note the general emphasis laid on "unity" and avoidance of "promiscuity."

[17] This refers to the period before the *chikula* rites, while the novices' wounds are healing. They must remain in the lodge precincts during this time and not go hunting in the bush.

The interdiction against divulging the secrets of the lodge has little force today, as a result both of the influence of missionaries and of the scepticism resulting from the crucial experience of labor migration.

I returned to the lodge a week after my last visit and found many changes there. The *mukoleku* frame, "forgotten" on the day of circumcision, had been erected shortly after I had left the previous week. It was clearly made of *Mukula* wood, and the novices' ragged clothes were now draped neatly over the crossbar, instead of lying higgledy-piggledy on the path where they had been torn off on the way to the operation. Women were forbidden to pass beyond it.

A fence of leafy branches called *chipang'u chanyadi* had been built along the old path to hide the lodge from passers-by. Between fence and lodge the bush had been completely cleared. A table of woven *mukula* twigs, called *kaweji,* had been placed to the right of the lodge door. Beneath it lay half-eaten balls of cassava mush and scraps of other food. These had to remain there until the end of *Mukanda.* Only novices were allowed to eat these balls which were openly compared with testicles by my companions from Mukanza and Kafumbu Villages. (See Plate 5 showing table and half-eaten food.)

On the higher branches of one tree in the clearing hung small birds snared or shot by the guardians, and near its foot were hung small rodents trapped by them. These would be used as relish. Not far from the fence was a long fire, called *lwowa.* Novices had to sit along the lodge side of this fire to receive instruction from the elders who sat facing them. No novice could pass beyond it into the space between *lwowa* and fence.

From behind the lodge came a grunting sound which Kasonda, who was with me, likened to that of a bush-pig (*chombu*). I went behind and saw one of the junior guardians (from Machamba Village) whirling a "bull-roarer," a fish-shaped piece of carved *mukula* [18] wood, around his head. He told me that it was called *"ndumba mwila." Ndumba* means "lion," but nobody could tell me the meaning of *mwila* except that it was a word "from long, long ago." The novices later sang a song about *ndumba mwila,* as follows: *Ndumba kanyaṁa kamafumbu ndumba wo-o ehe ndumbo katuka wudanyi oho ndumba o-o oho.* The lion (is) the animal of round pad marks, the lion rises up and catches someone, the lion.

[18] I was told by the Lodge Instructor that *kapwipu* wood is sometimes used for this purpose.

Like bull-roarers all over the world, this one, I was informed, had the function of frightening novices and their mothers. In the past the latter were told that a monster had come to swallow up their sons. The men had a good, knowing laugh at that one.

The sacred area behind the lodge, strictly tabooed to all the novices, was itself divided into two. The space between the *mukula* log and the lodge could be entered by junior guardians, but they could not pass beyond the log into the "*ifwilu*" proper. The guardian who had swung the bull-roarer had to stay in this section. Senior guardians and other elders could enter the *ifwilu,* but only circumcisers and very senior men, who had attended many performances, could come close to the *mudyi* tree beneath which *kambanji* had been circumcised, the sacred focus of the whole *Mukanda.* On this tree were now placed the *lwalu* basket of the senior circumciser (Nyaluhana), and in a fork two new *tudiwu* containers which, I was told, held the foreskins of the boys recently circumcised. On the tree were also placed skeins of bark-strings wound round sticks. These were taken from *katochi* trees and would be used in the making of *makishi* costumes.

While we were standing near the *mudyi* tree the Lodge Instructor, Kutona, asked me if Europeans knew of medicines "to give them a strong erection." I said that they had such medicines, but that people bought them privately, for "it was a matter of much shame." He replied that "African people" felt little shame about using such medicines. The best aphrodisiac was that given to a young bridegroom (*kalemba*) at his first marriage, when he was about to sleep with a girl who had just completed her puberty rites. This consisted of three pots of warm medicine, containing respectively pounded bark-scrapings and leaves of *kapwipu, mubang'a,* and *chikoli.* These were all "important *Mukanda* trees" which, being hard and strong themselves, would give a man a hard and strong penis, and would enable him to copulate many times in a single night, pausing only for urination. Indeed, if he could not act thus, his wife would despise him and signify her scorn to her ritual instructress (*nkong'u*), who would come early in the morning, by holding up a bent piece of grass behind his back for her secret inspection. I mention this conversation because it indicates the connection that Ndembu make between male and female initiation.

I noticed a red *nduwa* (lourie) feather inserted in the mouth of one of the *tudiwu* containers, and was told that it was Sampasa's.

The Lodge Instructor then mentioned that the boys' cuts were regularly washed with pounded leaf medicine (*nsompu*) taken from the following trees and shrubs: *mubang'a, muneku, kakenineki, chikwata* (fruits as well) and *musong'asong'a.* He said that, after the lodge was made, Nyaluhana had put a potsherd containing "medicine of *chikoli* and *ileng'i*" in the lodge to prevent the novices having bad dreams about their operation. On the novices' fence were hung the sticks of *katochi* from which the bark had been spirally stripped.

I discussed several of the matters mentioned with the lodge elders. They told me that the special term for the novices' food used in *Mukanda* was *nkalata.* Before *chikula,* the mothers cook collectively for all the novices. After *chikula,* each mother cooks for her own son only.

I was told that the *nkala* stub stands for the novice's penis—"if a boy leaves his *nkala* he will leave his penis." He must rest his head on the *nkala* at night and sit on it at meals and while resting. When he stands in the lodge he must place one foot on it. After *chikula,* novices are allowed to leave their *ankala* at the lodge when they hunt in the bush, but they must sit on them when they return, before they do anything else.

The ingredients of the medicine for washing the circumcision wounds were explained to me by the elders of Mukanza Village when I returned.

*Mubang'a* wood is strong. *Muneku* comes from *kunekuka namuchima,* "to change one's mind, think better of." It has the property of causing a witch or sorcerer to change his mind and withdraw if he wishes to harm the novice. *Kakenineki* has big white flowers which "laugh aloud" (*ku-kenama*). Because they are white and swell up, they make the medicine give strength and good luck. *Chikwata* has thorns to catch people strongly. *Musong'asong'a* is called *muvulama,* from *ku-vulama,* to forget. It means to make a witch "forget" to bewitch the novices. *Chikoli* has a very hard wood like *mubang'a.* Neither wind nor rain nor ants can eat it. It gives a hard penis and a strong body.

Both *muneku* and *muvulama* are used at funerary rites where it is thought that many witches and sorcerers are gathered to eat the corpse. They are used to protect members of the funeral camp against witches.

At the lodge I was told that in the past, *katochi* sticks were "used to make fire," presumably as fire drills. At *kwidisha* the novices take *katochi* sticks when they are carried back to their mothers and bang them behind their heads. *Ileng'i* is used in many medicines, not only because its canes "cut" and "stab" (*ku-tapa*) but also because it grows very fast. Children treated with it will also grow very fast, it is believed.

The elders also told me that the guardians of the boys were often their own fathers, their circumcised older brothers, or "just special friends." Table I indicates clearly the importance of sibling and father/son ties in allocating the role of guardian. It will be noted from Diagram 4 that in this lodge five of the nine guardians looked after their uterine brothers, and one after his classificatory "brothers." Since

*Table 1.* The relationship of novices to guardians in *Mukanda*

| Relationship | No. | Relationship | No. |
|---|---|---|---|
| Brothers | 7 | brothers and classificatory brothers | 10 |
| Mother's sister's sons | 3 | | |
| Sons | 3 | sons and classificatory sons | 5 |
| Mother's mother's sister's daughter's daughter's son | 1 | | |
| "Son" | 1 | | |
| Mother's brother's son | 1 | cross-cousin | 1 |
| Daughter's son | 1 | grandson | 1 |
| No relative | 2 | | 2 |
| Total | 19 | | 19 |

guardians sleep in the same group as their charges, and since brothers are often initiated together, most sleeping groups are dominantly sets of brothers. Two of the guardians, including the Lodge Instructor, were looking after their own sons. I was assured that maternal uncles seldom look after their nephews, "because maternal uncles may become their fathers-in-law, and it would be shameful for them to share the matters of the lodge together." It is also possible (my own view) that since maternal uncles are "male mothers" the ritual separation from mothers partially applies to them also, although as males they are allowed to visit the lodge.

I was informed by the lodge officials that two days after circumcision the novices were taken to a river to wash. There the following medicines were applied to the penis: *musenji* bark scrapings; *musafwa* bark, pounded, in cold water; *kasasanji* leaves chewed then bandaged round the glans. All these had astringent and drying properties.

Next, I was given a much fuller list of food taboos. These took effect from the time that *kambanji* first ceremonially summoned the Senior Circumciser. They included the flesh of a wide range of striped and spotted animals and birds. To eat them would bring leprosy. Among them were zebra, bushbuck, serval cats, striped mice, a striped kingfisher, and a songbird with a spotted head called *mulundu*. Another group of birds and fish had red markings; eating them would cause excessive bleeding at circumcision. They included the red-legged bare-throated francolin, the red-winged lourie, and a red-breasted species of bream. Permission to eat these could be obtained during *Mukanda* if *ku-seng'ula* medicine was first applied by spitting. Most of the food taboos held good after *Mukanda* but were gradually relaxed as men grew older. Nevertheless, Kasonda had not yet eaten zebra meat thirty years after circumcision, even though some had recently been offered to him by an Angolan meat hawker. The lodge itself was sometimes called "the elephant" (*nzovu*).

My wife discussed the role of the novices' mothers with the women at the parents' camp, writing down texts of their answers. She confirmed that until *chikula* all the women cooked together for the novices, not for their own children only. If a mother lived far away, say in another chiefdom, the others would cook for her child afterwards or she could arrange for a kinswoman living locally to do it. If a boy's father was at the camp, his wife would cook for him in the camp as well as for the novices. If he remained in his village, his other wife or wives would cook for him, or, if there were none, his sister or niece.

Mothers must not use salt in cooking "until the *makishi* come out at *chikula*." Salt is "*wawutowala*" and tastes like blood (*neyi mashi*). If either the novices or their mothers ate salt, the boys' cuts would not heal. This would also be the case if the mothers slept with their husbands before *chikula*. Furthermore, if the mothers ate salt they would break out in boils when they were washed with medicine at *chikula*.

It will be remembered in this connection that semen is thought of as a kind of blood "mixed with water." One of the songs sung at the *Wubwang'u* or twin ritual refers to sexual intercourse as being like "sweet honey" (*wuchi wawutowala*). *Ku-towala*, in fact, means both "sweet" and "salty." Male informants have told me that the sexual fluids are "salty." Thus it would appear that Ndembu make a connection between the ideas "blood," "semen," "salt," and "intercourse." The fact that both intercourse and the eating of salt are tabooed means more, therefore, than the mere abstention from different kinds of pleasure while the novices are in discomfort. The prohibitions are intrinsically related.

The women told my wife that, far from dreading the appearance of masked *makishi,* who would appear at *chikula,* they wanted them to come, for it meant that the boys' wounds had healed and that the taboos would be lifted on sexual intercourse and the eating of salt. They confessed that they "felt a little fear of the *makishi*" who were "dead people" (*afu*) of "long ago" (*ahashankulu*).

Kasonda and I made several more visits to the lodge before *chikula.* On the last visit I made, about a week before *chikula,* the costume of the single *ikishi* was almost completed, but its mask had not yet been carved.

On one occasion, we had with us a man from Kafumbu Village who had not been present on the day of circumcision. The novices were standing on their own side of the long *lwowa* (or *mwowa*) fire in the lodge enclosure when we arrived. Seeing this man, Kantumoya, they all seized switches of pliant wood that were lying around and threatened to beat him, crying out in unison, "*towolola* (display your penis)." At circumcision, all men present must do this to prove that they have been circumcised. Kantumoya, not having established his circumcised state until then, was obliged to show the novices his penis. In revenge, he grabbed hold of an *nkala* stub held by the nearest novice and shouted "*zandamenu!* (lift a leg)." All the novices promptly either stood on one leg or lay down with one leg in the air. Then Kantumoya picked up an ax handle from the enclosure and ran with it to the dying-place. While he remained there the boys were compelled to retain their stance. Indeed, if any man is present who has been circumcised at an earlier date than the others, all his juniors must take one leg off the ground when he shouts "*zandamenu!*" If an initiated man seizes two *ankala* stubs, the novices must lie down with both legs held in the air. When Kantumoya returned from the dying-place, he tossed the *nkala* back to its owner, and all the novices put theirs on the ground and stood and stamped on them.

When novices greeted their young initiated friends, they had to touch them lightly on the hands instead of gripping hard. If they gripped hands, this was said to delay the healing of their wounds.

A few of the boys had healed up by this time. These were allowed to go into the bush to catch animals and birds, and to fish with the guardians. Guardians skilled in bushcraft taught the novices how to track different kinds of game, how to make traps and snares properly, and the techniques of fishing. Any kills they made were hung up on the tree mentioned above and could only be eaten by guardians and novices.

Novices had to make set responses to riddles and formulas put to them by elders. If they were slow or failed to answer correctly, they were beaten. Formerly, it was said, they would have been punished as slaves were, by being hung by the neck in the fork of a tree.

Not only novices, but also junior guardians, were punished for breaches of lodge discipline. According to the lodge elders, the main purpose of seclusion was to teach junior guardians as well as novices to respect and obey their elders. They had to maintain a modest demeanor, only speak when spoken to, fetch and carry anything required at the double, and run errands. One junior guardian was brought before Nyaluhana and Wukengi at the parents' camp in my presence and was severely rebuked for talking loudly about lodge matters in the hearing of the women cooking at the "fire of *Mukanda.*" As punishment he had to carry all the water wanted by the novices for several days. The *Mukanda* officials could form an *ad hoc* court of their own, Nyaluhana said, and were not liable to the chief's jurisdiction on *Mukanda* matters. If a boy died during *Mukanda,* no action could be brought against these officials by his relatives in a chief's court. God (*Nzambi*) alone is responsible, he said. Junior guardians were held partly responsible for the good conduct of novices in their charge and could be ordered by senior guardians and other elders to beat them. They also had to keep watch in turn at night in case women or other unauthorized persons approached the lodge. Senior guardians wove the *makishi* costumes, junior guardians swung the bull-roarer.

Novices are given verbal instruction not only by the appointed lodge officials, but also by other elders from near and far who decide to visit the lodge. They are enjoined not to swear, to refrain from adultery when they leave *Mukanda,* not to steal, not to lie, to be brisk in performing tasks given them by senior men, to be hospitable, not to jeer at the aged, but to laugh and be affable with their peers. They are told to be brave, like lions, when they go hunting. What is there to fear, when they have known the circumciser's razor? They are warned not to dabble in sorcery.

Before *chikula,* however, punishment by beating tends to be light, I was told. Beating is frequent after *chikula,* and in the past they would have had to undertake such dangerous tasks as collecting honey from the nests of wild bees wearing only a *fwefweta* (grass girdle).

Most of White's remarks on seclusion refer to Luvale lodges, but he makes some references to Lunda lodges, and some of his observations cover practices common to Lunda, Luvale, Chokwe, and Luchazi. The following summary is taken from pp. 47–50 (1953) of his account.

The lodge is an oblong enclosure; the Lunda lodge has a single entrance only, in the front. White writes that at Mwinilunga, lodges are roofed over, but the one at Wukengi was open to the sky, as were others on which I have information at Nswanamundong'u and Ntambu Villages. In a Lunda lodge the individual fires of the novices are placed down the center of the lodge. White mentions that novices sleep in pens of sticks, in pairs; at Wukengi there were no pens. He also says that in all the lodges the guardians sleep in a row along the inside of the front wall and the novices in a row along the back wall. I did not see the lodge at night, but was assured by the officials that, as mentioned, guardians and novices slept together in groups of siblings and friends, around the fires. I have seen marks of burning on the legs of novices who were said to have slept too close to the fires.

White mentions that in Lunda lodges the place where the novices urinate (*chitekelelu*) is marked by a stake of *mubang'a* stuck in the ground. I was shown a *mubang'a* tree which the novices slapped as decribed before urinating. My informants' remark agrees with White's when he says that Lunda have to go outside to urinate at nights.

The word *lwowa* for the ritual fire, says White, is one of the esoteric terms of the rites and must not be used among women. Lunda lodges have only one *lwowa,* outside the lodge, and it runs lengthwise. A magic peg (*shiza*) is placed at either end to avert evil.[19] The fire serves as a gathering point for the occupants of the lodge; they warm themselves by it and stand by it to sing and cheer. Nothing must be burned on it or cooked on it; it must not be used to light tobacco—this point was not raised at Wukengi.

[19] Muchona told me that *shiza* is the same as *yikomu,* "pegs." They are hammered (*ku-popa*), not only at each end of the *lwowa,* but also at the "fire of *Mukanda.*"

White describes a point in the back wall of the lodge, called *ndambi* [20] marked by a projecting forked stick. It is a forbidden ritual spot. The novices must not look at it and hence when entering the lodge must lower their heads. Any food left over by the novices is taken and thrown over the *ndambi*. While the novices are outside the lodge during the daytime, they must always face away from the *ndambi,* which is symbolic of the childhood they have left behind them. As we have seen, in the lodge I visited, remnants of food are placed under the *kaweji* table beside the lodge door. I did not observe such a stick at Wukengi, but informants have told me that in the past it was customary to have one.

In Lunda lodges, according to White, a stake called *mwima* is placed outside the lodge at the back near the *ndambi*. On it is placed a flat basket containing medicines provided by the circumciser, the unwashed knife of the circumciser, a small calabash of medicine used by him to anoint the backs of the novices, and the red wing feather of a lourie. According to my observations and information, the *mwima* stake was placed on the *mudyi* tree under which *kambanji* was circumcised, and was also called *muchanka waMukanda*. The circumciser washed his knife immediately after the operation and gave novices their first meal from it, there was no calabash of medicine on the *lwalu* and the lourie feather was inserted into Sampasa's *kadiwu* container.

White's observations agree with my own when he writes that the novices wear no clothes in the first period of seclusion; but their penes were not enclosed in leaves tied with bark rope, as he states, at any rate after the first few days. When the guardians dress the wounds, the novices must not look at the wounds; I did not observe the process of dressing the wounds.

According to White, the novices sleep with a stick to keep their legs from chafing the wound; this stick is always called "dog." This probably refers to Luvale. Among Ndembu the stick or stub is called *nkala,* "mongoose" and is said to be used as a pillow.

I can confirm White's remarks that it is not permitted in Lunda lodges for infants to visit and that a stranger is required to exhibit his penis if there is doubt as to whether he is circumcised. White says

[20] Muchona said that *ndambi* meant the bits of food themselves thrown over the lodge.

that the Lunda term for this is *kutoholola* (which I heard as *kutowolola*).

The novices may not wash during this period, writes White; the "blood friendship" which is implicit in those who have shared the rite together is commonly interpreted as being symbolized by the fact that they have eaten each other's uncleanness during this period when eating together.

According to White, contact with fire is forbidden to the novices before they have healed; they may not gather firewood and may not touch dead embers of fire or stir up their fires at night themselves; the attendants must collect the firewood and at night, if his fire is low, the novice must arouse his *chilombola* to stir it up. Contact with fire is deemed likely to impede effective healing (see Turner, *Drums of Affliction,* Chapter VIII).

In considering White's observations in connection with my own, it would appear that while there are many common features, there is a good deal of variation not only between these tribes but also within each tribe from one performance to another. The same ideas and symbolic themes may be represented by different symbols in different performances.

My own observations on *chikula* are rather scanty because I missed the first part of the rites and omitted to get a full description of them from informants. I will give a generalized picture of what I have gleaned about the first part of the rites from various informants, including Chief Ikelenge, Kasonda, and Sakutoha, and then give my own observations of the later stages.

When the novices are adjudged to be fully recovered from the wounds and shock of circumcision, and when the *makishi* costumes and masks have been made, the Lodge Instructor asks the Establisher to tell the novices' mothers and other women to brew much beer—say ten or twelve calabashes for the *chikula* rites. Chief Ikelenge told me that these rites were called *chikosa chikula,* and both he and Kasonda agree that there are traditionally two *chikula* rituals, *chikula chanyanya,* or "small *chikula,*" when the novices are first washed ritually and the *makishi* first appear, and *chikula cheneni,* which comes between *chikula chanyanya* and the concluding rites of *kwidisha.*

The women are told that if beer is poured in the dying-place, the *makishi* will come out of the ground and begin to dance. Like the women, the novices believe that the *makishi* are "dead people" (*afu*).

They are also informed that the Lodge Instructor is going to pray with *mpemba* in the dying-place to an *ikishi,* "which is a terrible thing that stays under the ground" (*kukalung'a kachinana,* "in the red grave"). Early in the morning of the *chikula,* the novices see many guardians going behind the lodge. They see calabashes of beer taken behind. Then loud singing begins. The children are lifted on the backs of guardians and other men. Others stand behind to prevent them running away. They are greatly afraid, but must stay facing the lodge. Suddenly, two *makishi,* the first one called *Mvweng'i,* then a second called *Katotoji,* appear, led by the Lodge Instructor. They swiftly approach the boys and beat them with their sticks. The fathers console their boys, telling them they will not be beaten again by the *makishi.* After this, the *makishi,* accompanied by elders, go to the "fire of *Mukanda.*" There all the women in the vicinage are obliged to be present. Unlike Luvale *makishi,* the Ndembu ones do not beat the women, for it is said that if women touch them they will contract leprosy. The women must gather around the *makishi* and sing while the latter conduct in dumb show. The *makishi* bring salt with them, which is handed out by their accompanying guardians to all the fathers and mothers of novices. Then the *makishi* are led to the village *nyiyombu* tree-shrines and given the names of remote male ancestors.

At some time, either before or after the appearance of the *makishi,* the novices were anointed with *ku-seng'ula* medicine, made from *mukombukombu* and *mututambululu* leaves chewed up by the Lodge Instructor and spat on the wrists, inner elbow joints, shoulders, and behind the ears of the novices. This was to prevent them dreaming about the *makishi.* Uncircumcised boys and youths who had not taken part in the earlier stages of the ritual were similarly treated at the parents' camp. When the medicine is applied the *ikishi* leans close to the youngster treated, almost touching him.

On the same morning, after the coming of the *makishi,* the novices are taken to a stream and totally immersed in it. Then they are washed by the Lodge Instructor with a new *nsompu* medicine called *yitumbu yachikula,* consisting of the pounded leaves of *musoli, munjimbi, museng'u, kabalabala, muhotuhotu, mubang'a, musesi wehata, musesi wezenzela, mulumbulumbu, muhuma,* and *mukonkola.* The medicine is kept in the *lwalu* basket used by the Senior Circumciser at circumcision.

The novices now dig up the roots of a certain tree, extract fibers from them, and make themselves skirts called *fwefweta,* which they must wear until *kwidisha*. They are then sent into the bush to trap small animals and snare birds on their own account, the catch going to the guardians.

Later that day the *makishi* dance again in the parents' camp and the sponsoring village. The novices' parents and the circumcisers and their wives are expected to have ritual intercourse that night. The novices' mothers cook food for the boys containing the salt given to them by the *makishi*.

I have collected a number of texts on *makishi*, describing their general form and functions, differences between specific *makishi*, and the behavior of those who dance in the costumes.

Muchona discusses the problem of the relationship between ancestor shade (*mukishi*) and the dancing mask and costume (*ikishi*)—a problem that perplexes and divides Ndembu quite as much as it does anthropologists. He told me: "*Mukishi ona wafwili iyanatunguwu mwikishi yamwekani kumesu anyana nikumesu awambanda nanyanta*. (A shade is someone who died made up into [the form of] an *ikishi* [costume] which is visible before children and before women and chiefs)." He went on to say that the dancer represents the "body of the shade" (*mujimba wamukishi*). "That shade (*mukishi*) came from the *muyombu* tree planted in the dying-place at circumcision. That is where the Lodge Instructor prayed." He continued:

The shade of *ikishi* (*mukishi wekishi*) is for famous men such as chiefs, hunters, rich men, men with many children or who have important ancestors (*ankakulula*). The *ikishi* dancer is supposed to be helped by that shade.

Up to four *makishi* come to visit the novices before *chikula chanyanya*. Before they come, the boys are given *ku-seng'ula* medicine, so that they may not be afraid. The first time they are seen, they beat the children, not afterwards.

A woman would contract leprosy if she slept with an *ikishi* dancer. Such a dancer must wash with *chikula* medicine before he returns to the village after dancing. The medicine is to purify or cleanse himself on the body (*yitumbu yakuditookesha nachu mujimba hela yakudikosa nachu hamujimba*).

According to Muchona:

*Katotoji* should be the first *ikishi* to appear to the novices. He wears an *nkambi* kilt of stiff grasses, like the novices at *kwidisha*. Like the novices also he carries two sticks and beats them together. He is the cleverest one, he beats the boys with his sticks, or anyone who laughs at him. He moves very quickly. *Chafwana!* (It is terrible or dangerous!)

The song sung by women for *Katotoji* runs as follows: "*Katotoji wenze-e woho wenze-e wajila mwikeki wenze woho wenze-e mwitala weng'ilang'a wenze wohoho wenze* (*Katotoji* comes. He comes, he prevents [people from standing] in the veranda, he comes into the hut, he enters, he comes, he comes)."

His behavior was further described by Muchona as "being completely fierce all the time (*ku-zuwang'ang'a chikupu*)." He makes people run "by acting in a mad way." He derived the name "*Katotoji*" from *ku-totola* "to go on chopping trees" (*to-to-to*), abandoning them without cutting them down—a reference to circumcision.

The other authentic Ndembu *ikishi*—most of the ones seen today in Mwinilunga, he told me, were borrowed from Luvale—is *Mvweng'i,* which he described as "a wide one with many strings hanging down." He is "the chief of the *makishi. Mvweng'i* feels heavy and wears an *nkambi* kilt and strings. He carries an *mpwambu* hunting bell. He looks this way and that, and makes people dream. His whole face looks as though it were blinking. He is called *nkaka* 'grandfather.' " They sing for him as follows:

*Kako nkaka eyo nkaka eyo eyo nkaka yetu nenzi, eyo eyo, nkata yetu*
Grandfather, o grandfather, our grandfather has come, our grandfather
*mwanta; mbwemboye mbwemboye yawume-e mwang'u watulemba mbwemboye*
chief; the glans penis, the glans is dry, a scattering of *tulemba* spirits, the glans
*yawumi. Wenze wawani ikishi wawombe-e ohohoho wenze, wawani ikishi.*
is dry. He comes that you may find an *ikishi,* he goes secretly, he comes that you may find an *ikishi.*

The song represents the healing of the boy's cuts. *Tulemba* are modes of manifestation of ancestor shades, or possibly in the far past, nature-spirits, which cause the death of infants and are propitiated in the ritual of the women's cult *Kalemba.* The song would appear to mean that influences inimical to the boys' welfare, represented by *tulemba,* are dispersed by the arrival of the *makishi,* which show that the boys are healed up. *Mvweng'i* himself is thought to be dangerous to women's fertility, for women who have miscarriages are believed to dream of *Mvweng'i.* The *Isoma* ritual to propitiate ancestor shades, who "have come out in *Isoma* or *Kabwiza,*" contains several references to *Mukanda*: the circumcision song, "*kwalamo-o,*" is sung when a red cock is sacrificed near the end of the performance, and the *Isoma*

5. Utensils employed for carrying food to the novices from the "fire of *Mukanda*" at the camp where their mothers dwell and cook for them during their seclusion. Uneaten food is not consumed later or thrown away but collected under the framework.

6. The *ikishi* Chizaluki surveys a village in the neighborhood of the circumcision lodge, fly-switch in hand. Note the beard, symbol of chiefly authority.

7. Chizaluki dances in a village, while women sing his "theme" song.

8. An elder from the circumcision lodge blows medicine in a baby's ear so that the latter "will not dream" about Chizaluki.

mode of dancing is a gentle rhythmical swaying, called *ku-punjila,* which resembles the swaying of the *Mvweng'i ikishi* dancer.

Other *makishi* that appear occasionally at Ndembu rituals, according to Muchona, include: *Mudimbula,* similar to *Katotoji* with a long tapering pipe on the top of the head; *Chikumbu,* "the bald one" (baldness is the mark of an elder, say Ndembu), called *kashinakaji,* "the old man (or woman in other contexts)" or *mukulumpi,* "the elder," for *Chikumbu* "walks like an old man, doddering and nodding sleepily"; and *Chizaluki* "the mad one," which appeared at Wukengi Farm (see Plate 6). These are borrowed *makishi;* Ndembu and other Lunda generally have few *makishi,* in contrast to the other Balovale tribes, who sometimes have a dozen or more at a single performance. Traditionally, indeed, Ndembu have only *Katotoji* and *Mvweng'i.* Recently, Ndembu have also borrowed the Luvale *Mwana Pwevo* "the young woman," under the name of *Chileya yawambanda* "the fool of the women."

Sandombu, one of my Mukanza Village informants who had danced *Katotoji* himself on various occasions, spoke of the role of *ikishi* dancers in the following terms:

> If the shade to whose name one succeeds wishes one to dance in an *ikishi* costume, it will sway about inside.
>
> The costume (*ikishi*) is made at the lodge. When it is completed then you will feign (*ku-lumbisha*) that it has a different name. For example, Lupinda, that Lupinda who has died, he is the one you have pretended has come into the *ikishi.* You come with him (from the lodge) into a village, you tell lies about him (to the effect) that he is Lupinda who died long ago. All the people assemble to see that Lupinda. They bring a mat to put near the *nyiyombu* trees, they bring a stool to put on the mat, they bring a goat or two fowls, they bring *mpemba* powder, they pray to the shade they have pretended is in the *ikishi.* They pray and give him that goat. That spirit (*mukishi,* i.e., the dancer impersonating the shade) takes his goat off with him to his guardians. They take it to the novices, kill and eat it. That day they pray for him, he cannot dance but must first sleep. Later, on another day, women will dance and clap hands and sing, and men will play the drums. He goes to dance in all the villages. He is given presents of money or cloth. He takes them to *Mukanda,* puts them down and takes off his *ikishi* (costume). He goes to his own village.

*Makishi,* I was told by Nyaluhana, are believed by women and novices to die after the *ku-tomboka* dance performed by initiated novices at the end of *kwidisha.* Some of the masks are concealed near a burned lodge in calabashes and can be used again at subsequent performances. The mask is called *kumesu ekishi,* "the face of the *ikishi*" or *kumesu achileng'aleng'a* (from *ku-leng'a,* "to cut bark ropes in strips"; this refers to the *makishi* costumes of bark string), while the costume is *mujimba wekishi,* "the body of the *ikishi.*" Other informants told me that the mask is concealed in the dancer's own village, sometimes in a calabash hidden in the thatch of the *chota* or men's shelter, which women are not supposed to enter (although I have seen older women sitting in men's shelters when there were few people about).

The meaning of the *makishi* and of masks in initiation rites has been touched upon in an earlier, analytical chapter (p. 72). Here I have simply assembled what exegetic data I was able to collect from the Ndembu about them. Its thinness is in marked contrast to other classes of interpretations.

Kasonda and I were unable to attend the earlier *chikula* rites, for, as frequently happens in field work, I had had to make observations of an important ritual elsewhere at the time of their performance. We arrived at the "fire of *Mukanda*" at about 8:30 A.M. on July 20. Many women were pounding cassava at the parents' camp for the novices and also for the assembled visitors. The lodge officials were waiting for a boy who had been sent to a store at the Boma to buy a white cloth for the *ikishi.*

Wukengi told me that the previous day at about 4 P.M. they had performed the *chikula chanyanya* rites. The *ikishi Chizaluki* had appeared briefly, he said, and Sampasa had given salt to the novices' parents on behalf of the *ikishi.* He had also washed them on the face and neck with *chikula* medicine collected in his *lwalu* basket.

While we were waiting, a man quietly walked up, carrying a gnu-tail switch and a carved walking stick (*mbwechi*). I recognized him as the older brother of the most famous dancer in Mwinilunga District, Kanseng'ula. He sat down with the elders for a while, then quietly slipped away in the direction of the lodge. Musona whispered that he thought this man would dance *Chizaluki.*

Sampasa next washed a few men and women with *chikula* medicine. These were people who had been unable to go to the rites on the previous day. When he had finished, he poured what remained of the medicine on the *chikoli* tree in the middle of the clearing. Two junior guardians collected the novices' food and advanced slowly with it to the lodge, while the boys sang. They also took Sampasa's leaf-broom with them. I noticed that all the novices' mothers had been anointed with *mpemba* clay beside their orbits.

I fell into conversation with an underground worker on leave from the Nchanga Mine. He told me that in over ten years on the mine he had saved about £300—he drove an engine towing trucks of ore—and wanted eventually to come home and set up as a trader. Suddenly he pointed out that the *ikishi* was coming. As is customary with *makishi,* he came from an unexpected direction—from Wukengi Village and not from the lodge or bush. He was dressed in a costume of woven *katochi* bark-strings, decorated with white, red, and black designs, and carried an eland-tail switch. At the back of the painted mask was attached the complete skin of a *kambunji* mongoose (the flesh of which is tabooed at *Mukanda*) and a beard of sable antelope hair adorned the "face" (see Plate 7). A circle of people, women to one side, men to the other, formed up, and the *ikishi* entered it. Men sang and clapped as well as women, and I was told that this was done only when an *ikishi* is dancing. Then parents took uncircumcised children, sobbing and wailing with terror, to the *ikishi*. The Lodge Instructor stood beside *Chizaluki* and applied *ku-seng'ula* medicine by spitting, as already described, to prevent them from having nightmares (see Plate 8). There was a lot of criticism of the dancer's performance; it was said that being a Lunda he could not dance in Luvale fashion.

After about a quarter of an hour, Sampasa led the *ikishi* off to the *nyiyombu* trees in Wukengi Farm. All the *Mukanda* officials with other elders accompanied them. At the shrines, Nyaluhana gave the *ikishi* the name "Makana." This name belonged to one of the ancient Kanongeshas, senior chiefs of the Ndembu. Makana was also a matrilineal predecessor of Nyaluhana himself. Nyaluhana prayed to Makana's shade (*mukishi*) with *mpemba,* and as he did so the *ikishi* looked up at the sky. Then he was led back to the camp and the women were informed that he was "really Makana."

I asked Sampasa and Nyaluhana why there was only a single *ikishi* and that a Luvale one. They replied that most of the men were away at work on the Copperbelt or in local employment. There were only enough available to make a single costume. Nor were dancers who knew the correct *ikishi* movements readily available. As it was, they had to call on the services of a Luvale carpenter and woodcarver to make the mask.

The *ikishi* dancer, bow in hand, danced the *Wubinda* hunting dance several times. Younger men called out to the women to sing modern "*chikinta*" songs (see p. 211), but Nyaluhana put a stop to this. Kasonda told me that the *ikishi* dancer usually has several cupfuls of beer at the dying-place before he comes out. The guardians join him in drinking three or four calabashes—just to put them in the right mood, so to speak.

Nyaluhana told me that the lodge is burned about two hours before dawn on the day after the boys have first been seen by their mothers. The dying-place is abandoned and treated like a graveyard. It is more dangerous than a graveyard, however, for neither women nor the former novices should enter it lest they contract leprosy. The site of the parents' camp is allowed to revert to bush, after *Mukanda*.

Later, when an uncircumcised boy tried to approach the fence around the novices' enclosure, Nyaluhana in a towering rage chased him away with sticks and stones and a volley of curses. They tried to catch him, to bring him close to the *ikishi*, who would "mop and mow" at him, but he had judiciously disappeared.

Eventually, the *ikishi* returned to the dying-place and revealed himself as Kanseng'ula's brother, when he stripped off his costume. We had a few beers with him and set off, not altogether steadily, homeward.

Chimwang'a provides information about some eating customs of the boys after *chikula*:

*Neyi anyadi analuki dehi akuyiletela kudya nachu yakulung'a*
When the novices have already been healed up, they bring food for them seasoned with

*mung'wa. Mukwakutwala kudya wukuya nakwimba kamina kakutwala nachu*
salt. The one who takes food will go and sing a song to accompany

*nshima iku nasendi nshima hamutu hela hamafwiji. Chatumbulayi*
the mush he takes, carrying it on the head or on the shoulders. When he has sung

*kamina wukwimbila anyadi, anyadi akwakwija kamina, kamina kanowu*
a song, he will sing for the novices, the novices will respond with a song, the special song (for when)

*wudinakwinza nanshima. Owu iyala wukwila imbe-e ninichi chakushikayi*
he is coming with mush. That man goes on singing until he has reached

*kudi anyadi. Anyadi chakumonawu nshima hiyakwimba embang'a kamina kawu*
the novices. When the novices have seen the mush they sing their song

*nawu ntombu nshima, ntombu nkalata,*[21] *eyo nshima yetu. Ona wukwinza*
"Tributary slave (with) mush, slave (with) mush, yes, (it is) our mush." That man will come

*nanshima iku nakwinza kwakwihi anyadi ejima akwimana; neyi nshima*
with the mush and when he approaches the novices they will all stand up; when the mush

*anatuli dehi anyadi ejima akuhamina hankala jawu, akushakama ejima*
is put down already all the novices will climb on their *nkala* stubs, they will all sit

*hankala akuyanzang'ana nshima chikanka chimu hejiku niyakudya nachu*
on the stubs, they will divide the mush, one piece at a fire,

*chochina hohu hamajiku ejima. Anyadi ejima ching'a kudya chachiwahi*
and will eat in just the same way at all the fires. All the novices must eat well,

*nakumwena nzo o nakubula kwinyisha kudya. Neyi anamanishi dehi*
be completely silent, and not belittle the food. When they have

*kudya ejima wawu akunyamukila hamu hiyahuya nakunoka mumashina*
eaten, all of them, they must hurry off together to rest under

*anyitondu muwulelu. Namelele akwilu mwowumu ilang'a akushiya hohu*
the trees in the shade. In the evening they will act in the same fashion but will leave only,

*mwana himwana kashima kakunata nachu kang'eli mulong'a*
each boy separately, a little piece of mush to throw with a twig called *kang'eli*, because

*itang'wa dinayi dehi. Chakumanishawu kudya namelela anyadi ejima*
the sun has already gone. When they have finished eating in the evening, all the novices

*akwimba nawu dayawo dayo, itang'wa detu daya dayawo dayo, kang'eli*
will sing: "It went, it went, our sun went, went, went, the twig
*wayo kang'eli wayo kukukuwo.*
went, the twig went." (After this song the novices throw their
*kang'eli* twigs backwards over their shoulders into the dying-place behind the lodge.)

*Habudidi anyadi chakumonawu itang'wa embang'a kamina nawu*
Early in the morning when the novices have seen the sun they sing:

[21] Esoteric term used in lodge for cassava mush.

*Denzawo denza itang'wa detu denza denzawo denza.*
"It came, it came, our sun, it came, came, came."

*Anyadi akwing'ila mung'ula namwana akuwana mulong'a ching'a*
Novices who will enter the lodge at midday will find a case (i.e., have a case brought against them).

*hakukama hohu hela mwadi kuya kwifwilu chinjila hela kuya kumukala*
they must sleep only. It is taboo for a novice to go to the dying-place or to the village.

*Anyadi akula dehi ayang'a mwisang'a neyi aluka dehi nakulowa*
Older novices go into the bush when they are healed to catch

*anshi hela kufunda amfwa hela kuhang'a ansenji akuleta yawu akudya*
fish on hooks or dig up mice or chase cane-rats, they bring their

*nachu. Kwejima kwayang'awu anyadi ching'a kuya nakwimba tumina*
own and will eat it. Wherever the novices go they must go singing songs

*nihakuya nihakwinzu nawu.*
both going and returning.

At Wukengi Farm I was assured that very little esoteric instruction was given to the boys. In the past, however, the novices were asked to explain riddles, many of them in a secret language, possibly containing archaic words. For example, there was the mystery (*mpang'u*) of the three rivers: the river of the red water (*kachinana*),[22] of the white water (*katooka*), and of the black water (*keyila*). This mystery was taught in three different kinds of ritual, *Mukanda, Mung'ong'i* (performed at the death of a member of the male *Mung'ong'i* society), and *Chiwila* (performed at the death of a member of the female *Chiwila* society). *Chiwila* is no longer enacted in Mwinilunga, but one of the women at Mukanza Village had been initiated into it as a young girl in Ndembu territory in Angola. This woman, Nyakalusa, described to me how the novices, both boys and girls at *Chiwila*, were taught the mystery of the "river of blood" (*kalong'a kamashi*) or of redness (*kachinana*). She said that the novices (*anyadi*—as in Mukanda) were taken to a long roofed but unwalled shelter. The senior officiant, with the title *Samazembi*, took a hoe and dug a trench inside the hut. It was shaped "like a cross" (*neyi mwambu*), but it could also be shaped like an Ndembu ax (*chizemba*) or a hoe (*itemwa*). Then he took reeds (*mateti*) and planted them along both sides of the

[22] The prefix *ka-* is sometimes used to signify liquid.

trench. Next, he placed a large number of small horns, containing *nsompu,* pounded leaf-medicine, in lines on either side of the trench. Water was then poured into the trench. *Samazembi* beheaded a chicken and poured its blood into the "river" to redden it. Other red substances, such as powdered red clay (*ng'ula* or *mukundu*) and powdered *mukula* gum, were sprinkled in the water. *Samazembi* had his own calabash, full of medicine made of root-scrapings mixed with water. He washed his body with this and threw the residue into the "red river." Next, he prayed with *mpemba* to the spirits of those who had "passed through *Chiwila* long ago." After marking the novices with *mpemba* on the temples and by the orbits, he addressed them as follows:

Pay attention! This river is blood, it is very important, it is very dangerous. Don't speak of it in the village when you return. Beware! This is no ordinary river, God made it long, long ago. It is the river of God (*kalong'a kaNzambi*). You must not eat salt for many days, nor anything salty or sweet (*ku-towala*). Do not speak of these matters in public, in the village, that is very bad.

When he had finished, each novice bent down and took one of the small horns by the teeth, without using hands. They went outside and each of them bending backwards, threw his or her horn over the head, where it was caught by an adept standing just behind. They had to try to avoid spilling the contents. *Samazembi* collected all these horns and put them in a *katunda* medicine-hut privately. The medicine in them, called *nfunda,* as in *Mukanda* and containing some of the ashes of the dead person's hut, could be used again. It was mixed with fresh medicine whenever there was a new *Chiwila.*

Nyakalusa had little idea of what the "river of blood" meant, but Muchona, as usual, was helpful. He said that at *Mukanda* and *Mung'ong'i,* there were three rivers. The river of redness, made in the shape of an ax, represented "man and woman" (*iyala namumbanda*) or "copulation" (*ku-disunda*), the man being the ax-head with its tang and the wooden shaft. The river of whiteness (*katooka*) is the main trough. It is whitened with powdered *mpemba* and stands for "life" (*wumi*). The red and black rivers are joined to it like branches. The black river (*keyila*), blackened with charcoal, represents "death" (*ku-fwa*).

One of the riddles of the lodge is *katooka kusaloka,* which means "white water becoming restless at night." The correct answer is "semen." "White water" occurs again in a lodge incantation—both at *Mukanda* and *Mung'ong'i*—most of which was incomprehensible to Ndembu themselves:

*Katooki menji kansalu kelung'i chimbungu*[23] *chelung'a belang'ante-e*
White river water the little grass mat of the country, the cannibal

*mukayande-e*[24] *he-e kateti kasemena*[25] *mwikindu mwini kumwalula hinyi?*
of the country in suffering, the little reed of begetting in the basket, the owner who may find him?

*Apika kapumbi mujintiki samazedi ye-e* (meaning unknown).

According to Muchona:

The crossing of the father's and mother's blood (in the red river) means a child, a new life, a seed of life (*kabubu kawumi*). That is why the white river is joined to the river of blood. To have a child is very lucky for men and women, for a son gives things to his father, and also a daughter. The mother is like a pot only, the child's body comes from the father. God breathes life (*wumi*) into a child. A man begets (*kusema*) children, but they are the woman's because she nurses them, she feeds them with her breasts (*mayeli*); without her breasts they would die. As Luvale say *kusema kwandemba nyana yachali,* "the cock begets children, but they are the hen's for she feeds them."

White mentions a number of tricks (called by Luvale *jipango*) played on novices in the lodge.

A novice may be given a long basket and told to go and fill it with mushrooms, which are in any case non-existent during the cold dry weather. Unless his relatives run to the village and bring a fowl to redeem him, the novice will be beaten on his return. A similar trick is called shooting an arrow at night; a *chilombola* shoots an arrow into the darkness and all run to find it. If it is not found, the novice will be beaten; he may be redeemed again by the payment of a fowl or in some cases if forewarned, his relatives may have hidden an arrow nearby, and produce this instead. The incidence of these tricks is variable and it seems possible that they are being discontinued.

[23] *Chimbungu* is a monster that eats human flesh. It is sometimes applied to the hyena.

[24] *Kayaṇda* is "suffering."

[25] *Kateti kasemena* may stand for "the little reed of giving birth."

The novices are taught most kinds of Ndembu dances, such as hunting dances and songs. They are also taught dances peculiar to *Mukanda,* such as *ku-kinda* (which involves movement of the shoulders and arms), and *ku-kinka,* to make the grass kilt whirl out like a wheel as they sway from side to side. Most important from the point of view of *kwidisha* is to learn how to dance *ku-tomboka,* the solo war dance with an ax, for each boy has to do this on the last day of *Mukanda.*

On July 31 and August 1 the *ikishi* from Wukeng'i's *Mukanda* danced around many of the neighboring villages, both in the vicinage of Nyaluhana and in adjacent vicinages. The original dancer had died a week or two earlier, and a new dancer had taken over. The second day, he came to Mukanza Village, accompanied by various guardians. One of them collected *nyishing'a* payments from the villagers and spat *ku-seng'ula* medicine on uninitiated boys in return for small payments by their fathers.

### KWIDISHA: THE RITES OF RETURN

The Rites of Return I observed at Wukengi were said to include the rites of *chikula cheneni,* or "great" *chikula.* These preceded the return of the novices to their mothers. I shall principally record my own observations, interlacing these with comments and indigenous exegesis.

Before dawn on August 8, 1953, Kasonda and I set out to walk the nine miles between Mukanza Village and Wukengi Farm. At 6 A.M. the novices, still wearing their *fwefweta* fibre girdles, were taken to a site in the bush about two hundred yards to the left of the lodge, called *katewu kanyanya,* literally "the small shaving place." About two and a half hours later they were washed with the same medicine that had been applied to them after circumcision. Their kilts of stiff grass (*nkambi*), to be used at *kwidisha* proper, were neatly arrayed beside them.

After chatting with the boys, who all seemed to be in excellent health, we were called by Wukengi to drink beer with the lodge officials and other elders at the parents' camp. On this penultimate day, a good deal of stocktaking about the course of events was going on. For example, Headman Machamba and his close kinsman Towel drank with me and whispered that their village, which belonged to the matrilineage of Mwenilunga, the first Ndembu owner of the land, should have sponsored *Mukanda,* but that Nyaluhana had usurped their prerogative because he was a matrilineal kinsman of the reigning Chief Kanongesha. Later, Sampasa and Nyachiu joined us, and the anti-Nyaluhana sentiments fairly tumbled out. Sampasa claimed that he had been regarded by most people as the Senior Circumciser, but that Nyaluhana had taken over at the crucial moments before the operation. Indeed, the *Mukanda* had been first proposed by the mother of an uncircumcised boy from Sawiyembi Village. She had sent her son to Sampasa to inaugurate *Mukanda* formally. Later, Wukengi himself had agreed, when he became Establisher, that Sampasa should be Senior Circumciser, giving him an arrow and a knife to signify his assent. Later, under pressure from Nyaluhana, he changed his mind and yielded the office to the old man, his uncle.

Nyaluhana himself arrived while the others were in process of agreeing that he was a very powerful sorcerer. He began to scold Machamba, half humorously, for not having invited him to have a drink too, but he had come to invite me to see what was going on in the dying-place. As we went off, a quarrel broke out between Towel, from Machamba, and Philemon, from Nyaluhana Village. Towel alleged that Philemon had agreed to make up four pairs of shorts for his sons to wear for their *ku-tomboka* dance and had deliberately delayed doing so. In answer, Philemon quietly produced the shorts.

At *ifwilu,* a new dancer was donning the *Chizaluki* costume. He proved to be the best yet tried. A great deal of chaffing and fooling about was going on among the younger men around the *ikishi.* I noticed that the *mukoleku* had been broken down and that the medicine calabash which had previously stood beside the *muyombu* tree in the *ifwilu* had been placed inverted on top of the tree. Nyaluhana pointed to *Kambanji's* withered bed of leaves and said that some of the leaves would soon be burned to form an ingredient of *nfunda* medicine. The *ikishi* dancer put a white cloth around his waist to hide his shorts which were visible through the costume.

At about midday I returned to the "fire of *Mukanda*" to find the novices' mothers cooking their sons' last seclusion meal on it. When they had finished, Wukengi, the Establisher, kindled a new fire near the path along which the novices had been taken to be circumcised. Men and women were now mixing freely and chatting blithely together, in contrast to the marked sexual segregation just before circumcision. From time to time the *ikishi* dancer came in, beckoned women around him, and conducted their singing and clapping. Little children of both sexes ran shrieking to their mothers whenever he made one of his unexpected visits from the bush.

With regard to the new fire, Kasonda told me that the correct custom would have been for the circumcisers to spend the night around the new fire for cooking the novices' food and for the novices to gather around the fire used by the circumcisers on the night before the operation. In point of fact, the novices were to spend the night by the new fire, and the circumcisers by their *kwing'ija* one.

At about 3:30 P.M., a fence (*chipang'u*) was erected on the side of the "fire of *Mukanda*" nearest to the *katewu kanyanya* in the bush where the novices were being prepared for their entry. An open space was left in the fence for the novices to pass through.

Meanwhile, at the *katewu* the novices were being decorated for their first public appearance. The scene resembled that in the dressing room before a play. The boys were being spotted and circled with *mpemba* by their guardians. Their *nisweswa* sticks were tidily piled beside them. Furious arguments were going on about the decoration, some holding that they should be striped with alternate bands of red and white clay, others that they should have white stripes only,[26] but Nyaluhana insisted on spots. Their faces were also spotted, though some had "spectacles" of white clay drawn on them, a motif that recurred the following day on many women's faces at the *ku-tomboka* dance. The same motif is characteristic of the *Wubwang'u* twin ritual.

The *nkambi* kilts of stiff grass were being fitted when I arrived. Some of the boys wore the tattered shorts that had been discarded on the day of circumcision and later hung on the *mukoleku*. Traditionally, they should have worn *fwefweta* girdles. Nyaluhana raged at those guardians who fitted kilts over shorts, telling them that they were "worthless" (*mukunkulwayi*). He went away in a huff and immediately a fight broke out between a guardian from Nyaluhana Village and one from Sawiyembi Village over the matter. They were separated and pacified by the Lodge Instructor. (See Plate 10 for fitting of kilts.)

One man, from Mukoma Village, was dressed like a woman with blouse, skirt and headband. I asked a guardian if this was a *kwidisha* custom, and he replied laughingly that it "was only his liver" (*muchima windi hohu*), his personal foible. However, another guardian told me

[26] The term for "stripes" is *nyilenji*. To stripe novices is *ku-leng'a anyadi*.

that he had enacted *"Nyakayowa"* just previously, while I had been away. I had already collected fragments of information about *Nyakayowa,* and later took the opportunity to expand it. Here is what I was told.

According to Muchona, the term *"Nyakayowa"* is used in the lodge for "woman" and the ordinary term *mumbanda* is taboo. *"Nyakayowa,"* he said, "is the symbol (*chinjikijilu*) for woman. With her each boy must leave his sickness, pain, impotence, bad luck, and all bad things. She is the first woman for a boy."

Kasonda told me that "the proper custom" was for the Lodge Instructor at the *katewu kanyanya* first to give the novices some tortoise (*mbachi*) meat to eat "to give them a strong penis." Then just after midday, one of the elders covers himself with a blanket, makes a hole in it, and thrusts his penis through the hole. This elder is *Nyakayowa.* He sits on the ground, legs apart, and all the novices in turn, *kambanji* leading, mime copulation with him. Then each novice is given a small round cucumber, of a species called *katanda,* or a fruit called *ihwila,* and is told to make a hole in it and feign intercourse with it. White (1953, 52) mentions that (in Luvale lodges) "if a novice is too young to find a woman easily the *chilombola* takes him into the bush and carves a vagina in a cucumber or small pumpkin and the novice has connection with this to remove the taint of the *chikula.* The cucumber is known as *kashinakazi* (the old woman)."

According to Kasonda, after this episode *Nyakayowa* says: "Today you will return to mother. The guardians will carry back different children from those they have been tending. How the mothers will weep when they see different children on the guardians' backs! But this is the custom of *Mukanda.*"

After this, the Senior Circumciser makes an incision in the novices' brows and above their navels, and rubs in *nfunda* medicine. They are also given *nfunda* to lick from his circumcising knife. This is "to give them their bodies back again."

Some informants said at Wukengi Village itself, during the night dance before *ku-tomboka,* that the boys were also given ashes of *kukolisha* medicine to eat, just before they swallowed a few grains each of *nfunda.* All these acts signify that the novices are cured of their circumcision wounds and are potentially sexually capable. Since the age of circumcision is now so low (the average age at Wukengi was about eight), it is likely that this custom is a survival from a period when novices were older.

At last the time came for bringing the boys to the parents' camp.

Each guardian took charge of another's novice, picked him up and seated him on his shoulders. The boys with bent heads, spotted all over, with clacking *nisweswa* sticks, were still quite recognizable, even to me. I think the significance of the disguise must be mystical—for their mothers they are changed persons, they are no longer children, they have entered the adult male moral community. No mother would at any rate have had the slightest difficulty in recognizing her own child. Before the line of guardians advanced, there was another dispute about custom. Some said that the *nisweswa* sticks should first have been wrapped round with bark-string and placed in the lodge fire. When the string was removed there would then have been alternate bands of black and white. Others said that each novice should have had one white and one black stick. As it was, the sticks were completely white.

It was too late to do anything about it anyway and the long line of burdened guardians started to run rapidly to the new *chipang'u* fence. An escort of men hurried along on either side. When they entered the camp site, drums began to thud rapidly and a close throng of mothers advanced on the column, which began to circle around the *chikoli* tree. At first the mothers wailed, then their mourning turned to songs of rejoicing [27] as each realized that her son was safe and well. It is impossible to describe adequately the ensuing scene of complete, uninhibited jubilation. The guardians ran around in an inner circle, the mothers danced beside them waving scarves, cloths, anything they could lay hands on, while other female relatives and friends made up an outer ring of joyful chanting dancers. The men stood outside the whirl, laughing with pure pleasure. Dust rose in clouds. (See Plate 11 for guardians carrying novices.)

After three or four turns around the *chikoli*, the male procession headed off once more into the bush. First, the novices were taken into the lodge which they circled clockwise inside; then they were carried to a new site in the bush on the opposite side of the village path from the *katewu kanyanya*. This site was known as *ifwotu* (from *ku-fwota*, "to precede"). There they had to wait until sunset before being brought in triumph to their new fire at the parents' camp. Meanwhile, the mothers and other women were still dancing merrily round the drums at *chikoli*.

At sunset the boys were borne into the camp again, this time on

[27] The most important of these is: "*Twamuswekeli, tunamusololi*," "we hid him away, (now) we have produced him to view."

their own guardians' backs. Some were waving Union Jacks supplied by their parents. Once more the women rejoiced around them. At last they were taken to their new fire, where their mothers and sisters fussed over them, each being treated like a little prince. Then the *ikishi* came to them and greeted each one individually in ritual order of precedence.

By this time a huge crowd had arrived, about twice as large as at *kwing'ija*. This was partly because a new road was in process of construction from the Boma to Chief Kanongesha's capital village, and it was just passing Nyaluhana Village at that time. All the laborers and capitaos came to the dance, in expectation of beer, women, and song. Many clerks, messengers, and storemen came from the Boma itself, for it was reported far and wide that there would be plenty to drink. Calabashes of beer were divided among many groups and *Chikinta* began. The great drummer Shem from Shika Village, whose wife was a patient at the *Nkula* ritual described in *Drums of Affliction,* Chapter III, settled himself to play all night long without a break. Periodically, the general dance was interrupted by *ing'ung'u,* at which the novices and other young lads had to be carried, as mentioned earlier. Sometimes the novices danced *ku-kinda* and gracefully swirled their kilts in unison. In the lodge sat several elders, drinking ritual beer. They had a red chicken ready to kill when the lodge would be burned.

All the usual features of a Ndembu night dance were present—the desperate search for beer as it grew less and less, the jealous fights and wife-beatings, the flirtations and clandestine trysts of young lovers in the bush. Moreover, there was now no sexual taboo on the parents of novices.

Shortly after the morning star was seen to rise slowly above the trees, at about 4 A.M., everyone in the camp shouted, *"Tendenu! Kwocha dehi!"* "Hide yourselves! Burning already!" I looked towards the lodge and saw a great sheet of flame through the trees. Everyone was madly shouting. Young boys, including even those who had attended several performances of *Mukanda,* crouched down with averted eyes and hands behind their heads. The penalty for seeing *ng'ula* burn, if one is uninitiated or young, is madness or leprosy. The stripes of flame will produce, it is thought, stripes of leprosy. All the novices were covered up by reed mats. Their parents were banging these mats with the flat of their hands and yelling *"Tendenu-u!"* Others clapped their hands. Only the older women were allowed to see the flames, though I saw many young ones doing so.

In the first light of dawn, the novices, still wearing their *nkambi* kilts, were carried by their guardians to the Kachibamba Plain, to wash in the river of that name. Three fires were lit near the river, and beside them the novices were stripped of kilts, *fwefweta* girdles, and any bits of cloth they happened to be wearing despite Nyaluhana's ban. Then they were rushed off naked to the river and told to wash themselves completely. Their ritual clothing had been rolled up into two neat bundles, and these were flung into the stream by the Lodge Instructor. The younger guardians also washed themselves. Then everyone hurried back to the fires and the boys dried themselves in the heat. It was extremely chilly at that dawn hour. The novices' new clothes would only be given them when they went to the *katewu keneni,* "the great shaving-place" whence they would sally for the final rites. The washing was called, in the argot of *Mukanda, ku-tapa tuloya,* "killing catfish."

Everyone huddled around the fire and gossiped cheerfully. The sense of strain had completely gone, as well as the rancors of the previous day. Some said that they were looking forward to living quietly in their own villages again. Ndembu present accused the Kawiku jokingly of always brawling, cursing, and drinking, but Kasonda, an Kawiku himself, mildly remarked that he had seen none of the Kawiku fighting during the night, but that he had heard Nyaluhana, Machamba, and other Ndembu quarreling loudly.

Once dry, the boys walked—they had ceased to be carried from the time of their arrival at the fires—with their guardians to the new *katewu keneni.* We took a circuitous route back to avoid meeting women, for *Mukanda* was not yet at an end.

*Katewu keneni* was sited at no great distance from the parents' camp. The novices' hair was shaved around the hairline, combed, and oiled with castor oil (*imonu*). Their limbs were rubbed with oil, and colored beads were fixed in a circular design on their heads with a string across the top. At the new fire for the novices, their mothers prepared a big meal for them, with large quantities of meat. Several chickens were cooked. The guardians carried the food in for the last time and set it out in a long line. The meal was provided by the parents of the novices for the whole group. It was taboo to break the bones of the chickens as this would put the boys' potency in jeopardy. The boys' fathers then dressed them personally in completely new clothes, bought or made for the occasion, and they rested for a while before the *ku-tomboka* dance.

I have already described how new *nfunda* is prepared. When the lodge was burned, the red chicken was sacrificed. Its intestines were carefully removed and the blood gushing from its neck collected. This blood, it was said, would give strength to the medicine.

Meanwhile at the *katewu keneni,* the Lodge Instructor made a final speech to the novices. He had previously (some said during the morning of the previous day at the *katewu kanyanya*) sworn the boys to secrecy on a stick of *mukula wood*[28] on penalty of idiocy, leprosy, or madness if they divulged lodge matters to unauthorized persons. Now, as closely as I was able to record his words, he said:

*Ilang'enu anyadi yami nayilamang'a natalang'a; neyi ifuku dinu*
But you my novices, I care for and look after you; when today you

*himukuwudyika himukuya kudi amama jenu, kwosi mwana ona wunafwi nehi.*
will emerge and go to your mothers, not a single child has died.

*Munawudyiki ejimu wenu wuseng'useng'useng'u. Dichi ching'a chimukuya*
All of you have emerged in the best possible condition. Therefore when you must go

*kudi amama jenu nikudi atata jenu eng'a mwiluki nyidimu yamvwali jenu*
to your mothers and your fathers, yes, you have known the work of your mothers

*niatata jenu, kanda nawa mfumwa twbwiku aha-a.*
and of your fathers, but not yet (of) the Lodge Instructor, indeed no!

*Ami kwami nukuya kumukala wami nakushakami, enu nenu hukumwang'ala*
I for my part will go to my village to rest, for yours you will disperse

*kunyikala jenu mwiyi chachiwani. Mwakula dehi mwakula dehi, kanda*
to your villages, may you go well. You are mature, you are mature, already, (but)

*wakashikeni hadi mumbanda wumutuli chikula chaMukanda. Ching'a*
you should not yet have intercourse with a woman—you may give her (the taint of) *chikula* of *Mukanda* (i.e., leprosy). You must

[28] According to Muchona, the Lodge Instructor rubs the *mukula* stick horizontally along the ground, just as diviners do who practice divination with a pounding-pole (*mwishi*), stopping at each point he makes.

*mukami nawufuku halehi. Neyi wunakeng'i mumbanda wuyeng'a*
sleep at night (alone) for a long time. When you want a woman you may (then) go

*nakumukama windi. Enu anyana ejima wenu chikumwang'ala kunyikala*
and sleep with her. All you children, when you have dispersed to your villages

*yenu kanda mudimbalaku, kasenda, mbang'ala, nduwa, nchawa nawa kanda;*
do not cheat—(in the matter of eating) blue duiker, guinea fowl, lourie; nor of firewood too;

*kanda mwota mukulaku ni kabalabala kanda mukwota hanuku, ching'a*
do not warm yourself at *mukula* (firewood) nor *kabalabala* (firewood), you must

*mujili chenochu. Mukunkulwayi mukukwata mbumba.*
observe these taboos. Otherwise you will catch leprosy.

Muchona told me that *ikunyi* firewood is also tabooed.

At about 11 A.M. the novices were carried into the camp site for the last time, in new outfits of clothes, oiled, decorated with beads, and shaved around the hairline. The women rushed to greet them and the scarf-waving and joyful singing were repeated. The novices were taken to a single long mat where they were made to sit down in a row. They bowed their heads in the characteristic ritual attitude of modesty. Colored beads encircled their wrists. A long lane of people was made between their mat and the *chikoli* tree. Stools and chairs were placed just in front of the *chikoli* for the lodge officials and circumcisers. On one side of the lane stood most of the women, and on the other, all the men and many women, too, for they outnumbered the men.

Now the *ku-tomboka* dance began. Each boy was decorated with red clay (*ng'ula*) by the orbits and on the brow. As each danced in turn from the mat to the waiting officials, he brandished in his right hand Nyaluhana's long knife of authority. Before dancing, he was required to go to the circumcisers and strike a number of metal tools and implements carried by the circumcisers in order of precedence, beginning with Nyaluhana. These included penknives and ax-blades. Those who had shown themselves during seclusion unable to dance *ku-tomboka* adequately, found other boys to dance in their stead, and on one occasion a grown man substituted for a novice. *Kambanji* himself did not dance, as he was said to be clumsy. In fact, for some time the Kawiku lad from Kafumbu Village had proved to be the brightest and best novice, and he danced as *kambanji* (see Plate 12).

Money was thrown into a plate to "help" the boys and guardians, as at *Nkang'a*. The general atmosphere closely resembled that of a children's talent competition in our own society. Each boy's performance was carefully scrutinized and indulgently or critically commented on. *Kajika* provided a surprise, for he turned out to be none other than Wukengi's son, who had begun as *mwanta waMukanda,* the second novice in order of importance. His action at circumcision and his subsequent lack of skill and enterprise at the lodge had been his undoing. When he brought the proceedings to an end by thrusting the knife in the ground before Nyaluhana, *Mukanda* was officially over. All that now remained was for the boys to go home with their guardians to their respective villages, where a further celebration awaited them. Guardians and their charges become special friends for the rest of their lives, it is said.

I was told by Kasonda and Chief Ikelenge that when a chief is present at *ku-tomboka,* the novices retire to their mat after the dance is finished. *Kambanji* then comes forward and addresses the chief as follows: "I am now a big man, I myself. You are a fool and a rogue, no good at all. From now on take care not to eat all your food by yourself, but share some of it with your children!" Then the Lodge Instructor leads the novices to the Establisher who says to the chief, "O chief, we came to ask you for fire. You gave us fire, we have looked after these children well. Now count them. Not one is missing." The chief then says: "All the parents must pay the circumcisers."

According to my informants, the *ambimbi* would be paid after *Mukanda* in their own villages, by the Establisher and the Lodge Instructor. Senior Circumcisers are usually given a goat or a sheep, two calabashes of beer, and two large baskets of cassava meal, which they share with their *yifukaminu* and assistants. The guardians are paid privately by the parents of the novices they have looked after. The Lodge Instructor receives a present similar to that of a Senior Circumciser, both being paid out of the food and goods contributed by the villages sending novices. The Establisher's only reward is the glory of having held a successful *Mukanda.*

## *Some Analytical Comments*

When I came to examine the data I had collected on this single performance of the *Mukanda,* I found myself in a quandary about the most fruitful mode of presentation. For the mode of presentation depends on the mode of analysis. I had brought into the field with me two distinct theoretical orientations, and these determined the kinds of data I collected and to some extent predetermined the sorts of analysis I expected to make. On the one hand, following in the tradition of Rhodes-Livingstone Institute research, I collected the kind of data that would have enabled me to analyze the structure of the social system in which *Mukanda* occurred. I recorded genealogies, made hut diagrams, discovered political ties and cleavages between groups and subgroups, and noted the social characteristics of the ritual participants. On the other hand, I recorded ritual details, their interpretation by experts and laymen, and those items of secular behavior directly related to the servicing and maintenance of the ritual complex.

From the first set of data, I was able to abstract a system of social relationships between the participants and to relate this specific system to what I already knew about the general principles underlying Ndembu social structure. From the second set of data, I was able to exhibit *Mukanda* as a system of customs governed by the same principles that I had already isolated in the analysis of many kinds of Ndembu ritual. I was then left with two virtually autonomous spheres of study, one of the social, the other of the cultural structure of *Mukanda*.

Yet, during the period of *Mukanda*, I had felt keenly that most of the events I had observed, not only at sacred sites and during sacred phases but also at other places and times in the sociogeographical area primarily concerned with its performance, were significantly interconnected with one another. Such events exhibited a dynamic interdependence, and I felt that it was incumbent upon me to expose the grounds of this interdependence. A simile that occurred to me likened the cultural structure of *Mukanda* to a musical score and its performers to an orchestra. I wanted to find some way of expressing and analyzing the dynamic interdependence of score and orchestra manifested in the unique performance. Furthermore, I wanted to find a theoretical framework that would have enabled me to understand why it was that certain persons and sections of the orchestra were obviously out of sympathy with the conductor or with one another, though all were obviously skilled musicians and well rehearsed in the details of the score. Neither the properties of the orchestra *qua* social group nor the properties of the score, taken in isolation from one another, seemed able to account fully for the observed behavior, the hesitancies in certain passages, the lapses in rapport between conductor and sections, or the exchanged grimaces and sympathetic smiles between performers. Similarly, it became clear to me that the events both in and out of a ritual context I observed at *Mukanda* were influenced by the structure of a field that included both ritual and social components.

When I first read Kurt Lewin's *Field Theory in Social Science* (1949), I realized that an important advance had been made in the analysis of social life. Lewin found it possible to link in a definite manner, by means of his "field theoretical" approach, a variety of facts of individual and social psychology, which, from a classificatory point of view, seem to have little in common. He was able to do so by regarding the barrier between individual and environment as indefinite and unstable. His approach requires the consideration of an organism-environment field, the properties of which are studied as field properties and not as the properties of either organism or environment taken separately. The flow of events within the field is always directed to some extent by the relations between the outer and inner structures.

According to Lewin, "a basic tool for the analysis of *group* life is the representation of the group and its setting as a 'social field.'" Any event or happening in this field he views as "occurring in, and being the result of, a totality of coexisting social entities, such as groups, subgroups, members, barriers, channels of communication, etc." This totality has "structure," which he regards as "the relative position of the entities, which are parts of the field."

I realized after reading Lewin that the behavior I had been observing during *Mukanda* became, to a large extent, intelligible if it was regarded as occurring in a social field made up, on the one hand, of the generic beliefs and practices of *Mukanda,* and, on the other, of its specific social setting. In practice these major sets of determinants could not be clearly demarcated from one another. Since the predominant activity within this field was the performance of a protracted ritual, it seemed appropriate to call it the "ritual field" of *Mukanda.* What, then, were the major properties and relationships of that ritual field?

First, the spatial limits of the ritual field had to be considered. These were fluid, varying from situation to situation, but corresponding approximately to the boundaries of a vicinage, which I have defined elsewhere as a discrete cluster of villages. All the boys to be circumcised came from the vicinage, as did the majority of the officiants. At the great public ceremonies that preceded and terminated *Mukanda* proper, however, people from several vicinages, and even chiefdoms, attended, and during one phase of the seclusion period, masked dancers from the lodge visited villages in adjacent vicinages. The boundary of the ritual field was therefore vague and variable. Nevertheless, for most of the ritual, the effective boundary of the ritual field tended to overlap the perimeter of the vicinage.

Now the Ndembu vicinage has certain general properties that crucially affect the structure of the ritual field of any performance of *Mukanda*. It consists, as we have said, of a number of villages—anything from two to over a dozen, separated from one another by variable distances of fifty yards to a couple of miles. Few of these villages are interlinked by matrilineal ties, that is, by the dominant principle of descent. Most of them have only short histories of local settlement and have come from other vicinages or chiefdoms. Such villages soon become interlinked by a complex network of marriages, and affinity assumes a political significance. Since marriage is virilocal, and most marriages occur within the vicinage, most villages rear as their seminal "children" the junior matrilineal members of the other villages. I mention this because it is an important feature of *Mukanda* that fathers protect and tend their sons during circumcision and seclusion. The father-son link which is crucial for the integration of the vicinage is also stressed in the ritual custom.

As I have shown in *Schism and Continuity in an African Society,* vicinages are unstable groupings, for villages frequently split through time and wander over land. The split-off section or migrant village often changes its vicinage affiliation. These characteristics of the vicinage, its instability and transience, render political control by any one headman over the others impossible. No clearly dominant criterion exists to validate such authority. As in other sets of Ndembu social relations, we find rather the coexistence and situational competition of several principles that confer prestige but not control. Thus, in each vicinage there are usually two or more villages that claim moral preeminence over the others, each advancing its claim by virtue of a single criterion. One village, for example, might claim seniority on the grounds that it has resided for a longer time in the territory occupied by the contemporary vicinage than any other village. Its claim may be countered by a later-arriving village, the lineage core of which is closely related to the Ndembu Senior Chief or to the Government

Subchief of the area (which includes several vicinages). The conflict between them is pertinent to the analysis of *Mukanda,* for the headman sponsoring this ritual thereby obtains general recognition in and outside his vicinage as its moral leader, if not as its political head. Thus, every *Mukanda* is preceded by faction struggles for the right to sponsor it. Each important headman tries to exploit his ties of kinship, affinity, and friendship with members of other villages to strengthen his following. He may also attempt to win the favor of his local chief, who must ritually inaugurate *Mukanda.* On the outcome of this struggle depends the specific allocation of ritual roles, for the most important fall to members of the victor's faction.

In delimiting the ritual field, the structure of the village and the pattern of intervillage relationships have also to be considered. Villages are the major local subdivisions of the vicinage and must be considered both in terms of their interdependence with that wider grouping and with regard to their degree of autonomy within it. Furthermore, they must be examined from the standpoint both of their interdependence with and independence from each other, that is, of their relationship with structurally equivalent groups.

Membership of villages helps to shape the composition of the ritual assembly at *Mukanda* and is an important factor in the disputes that arise in the secular intervals between sacred phases and episodes. Indeed, what is more important than the general characteristics of village structure in this kind of ritual is the specific content of intravillage and intervillage relationships during the period of *Mukanda.* This content includes the contemporary interests, ambitions, desires, and goals of the individuals and groupings who participate in such relationships. It also includes patterns of interaction inherited from the immediate past: personal grudges, memories of situations of blood vengeance, and corporate rivalries over property or over the allegiance of individuals. In other words, when we analyze the structure of a social field, we must regard as crucial properties of that field not only spatial relations and the framework of persisting relationships which anthropologists call "structural," but also the "directed entities" at any given time operative in that field, the purposive activities of individuals and groups, in pursuit of their contemporary and long-term interests and aims.

One aspect of the enduring structure of Ndembu society assumes heightened significance in this kind of ritual field. I refer to categorical relationships which stress likeness rather than interdependence as the basis for classification. *Mukanda* has the prominent characteristic of expressing in its symbolism and role-pattern not the unity, exclusiveness, and constancy of corporate groups but rather such widespread classes as men, women, elders, children, the married, the unmarried, and so on. Such categories cut across and interlink the memberships of corporate groups. In a sense they represent, when ritualized, the unity and continuity of the widest society, since they tend to represent the universal constants and differentiae of human society, age, sex, and somatic features. By emphasizing these in the sacred context of a great public ritual, the divisions and oppositions between corporate groups and between the total social system, viewed as a configuration of groups and all or any of its component groups, are "played down" and forced out of the center of ritual attention. On the other hand, the categorical relationships are ritualized in opposed pairs (men and women, old and young, circumcised and uncircumcised, etc.), and in this way a transference is made from struggles between corporate groups to the polarization of social categories. However, it must be emphasized that *Mukanda* is dominantly a repressive ritual, and not a ritual of rebellion or an acting out of socially illicit impulses. On the whole, conflict is excluded from the stereotyped behavior exhibited in ritual events. On the one hand, the severe physical danger to the novices, and, on the other, the danger of fights breaking out between corporate groupings in the secular interstices of the ritual situation are partially countered by a strong stress on the need for social categories to cooperate. Harsh penalties are exacted upon those who disobey ritual officiants, and dreadful supernatural sanctions are believed to punish taboo-breaking. By these means, the opposition between social categories is confined within narrow limits, and in the ritual situation their interdependence, rather than their mutual antagonism, is emphasized.

Although specific corporate groups do not receive expression in the ritual customs of *Mukanda,* certain typical kinship relationships are vividly represented. These are the parent-child relationships. One of the aims of *Mukanda,* as we have seen, is to modify the relationship between mother and son, and between father and son, in the sense that after *Mukanda* the relationships between occupants of these three social positions are guided by different values and directed towards different goals than those which prevailed before that ritual. From being "unclean" children, partially effeminized by constant contact with their mothers and other women, boys are converted by the mystical efficacy of ritual into purified members of a male moral community, able to begin to take their part in the jural, political, and ritual affairs of Ndembu society. This change has repercussions within their relationships to their parents. These repercussions not only reshape the structure of the elementary family, that is, the modes of interlinkage between sons and parents, but also reshape extrafamilial links of matrilineal descent and patrilateral affiliation. For a boy is linked through each of his parents to different kinds of corporate groups: through his mother to the matrilineal nucleus of a village, and through his father not only to another village, but also, by extension, to units of the wider society, vicinage, chiefdom, tribe. *Mukanda* strengthens the wider and reduces the narrower loyalties. Matriliny is the principle governing the persistence of narrow local units through time. It is a principle of cardinal importance in Ndembu society and is ritualized in a great number of contexts. Nevertheless, in *Mukanda,* emphasis is laid on the unity of males, irrespective of their matrilineal interconnections. The father-son tie assumes special prominence and is almost regarded as representative of the values and norms governing the relationships of the widest Ndembu community. It is a ligament binding local groups into a tribal community. The separation of men and women in *Mukanda* is not only a ritualized expression, indeed an exaggeration, of the physical and psychological differences between men and women, but it also utilizes the idiom of sexuality to represent the difference between opposed modes of ordering social relations, which in Ndembu culture have become associated with descent through parents of opposite sex. The mother-son and father-son relationships have, in *Mukanda,* become symbols of wider and more complex relationships.

I have stated some of the major spatial and structural properties of the ritual field of the *Mukanda* I studied, and I indicated that the general characteristics of Ndembu social structure were here combined in an idiosyncratic way, consonant with the interests and purposes of members of the contemporary community. I showed in the first section how the actually existing social relationships were specifically aligned. Now I would like to point out that from the standpoint of our analysis these spatial and structural properties really relate to what Lewin would call a "power field," rather than "force field." The concept of "power" refers to "a possibility of inducing forces" of a certain magnitude on another person or group. It does not mean that group A actually exerts pressure on group B. I have described a power field, the boundaries of which were roughly coterminous with a Ndembu vicinage, containing villages of various sizes, some of which claimed moral leadership of the vicinage by various criteria and which were interlinked with one another by ties of kinship and affinity of variable number and efficacy. I have discussed other groupings and relationships in the structure of this power field.

Now the decision to perform *Mukanda* converted this power field into a "force field." Lewin defines force as a "tendency to locomotion" where locomotion refers to a "relation of positions at different times." What does this mean for us in analyzing *Mukanda*? It means, on the one hand, that the various component groupings put their "power" to the test, in competition for the leading ritual roles. Forces are goal-directed, and goals determine the structure of particular force fields. In this situation, the participants in *Mukanda*, individually or in sections and factions, competed for common goals, namely, major ritual roles, in order to obtain prestige. The concept of "force field" implies more than this at *Mukanda*. More than the teleology of struggle for short-term benefits is meant here. For the complex sequence of ritual events that make up *Mukanda* is associated with other than particularistic ends. In an important respect, *Mukanda* is a cybernetic custom-directed "mechanism" for restoring a state of dynamic equilibrium between crucial structural components of a region of Ndembu society that has been disturbed by the growing up of a large number of boys. Too many "unclean" (*anabulakutooka*) boys are "hanging around" the women's kitchens. Not enough youths are sitting in the village forum (*chota*) and participating in its adult affairs. It is in the general interest of many villages to bring these boys into the adult fold and thus to correct the obstructions in the course of regular social life brought about by their presence. Given the belief that uncircumcised Ndembu males are both unclean and immature, the natural increase of such persons must lead to a numerical imbalance, and also to an imbalance in social influence, between men and women. Uncircumcised boys belong to the women's sphere of activities and their attachment to this sphere becomes greater as time passes. At any given time, the nuclear constellation of social relationships in a village is between male kin, matrilineally or patrilaterally attached to its headman, but relationships of authority-respect and superordination-subordination concern only the circumcised. If "structural relationships" may be defined as social relationships that are given a high degree of constancy and consistency by norms sanctioned by organized force, withdrawal of reciprocity, and/or by mystical agencies, it may be said that only circumcised men participate in such relationships. Men do not normally order about or chastise uncircumcised children. Ancestral spirits are not believed to afflict uncircumcised boys with illness or misfortune for their own misdemeanours, since they are not regarded as responsible persons. Children are not entitled to suffer. Such boys may, however, be afflicted for the misdemeanours of their mothers, since they are regarded as part of the social personality of their mothers. After the boys have been purified and rendered "men" by *Mukanda* they must obey their elders, fulfill the norms governing each category of kinship relationship, and may be punished for disobedience by any male senior to them. They can also be afflicted by the spirits as independent persons or as representatives of structured subgroupings of Ndembu society. If there is an undue preponderance of uncircumcised boys in a village or in a vicinage, therefore, there may not be enough initiated boys to perform routine tasks of village maintenance, and there may exist a tendency for uncircumcised boys to become increasingly less amenable to the discipline whereby structural relationships are maintained. Prolonged attachment to mother and to the women's sphere is symbolized in the fact that the foreskin is compared to the *labia majora*. When the foreskin is removed by circumcision the effeminacy of the child is symbolically removed with it. The physical operation itself is symbolic of a change of social status.

Thus, there are two main categories of forces in the ritual field of *Mukanda,* associated with two types of goals. One type of goal is concerned with the maintenance of the traditional structure of Ndembu society. The means employed is a bounded sequence of ritual customs directed to the correction of a deviationary drift towards numerical imbalance between socially recognized categories of Ndembu. Ndembu themselves do not formulate the situation at this level of abstraction. They say that "there are many children (*atwansi*) in the villages who have not been cut (*ku-ketula*) or circumcised (*kwalama* or *kwadika*), and so the elders of the vicinage feel that it would be good to circumcise them." Pressed a little further, Ndembu admit that it is inconvenient if there are many uncircumcised boys in a village, for circumcised men may not eat food cooked on a fire used for cooking such boys' meals nor use a platter on which they have eaten. Again, they will say that the boys in a village get sharply divided into circumcised and uncircumcised, and that the former mock the latter. This division cuts across groups of siblings, and it is felt to be inappropriate that brothers should revile brothers. Uterine brothers and the male children of sisters form the principal unit in founding a new village, and in other contexts also the principle of the unity of brothers is strongly stressed. We have seen that older brothers or parallel cousins frequently act as guardians (*ayilombweji*) for their younger brothers or cousins in the seclusion period following circumcision. In this way, they are brought into a close helpful relationship with their junior siblings, which to some extent tends to overcome their earlier cleavage.

Customary beliefs about the function of *Mukanda,* then, give rise to a situation of both moral and physical discomfort when there are many uncircumcised boys in a vicinage. It is this feeling of discomfort, associated no doubt with anxiety on the part of their fathers about whether the boys are becoming too closely attached to their mothers, and with irritation among the men generally that there are so many undisciplined youngsters around, that sets the prevailing tone of vicinage life. In such an atmosphere, the suggestion by a responsible adult that *Mukanda* should be performed is received with a certain amount of relief, although this is tempered by the knowledge that *Mukanda* is a difficult and dangerous ritual to undertake and that it involves the participation over several months of almost everyone in the vicinage in some capacity or other. Human beings everywhere like to feel secure about the functioning of certain dominant social relationships. If these work smoothly, and, so to speak, unobtrusively, they are the better able to pursue their personal and sectional aims. If they feel that custom is, on the whole, being upheld and observed, they are the better able to predict the outcome of activities set in train to achieve their particular goals. They may well feel that the totality of social interactions in which they participate in overlapping time cycles has a "framework." Certain actions and transactions are obligatory, however onerous they may seem to the individuals who perform them. If these are left undone or are done inadequately, the framework can no longer be relied upon as a safeguard and standard of general social intercourse. Insecurity and instability result when the interactions through which crucial "structural" customs are maintained and expressed fail repeatedly to be performed. Now *Mukanda,* as stated above, is a mechanism "built-in" to the system of customs which give a measure of form and repetitiveness to Ndembu social interactions. It is a mechanism that temporarily abolishes or minimizes errors and deflections from normatively expected behavior. Such errors are not here to be regarded as overt, dramatic breaches of norm or challenges to values, but rather as a drift away from a state of ideal complacency or equilibrium. Other kinds of mechanism than *Mukanda,* both jural and ritual, are indeed available in Ndembu culture for redressing breaches of norms. *Mukanda,* like rituals in many other societies which are connected with the sociobiological maturation of broad categories of individuals, is a corrective rather than a redressive mechanism, a response to cumulative mass pressures and not to specific emergencies.

The other set of goal-directed forces in the ritual field of *Mukanda* is constituted by the carrying forward into that field of all kinds of private pursuits of scarce values from the pre-existing state of the vicinage field. Individuals and groups saw in *Mukanda* not only a means of correcting and adjusting the wider framework of their social relationships, but also of augmenting their own prestige or establishing their claim to certain rights in subsequent secular and ritual situations. They also saw in it an opportunity to reduce the prestige and damage the future claims of rivals.

In dynamic terms, the ritual field of the *Mukanda* I am discussing represents the overlapping of two force fields, each oriented towards different and even contradictory sets of goals. I say "contradictory," for the same persons were at one and the same time motivated to act for the general good of the vicinage and to compete with one another for scarce values. If one were in a position to examine every item of public behavior during the period and in the site of *Mukanda,* one would undoubtedly find that one class of actions was guided by the aims and values of *Mukanda,* another class by private and sectional strivings, while yet another represented a series of compromises between these altruistic and selfish tendencies. If one could have access to the private opinions of the participants, it could probably be inferred that ideals and selfish motives confronted one another in each psyche before almost every act. My own observations and records of a few confidential conversations would lend support to this point of view.

However, it must be clearly understood that I am not positing a simple dichotomy between "ideals," as embodied in the customs of *Mukanda,* and "selfish or partisan interests," as expressed in certain kinds of behavior. For the principles, consciously recognized or implicitly obeyed, which govern social interaction, are never in any society so interrelated that the kind of behavior each instigates falls harmoniously into place with behavior according to other principles. Even where each principle controls a separate field of activity, nevertheless activity fields are intercalated by individuals pursuing their life goals. Wherever a principle "leaks" into an "alien" activity field it modifies the behavior of persons who pursue their aims in that field. It often happens that in practice the intruding principle, highly valued in its original activity field, exercises a stronger influence on behavior than the principle normally dominant. Thus, the principle of matriliny, which should govern only relationships arising from descent in the case of married Ndembu women, sometimes ousts the principle of virilocality as a determinant of residence. I write as though I have personified principles, but this is merely a convenient device for expressing a very complex interrelation of variables. In reality, tensions within individuals and between groups generate behavior that renders already established principles operative or inoperative. Even where behavior is principled and is not entirely self-seeking, the principles that support it may be discrepant and induce the actors to pursue mutually inconsistent or even contradictory aims at the same time and with regard to the same people. It is arguable that without a certain "looseness of fit" or discrepancy between its principles of organization, there would not be such a thing as a "society," for a society is essentially a whole hierarchy of corrective and adaptive activities, in which each more inclusive activity corrects or redresses the deflections or breaches of the activity below it in the hierarchy. There is never in this hierarchy such a thing as the radical correction of deviation or the complete restoration of breach. Biopsychological needs and drives, on the one hand, and external sociocultural stimuli, on the other, ensure the immortality of disturbance in each society, but the activities that make up a society are patterned by custom, and pattern only emerges in corrective and adjustive situations. Society is a process, a process of adaptation that can never be completely consummated since it involves as many specialized adaptations as there are specialized influences in the environment to be met, as Herbert Spencer wrote a century ago. An essential feature of the process that is society is the discrepancy between its structuring principles. The conflicts between persons and groups that are provoked by such discrepancy continually call into play the corrective and adaptive activities whose hierarchy summates human social life.

The ritual field of *Mukanda,* then, exhibits certain relatively constant properties and relationships, such as its spatial coordinates and customary principles of social organization. It also exhibits, as we have seen, dynamic properties in the form of aim-directed chains of activities. These aim-directed activities can be envisaged as force fields which overlap and interpenetrate. The circumcision ritual itself, with its aim of purifying and conferring social manhood on uncircumcised boys, establishes one such force field. The kinds of relationships handled by this ritual tend to be categorical relationships, and the overt expression of corporate relationships is concomitantly suppressed. Private and sectional aims set up an antithetical force field. In this field the units of structure and struggle tend to be just those units and relationships that are suppressed by the ritual, that is, those of a corporate character. This meant that since there could be no licit admission of the tensions between corporate groups, behavior indicative of such tensions was on the whole excluded from the "sacred" episodes of *Mukanda*, but it could be clearly observed in the secular intervals between such episodes and in those regions of the ritual field which had not been sacralized. It is perhaps hardly correct to speak of "secular" and "sacred" behavior in the ritual field of *Mukanda*. All behavior I observed in the neighborhood of the main ritual sites and between rites was directed by the relations between the structural and dynamic components of the total field. Behavior characteristic of the social relationships suppressed by ritual custom flourished outside the jurisdiction of such custom. Ritual custom itself was modified and even distorted from the "ideal pattern" which one could elicit from the accounts of ritual specialists under placid interview conditions. It was modified by the purposive activities of persons and groups organized according to the very principles repressed by overt ritual custom. Shifts in the balance of power between structural components of the power field of the vicinage are referable to the force field of interests which exerted pressure on the structure of forces directed towards the ends of the ritual proper. There were regions of the total field where the structures of the two major force fields tended to coincide, but there were also regions of stress and discrepancy between them. The methods of analysis that have become established in anthropology cannot provide adequate constructs to explain the relationships between the interacting factors that determine successive and simultaneous events in a behavioral field of this type. If, on the one hand, one abstracts that behavior which can clearly be classified as "ritualistic," that is, prescribed formal behavior not given over to technological routine but having reference to beliefs in mystical agencies, one gains possession of a set of data useful primarily in comparative cultural analysis. One can compare the observed ritual behavior with other observations of the same kind of ritual and with informants' accounts of that kind of ritual. From these observations and accounts one can construct two types of model. From repeated observations of the same kind of ritual, one can make tentative statements about its "real pattern" at a given time, the accuracy of this model varying with the number of observed instances. From informants' statements one can make a similar model of the "ideal pattern." Then, if one wishes, one can estimate the degree and kind of deviation between the specific instance and both types of model.

If, on the other hand, one abstracts the kind of data that one can label as "structural," that can be reasonably related to the constant and consistent relationships between persons, groups, and categories, one gains possession of data pertinent to the construction of two similar models at a different level of abstraction from the pair of cultural models.

From the first pair of models, one can demonstrate that deviation exists between specific instance and real and ideal normative patterns, and show where precisely it occurs, but one cannot show why it occurs, what are the causative factors behind it. From the second pair of models, one can exhibit which features of the structure of the total social system receive expression in the given kind of ritual. Where deviation exists between ideal and real patterns, one can speculate whether this is due to the intrinsic nature of ritual, which perhaps always allows in its symbolic pattern a high degree of leeway to accommodate local and situational variations in the structure of the groups performing it, or whether social change is the factor responsible for marked divergence. However, it is of the very essence of structural analysis that it regards as irrelevant items of behavior that are never or seldom repeated, the "unique events" of which social life is full. Yet it may be just such items of behavior which have the highest significance for the study of society regarded as a process. A further objection to the kind of abstracting activity that leads to the framing of models, often on assumptions borrowed from the study of two dimensional figures, is that the structural and cultural models cannot be compared with one another, for they belong to different planes of analysis.

It is doubtful whether fruitful problems can still be posed in terms of the culture-structure dichotomy. If society is conceived as a hierarchy of activities, or as a process of adaptation to innumerable and ever-renewed stimuli from the "environment," then "culture" becomes a property of a single important class of activities, and "structure" becomes a term signifying a certain constancy in the positions of active individuals relative to one another over a period of time. To conceive society thus as the motion of entities under the influence of forces is to allow scope for the systematic treatment of modes of motion that are not directly determined by "culture." The idiosyncratic behavior of individuals can now be handled within the analytical context of "activity field," for the consequences and implications of this kind of behavior are related to the constant and dynamic properties of such a field.

The sorts of "constructs" or "elements of construction" (to use Lewin's term) I have in mind are not general concepts based on abstraction from individual differences, in such a way that there is no logical path back from the "taxonomic" abstraction to the individual case. Rather, like Lewin, I believe that the individual case, "the unique event," the particular relationship, may be represented by the aid of a few constructive elements or their properties. Such elements and properties refer to activity fields as dynamic wholes. A total activity field or situation must first be characterized, not as an aggregate of isolated elements, but in terms of the kinds of interdependences, spatial and temporal, that expresses its operative unity. Only when this has been done, is it possible fruitfully to examine aspects and phases of the situation. Each individual instance may then be represented as a specific spatio-temporal nexus of "field" constructs. For *Mukanda,* what are the constructs and their properties?

The period of *Mukanda,* including preparations for it and its immediate sequelae, corresponds to the time of the situation. The vicinage in which it was performed locates it in space. Both its "time" and "space" have limits or boundaries. These have their conditions. Among these conditions are their degree of permeability or impermeability. *Mukanda,* for example, has its aspect of temporal uniqueness, in so far as it involves the suspension of many activities hitherto performed, but it also constitutes a phase in a social process of greater inclusiveness, and many of its distinctive activities have reference to activities typical of that wider process. The initial limits of *Mukanda,* therefore, terminate certain series of activities and mark the commencement of other series. The final limits of *Mukanda* reverse this

9. Chizaluki dances *Wubinda,* the initiated hunters' dance.

10. Novices undergoing decorative disguise for the "coming-out" ritual.

11. Novices decorated in patterns of white clay, and clacking ritual wands, being carried into the view of their mothers for the first time on the shoulders of different guardians from those appointed to look after them.

12. *Kambanji,* the bravest and cleverest novice, leads the others in dancing the *ku-tomboka* solo war-dance before the assembled vicinage at the coming-out ritual of *Mukanda.*

order. During the time of *Mukanda,* there are also mediate limits, at which certain activities characteristic of preritual time are resumed, and ritual activities discontinued. These mediate limits are concerned with the relation between ritual time and nonritual time, and not with the phases of ritual time itself. *Mukanda,* moreover, has its aspect of spatial autonomy, as we have seen above. Its effective boundary with the environing society coincides with that of the vicinage. However, since *Mukanda* is, in principle, a tribal ritual, several members of its personnel came from outside the vicinage, and during one phase of its performance, *Mukanda* was "taken" to adjoining vicinages. Within the situation of *Mukanda,* too, there are boundaries that demarcate areas of ritual space. Some of these boundaries also delimit *Mukanda* from the environing sociogeographical region, in that they allow selective entry into esoteric areas of specific categories of persons from that region, namely, to circumcised males.

Having established the temporal limits and spatial boundaries of the *Mukanda* situation and their conditions, the next step is to consider what are its constructional elements. Priority must be given, I think, to those elements that organize behavior in a ritual setting. What might be called the esemplastic elements, the unifying factors, of *Mukanda,* are the goals of the ritual behavior. These may be divided into explicit and implicit. The explicit goals are those which can be verbalized by the majority of participants. The implicit goals may be further divided into unavowed and unconscious. Unavowed goals can be verbalized by a minority of intelligent informants and are concerned with the readjustment of social relationships in the field. Unconscious goals cannot be verbalized but betray themselves in the form of ritual symbolism and in the comparative study of discrepancies in the meanings of symbols given by informants in different ritual contexts. Such goals are concerned with the adaptation of the psychobiological disposition of the individual to the general conditions of human social existence, for example, with adapting that disposition to the exigencies of the incest taboo which it seems, on the evidence of depth psychology, to find innately uncongenial.

Goals are distributed through the duration of *Mukanda,* in such a way that persons, resources, and activities are mobilized to attain instrumental goals, which, when attained, are seen as means to further goals. Thus one of the first explicit goals of *Mukanda* is to circumcise the boys without mishap. This accomplished, the next aim is to see that the boys are properly healed. When this has been done, the next aim is to see that the boys are properly instructed, and so on, until the final goal, that of returning the boys to society as purified and socially mature tribesmen, has been effected. Each aim or goal focuses a force field of specific structure, and there is a logical progression from mediate goals to final goal. The goal structure of Mukanda may then be likened to a many-step rocket, each step of which increases velocity in order to build up a momentum adequate to reach a target.

Interpenetrating the gradient of explicit goals are implicit goals of both categories. Thus, those who circumcise aim explicitly at bringing the boys to life as men. Unconsciously, however, as songs and symbolism indicate, the older men go as near as they dare to castrating or killing the boys. Infantile and archaic impulses seek gratification in the ritual situation in directions and by means quite opposite to those prescribed by the explicit goal structure. Indeed, I would argue that the symbol form which is characteristic of ritual represents a conjunction of opposite tendencies. Contrary goals are represented by the same form, which owes much of its apparent obscurity to this antilogical property. In most kinds of ritual, the sequence of explicit goals is "logical," if their premises are accepted, but the symbolism of the same rituals must remain enigmatic unless one postulates the existence of implicit goals which often run counter to the explicit ones.

The goals of the ritual itself, expressed in words or buried in symbols, structure relationships for a determinate period of time. Preexistent forms of groupings and relationships are realigned in a new structure of relationships established in goal-directed behavior. A force field is superimposed on the network of intervillage interactions within a vicinage. This force field is characterized by a specific role structure of officials, novices, and other participants. Each ritual role itself becomes a goal to be attained, and when attained, a part to be played competitively in relation to other roles, and successfully—to demonstrate the importance of the actor. In other words, the ritual force field supplies what Lewin would call a set of "positive valences" for members of the vicinage field. A positive valence is "a region (which may represent an activity, a social position, an object, or any other possible goal) which is attractive to (a given) person (or group)." Thus, the same set of goal-directed activity patterns which make up the ritual proper both covers up and activates the antecedent power field of vicinage interrelations. The system of vicinage interrelations becomes a vicinage force field or rather a set of interpenetrating force fields. This set of interpenetrating force fields is subordinated to the esemplastic goals of the ritual force field. The ritual force field is characterized by a cooperative atmosphere; the vicinage force fields are typified by a competitive atmosphere. Values held in common by all Ndembu determine that the attainment of the ritual goals has priority over the attainment of prestige in the ritual situation by specific groups and persons. Individuals and factions have to accept the frustration of their ambitious strivings in the interests of what is regarded as the general welfare of the widest community.

The subjacent force fields with their competitive goals are no merely arbitrary features of the total ritual field, but integral parts of it. Many kinds of ritual contain observances that express conflict and struggle. Such stereotyped forms may well induce the feelings they portray in the psyches of the participants. Professor Gluckman has analyzed such "rituals of rebellion" in a masterly fashion in *Custom and Conflict in African Society* (1955), and in his Frazer Lecture (1954). However, where rituals exclude the expression of certain kinds of conflict and competition from their overt and licit structure, I would postulate that their contextual situations are full of just those kinds of conflict and competition that are excluded. The extreme case is found in puritanical Protestantism which in its ritual structure suppressed parent-child and sibling competition and enjoined dependence and collaboration in these relationships. In the environing secular life, however, fierce competition reigned, the classical *bellum omnium contra omnes* of nascent capitalism. This competition existed between entrepreneurs and their parents or brothers-surrogates in the national economic system.

Among the elements of construction of the ritual field of *Mukanda* are various kinds of social grouping. If we regard the vicinage just before *Mukanda* was performed as a power field, that is, a set of "possibilities of inducing forces" of various sorts and magnitudes, we must examine the power units and their interrelations. The dominant power units in a Ndembu vicinage field are villages, and so we must say something about their general structure and the characteristic form of their interdependence. Since we are considering a specific activity field, we must also discuss the content of the actually existing relationships between the villages in this field. We must deal with general form, with patterned interdependence, and also with idiosyncratic content and with specific properties.

I began the analysis by setting out the main general and specific features of village relationships in the vicinage where the *Mukanda* I discussed took place. I called this set of relationships a "power field"—after Lewin—rather than a "social system" in order to bring out the point that this is a study in social dynamics, and not in social statics. Although "power field" does not have the same conceptual dimension as that of "force field," it still implies the possibility of motion. Nevertheless, to investigate the state of the vicinage as it was just before and during the preparations for *Mukanda* was to make something closely resembling a structuralist analysis. The major difference between this and an orthodox structuralist analysis is that I discussed the contemporary state of power relations between the real groups in the field, as well as examined the traditional principles of organization that govern the relatively constant interdependencies of person and groups. Since I have made my abstraction from reality with reference to a particular place and time, I could not exhibit the vicinage power field as a balance of power, but rather as an imbalance of power, an unsteady state, which the process of *Mukanda* ritual would shortly transform into overlapping and interpenetrating force fields, rife with struggles between individuals and groups. "Power equilibria" and "steady states" refer to ideal models and seldom to social reality which at any given time exhibits disequilibrium and deviation from norm.

## BIBLIOGRAPHY

Baumann, H. 1932. "Die Mannbarkeitsfeiern bei den Tsokwe," *Baessler Archiv,* XV, No. 1.

Borgonjon, R. J. F. 1945. "De Besnijdnis bij den Tutschokwe," *Aequatoria,* VIII, Nos. 1 and 2.

Colson, E. 1962. *The Plateau Tonga of Northern Rhodesia, Social and Religious Studies.* Manchester University Press.

Delille, A. 1930. "Besnijdnis bij de Alundas en Aluenas in de strak ten Zuiden van Belgisch Kongo," *Anthropos,* XXV, Nos. 5–6.

——. 1944. "Over de Mukanda en Zemba bij de Tshokwe," *Aequatoria,* VII, No. 2.

Gluckman, M. 1949. "The Role of the Sexes in Wiko Circumcision Ceremonies," in *Social Structure.* London: Oxford University Press.

——. 1954. *Rituals of Rebellion in South-East Africa.* Manchester University Press.

——. 1955. *Custom and Conflict in Africa.* Oxford: Blackwell.

Hambly, W. D. 1935. "Tribal Initiation of Boys in Angola," *The American Anthropologist,* XXXVII.

Holdgredge, C. P., and Young, Kimball. 1927. "Circumcision Rites among the Bajok," *American Anthropologist*, N.S. XXIX.

Lewin, K. 1949. *Field Theory in Social Science*. London: Tavistock Publications.

Tucker, J. T. 1949. "Initiation Ceremonies for Lwimbi Boys," *Africa*, XIX.

Turner, V. W. 1957. *Schism and Continuity in an African Society: A Study of Ndembu Village Life*. Manchester University Press.

——. 1962a. *Chihamba, the White Spirit* (Rhodes-Livingstone Paper 33). Manchester University Press.

——. 1962b. "Three Symbols of Passage in Ndembu Circumcision Ritual," in M. Gluckman ed., *Essays in the Ritual of Social Relations*. Manchester University Press.

——. 1968. *The Drums of Affliction*. Oxford: The Clarendon Press for the International African Institute.

White, C. M. N. 1953. "Notes on the Circumcision Rites of the Balovale Tribes," *African Studies*, XII, No. 2.

——. 1961. *Elements in Luvale Beliefs and Rituals* (Rhodes-Livingstone Paper 32). Manchester University Press.

CHAPTER VIII

# Themes in the Symbolism of Ndembu Hunting Ritual*

FOR the Ndembu tribe of Zambia the hunt is more than a food quest; it is a religious activity. It is preceded and followed by the performance of rites and is believed to be beset with perils of an ultrahuman order. I have discussed the social importance of hunting among the Ndembu in a number of previous publications (1953, 1957, 1961), and will therefore confine myself to repeating that this importance does not derive from the objective contribution to the food supply made by the chase. It arises partly from the high ritual status of the hunter and partly from the fact that, for the Ndembu, hunting epitomizes masculinity in a society jurally dominated by the principle of matrilineal descent. In agricultural production (mainly the cultivation of cassava, finger millet, and maize), and in the preparation of food, women's work has major importance, though men today are increasingly drawn into the cultivation of crops for cash while hunting declines with the shooting out of game.

Ndembu recognize two main branches of hunting: (1) *Wubinda,* which includes every recognized technique for killing animals and birds—firearms, bows and arrows, spears, snares, traps, pitfalls, nets, the use of birdlime, etc.; (2) *Wuyanga,* the skilled use of guns. Although women and children snare small animals and birds, this activity is not described as *Wubinda*; the term is reserved for the killing or catching of bigger game. Forest game is hunted all year

* First published in the *Anthropological Quarterly,* XXXV, No. 2 (1962).

round, except at the height of the rainy season, but animals are hunted on the plains which stretch around the upper reaches of rivers —most of the Ndembu territory in Mwinilunga District in northwestern Zambia lies on the Congo-Zambezi watershed and is therefore an area of river sources—mainly when the grass has grown long enough to give the hunter adequate cover.

During the period of my field research, guns were by no means plentiful among the Ndembu. According to the 1951 District Report (kindly made available to me by Mr. R. C. Dening, then District Commissioner), 68 breechloading guns and 1,154 muzzle-loading guns had been registered at District Headquarters. These figures refer to the whole of Mwinilunga District, which includes not only 18,346 Ndembu, but also 13,107 Kosa people. The total taxpaying population of adult males was recorded as 10,542. The ratio of approximately one gun to nine adult males is probably not incorrect. Quite a high proportion of the guns are ancient flintlocks, used as currency in the nineteenth century slave trade, and are inefficient and dangerous to use. Thus few men can hope to possess guns, and of these, fewer still become really proficient hunters.

To the two main branches of hunting correspond two cults, also called *Wubinda* and *Wuyang'a,* and the latter has many of the characteristics not merely of a profession but even of a vocation. The gun-hunter (*chiyang'a*) is often a solitary adept who spends much of his time alone or accompanied by a single apprentice—(who is also a candidate for admission to the cult)—in the wild bush with all its visible and invisible dangers. He is assisted by the guardian shade of a deceased hunter kinsman and by magical charms, he performs rites to propitiate the shades of hunter-dead before he ventures into the bush, and he is believed to encounter there the inimical powers of witches, sorcerers, ghosts, werelions, and persecuting ancestors.

A *chiyang'a* is also a *chibinda* (a hunter with bows and traps), but not every *chibinda* is a *chiyang'a. Wubinda* is the older cult and is said to have come with the forbears of the Ndembu when they migrated from the kingdom of Mwantiyanvwa, the great Lunda chief in Katanga, more than two centuries ago. *Wuyang'a* is believed to have been introduced, along with the first muzzle-loading guns, by Ovimbundu traders who came regularly from Kasanji and Bihe in western Angola to purchase slaves and beeswax in the mid-nineteenth century. It shares many features of its symbolism with *Wubinda* on which it must have been speedily grafted.

## *Ritual of Affliction*

*Wubinda* belongs to the category of Ndembu ritual that I have called "ritual of affliction" (see pp. 9–10). The rites belonging to this category are performed to propitiate or exorcise ancestor shades that are believed to bring misfortune, illness, or reproductive disorders. The victims are their living kin. The alleged motives for afflicting vary, but it is commonly said that the victim has neglected to make offerings to the shade at its shrine or has forgotten the shade "in his heart." Affliction is conceived to be a sharp rebuke for such negligence. In almost every case I have been able to observe of illness or misfortune treated by ritual of affliction, there has been an additional factor of social disturbance. The victim has here been afflicted as a representative of a quarrel-ridden social group (a village, matrilineal descent group, or extended family), even if he or she is not held to be personally blameworthy. I have heard it suggested that such affliction is "good" ( *wahi*) because the ritual to remove it "brings to light" (*kusolola*) and so dispels the quarrels (*madombu*) and grudges (*yitela*) in the group.

There are various modes of affliction. Women, for example, are afflicted by ancestor shades (*akishi,* singular *mukishi*) with a number of clearly defined reproductive troubles, each kind corresponding to a named mode of affliction. For example, an ancestress "coming out in (the mode of) *Nkula*" (as Ndembu put it) afflicts her kinswoman (nearly always in the matrilineal line) with menstrual disorders. The rites to propitiate such shade manifestations might be termed "gynecological" rites. Hunters, too, are afflicted with different kinds of bad luck in the chase by dead hunter kinsmen (patrilateral as well as matrilineal).

To each mode of manifestation there corresponds a curative rite which bears its name. Thus "*Nkula*" is performed to cure a patient "caught" by the "*Nkula*" manifestation. *Nkula* cult members are recruited from those who have been its former patients. The patient is thus also a candidate for admission to the cult association, while the doctor is simultaneously an adept. Such associations of adepts cut across corporate groups with a kinship or local basis and across one another. They are called into transient being and action by a diviner's verdict. The divination séance itself may be regarded as a phase in a social process: (1) the beginning of a person's illness, reproductive trouble, or misfortune at hunting; (2) informal or formal discussion in the local community as to what is to be done; (3) representatives of the community are sent to a diviner; (4) a séance terminated by the diviner's diagnosis of the nature, cause, and agency of affliction and his recommendation that a certain type of rite should be performed; (5) the actual performance of that rite.

## Wubinda

The cult of *Wubinda* is an assemblage of five rites called respectively: *Mukala, Chitampakasa, Kalombu, Mundeli,* and *Ntambu.* Each of these names denotes a specific manifestation of a hunter ancestor, and much of the symbolism of the propitiatory rite is expressive of the attributes of that manifestation. Thus the senior adept in the *Mukala* rite makes whistling noises and at one stage wears strips of hide, each with a ridge of fur, because the *Mukala* manifestation is thought to whistle game away from the hunter and to wear these "*mazang'a,*" part of the garb of hunters in bygone times. *Mukala* may be performed for a young man who has just started to hunt seriously, though spirits may manifest themselves in this mode, so Ndembu think, to established hunters as well. The other modes of affliction affect only experienced hunters who have already been accorded cult names.

## Wuyang'a

The cult of *Wuyang'a* differs from *Wubinda* in that it consists of a graded series of four rites, each of which indicates the attainment of a certain degree both of proficiency in killing animals and of esoteric knowledge of the cult mysteries. These grades of initiation into *Wuyang'a* are as follows. (1) *Kuwelesha,* "causing to be washed"—in this case with pounded leaf medicine (*nsompu*). Here the novice or apprentice in "huntsmanship" (as *Wuyang'a* might be termed), having enjoyed a measure of success in shooting animals with an inherited or borrowed gun, is deemed worthy of being washed with a decoction of bark-scrapings and leaves taken from a number of tree species, each of which is thought to impart some aspect of "huntsmanship" to the would-be hunter. (2) If the young hunter has demonstrated his prowess he undergoes *Kusukula,* "initiation (into huntsmanship)." At the end of this rite he takes a special hunter-name from a collection of names reserved for initiated hunters. (3) *Kutelekesha,* "causing to cook (meat)": this is both a celebration of the hunter's skill and success over a long period and a feast in honor of his guardian ancestor spirit who has provided him—and through him his dependents and fellow villagers—with a regular supply of meat. In the course of this rite much meat is given by its sponsor to hunter adepts and to the general public. (4) *Mwima,* "ripeness" (from *kwima,* "to bear fruit"): this is the *dernier cri* in praise and self-praise for a gun-hunter. Only the greatest hunters are bold enough to hold *Mwima* which is a sign that a man has "finished huntsmanship." Incidentally, the term *mwima* is also applied to the forked branch shrine planted in honor of a hunter's shade. We shall shortly discuss this structure in detail, but it is worth mentioning in passing that the "fruit" borne by it are trophies of the chase, the heads and entrails of antelope and other game. In all this an important analogy is made by Ndembu between what they consider is woman's dominant role, the bearing of children, and man's, which is the bringing home of carcasses from the hunt. In hunters' and women's rites of affliction the same symbols stand respectively for a multiplicity of kills and a multiplicity of children. Women do not possess a *mwima,* and indeed their reproductive powers are endangered by close contact with "the things of huntsmanship," but the values associated with *mwima* are those which assert a parallel between the many kills desired for a male hunter and the many new lives desired for a mother.

## *Hunting Rites*

Since space is limited I can do little more here than indicate a few of the main themes running through the symbolism of *Wubinda* and *Wuyang'a* and of the mortuary rites of professional hunters. I have discussed (pp. 50–57) the semantic structure and properties of some of the principal symbols found in Ndembu ritual and there distinguished between three "levels" or "fields" of meaning possessed by such symbols. I pointed out that many ritual symbols are multivocal or polysemous, that is, they stand for many objects, activities and, relationships—there is not a one-to-one relationship between symbol and referent but a one-to-many relationship. Each major symbol has a "fan" or "spectrum" of referents (*denotata* and *connotata*), which tend to be interlinked by what is usually a simple mode of association, its very simplicity enabling it to interconnect a wide variety of referents. Some of the symbols we shall shortly consider have this polysemous character. I shall consider them first on the level of their exegetical meaning, secondly in their operational meaning, and thirdly in their positional meaning. The first level, briefly, represents the interpretations of my Ndembu informants—in this case of hunter adepts—the second results from equating a symbol's meaning with its use, by noting what Ndembu do with it, and not only what they say about it, while the third level of meaning consists in examining a symbol's relationship to others belonging to the same complex or *Gestalt* of symbols. I hope to show that this set of methodological tools has its uses in exposing to view the deeper layers of a society's system of values.

Simply because each ritual symbol is so dense with significance, the task of presenting, classifying, and analyzing the referents of even a few interrelated symbols is necessarily a long one. For ritual, in one important aspect, is quintessential custom; what is distributed through many fields and situations of secular life is condensed into a few symbolic actions and objects. For every kind of hunting rite, itself an epitome of a whole sector of Ndembu culture, a quintessential feature is the temporary shrine erected to the hunter ancestor, who is either afflicting his living kinsman with bad luck or has already been propitiated and is regarded as the source of his good fortune in killing game. This shrine typically has three main components and may be associated with further symbolic units according to the specific rite that is performed. These three components are : (1) a forked branch known as *chishing'a, muchanka,* or, as we have seen, in the case of a supreme hunter, *mwima*; (2) a small piece of termitary earth trimmed into a square of rectangular shape and laid at the base of the forked branch, which is firmly planted in the ground, facing the ritual assembly or "congregation"; (3) a braid of grass, of the *kaswamang'wadyi* species, which grows to a considerable height on the plains.

## *The Exegetical Meaning of* Chishing'a

Each of these components is a complete system of meaning and may be analyzed at the three levels of interpretation discussed earlier. Let us, then, consider the forked branch at the level of indigenous exegesis. In explaining what a symbolic object stands for, Ndembu normally look to two of its characteristics, its name and its natural properties, as the *fons et origo* of interpretation. Let us then consider the name *chishing'a,* commonly applied to these shrines. My informants are in general agreement that the term is derived from the reflexive form of the verb *ku-shing'a* or *ku-shing'ana,* "to curse," namely, *kudishing'a,* which means "to curse one another." This may well be an instance of fictitious etymologizing (see Turner 1961, 57), but fictitious eymology, like homonymy (i.e., increasing the senses possessed by a word by adding to them those of a word of the same form but different derivation), is a device whereby the semantic wealth of a word or symbol may be augmented. Whether this is the case or not, my informants are also in agreement in stating that "meat (*mbiji*) is a cause of quarrels (*madombu*), and in quarrels people curse one another"—with implications of the use of sorcery.

"Meat is a cause of quarrels" in two basic situations. In the first place, hunters often conceal from their fellow villagers that they have made a kill, pleading dolefully that they have had no luck. Meanwhile, they have divided the meat secretly among the members of their elementary family and personal friends, instead of distributing customarily specified joints among the members of their village matrilineage. If this is later discovered, grudges (*yitela*) will develop, leading to the invocation of ghosts to kill the hunter, if the situation is not remedied. Such an invocation is known as *ku-shing'ana,* a "curse." In the second place, even when the meat is distributed in public, villagers tend to quarrel about the amount given to them; for example, a classificatory mother's brother will demand an equal share with a full mother's brother. Thus jealousy (of the hunter's prowess), envy over the distribution of meat, hatred of the hunter by those who have been cheated, and quarreling between individuals and factions over amounts (quite a bunch of deadly sins, not to mention greed!) are regularly associated with the hunter's role. One informant told me, "a hunter eats good meat while others starve, and they say that he ought to find bad luck because he does not give them meat." Another said that "hunting is sorcery (*wuloji*), for hunters have snake-familiars (*malomba*) which kill their relatives to increase their (the hunters') power." For each tuft of the victim's hair the hunter is said to acquire the power (*ng'ovu*) to kill an animal. Far from feeling shame on account of their bad reputation, hunters, like big businessmen, seem often to rejoice in being known as "hard guys" and in song and invocation to hunter spirits refer to themselves by terms normally considered opprobrious, such as "adulterers who sleep with ten women a day" and "great thieves." They take pride in the envy directed against them for they say that only those who are successful are envied. To be "cursed" is part of what they term their "pride" or "dignity" or "self-praise of huntsmanship" (*kudilemesha* or *kudivumbika kwaWuyang'a*). Yet there is ambivalence in Ndembu society's attitude towards the hunter for he is, when all is said and done, the provider of the most prized food of all.

There was no agreement about the meaning of the word *muchanka.* One informant said that it was "an old word for the way animals move when a hunter is chasing them." *Mwima,* as we have seen, means "ripeness" or "bearing fruit," and this may refer to the skulls of buck and other trophies "borne" by the forked branch.

The name *chishing'a,* then, is heavily charged with the irony of huntsmanship. The meaning of the hunter as provider of blessings is expressed by language of quite opposite tendency. Let us now consider the natural properties of the forked branch. These provide further sources of meaning. They may be subdivided into two aspects: the species of trees used for the *chishing'a* and the shape of the *chishing'a.*

Trees, bushes, and herbs play the important part in Ndembu ritual that they play in the ritual of other forest Bantu. Each species is thought to have its own virtues, both for treating illness and in religious rites, but there is a crucial distinction to be made between these two major uses. When trees are used in the empirical treatment of illness, usually in the form of pounded leaves, scrapings of bark, and sliced roots mixed with hot or cold water, emphasis is laid on their directly physical effects on the senses. Thus in the treatment of pyorrhea, "medicine" (*yitumbu*) made from the sliced roots of various trees is heated and the patient is made to rinse his mouth with it. The aim of the treatment is "to remove pain so that the bad teeth will fall out by themselves." Among the ingredients are the roots of the *mwalu* tree, which is used "because it is bitter and can kill the disease." (*Musong'u,* a "disease," has certain animal and human characteristics; it can "move," "curl up," "think," "go away," "die.") *Musosu* is used because it is rather "sweet" and deadens pain. *Kambanjibanji* is "hot" (*yeya*) and drives off the disease. *Kapepi* is used "because it sets the teeth on edge by its bitterness (*wukawu*), so that the bad ones drop out."

Now the same term, *yitumbu,* is applied to pounded vegetable medicines used as potions and lotions in religious rites, but the nature of the association-chains in these rites is quite different. Here certain selected natural properties of the tree are regularly connected with values, moral qualities, principles of social organization, and with religious beliefs. I have many statements from informants that actually identify the *yitumbu* used in a rite of affliction with the mode of affliction in which an ancestor spirit has "emerged." Thus, the leaves of trees that secrete red gum or have red wood or roots are used in the "medicine" with which a woman patient is washed in the *Nkula* rite. An ancestress who "comes out in *Nkula*," as Ndembu say, afflicts her victim with menorrhagia and other periodic disorders involving the loss of blood which, so the people think, should cohere around the implanted "seed of life" (*kabubu kawumi*) to form an infant. The patient is exposed to a hot fire so that fragments of leaves should adhere to her when the medicine has dried. These fragments are said to be a "symbol (*chinjikijilu*) of the shade (*mukishi*) in Nkula." The "red" properties of this mode of affliction are here represented by the green leaves of trees that are ritually standardized as "red" (*-chinana*). "Redness" is a complex concept in Ndembu ritual, and in *Nkula* alone it stands for (1) menstrual blood; (2) maternal blood, "that is clear and good and shown at parturition"; (3) the principle of matriliny itself—a matrilineage is called *ivumu*, "a womb"; (4) the *Nkula* cult; (5) the historical continuity of the Ndembu with the great Lunda empire, whose foundress, Luweji Ankonde, suffered from menorrhagia and was cured by the first *Nkula* rite. In the hunting cults, "redness" has a further "fan" of referents, associated mainly with the shedding of the blood of animals. The forked branch shrine, though it is frequently splashed with offerings of blood, is not a red symbol but, in terms of its color symbolism, a white one. It is made from five species of trees. These are not used interchangeably, but the kind of rite determines the kind of shrine tree. The same species also provide ingredients for hunting "medicines," of the ritual type we have just been discussing. Whether these species are used for medicines or shrines their referents remain the same.

The five[1] species are: *Musoli* (*Vangueriopsis lanciflora*); *Museng'u* (*Ochna* sp.); *Kapwipu* (*Swartzia madagascariensis*); *Kapepi* (*Hymenocardia mollis*); and *Mubula* (*Uapaca* sp.).

### MUSOLI

*Musoli* is employed as "medicine" in rites to restore female fertility as well as in hunting rites. This tree has edible yellow fruit, much appreciated by duiker and other woodland buck during the early

[1] Some informants have told me that the *kabalabala* tree is also made into a *chishing'a,* but I have no detailed information on this point.

rains. Snares are set beneath *musoli* trees to trap these animals. Ndembu say that the name *musoli,* derived from *ku-solola,* "to make visible" or "reveal," is connected with the capacity of the tree to draw forth animals from their hiding places in the bush and make them visible to hunters. This is a "natural" capacity of the tree, as we would say, but Ndembu see in it something more. It is for them a particular instance of a power underlying all life, the power of "making visible." Thus, *musoli* medicine is given to a barren woman so that she will "make children visible" (*ku-solola anyana*) and to a hunter "to make animals visible" (*ku-solola anyama*) for him. *Musoli* has the further sense in the hunting rites of "producing to view a large gathering of people" (*ku-solola luntu lweneni* or *chipompelu cheneni*). The reasoning behind this is that just as the many fruits of the *musoli* bring out of hiding many animals, so will its ritual use bring many people to praise the hunter who has sponsored the rite, and who (it is implied) has killed many animals. The *musoli* tree, therefore, represents the prowess of the hunter at his profession and the fame (*mpuhu*) it confers on him.

### MUSENG'U

The Ndembu derive the name of this species from *ku-seng'uka,* "to multiply." The tree bears a great number of tiny black edible fruits, and informants connect this prolificity with its name. It is also connected with the term *ku-seng'ula,* "to bless"—in practice by blowing "medicine" in the ears. Like *musoli, museng'u* is used in both hunting and "gynecological" rites; in the former it represents "a multiplicity of kills," in the latter "a multiplicity of offspring."

### KAPWIPU

This tree is also known as *mutete,* and it is from this ritual usage that Ndembu normally commence its exegesis. *Mutete* itself is the first word of a phrase *mutete manyangi wuta wachashi,* literally, "the one who cuts huntsmanship" (i.e., "cuts up and distributes meat"), "the empty gun," or "the gun that misses its aim." In explanation of this phrase an informant told me: "A hunter was in the habit of killing many animals, but then he missed his aim once or twice. Others told him to hold his gun correctly, for the shaking of his mind caused him to miss. They played a hunting drum (i.e., performed *Wuyang'a* or *Wubinda* rites) for him and instructed him to shoot properly. After this, he never missed. So he praised himself thus: 'At first I killed animals, later I failed to do so, then after missing I killed again.' "

The *mutete* tree, then, epitomizes the whole process of *Wubinda*—hunting as a set of rites of affliction. Good luck depends on the favor of hunter ancestors, and they will withdraw their assistance from you, sometimes to punish you for distributing meat unfairly, sometimes because a ritually impure person such as a woman or an uncircumcised boy has eaten the sacred portions of meat (head, lungs, entrails), called *yijila* ("tabooed things"), reserved for the hunter. This withdrawal, and even active persecution, is something other than merely punitive. For the Ndembu have the notion that affliction is also a sign of election. The afflicting ancestor shade wishes to become "your shade" (*mukishi weyi*), in other words your guardian or patron shade. First, however, you must do something for him; you must perform rites for him, both private and public, and demonstrate that you have "not forgotten him in your liver" (the seat of the emotions in Ndembu belief), by making offerings either on his grave, if it can be found, or on a *chishing'a* specially planted to him. The identity of the hunter shade is established by divination, as also is the mode in which he is manifesting his displeasure. At the public phase of the rite, it is considered pleasing to the shade to mention his name often in invocations and praises. This is considered a form of *ku-solola,* of "revelation." If the shade has been placated he will "help you to kill many animals" and so contribute to your eventual fame as a great *"Mwima"* hunter. The motto of the Ndembu might well be "you must suffer to succeed." It is this theme that is so signally represented by the *kapwipu* or *mutete* tree. In this case, it is the "name only" (*ijina hohu*) that determines the chain of associations, not the properties of the species, but we shall see that *kapwipu* shares certain physical properties with the other species mentioned which make it suitable for use as a *"chishing'a."*

### KAPEPI AND MUBULA

I must discuss these species briefly, owing to shortage of space, and say that *kapepi* is connected with terms meaning "wind" and "breath" and stands for the desired invisibility and ubiquity of the hunter. *Mubula,* another fruit tree, is etymologically connected with *ku-bula,* "to make fire by steel, flint and dry-moss tinder" as hunters do in the bush; it also refers to the firing of their flintlocks.

## *The Shape of* Chishing'a

A *chishing'a* is a branch forked in one or more places, stripped of all its leaves and bark. The species I have mentioned are said to be termite-resistant and to have a "strong wood," representing the "strength" (*wukolu*) of huntsmanship. It has been said to me repeatedly by Ndembu hunters that string cannot be made out of the bark of any of the trees used for these shrines. "If they were string-trees, they would tie up (*ku-kasila*) the huntsmanship of the candidate." In just the same way, string bearing trees may not be used in gynecological ritual for fear of "tying up" the fertility of the patients.

The prongs of the extremities of the branches are sharpened by the knives of hunter adepts. This is to represent the "sharpness" or "keenness" (*ku-wambuka*) of huntsmanship. As informants said: *Wubinda wawambuka nang'ovu*" ("huntsmanship is sharp with power"). The causative form of *wambuka, wambwisha,* means "to whet a knife," and it is as though the hunters were trying to "whet" the candidate's huntsmanship. Forked-branch shrines are common throughout Africa, and they are by no means always associated with hunting cults. What is interesting in the present context is that Ndembu ascribe to such shrines senses that express the values of their hunting culture. One of the marks of a viable ritual symbol may be said to be its capacity to move from society to society without marked change in form but with many changes in meaning. Though referents are lost in transference, new referents are readily acquired. Certain symbols arouse an almost universal response, much as music does. This is a problem that would repay investigation in terms of a detailed comparative study.

The whiteness of the exposed wood in each species of *chishing'a* is also held to be significant by Ndembu informants. Whiteness (*wutooka*) in Ndembu ritual has many connotations. These include: strength, health, good luck, ritual purity, authority, good will between the ancestors and the living, the clear and known as opposed to the obscure and unknown, life, power, breast milk, seminal fluid, the whiteness of cassava meal and roots. In the context of hunting ritual the qualities of health, strength, toughness, luck at the hunt, virility, and a state of *bon rapport* with the ancestors tend to receive special stress among the "white" senses.

## *The Operational Meaning of* Chishing'a

The way a symbolic object is used, I have suggested, forms an important part of its meaning. Before we can fully appreciate what the *chishing'a* "means" to Ndembu, therefore, we must enquire how it is collected, set up, and thereafter utilized. A *chishing'a* may be cut: (1) by a solitary hunter; (2) by a hunter and the "great hunter" who is training him, known as his "mother of huntsmanship" (*mama daWuyang'a*)—for among the matrilineal Ndembu the term "mother" refers to one who nourishes with knowledge as well as with milk and is used metaphorically of male authority figures and teachers; and (3) by a group of hunter adepts. When the latter collect a *chishing'a,* one hunter lays his ax to the root while the others seize hold of the branches and bear down on them while they sing the melancholy, nostalgic songs of their cult. A hunter adept explained this as follows: "the hunters pull down the tree together to prevent it falling by itself—if it fell of its own accord the huntsmanship would be lost." Here again we find "huntsmanship" (*Wuyang'a* or *Wubinda*) being regarded almost as though it had physical properties, like a fluid that may be spilled, or a charge of electricity that may be carelessly expended.

The operational level of meaning is the level on which we may observe most clearly the sociological concomitants of ritual symbolism, for we observe not only what is done with the symbol but who does it. Here the unity and exclusiveness of the hunters' cult association is clearly portrayed. This is further exemplified in the setting up of the *chishing'a* in some of the rites. For example, in *Mwima,* the celebration of a great hunter's prowess, the hunters excavate a hole with their gun butts, then lift up the *chishing'a* collectively by means of their gun barrels, place it in the hole, and tamp it in firmly all together with their hands.

This *chishing'a,* and indeed the *ayishing'a* (the plural form) of all *Wuyang'a* rites, is planted in the hunter's village near the shrine trees planted to his matrilineal ancestors. But for many of the rites of *Wubinda,* the generic cult, the *ayishing'a* are inserted in large termite hills in the bush. *Ayishing'a* are also inserted in hunter's graves located at the fork of two paths leading from the village. It is of these *ayishing'a* that Ndembu say: "*Chishing'a* is the first place to which a hunter brings meat when he has made a kill. It is a *mutulelewa,* a place where meat is put. The whole carcass is put there before the hunter takes it to village to be eaten." The sacred portions of the animal, mentioned above, are placed on the *chishing'a,* as an offering to the hunter ancestor. In the *Mukala* rite, for example, when a hunter has made a kill, he washes the *chishing'a* with blood, impales pieces of *yijila* on the prongs, and expresses his gratitude to the patron spirit who has manifested himself in the form of *Mukala,* a mischievous entity which drives and whistles the game away from the hunter until propitiated. When the hunter, on learning from a diviner that he is being afflicted by an ancestor in the form of *Mukala,* first sets up a *chishing'a,* he chooses one of *musoli* wood, plants it, and invokes the shade manifestation as follows: "You, my kinsman who have already died, if you are the one who has come out in *Mukala,* now listen to me. Tomorrow, when I go into the bush to look for animals, you must cause me to see them quickly. I must kill animals by gun or trap." He then puts some powdered white clay (*mpemba* or *mpeza*) in his mouth and draws a line with the moistened clay from the *chishing'a* towards himself, places some on his temples, down the center of his brow, spits some on his shoulders, and draws a line of white upwards from his navel. "He puts it on his temples, beside his eyes," an informant said, "to see everything perfectly clearly (to spot animals in hiding or at a distance), on his brow that his face should be white or lucky, on his shoulders because he carries his gun and meat on them, and on his stomach, that there might be food in it." Then the hunter spits white powder on the *chishing'a.*

The hunt that follows may be regarded not merely as a utilitarian food quest but as some sort of a rite of sacrifice. It is not strictly comparable to the sacrifice of pastoral peoples, who give to the Deity or the ancestors a valuable animal as a token of their homage, penitence, and atonement, for the hunter has no animal to offer. The animal must first be given to him by the hunter shade, and this is already a sign of partial reconciliation, of the shade's provisional approval of the hunter's worthy intention. Nevertheless, until the hunter has made his offering of the blood and *yijila* at the *chishing'a* shrine he has not fully demonstrated his intention to propitiate and revere his ancestor. It is as though the shade, in giving him an animal, were putting his expression of good will to the test. Moreover, there is an element of gift exchange, of transaction, about the relationship between shade and hunter that contrasts with the attitudes of submission and adoration found in fully developed sacrifice to a deity.

Among the Ndembu, the ancestors do not represent or embody the moral order so much as continue after death to interact with their living kin, in terms of their human likes and dislikes. In most ritual contexts, not remote ancestors but the spirits of the comparatively recently dead are involved, and these shades are believed to afflict the living not only in punishment for wrongdoing but also because they themselves still harbor ill will against them on account of quarrels they took part in when they were alive. For the Ndembu, the moral order is felt to transcend both the living and their deceased kin, to be in fact something axiomatic in terms of which both the living and the spirits of their ancestors must seek to become reconciled (see above pp. 49–50). The mutual bargaining that for Ndembu characterizes the dealings of dead with living has a severely practical aspect. If the dead use their powers of invisibility and panic-making to drive animals towards the hunter, he will feed them with blood and cause their names to be remembered among men. For the dead depend on the living—to be sustained by food, offerings, and memories—and the living depend on the dead—for strength, health, fertility, fame, and good fortune. The moral order that decrees piety to the dead and compassion for the living is felt to be higher than both and in some obscure way to be connected with the High God *Nzambi* or *Shakapang'a. Nzambi* is not directly worshipped; "He is so far away," the people say.

## *The Positional Meaning of* Chishing'a

A major—one might even call it nuclear—symbol like *chishing'a* is nearly always found in regular association with other symbols which, like adjectives in language, qualify or extend its meaning. I have mentioned earlier that a hunter's shrine typically consists of a *chishing'a,* together with a small piece of termites' nest and a braid of *kaswamang'wadyi* grass. Small termitaries, known as *mafwamfwa* (singular, *ifwamfwa*), domed or finger-shaped, are a familiar feature of the Ndembu woodlands and plain margins. In circumcision and funerary rites they have an explicitly phallic significance. The swarming life within them is pointed out as a sign of "procreation" (*lusemu*). In hunting rites, the *ifwamfwa* is usually shaped into a cube and is either placed just in front of the *chishing'a,* or the branch is inserted in a hole in it (e.g., at *Kusukula*). Such a cube is called *katala kamukishi,* "the little hut of the ancestor shade." The shade is thought to visit its "hut" during and after the rite. The small termitary also represents in hunting rites the large termite hills (*tuwumbu,* singular *kawumbu*), sometimes fifteen feet or so in height, which stud the Mwinilunga bush. Informants say: "A termite hill is a favored site for hunter shades, who like to live on high places and, like lions, climb up them to see if there is game about." It was also pointed out to me that hunters hide themselves behind termitaries, large and small, when they stalk their quarry. Finally, in some *Wuyang'a* rites (such as *Mwima*) the termitaries are called *yimbumba,* a term that represents a dome-shaped cover of molded moistened earth raised on graves. The same term is applied to small termitaries placed in a ring round a dead hunter's head, which is allowed to appear above the surface of his grave. Hunters are buried, sitting upright, "like alert lions," and an opening is made in the ring of termitaries, "so that they may see clearly." Thus the symbolism of the termitary includes in its exegetical meaning references to burial practices peculiar to hunters, to the hunter's stealthy pursuit of game, to his vigilance, to his leonine traits (indeed the very name of the rite *Ntambu* signifies "the lion"), and to the feeling that his proper "home" is in the bush (represented by the termitary "hut") rather than in the village. Besides these senses there are overtones of fertility and virility from other rites in which termitaries represent these qualities.

The braid (*chibaba*) of *kaswamang'wadyi* grass is placed underneath the first fork (*mpanda*) of the *chishing'a.* Its name is derived from *ku-swama,* "to hide," and *ng'wadyi,* "the bare-throated francolin." At *Kutelekesha,* in the course of invoking hunter ancestors, the hunters say: "Today this grass is *kaswamang'wadyi* where all the animals and birds in the bush conceal themselves. If an animal is hidden in the grass, may we hunters be quick to see it, that we may shoot and kill it and be well pleased. May we carry it back and eat its meat. Do not hide it from us. It must appear, you must reveal it quickly (*muyisololi swayiswayi*)." The familiar theme of "making visible" (*ku-solola*) is again exemplified. Ndembu believe that the use of this grass in ritual will make the hunter invisible to the game he stalks.

The twist of grass divides the *chishing'a* into two sections. This division has meaning for the Ndembu. Below the grass, ancestor spirits come "to drink blood." On the forks, trophies of the chase are hung. "The hunter must resemble the ancestor shades," I was told, "the animals will not see him on account of the grass." The prongs of the divided branch may be said to represent the hunter's power to kill animals, power that he obtains from the ancestors by feeding them with blood. The shades are believed to "emerge" (*kw-idikila*) from the earth in which they have been buried, into their "grave-hut," and ultimately into the *chishing'a* itself.

Features of the topography that have importance for hunters are thus represented in combination: *chishing'a* = forest; *ifwamfwa* = termitaries; and *kaswamang'wadyi* = grass plains. Here we have the familiar ritual principle of association by *pars pro toto*. When we consider these three symbols together, we must also note the important division between the visible animals and the invisible shades, whose property of invisibility is desired by the hunter so that he may approach and kill the game. These conjunctions and divisions are aspects of the positional meaning of *chishing'a*.

## *The Semantic Morphology of* Chishing'a

Although the *chishing'a* forked branch shrine is an important element of Ndembu hunting ritual, there are hundreds of other symbols in the system, some of which are full or partial expressions of the same basic themes, while others represent different themes. Each of the *Wubinda* rites, for example, has its own ritual "plot" and idiosyncratic character. *Chishing'a* may fairly be said to typify the hunting symbol, since it is found in every hunting rite.

Starkly simple in outward form, a mere forked stick bare of bark, it is, as we have seen, rich in meaning. Let me try to express this semantic wealth diagrammatically, so as to bring out the semantic structure of this symbol. (See Diagram 9.)

The following may be said to comprise part of the "meaning" of a *chishing'a:*

(1) Social Relationships
- (a) Between hunters and nonhunters;
- (b) Between hunter's elementary family and matrilineal kin;
- (c) Between full and classificatory matrikin of hunter;
- (d) Between hunter and "his" hunter ancestor shade (most frequently the mother's brother or father);
- (e) Between hunter and his instructor in "huntsmanship";
- (f) Between fellow members of the hunters' cults.

(2) Values
- (a) Toughness of mind and body;
- (b) Efficiency in providing meat;
- (c) Piety towards the hunter ancestors;
- (d) Making known or visible what is unknown and hidden;
- (e) Fertility (multiplicity, fruitfulness);
- (f) Hunters' skill in concealing themselves from animals;
- (g) Fairness in meat distribution;

(h) The sacredness of age and sex distinctions (taboos against eating of *yijila* by women and uncircumcised boys);
(i) Suffering that good may come of it;
(j) Acuity of hunter's responses;
(k) Skill in the use of weapons.

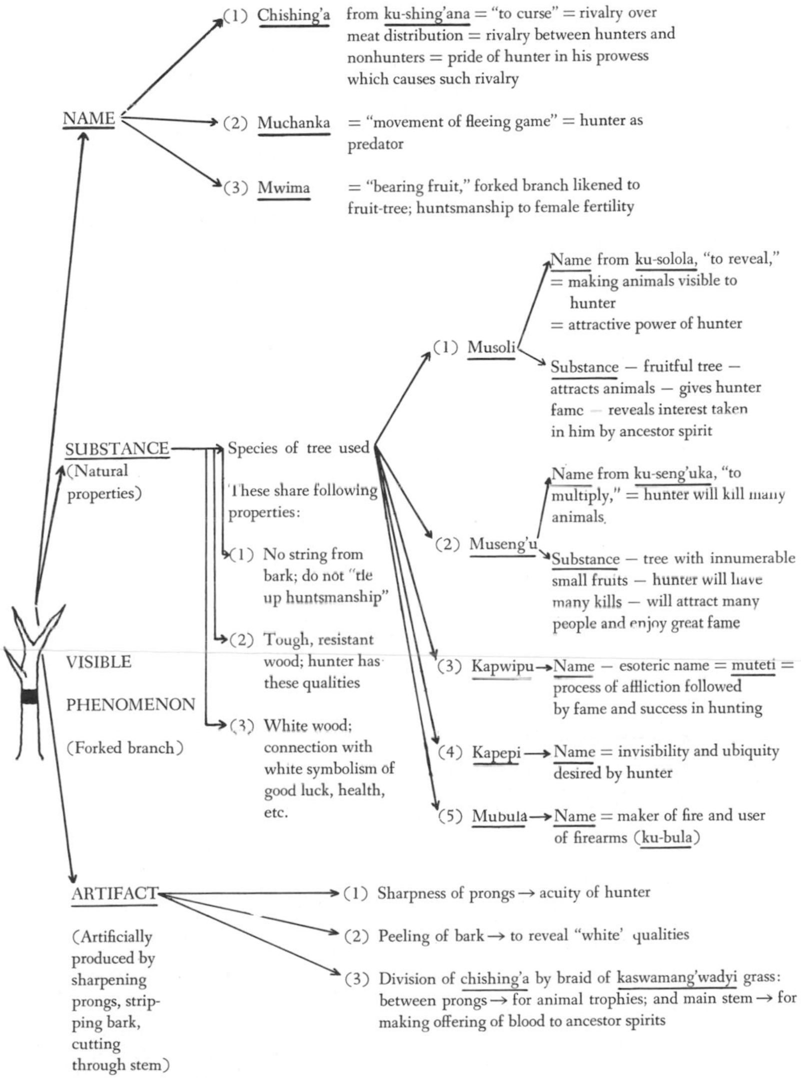


*Diagram 9*. Symbolism of *Chishing'a*

(3) Topographical Features
   (a) Forest;
   (b) Plains;
   (c) Termite hills and nests;
   (d) Burial sites.

All these referents,[2] merely at the level of Ndembu exegesis, are possessed by a piece of stick, a bit of grass, and a fragment of termitary. This is but a single example of the mighty synthesizing and focusing capacity of ritual symbolism. It might almost be said that the greater the symbol, the simpler its form. For a simple form is capable of supplying associative links of a very generalized character; it displays a feature or features that it shares, literally or analogically, with a wide variety of phenomena and ideas. Thus, the whiteness of *mpemba* clay recalls the whiteness of milk and of cassava meal and, more than these, such abstract ideas as freedom from impurity, goodness "without spot," and the like.

Finally, it must be stressed that the *chishing'a* is regarded by Ndembu not as an object of cognition, a mere set of referents to known phenomena, so much as a unitary power, conflating all the powers inherent in the activities, objects, relationships, and ideas it represents. What Ndembu see in a *chishing'a,* made visible for them in its furcate, ambivalent, and awe-inspiring nakedness, is the slaughterous power of *Wubinda* itself.

## BIBLIOGRAPHY

Turner, Victor W. 1953. *Lunda Rites and Ceremonies* (Occasional Papers of the Rhodes-Livingstone Museum, N.S. No. 10). Livingstone: Zambia.

——. 1957. *Schism and Continuity in an African Society: A Study of Ndembu Village Life*. Manchester University Press.

——. 1961. *Ndembu Divination: Its Symbolism and Techniques* (Rhodes-Livingstone Paper 31). Manchester University Press.

[2] And others—implicit in those aspects of the symbolism which connect it with such sectors of the ritual system as life crisis ritual, gynecological ritual, veneration of village ancestors, antiwitchcraft ritual, divination procedures, etc.

# CHAPTER IX

# Lunda Medicine and the Treatment of Disease*

In an illuminating appraisal of the literature on disease and treatment in primitive medicine, Erwin Ackerknecht (1946, 471) has pointed out that "most data on treatment, in general ethnographic monographs, consist of a list of drugs or other techniques used, of a list of the diseases in which they are applied, and of statements as to the possible objective effect that such measures have. It is obvious that such descriptions, valuable as they are, omit just the points needed for our special inquiry: *what are the the ideas underlying these therapeutic acts, and under what circumstances (with or without ritual) are they performed?*" (my italics). Since Ackerknecht wrote, there have been several praiseworthy attempts to answer his queries,[1] directly or by implication, but by and large there have been few systematic discussions of the relationship between the treatment of disease and

* First published as Rhodes-Livingstone Museum Occasional Paper No. 15 (Livingstone: Rhodes-Livingstone Museum, 1964). I am greatly indebted to Mr. Barrie Reynolds, Keeper of Ethnography at the Rhodes-Livingstone Museum, not only for personal encouragement in a field of data marginal to my main research, but also for enlisting the generous help of Mr. D. B. Fanshawe, Principal Scientific Officer in the Northern Rhodesia Forest Department, and of Dr. D. A. Cahal, formerly Regional Scientific Director in London of the Squibb Institute for Medical Research. These specialists, by commenting on botanical and medical aspects of the paper, have considerably strengthened its presentation.

[1] In the field of African studies there have been analyses of tribal therapies by Monica Wilson, S. F. Nadel, and Michael Gelfand.

the religious beliefs, ideas, and practices of a specific tribal society.

I am painfully aware that my own data on the treatment of disease, collected intermittently in the form of *ad hoc* observations and accounts by informants of varying intelligence and knowledge of tribal therapy, are relatively scanty and have many lacunae, but they are enough to demonstrate that Ndembu healing procedures are governed by the same principles and modes of classification as their religious rites and moral concepts. In this study I am not primarily concerned with the familiar problem of the extent to which primitive medicine is magico-religious or rational, for I am not a medical man and cannot say with authority just how "effective" a given procedure has been. My aim here is to reveal the ideas implicit in the Ndembu treatment of disease and to show that these ideas pervade wider realms of belief and action.

## *Disease, Misfortune, and Affliction*

In the first place Ndembu conceive disease or illness (*musong'u*) as a species of misfortune (*malwa, kuhalwa, kuyindama,* or *kubula kutooka*—this last term signifying "to lack whiteness or luck or purity"). Misfortune is a class term of which other species include: bad luck at hunting, reproductive disorders, physical accidents, and the loss of property. It might be argued that words such as "misfortune," "accident," "bad luck," "mischance" are erroneous translations of *malwa* and its synonyms, for there is indeed no concept of "accident" among the Ndembu, who seek to find a cause for every calamity; far from being "prelogical," they are obsessively logical, though on the basis of mystical premises, as Evans-Pritchard showed us (1937) in his classical study of Azande systems of belief. The Ndembu, like the Azande, consider that calamities and adversities of all kinds are caused by mystical forces generated or evoked and directed by conscious agents. These agents may be alive or dead, human or extrahuman. They may operate directly on their victims or indirectly through mystical intermediaries. Ancestral shades cause suffering directly; living sorcerers and witches work evil through medicines or familiars or through a combination of both. A person may also raise a "zombie" or "wraith" (*musalu*), an evil component of the personality which persists after death, by means of a curse and send it to kill someone against whom he has a grudge (*chitela*). However, shades, witches, sorcerers, and utterers of curses are not regarded as the sole causes of illness. For Ndembu talk of different kinds of *nyisong'u*, "illnesses" or "diseases," and recognize that specific symptoms are connected with each of them. At first I assumed that the Ndembu regarded these *nyisong'u* merely as conditions of the body and that they had been influenced in this respect by European notions, but when I inquired further I found that the *nyisong'u* appeared to be endowed with independent life and that part of the therapy consisted in using "bitter," "hot," or evil-smelling herbs to disgust and disconcert the *musong'u* and drive it away.

Yet Ndembu speak as though sorcery and witchcraft were always in the background where illness is concerned. Some sicknesses are so common that the element of the untoward which makes people immediately suspect sorcery or witchcraft is lacking. Nevertheless, if these become exceptionally severe or protracted, suspicion grows. There are certain classes of calamities that are believed *a priori* to have shades as their probable cause. These are female reproductive troubles, including menstrual disorders, frequent miscarriage and stillbirth, and lack of success at hunting. Illness may or may not be caused by shades. If the patient dreams of dead relatives while he is sick, the probability is that he is being afflicted by an ancestral shade, but the possibility of sorcery or witchcraft cannot be ruled out even here, for these evildoers are notorious deceivers and illusionists. Thus it is usual for the relatives of a person to seek out a diviner. The diviner, by means of one or another of various techniques (see Turner 1961) diagnoses a mystical cause as responsible, and a rite is performed either to propitiate a specific manifestation of a shade or to exorcise the familiars of sorcery or witchcraft.

Consulting a diviner and sponsoring a curative rite are both costly and troublesome for marginal subsistence cultivators, and there are many herbalists and lay healers in the villages who claim to be able to dispel *nyisong'u*, whether these are associated with shades and witches or not. Some Ndembu believe that all ailments are mystically caused but that most are brought on by "only little grudges" and can be dealt with by local herbalists in their early stages. It is thought that the familiars of witchcraft and sorcery are activated only by sudden violent anger or by long-cherished, smoldering "grudges" (*yitela*), resulting from some affront or the product of jealousy or envy. A minor grudge or quarrel might induce a sorcerer to send a minor ailment against his rival, but in this case there is little public interest in who did it. It is mainly a matter for the patient and his close kin and affines who desire the restoration of his health.

Some illnesses are believed to be caused by the breach of a ritual prohibition which is disclosed by the nature of its symptoms. For example, leprosy (*mbumba*) is thought to be the result of transgressing one of the taboos of *Mukanda,* the boys' circumcision ceremony. A form of fever, associated with foaming at the mouth and believed to attack only young children, is said to be caused by eating the meat of the hyrax (*chibatata*) or wild pig (*chombu*). Other diseases, such as elephantiasis of the scrotum, may result, according to Ndembu ideas, from coming in contact with protective medicine against adultery, though it is conceded that the disease may not always have this cause, for a newborn child may have it.

Other diseases again, such as tuberculosis (*musong'u wantulu,* "the disease of the chest") and dysentery (*kapokota*) are held to have been imported by the Europeans, though treatments based on traditional Ndembu pharmacological principles have been developed to cope with them, as we shall see. These may or may not be connected by Ndembu with indigenous notions of witchcraft or spirit possession. In the case of severe tuberculosis the rite of *Tukuka,* introduced from the Chokwe and Luvale territories, is often performed. Its aim is to propitiate the souls of living aliens, but principally those of Europeans, which are believed to fly about at night, to possess Ndembu, causing them to tremble violently and to feed on their lungs.[2] Nevertheless, before Ndembu have recourse to *Tukuka* specialists, they treat tuberculosis as if it were *musong'u* with herbal and other kinds of "medicines."

Ackerknecht has shown (1946, 472) that of the diseases regarded as "natural" by primitives, three groups seem to stand out: "the very slight diseases (colds); the very common diseases (old age, tuberculosis, venereal diseases, malaria, filariasis, yaws, food poisoning, sunstroke, skin diseases); and the diseases imported by the Whites." Children's diseases are often added to the very common diseases. The word "natural" is not apposite here, for Ndembu do not distinguish, as we do, between natural and supernatural orders. For them there is only a single cosmic order, though some parts of it are "quite clear" and others are "dark" and obscure, some things are visible and others cannot be seen. The process of therapy, as we shall see, is partly a

[2] H. Baumann mentions (1935, 205–206) that the Chokwe themselves connect *Tukuka* with Europeans, and that two clay models of bellows (representing lungs?) "are important for the cult."

process of making hidden and secret things visible and thereby accessible, if they are harmful, to redressive and remedial action. Ackerknecht's formulation would fit the Ndembu facts if we substituted for "natural diseases" the phrase "diseases in their own right," that is to say, not as brought on by spirits or witches. Perhaps the only instance of disease regarded as inexplicable in its origin, if not natural, is the influenza epidemic of 1918 which followed the First World War and swept destructively through Ndembu territory, as it did through the rest of the world.

## *Color Symbolism, Medicines, and Treatment*

The classification of reality in terms of the tripartite color division between white, red, and black, which I have discussed elsewhere, is also of crucial importance in therapeutic procedures. For among the many senses of whiteness are: strength (*wukolu*), life (*wumi*), health (*kuhanda*), making visible (*kusolola*), sweeping clean (*kukomba*), and washing (impurities from) oneself (*kuwela*). It also stands for "prosperity" and "freedom from misfortune." Thus the state of health is a "white," "clean," and "pure" state. The state of ill health is, on the contrary, a "black" state, and indeed one of the attributes of blackness is "having diseases" (*yikweti yikatu*—from the verb *kukata,* "to be ill"; *yikatu* is synonymous with *musong'u*). "Black" is also to "lack luck" (*kubulu kutooku*) or "purity," to have "sufferings" (*yihung'u*) and "misfortune" (*malwa*). It also represents "darkness" (*mwidima*) and "what is secret" (*chakujinda*) or "what is hidden" (*chakusweka*). One of the aims of therapy, therefore, is to restore his former "whiteness" to the patient who is in a "black" state. Symbolic actions directed to that end include sweeping the patient's body with a medicine broom to get rid of the "impure things" on it or in it and washing him with decoctions of pounded herbs. Some medicines are literally "white" substances, made from plants with white bark, wood, roots or fruits, or from birds or animals with white feathers or fur. Others have analogous qualities to "whiteness" or "purity," like the tree *mukombukombu* (*Tricalysia angolensis* [*Leptactina*]), whose leaves are used in the making of a medicine broom (*chisampu*). The name of this tree is homonymous with *kukomba* (to sweep), and from the name alone, and not from any physical property of the tree—its leaves are small and unsuitable for sweeping—*mukombukombu* has acquired its ritual role as an instrument of purification.

However, "to make white" (*kutookisha*) is more than these: it is to make clear and explicit, to leave nothing hidden or confused. The herbal and other "medicines" applied to the patient as potions, lotions, or poultices are substances each of which has its own specific "virtue" —each reveals either some aspect of the disease or points forward to some aspect of the desired state of health or "whiteness." The pharmacopoeia for each disease is nothing less than a description of the disease in symbolic terms and a statement of the attributes of health and wholeness. Behind the symbols and their interpretation lies the pattern of values peculiar to Ndembu, the fundamental frame of their thinking and feeling. Thus, the act of treatment is itself a "white" action, directed against the "black" action of the disease.

Redness also has its part to play in therapy, its usual equivocal part. For in some respects, it represents, as we have seen, "power" (*ng'ovu*), "life" (*wumi*), the strength and joy that comes from eating the flesh of animals, and the blood tie linking together matrilineal kin and mother and child. It also stands for murder, necrophagous witchcraft, and the impure blood of menstruation. Thus some diseases, in addition to being "black," also have a "red" lethal charcter. Bilharziasis (*kaseli kamashi*) is such a disease for one of its symptoms is blood (*mashi*) in the urine. The use of certain red medicines in its treatment is therefore appropriate, for these "reveal" the essential character of the disease.

Although this fundamental classification governs the symbolic articles and symbolic actions of Ndembu treatments, nevertheless there are other features to be considered here. Most important is the Ndembu concept of "medicines." C. M. N. White has outlined the main features of Luvale beliefs in medicines (1961, 35–38) and for the most part his conclusions apply to the Ndembu, who are neighbors of the Luvale. Like the Luvale, Ndembu distinguish between two classes of medicines, *yitumbu* (Luvale *vitumbo*) and *mpelu* (Luvale *lupelo*). White describes the former as "of vegetable or inorganic nature" and the latter as "organic material." I would like to distinguish these classes further by the mode of association thought to exist between the symbol and its object and associated concepts. In the case of *yitumbu,* the associative link is dominantly one of sympathy; the symbol shares an aspect of the object's existence or state. For example, the root of the *kapumbwa* plant (*Ancylobothrys amoena*) secretes white gum which resembles pus (*mashina*). *Yitumbu* made from this root is used in the treatment of gonorrhea (*kaseli kamashina*), one symptom of which for Ndembu is the presence of pus in the urine. In the case of *mpelu,* the associative link is one of contagion—to borrow a useful term from Sir James Frazer which indicates that the symbol has in fact been part of the object it signifies or has been in close physical contact with it. Thus, as part of the materia medica employed to cure tuberculosis, we find portions of the diaphragm of an antbear (*itandantulu dachibudi*). This animal has a strong chest and *mpelu* taken from it will, so it is believed, strengthen the chest of the patient. Similarly, the hair of an albino (*mwabi*) is considered "strengthening," for an albino is a "white" or auspicious being.

*Yitumbu* has much the same range of senses as the East Central Bantu term *muti* which Goodall, writing of the Bemba, defined (1921, 80) as "medicine, simple, charm, drug, poison (almost entirely prepared from the bark, leaves, wood or roots of trees)." Here I shall be concerned only with its use as medicine, drug, and simple, not as poison or charm.

I propose to describe a series of diseases and their treatments, just as my informants told me of them. In the course of these accounts, we shall encounter different kinds and classes of medicines and ways in which they are applied. It is in these contexts of situation that we shall get to understand their properties and uses best.

## *Inventory of Diseases*

The following list of diseases makes no claim to completeness or even adequacy, but it represents some of the more common types which spring readily to the mind of a Kandembu. I give the vernacular term for the disease, informants' comments on its name and symptoms (*yuma yakutiyayi muntu mumujimba hakukata*), and finally the term by which it is known in English. In this matter of translation I have followed the advice of Dr. Cahal who points out that the *chimbuki* treats symptoms and signs, not specific diseases. The vernacular terms correspond to symptoms. Thus *kaseli kamashi* is hematuria, not necessarily bilharziasis, although bilharziasis may well be the most common cause of hematuria among the Ndembu.

*Mbumba yaluzong'a* or *mbumba yachula*

"This disease causes people to lose toes and fingers. They have white spots." [Almost certainly leprosy.]

*Mbumba yichinana*

"Red leprosy." [Possibly yaws.]

*Kaseli kamashi*

"Blood is seen in the urine." [Hematuria.]

*Kaseli kamashina*

"There is pus in the urine." [Pyuria.]

*Musong'u wantulu*

"The disease of the chest; the patient spits blood." [Chest disease (hemoptysis).]

*Musong'u wamesesi*

"The disease of sore eyes. A cream-colored liquid, called *mpota* comes out of the eyes. A white film covers the eyes. But only a few go blind with it." [Possibly conjunctivo-keratitis and corneal opacities.]

*Musong'u wamatu*

"Disease of the ears. Pus comes out of the ear, following earache. The patient may become deaf (*wajika matu*)." [Otitis media.]

*Musong'u wevumu*

"Disease of the stomach. There are several kinds: (1) pains in the stomach; (2) inability to defecate; (3) a 'running' stomach; (4) '*Kapokota,*' a disease which perforates the intestine. This disease comes from the Northern Rhodesian Copperbelt." [(1) Stomach ache; (2) constipation; (3) diarrhea; (4) dysentery.]

*Musong'u wakalepa*

"The patient cannot move. This disease is incurable, and has been known by Ndembu from time immemorial." [Paralysis.]

*Musong'u wakuzaluka*

"The patient talks much, sleeps or goes away without giving warning, curses wildly. Once there was a woman called Nyasoneka of Nswanakamawu Village in Chief Mukang'ala's area. Her illness started with a headache. Then she had great fever. Her relatives thought she had some ordinary illness. After some months she became weak and tired. This was followed by a time when she stole food. Then she grew garrulous and began to tell lies. She did not seem to take any notice of the opinions of others. She took to sleeping in different villages, a night in each. Finally she went away into the bush where she got lost and died—no one found her body. People generally reckoned her to be mad (*kuzaluka*). About four years elapsed from the beginning of her illness to her death." [Insanity.]

*Musong'u wanyima*

"Disease of the back. The patient feels a pain in the back which gradually grows worse. In bad cases the person's back becomes bent (*wukuheng'a nyima*)." [Backache.]

*Musong'u wachinkomya*

"This is to fall down in a fit (*kukonya*)." [Epilepsy.]

*Musong'u wawansi*

"The disease of childhood. First the child cries a lot. This is followed by shivering and fever. After one day it begins to move its limbs convulsively. If the disease started in the morning, it will do this once that day, but on the following day will do it twice or thrice. These limb movements will continue for two or three weeks and then stop. If it goes on for longer the people will think it is epilepsy. This disease is caused by eating the flesh of the hyrax or of the wild pig, for these animals make a bubbling sound and move their limbs independently of their bodies." [?]

*Musong'u wakanwa*

"Disease of the mouth. It starts with a pain in the gums, with small boils (*mabobela*). The gums become swollen and discharge blood and pus. Teeth drop out." [Pyorrhea.]

*Musong'u wachingongu*

"Disease of smallpox. *Tungongu* are small tattoo marks, the raised scars of tattooing, i.e., cheloids. The patient is isolated from the village and treated in the bush (European influence?)." [Probably smallpox, with occasionally severe chickenpox being included.]

*Musong'u wamutu*

"Disease of the head. A person first feels very cold and his head feels very heavy. Then he has pain in his whole body. Sometimes it ends in death. Since much pain is felt in the temples, incisions are made in them and medicines are rubbed in." [Headache with fever.]

*Musong'u watupepa*

"A person feels sharp pains in his feet, just as when one suddenly withdraws one's feet from the neighborhood of a hot fire in very cold weather. The pain proceeds up the leg to the hips where it stops. He cannot walk. The cure is to keep the feet warm." [Severe cramps.]

*Musong'u wawunonu* (also called *musong'u wakaswendi*)

"Pus flows from the genitals, and from the ears, nose and throat." [Possibly Lymphogranuloma venereum.]

*Musong'u wampang'a*

"It attacks the testicles and causes them to swell." [Swelling of the scrotum; it probably includes hydrocele, hernia, varicocele, as well as elephantiasis.]

*Musong'u wanshing'u*

"A person feels as though the inside of his neck is broken." [Stiff neck.]

*Musong'u wakunong'oka*

"A person often falls into a doze." [Possibly sleeping sickness, but may also include encephalitis, some forms of epilepsy, and brain tumors.]

## *Treatment of Specific Diseases*

I now present some accounts of treatments given to me by a number of informants, including Muchona, my best informant on ritual and medicine, Kasonda my cook, Ihembi, a famed doctor and herbalist, Sandombu, the principal "actor" in the "social dramas" of my book *Schism and Continuity,* Chakadyi, a village headman, Windson Kashinakaji, a village schoolmaster, and Jackson, a young educated man.

### MBUMBA YALUZONG'A, LEPROSY

"Leprosy attacks a woman if she walks in the former site of a circumcision lodge, where the men were making *nfunda* medicine (the major protective medicine of the lodge which contains cindered foreskins, the urine of apprentice-circumcisers, the ashes of the burned lodge and of various sacred fires, and a number of other highly dangerous symbolic substances). *Mbumba* attacks people in the air where the boys were circumcised (a site known as *ifwilu,* the place of dying). But if your blood can fight *mbumba* you will not be attacked."

The curative procedure is as follows. "First you collect medicines (*kuhuka yitumbu*). The first thing is to go to a former circumcision site (*ifwilu*) to the *mudyi* tree (*Diplorryncus condylocarpon*) under which *Kambanji* (war leader), the senior novice, was circumcised and take a single piece of its root.

"Next you go to the streamside evergreen forest (*itu*) where the *mbumba yachula* tree (*Landolphia rubescens*) grows. (This means 'leprosy of the frog' and refers to the pale mottlings and spots on a frog's skin which resembles the marks of leprosy.) A branch of this tree is cut, and some bark scrapings (*nyemba*) are removed by an ax (*kazemba*) or knife (*mpoku*). These are put either in a potsherd (*chizanda*), a round, flat winnowing basket (*lwalu*), or any kind of discarded basket.

"Next a root (*muzaji* or *muji*) of *kavulawumi* (*Maprounea africana*) is collected. After this they go to the former site of the fire near which the novice *Kambanji* slept at a lodge and take a root from the ground beneath it, of any species. They also take a root of any species from the earth beneath the fire of the novice called *kajika* ('the little-one-who-closes'), who was the last to be circumcised. They then go into the bush to find the tree with white-spotted bark (called *mutondu wamabeng'a*, 'the tree of spots') and collect bark-scrapings.

"They return, scrape the skin from the roots and burn the bark and root-scrapings they have collected. The ashes are then mixed with castor oil (*imonu*) to form an ointment.

"Now the patient is brought and the doctors (*ayimbuki* or *ayimbanda*) make circular cuts around the sores and patches or spots (*mabeng'a ambumba*) of leprosy. They rub the ointment into these incisions, then rub what is left into the patient's whole body."

No explanations were given of the significance of these actions and medicines, but it is clear that the main principle underlying the treatment is to collect a number of substances that exhibit sympathetic associations with leprosy, or with boys' circumcision (of which one of the main mystical sanctions is leprosy), and to incinerate these, thereby destroying the disease (by sympathetic magic). This would be in accordance with the principle underlying the burning of the seclusion lodge (*ng'ula*) itself. It is said that "all diseases are burned if they are thrown into the burning *ng'ula*," presumably in symbolic guise.

It is interesting that *mudyi*, normally employed in ritual to signify such "good" things as "mother's milk," "womanhood," "matriliny" and "tribal custom" should here be connected with leprosy. *Mudyi* is a "white" symbol according to Ndembu principles of classification, and leprosy is a "white" disease, so that it would appear that whiteness (*wutooka*) is ambivalent in meaning. It is said that if a novice dies during *Mukanda*, no case may be brought against the lodge officials for compensation, since "God (*Nzambi*) took him." God is represented by white symbols, and it is likely that leprosy, a ritual sanction in other contexts also—if a Paramount Chief's *lukanu* bracelet of royalty is polluted the incumbent will become a leper—is regarded as a divine punishment, a punishment by the *Deus absconditus*.

### KASELI KAMASHI, HEMATURIA
(probably caused by bilharzia)

"Doctors begin to give medicines to the patient when they see that his urine contains blood or pus. If they see blood they know that it is *kaseli kamashi;* if pus, that it is *kaseli kamashina* (gonorrhea).

"Red gum is collected from the *mupuchi* tree (*Brachystegia spiciformis*). Then some roots of the *katunya* tree (*Uvariastrom hexaloboides*) which grows on the banks of rivers, are dug up. Its roots are red. They are cut up into small pieces, mixed with *mupuchi* gum and put in water in a clay jug (*mulondu*). The jug is then warmed on a fire and when it is warm the patient drinks this medicine. He goes on taking it at intervals from two days to a week.

"If the patient does not get better the doctor collects the roots of the *wutotu* (*Gardenia imperialis*) and *kansanying'a* shrubs, which grow near rivers or on large termite-hills (*tuwumbu*). These are cut up, mixed with water in a jug, warmed, then drunk by the patient. *Wutotu* has white roots and produces white gum. *Kansanying'a* has white roots and stinks strongly (*kanunka hama*)." Other roots are used in this treatment but the informant who told me of it had forgotten them.

The beginnings of an explanation appear in this account, for the informant, unsolicited, thought it necessary to mention the color of the roots and gums employed as medicine. The red medicines seem to refer to the blood passed in the urine. *Wutotu* is used in the treatment of *kaseli kamashina,* thought by Ndembu to be closely connected with *kaseli kamashi.* The basic principle here seems to be homeopathic; give the patient a medicine that has similar properties to the symptoms of the disease and he will recover. It should be noted that medicine is in this instance taken internally—the *musong'u* affects the internal organs—whereas in the case of leprosy, medicines, representing spotted and discolored skin, were applied to the body surfaces.

### KASELI KAMASHINA, PYURIA

The doctor collects and cuts up *wutotu* and *kapumbwa* roots and puts them into an earthenware vessel (*nsaba*) or jug (*mulondu*). Water is added, the pot is warmed, and the patient drinks. This is repeated every day for several weeks. If the patient does not recover, the medicines of *kaseli kamashi* are tried. Sometimes a potion of *mudyi* (*Diplorrhyncus condylocarpon*) and *kajing'a ludi*[3] roots is given.

It was explained that in the context of *wumbuki*, "treatment with medicines," whitish exudations from trees and shrubs are called *mashina*, "pus," while red secretions are called *mashi*, "blood." The *kapumbwa* plant produces white gum, which drops on the ground and is said to resemble pus. *Mudyi*, of course, secretes a milky latex which in more auspicious ritual contexts represents mother's milk.

### MUSONG'U WANTULU, CHEST DISEASE (HEMOPTYSIS)

(*a*) *First potion.* "The doctor goes first to an old burrow where red army ants (*nsalafu*) live. He digs and finds roots in it, cuts them up, puts them in a clay jug with water, and gives this potion to the patient to drink."

An abandoned burrow, now inhabited by the migratory red ants, is known as *itala dawansalafu*, "the hut of the red ants." Roots that have come in contact with these ants share their characteristics, prominent among which is their sharp, needlelike bite. "The pain in the chest is like the bites of red ants."

(*b*) *Second potion.* "The doctor locates and cuts up roots of the *mukula* tree (*Pterocarpus angolensis*) and mixes them in a clay jug with the diaphragm of an antbear, *muhanu* (*Ficus* sp.) roots, and the scale of a pangolin. Water is added, the mixture is warmed, and the patient (*muyeji*) drinks."

"The *mukula* tree drops red gum; it is the tree of blood (indeed, it has many ritual uses with this significance; see Turner, 1962b). It represents the spitting of blood. The diaphragm of an antbear (*itandantulu dachibudi*) is used because the antbear has a strong chest and they want the patient to have a strong chest too. The scale (*ikalu*) of a pangolin (*nkaka*) is put in because the pangolin moves slowly and curls up if it sees anyone coming. A hunter can carry it easily curled up. In the same way, the disease can be caught and taken away to die. *Muhanu* roots are used because *muhanu* grows up a hole in another tree—it will break the obstruction in a patient's chest. It does not matter which of these two potions is given first."

Three of the ingredients listed above are classed as *mpelu* (pl.

[3] This is a creeper with small white, five-pointed starlike flowers, possibly *Strophanthus welwitschii*. Fanshawe suggests that *Kajing'a ludi* might also be applied to a *Landolphia* or *Apocynaceae* creeper (personal communication).

*jipelu*) i.e., as operating by contagious magic. These are the roots from the red ants' nest, and the portions of antbear and pangolin. It would seem logical to a European observer, once he knew that hemoptysis was likened to the biting of red ants, to suppose that the Ndembu used anteater medicines to destroy the disease just as anteaters consume ants, but no informant gave me this explanation. Moral: One should guess meanings as little as possible and collect native explanations, as Professor Monica Wilson has always urged (1957, 6).

#### MUSONG'U WAMATU, DISCHARGE FROM THE EARS (OTITIS MEDIA)

"Yellowish fruits of the *chikoli* tree (*Strychnos spinosa*) are cut in two, the pulp is stirred up and lukewarm water is poured into the fruit. It is then left to soak in thoroughly. After a time some drops of the juice are allowed to fall into the patient's affected ear.

"Alternatively, bark is scraped from the *Mushokotu* tree (*Faurea saligna*), mixed with water in a large clay pot, the mixture is warmed, and drops are inserted in the patient's ear."

No explanations of the use of these vegetable medicines in terms of sympathetic or contagious magic were forthcoming. I have known Ndembu, treated in this way, who asserted strongly that they experienced an improvement in their condition. It is possible that these medicines are employed because they are objectively effective.

#### MUSONG'U WEVUMU, DISEASE OF THE STOMACH

There are two kinds of this disease. One is for women and one is for children. The kind for women is called *chisumi* or *mukung'a*. It affects the stomach in a line that crosses it completely just above the navel in front. A woman may have this pain whether she is expecting a child or not. It is continuous until medicines are given. The one for children is called *musong'u wevumu* with no other name.

(*a*) *Chisumi* or *mukung'a*. "Two old potsherds (*yizanda*) or cooking pots (*manung'u*) are found in the village and taken by the doctor to a stream. One potsherd is put on either bank of the stream at a place where an old tree has fallen across the water. Bark from the root of any species of tree is scraped off and some scrapings are placed in both potsherds. Then warm water is poured in one, and cold water in the other. After that both potsherds are put on the same side of the stream. The roots used as medicine must go right across the stream. Water must have flowed over and pushed against them.

"When all has been made ready, the doctor and his helpers bring a razor (*ntewula*) and make two cuts in the woman's abdomen, one on each side of the navel. Then they fetch cupping horns (*tusumu*)[4] and the doctor (*chimbanda*) sucks (*ku-sumika*) one horn on the abdomen, and one on the woman's back immediately opposite. He waits for a short while, then grasps both horns at once, pulls them off abruptly and empties the blood into the stream.

"Next, the doctor makes an incision at the outer side of each of the two cuts on the patient's abdomen and others on the outer side of those on her back. The horns are applied and removed as before. Afterwards the doctor takes medicine from the potsherds and rubs it into the cuts. He then tells the patient to return to her village. Meanwhile, he remains at the site of the operation and makes a barrage (*kafuza*) across the stream just where he threw in the blood. Then he throws in the potsherds and the dregs of the medicine at the same place. But he does not throw the cupping horns away. When he is ready to go, he pulls the barrage away and releases the water. Everything he has thrown in is completely carried away.

"After he has returned to the village with his cupping horns, the doctor goes into the bush and collects the root of the *mwala* tree (*Afzelia quanzensis*), which is very bitter in taste. One large root is taken, cut up and warmed in an earthenware vessel (*nsaba*). It is then given to the patient to drink and she takes it for about a week.

"If there is no improvement he goes to a *mutata* tree (*Securidaca longipedunculata*), digs up and removes one long root which he cuts in pieces. These he puts in a pot with water, warms the medicine and gives it to the patient to drink. This she does for several days until she

[4] These are usually goats' horns with the tips removed. After they have been sucked on over an incision in the patient's body, the open top end is plugged with beeswax by the operator and left for a time before removal. *Tusumu* are used in several rites to suck from a patient's body substances that have been injected into it by magical or mystical means. For example, the upper middle incisor of a dead hunter is believed to "bite" (*ku-suma*) a living relative of that hunter for neglect of his memory or as a punishment for quarreling between kin. "Biting" means that the tooth burrows beneath the victim's skin causing intolerable pain. It is extracted by the joint action of ritual and cupping. Again, sorcerers are supposed to shoot teeth, pieces of human bone and soil from graves into the bodies of those they wish to kill. They use a miniature gun carved from a human tibia and known as the "night gun" (*wuta wawufuku*). A full description of night guns and the ways in which they are used may be found in Barrie Reynolds, 1963.

gets quite better. But if she is still sick, roots of *molu wawubwang'u* [5] are cut up and mixed with the chopped roots of the *kakwema* tree (*Uvaria angolensis* or *Enneastemon schweinforthii*). These are then heated in an earthenware vessel and given to the patient until she gets better, perhaps for as long as two weeks."

"The name *chisumi* is from *ku-suma,* 'to bite.' Its other name, *mukung'a,* is from *ku-kung'ama,* 'to lie across, traverse.' Thus the root used for medicine lies across the stream just as the disease lies across the stomach. *Ku-kung'ika* stands for the piling up of flotsam (*ntotu jahameji*) against the traversing root. This flotsam or rubbish resembles the disease. Medicine is rubbed into the cuts to rid the woman's stomach of the rubbish. When the doctor pulls down the barrage, the disease goes away like the rubbish.

"The bitterness (*kulula*) of the *mwala* root can kill the disease. *Mutata* has a very nasty smell. The woman should drink its medicine to make her stomach smell very much. The disease will smell it and die because of its stink. *Molu wawubwang'u* also has a strong smell to kill the disease. So has *kakwema.* Medicines that are used because they stink (*ku-nunka*) are called '*yitumbu yanunka* or *yitumbu yevumba.*'

"A disease (*musong'u*) is something which remains alive in the body. If it goes on and on the patient is *wahalwa* or *mukwakuyindama,* an inauspicious person." [6]

This treatment stands on the borderline between the taking of more or less rational therapeutic measures and the performance of a magical rite. The first part of the treatment consists almost entirely of acts in accordance with the principles of sympathetic magic. A pain "crosses" the stomach, which is like a stream in that through it fluids and solids pass, and from it (since it is thought to be continuous with the womb) flow children; hence a doctor goes to a stream with his patient and

[5] A creeper found near streams. It is hung around the shoulders of the patient-candidate in the *Wubwang'u* rite performed for mothers of twins—it is supposed also to whiten the milk of a mother who has been yielding "red" or "yellow" milk—the result of some infection of the mammary glands, no doubt.

[6] Ndembu mean many things by these terms. Such a person is in a "black," or impure and unhealthy state; he is either afflicted by an ancestral spirit in punishment of his own or of his kin-group's transgressions or is under attack by witchcraft or sorcery. In other words, the *musong'u* has been mystically intensified and is now associated with other malignant agencies.

performs symbolic actions indicative of the removal of obstructions that impede the flow of the water and cause flotsam (= the disease) to pile up. The symbolism of two banks or sides is repeated in another form with the cupping horns—one in front and one at the back of the patient—and in the cutting of incisions on either side of the navel. Some informants connected the treatment with dysmenorrhea, for it was also the cure for this. The disease was believed to hold up the normal flow of the menses and hence to cause temporary sterility, for Ndembu recognize that normal periodicity is a prerequisite of pregnancy. The pain, they feel, is connected with the damming up of the ordinary flow.

The quasi-rational aspect emerges in the second part of the treatment in which potions are given to the patient to drink. Given the premise that the disease is a living entity inhabiting the stomach, it is quite rational to suppose that bitter or evil-smelling substances, disliked on the whole by human beings, animals, and birds, will drive it away or kill it. I am in full agreement with Ackerknecht's strictures on Malinowski for calling "scientific" the rational elements in primitive medicine, for, as he says (1946, 489), "Practical behaviour is not yet science. A butcher is no scientist. Science, full of disinterested curiosity, aims primarily at truth, not at practical success or psychic relaxation . . . Science is unthinkable without the experiment . . . presupposes a quality of scepticism . . . is a late invention of humanity." This is very different from acting medically, as Rivers pointed out (1924, 52) with perfect logic and rationality, but on the basis of false, supernaturalistic premises. Yet it must be admitted that medicine in our culture relies to a certain extent on suggestion. The general practitioner in British rural areas administered "nasty" medicines, partly on account of their curative properties and partly to satisfy the patient that they were "strong" enough to "kill" the ailment.

For all I know, *mwala* root juice may be empirically effective in curing stomach-ache, but if this is so, it is effective for the wrong reasons. It is possible that many "medicines" have been tried out by Ndembu doctors and some have been found to procure relief, but the next step has not been to set up a series of carefully controlled experiments to isolate the substance causing the beneficial effect. Rather it is to examine the sensorily perceptible attributes of the plant to see which of them might be regarded as an expression or embodiment of auspicious mystical powers, or which of them exhibited some virtue opposed to the putative properties of the disease. It is a question of allocating the item to a pre-existent category and not of making new discoveries by the experimental method.

(*b*) *Musong'u wevumu watwansi.* "The doctor collects and cuts up long roots of *kapwipu* (*Swartzia madagascariensis*) and *musong'a-song'a* (or *lusong'wasong'wa, Ximenia americana*). The root skin (*nyemba*) of *kapwipu* is scraped off and put in two different potsherds. Hot water is put in one pot of *kapwipu* medicine, cold water in the other; the *musong'asong'a* medicine is dealt with likewise. The doctor and his child-patient then sit under the *kapwipu* tree from which medicine was obtained and the doctor makes incisions on the patient's stomach beside the navel and on his back, just as for *Chisumi,* and applies *tusumu* cupping horns. When a girdle of horn-scars has been made round the patient's waist, *kapwipu* medicine is rubbed into them. When all is over, the doctor (*chimbuki*) buries (*wavumbika* or *wajika*) the potsherd containers, together with the blood sucked from the patient and kept in a small calabash, in the hole in the ground left by the long taproot taken for medicine.

"Next day the same process is repeated under the *musong'asong'a* tree with medicine obtained from that tree.

"Afterwards roots of the *chiputa mazala* tree (*Erythrina tomentosa*) are cut up into pieces (*yikunku*), put into a clay pot, and heated until lukewarm (*kavuyenki*). The patient is then given this decoction to drink.

"If the disease continues, *kanshinshi* root medicine is given lukewarm to the patient as a draught. Finally, *kakung'ami* root medicine is given as a lukewarm potion."

The reasons for using these roots are as follows. "*Kapwipu* medicine is used because it is a hard tree. Hardness (*ku-kola*) represents health and strength. *Musong'asong'a* is used for the same reason. *Chiputa mazala* medicine is given because it has a strong smell, *kanshinshi* because it has both a strong smell and a bitter taste.

"*Kakung'ami* is used not only because of its stink, but also because of its bubbling sound (*chilulululu*—sounds of flatulence) which drives the disease to one side, so that it no longer lies across the stomach. The disease fears (*watiya woma*) the medicine. If the stomach cannot fight it the disease spreads right over it, but the medicine chases it into one place where it will die.

"When the doctor goes to the *kapwipu* tree, he makes an address (*ku-lang'ula*) before collecting this, the principal (*mukulumpi*) medicine of the treatment. He mentions the doctor who taught him how to administer it, the name of the patient, and the circumstances leading up to the treatment."

(*c*) When men have stomach ache, also called *musong'u wevumu*. "The doctor collects, cuts up, and puts in a pot with lukewarm water the roots of *katong'a* (*Strychnos cocculoides*), which are very bitter, and gives the potion to the patient to drink. *Mulolu* roots (*Annona nana*) may be given as a decoction, because they have a strong smell. If the disease continues, *chikwata* roots (*Zizyphus mucronata*) may be given as above, because they are a little bitter."

Ackerknecht has observed (1946, 482) that bloodletting "is effective in some diseases although we do not know why, and have discarded it (in the West), therefore, almost entirely. In most cases its magico-religious 'purificative' character or its objective to drive out disease demons is obvious." The use of cupping techniques among the Ndembu would provide an example of "magico-religious" beliefs. In the case of "stomach disease," one of the main aims is to introduce substances possessing mystical power into the body of the patient. Although this was not stated by Ndembu informants, it is probable that there is here some notion of "replacement." Blood is taken out (and in the case of (*b*) poured into the hole from which the medicine root was removed) and replaced by medicine which it is hoped will force away the disease or give toughness and health to the patient. We meet once more in these treatments the notion that a disease is animate and vulnerable to obnoxious tastes and smells.

## MUSONG'U WAMESESI, CONJUNCTIVO-KERATITIS, CORNEAL OPACITIES AND OTHER EYE DISEASES

Bark is scraped from the trunk of a *muhuma* tree (*strychnos spinosa* or *stropanthus welwitschii*) and mixed with warm water in a clay pot. The patient's eyes are then bathed in the lotion. If this is not enough, the tiny leaves of *lweng'eng'i* (*Dracaena reflexa*) are crushed between the fingers (a process known as *kuchikita*), put in a leaf-funnel (*lutotu*), and allowed to drop in the patient's eyes.

Finally, steam treatment may be tried. Leaves of the *wadikalanziza* tree, sometimes known as *kayiza* (*Strychnos stuhlmannii*), are collected, put in a pot with water, and heated to the boiling point. The patient covers his head with a blanket and puts his face in the rising steam (*luya*).

In the case of each of these three medicines, informants told me that the efficacy (*ng'ovu*) of the herb is derived from its "bitterness."

"Bitterness" is *wukawu* or the verbal noun *kulula*. Ndembu say that "*wukawu*" can "stick to" (*ku-lamata*) the disease, "like a leach" (*neyi izambu*), until it dies.

One informant gave me a little information about *kayiza*, which might help to identify it correctly. He said, "*Kayiza* is very bitter in taste. It can grow into a big tree. Its fruits when ripe are as black as ink. They blacken your tongue when you eat them. That is why it is called also *wadikalanziza*, from *wadikala*, 'you deny,' for you can't deny having eaten it since it makes your tongue black."

### MUSONG'U WAKUZALUKA, INSANITY

"The doctor first collects old bones of a mad dog. Then he goes to a *musoli* tree (*Vangueriopsis lanciflora*) and collects a root and some leaves. Next he takes a root and leaves of *ikamba dachihamba* (or *musambanjita*) (*Cryptosepalum maraviense*) and a root of *musong'a-song'a* (*Ximenia americana*), followed by leafy branches and roots of *mukombukombu* (*Tricalysia angolensis*), *mututambululu* (*Xylopia adoratissima*), and *muhotuhotu* (*Canthium venosum*). Next a root and leaves of *mukandachina* which grows on termite-hills are collected.

"The doctor then goes to a place where a wild pig (*chombu*) was lying or trampling and there collects grasses and twigs. The doctor and his assistants go to the termite-hill from which they obtained *mukandachina* (*Rhus longipes*, or possibly *Eriocoelum* sp.) medicine. There they cut up all the roots they have collected, mix them together well, and fill two pots (*mazawu*) with the mixture. Old calabashes (*yipwepu*) can be used. Then they add any part of a dead leopard, a piece of wild pig's meat, and a mad dog's bone to each pot. These portions are classed as *jipelu*. *Mpelu* from the coney or hyrax (*chibila, chibatata*), the mamba (*ntoka*), the lion (*mutupa*), and of a fish called *muvundu* are also added to the contents of each pot.

"Now water is brought and poured in each *izawu*. There is no pounding of the tree medicines (*nyitondu*) in a mortar, as is often done. A medicine broom (*chisampu*) is made of the leafy branches of *mukombukombu, muhotuhotu, mututambululu,* and *musoli*. Both pots contain only cold medicine, the pots must not be warmed. One pot is carried to the top of the termite-hill, the other is left at the foot of it. The patient, the crazy person, is made to kneel while the doctor gives him the medicine to drink, first from the pot at the top of the termitary, then from the one at the bottom. Then he sprinkles the patient's eyes and face with his medicine broom. He repeats this treatment twice a day until the patient is able to say that he has recovered. No drums are played at this treatment."

The procedure is explained thus. "The *musoli* tree is the *ishikenu*, 'the place of greeting,' where an invocation is made. It is the senior of the medicines. It has many edible fruits, yellow and purple, called *nsoli*, much eaten by duiker (*nkayi*) and other antelope from September to November. Its name is from *ku-solola*, 'to reveal.' Here it means 'to make everything clear,' for a mad person does not see things clearly.

"*Musambanjita* used to be a war medicine to make people invulnerable to bullets or spears. Here it does the eyes good, for a person suffering from this disease feels dizzy in the eyes. This medicine clears the eyes.

"*Musong'asong'a* feels bitter (*kutiya wukawu*) to the eyes. This tree produces red edible fruits—*ku-song'a* signifies 'to produce fruits.'

"*Mukandachina* is collected because it has the habit of growing on top of termite-hills. A mad person is like a person who passes above (things). (*Muntu wazaluka wudi neyi muntu wahita kwiwulu.*) He wanders about in the air (*mumpepela*), on the tops of hills and even of trees. He can do nothing in a peaceful way. It is seldom that he talks while sitting, but he talks in the air (while standing?). That is also why a pot of medicine is placed on top of a termitary. There is a *mukishi* [7] (a manifestation of) an ancestral spirit (in the form of a hunter of long ago), who also behaves like a mad person and ascends to the tops or crests of places.

"*Mpelu* taken from a leopard (*chisumpa*) is used because a leopard is like a madman and kills for no reason, only for sport (*nakuhema hohu*). *Mpelu* of a wild pig is used because it moves about just like a mad person (randomly). So does a coney.

"The *muvundu* fish may swim upside down, it changes its direction, it is a mad fish. Its name is connected with *ku-vundumuka*, 'to pack up and go away without giving any reason.'

"This disease of insanity comes in the air."

*The special case of rabies*. "If a person has been bitten by a mad dog, he will, in the first instance, be given a medicine to make him vomit.

[7] *Mukala* or *Kaluwi*, see above, p. 293.

"The doctor goes to a *kavulawumi* tree (*Maprounea africana*), digs down and exposes the root, and cuts off a piece about six inches long.

"He then scrapes off the skin or bark of the root with the help of an old piece of calabash and puts these scrapings (*nyemba*) in the sunshine to dry. When dry they are pounded into powder (*luseng'a*) in a mortar. The doctor next brings some thin cassava porridge (*kapudyi*), to which he adds the powder, mixing it in well.

"He gives this mixture to the patient to drink. After drinking, the patient vomits very much, and has frequent motions of the bowels.

"Another treatment is to cut up the root of *mudiansefu* (possibly *Craterosiphon quarrei*), which secretes a white gum, add water to the portions in a pot and boil for about a quarter of an hour. While the water is still boiling, *kapudyi* gruel is brought and the medicine is added to it hot. The patient must then drink it while it is still very hot. The medicine stays within a short while, then the patient vomits and excretes at short intervals until his stomach is cleared out.

"These emetics and aperients, *kavulawumi* and *mudiansefu*, are equally strong. If they fail, the full medicines for *musong'u wakuzaluka* are used."

My informants gave this explanation. "A person bitten by a mad dog froths at the mouth (*ku-tupula*), just like the dog. Such frothy saliva is called *izeng'i* (singular), while ordinary saliva is called *mazeng'i* (plural). 'To foam at the mouth like a madman' is *kutupula izeng'i-zeng'i*. The poison given to a man by a mad dog is just like arrow-poison (*wulembi*) taken from the *Strophanthus* plant (also *wulembi*)."

*The treatment of madness as a rite of affliction.*[8] "The drum (or rite) of mad ancestral spirits (*ng'oma yawakishi akuzaluka*) is 'played' (performed) if all these medicines fail. It is then supposed that the spirits of people who died insane have 'caught' (possessed) the patient."

My best informant, Muchona,[9] described the rite as follows:

"The relative responsible for the patient [literally the 'owner of the

[8] See my *Schism and Continuity* (1957, 292–303), for a discussion of this class of rites.

[9] A character sketch of Muchona appears above in "Muchona the Hornet, Interpreter of Religion," pp. 131–150, and his interpretations form a considerable part of *Ndembu Divination* (1961).

patient' (*mwenimuyeji*)] starts the proceedings by bringing the doctor (*chimbuki*—as in herbal therapy) a cock or a goat, which may be of any color. The doctor agrees and fetches *mpelu* made from an '*mpompa*' a wooden fetter used to fasten the limbs of madmen, slaves, and criminals.

"Next he goes to an old site of the *Mung'ong'i* cult rites [10] and collects five or six roots from any species of tree that grows there. What is important is not the species but the place—the *izembi* shelter of the sacred mysteries. Then he goes to the site of a former circumcision lodge and collects about six roots from the *ifwilu* or 'place of dying,' where the boys are actually circumcised.

"Next, he and his assistants (an assistant or apprentice doctor is called *kadiza,* 'one who is learning') go to a stream and collect in the gallery forest (*itu*) roots and leaves of the *kaleng'ang'ombi* thornbush.[11] Two clay pots are used, each containing the same medicine. One *izawu* pot is taken to the top of a termite-hill (*kawumbu*), the other is left on the ground. Then the goat's throat is cut and its blood poured in each pot. The pots contain cut and pounded roots collected by the doctor.

"Next the patient drinks from both pots. The whole following night is spent in splashing medicine (*ku-kupula*) on the patient's body, washing it with medicine, and giving him a medicine draught at intervals.

"Drums are played near the medicine pot on the ground. The site is in the bush not far from the village. They begin by singing *Mung'ong'i* songs, then *Mukanda* songs, and follow these with songs from the *Kayong'u* rite [Turner 1961, 23–26]—performed to propitiate an ancestral spirit which causes chest trouble and confers the power to divine by tossing symbolic objects in a basket—and from the *Kaluwi* or *Mukala* rite [see below p. 374] performed to placate a particularly

[10] A funerary association which performs elaborate initiation rites on the death of its members. Among the Northern Lunda, or Luunda, it appears to have been connected with circumcision; but among the Ndembu, and other Southern Lunda and such culturally similar tribes as the Luvale, Chokwe, and Luchazi, the circumcision rites, called *Mukanda,* are performed independently of *Mung'ong'i.*

[11] Used as a symbol during the rite accompanying circumcision and explained in terms of the foundation myth of *Mukanda.* For a fuller account, see above, pp. 219–220.

troublesome manifestation of a hunter ancestor. These spirits are regarded as 'mad' (*akuzaluka*), for they make those possessed[12] by them jerk about convulsively (*ku-zakuka*). Both patient and doctor jerk and shiver. The doctor must treat himself with medicine along with the patient, otherwise the mad spirit may possess him also. When he shivers, the spirit is temporarily in him too.

"After drumming, the doctor continues to administer these medicines to the patient, for days or maybe weeks, until he is better."

It is interesting to note in what respects the treatment of insanity as a "disease" (*musong'u*) resembles the rite of affliction, where madness is regarded as a sign and symptom of affliction by an ancestral spirit. Both procedures stress the opposition of "above" and "below" (*hewulu* as opposed to *hamaseki,* literally "in the air" and "on the ground"), both take place on and near termite-hills, both involve the splashing of the patient—although Muchona did not mention the collection of the usual components of a medicine broom, *mukombukombu, muhotuhotu,* and *mututambululu* fronds, this was probably done before the affliction rite.

There are also profound differences between them, for the rite deals with the spirit of a deceased kinsman as well as with a disease. Since ancestral spirits are said "to be pleased by the playing of drums," drumming and singing must accompany the administration of medicines. Indeed, among the objects in a diviner's basket, a piece of wood crudely carved to represent a drum stands for "rites to propitiate ancestral spirits" (Turner 1961, 65).

The slaughter of an animal or fowl is another recurrent feature of rites of affliction that is not found in the direct treatment of disease. It is not always easy to see such slaughters as "sacrifices," for often the animal or chicken represents the ancestral spirit himself. If there is sacrifice, it is a sacrifice (in symbolic guise) of the ancestor, not to the ancestor, on behalf of the ritual participants and as a sign of reconciliation and communion between the spirit and his kin. Nevertheless, however it may be regarded, the slaughter of an animal is a characteristic feature of manistic rites among the Ndembu.

There may be a connection with the slaughter of a goat at this rite and at *Kayong'u.* At *Kayong'u,* too, a cock is slaughtered by the patient himself, who bites the bird's head off. About this act Muchona

[12] Ndembu say *"waheta mukishi,"* "you have a spirit," when they wish to indicate possession by a spirit. Often, too, they speak of a spirit which "catches" (*wakwata*) a patient.

said (Turner 1961, 32), "*Kayong'u* makes a person a little mad. He feels as if he were drunk or epileptic." It looks as though the spirit responsible for insanity were a species of the *Kayong'u* manifestation. The classical association between soothsaying and madness is made in a tribal milieu, for *Kayong'u* is usually regarded as the mode of affliction assumed by a dead diviner's spirit.

This comparison of treatment and rite enables us to see that a "rite of affliction" is a combination of therapy, aimed at treating the pathological condition (cataract, madness, reproductive disorder) and religious service (veneration and propitiation of ancestral spirits). There has been a considerable fusion of these procedures, so that some medicines have become symbols for modes of spirit manifestation, while something of the "law" bound character of magic has influenced the relationship held to exist between ancestral spirits and their living kin. Thus it seems to be assumed that if one collects the medicines appropriate to a rite and applies them correctly, the ancestral spirit is more or less compelled to stop afflicting the patient. This situation differs at any rate from invocations made to village shrine trees, outside the rite of affliction context, in which appeals are made to ancestors to "change their livers" (i.e. "minds" ) and cease causing trouble to their relatives. Here "free will" apparently prevails over "necessity."

### MUSONG'U WANYIMA, BACKACHE

(*a*) "The doctor takes part of a broken hoe blade. Then he goes to a tree that has been struck by lightning and takes a portion of the splintered wood. After that he goes to an old village site to the place where a mortar once stood for pounding cassava roots and grain. There he digs and removes the first root he finds—of any species of tree.

"He now brings the patient and makes him lie under a *mudyi* tree (*Diplorrhyncus condylocarpon*) that is naturally bent. With his knife, he scrapes off bark from underneath the bend in the tree. Then he collects some bark scrapings (*nyemba*) from the upper side. His next task is to place a pounding pole (*mwishi*) at right angles to the tree. He then adds to the medicine in his basket (*lwalu*, a flat round winnowing basket) some scrapings from the top of a tortoise's shell.

"The patient is then allowed to leave the *mudyi* site for a moment while the doctor brings a potsherd (*chizanda*) in which he puts red *ing'aji* oil (palm oil?). He scrapes some iron dust from the broken hoe on to the oil. Then he burns the piece of lightning-struck tree and adds its ash to the mixture. In go the tortoise shell scrapings and finally the *nyemba* of the *mudyi* tree. The medicine is thoroughly mixed with the oil.

"The doctor then makes two or three lines of small incisions across the small of the patient's back, where the pain is, with his razor (*ntewula*). When the blood begins to ooze, the doctor rubs the medicine into those cuts. The medicine goes into the blood right to the part where the pain is felt.

"When that is done, the doctor takes the pounding pole (*mwishi*) and presses (*ku-kanda*) it on the patient's back where the incisions are. The doctor presses the pestle lengthwise on the back with both hands. He then puts the razor and medicines in a pot and removes them from the scene.

"Now the doctor tells the patient to hold the pounding pole up vertically and to go under the crook in the *mudyi* tree once more. The patient must then straighten himself up, with the help of the pounding pole, and push the *mudyi* up with his back (a process known as *kudyikanda*).

"Now he must address the tree (*ku-subwila mutondu*) as follows: 'I have already left this disease with you (*nakushiyili dehi musong'u*). I must go home feeling no more pain, because I have left it already with you.' Then the patient returns home bearing the pounding pole."

(*b*) *Another treatment*. "The doctor goes in the early morning to where a mortar stands. He gets women to shift its position, digs down and removes a piece of any root he finds there. Then he scrapes some dirt from the base of the mortar itself. He mixes the scrapings from the root and the earth scrapings with castor oil (*imonu*) or palm oil (*ing'aji*) in a potsherd.

"Next he makes the patient lie across the hole where he removed the root at the former site of the mortar. Then he makes three lines of cuts with his razor across the patient's back where he felt pain and rubs medicine into the incisions. After that, he orders the patient to pull himself upright by means of the pounding pole that usually goes with the mortar. He must then walk to his hut. He must leave the pounding pole upright [13] against a tree near his hut and never let it lie on its side."

In the first of these treatments "the doctor took a broken hoe blade

[13] To lean upright is *ku-kunjika*.

because hoe blades snap suddenly (*koto-o*) when people are digging. In the same way a person with backache (lumbago) feels as though he has suddenly been broken.

"A meal mortar is used because of the pounding (*ku-twa*). This represents 'hitting.' Having backache is like being hit very hard.

"A tortoise shell is used because a tortoise has a hard shell and a hard body, so he never feels backache. Its medicine strengthens the back.

"The *mudyi* tree has white gum, so it is a white or lucky tree. The patient leaves bad things with *mudyi*, and its whiteness gives him health (*wukolu*)."

In the second treatment, the earth from the mortar "is a kind of *mpelu* for strengthening (*nakukolesha*)."

"A lightning-smitten tree is used because lightning gives a sudden shock (expressed by the ideophone *bele-e*). 'To strike' is *kw-anda*. 'Thunder' is *chivumina*, 'to thunder' *ku-vuma* or *ku-dulumwina*. Lightning is an animal. A mole rat (*mpumba*) makes a sound similar to that of thunder. The lightning grows jealous and tries to hit the mole rat and kill it. That is why lightning follows the holes and 'hills' of mole rats all the way along."

The treatment for backache appears to be almost entirely magical. In less severe cases, it is possible to imagine that there may be some psychological benefit.

### MUSONG'U WACHINKONYA, EPILEPSY

"The doctor goes first to a *museng'u* tree (*Ochna pulchra*) and collects leaves which are rolled up into a curl backward from the tip (*mafu adikonya adivung'a mafunda*) to form bundles (*mafunda*).

"Next he brings an old calabash cut across (*chipwepu*) and puts into it both pounded and unpounded *museng'u* leaves. He then adds several kinds of *mpelu*: a portion of coney or hyrax (*chibatata*), a piece of the beak of a *samunkambu* bird, and the scale of a pangolin.

"The doctor then takes a reed (*iteti*) and blows into it to make the water (which contains all these ingredients) bubble (*wapepa mwiteti nakubukumwina meji*). At intervals he washes the patient's face with the bubbling, foaming water.

"If this treatment fails after several days, the doctor collects the same kinds of *jipelu*, then goes to a *mulendi* tree (*Sterculia quinqueloba*) and cuts from it a part of a root. Then he goes to a place where a lion, leopard, or wild pig has scratched and collects grass scratched by their claws or hooves. He brings along another *chipwepu* calabash, cuts the *mulendi* roots into pieces, and adds them to cold water in the *chipwepu*. Then he puts all the *jipelu* (including those of the previous treatment) in the medicine, adding thereto the scratched grass, and takes the *chipwepu* to the village ash pile (*izalelu*). He puts it on top of the ash pile and gives the patient medicine to drink from his cupped hand. After this, he washes the face, head, and chest of the patient, and repeats the treatment for several days."

The procedure is explained as follows. "*Museng'u* is used because the epileptic patient shoots out his arms, then folds them again like curled *museng'u* leaves.

"*Chibatata* (*mpelu*) is used because it is an animal which makes a sound like an epileptic.

"*Samunkambu* is a bird which flies up and down spasmodically, like an epileptic, making a whirring sound.

"The pangolin (*nkaka*) curls itself into a ball like an epileptic's spasm.

"The doctor blows through the reed so that the foam rises (*kulonda kafulolu*[14] *kanyamuki*), like the foam on an epileptic's lips.

"*Mulendi* is a very slippery or glossy (=*senena*) tree, difficult to climb. The patient's disease will slip down and fall just like the climber of *mulendi*.

"The scratched grass is used because a lion, leopard, or wild pig scratches just like an epileptic in his fit.

"The ash pile is used because everything is thrown there, so the disease should be thrown there too."

This is another treatment which appears to rely entirely upon the principles of contagious and sympathetic magic. It is possible that the more severe the disease, the greater the recourse to magical techniques (q.v., leprosy, insanity, lumbago).

### MUSONG'U WAKANWA, DISEASE OF THE MOUTH

(a variety of conditions, including pyorrhea and toothache)

(*a*) *For blisters in the mouth* (*mabobela mukanwa*). One educated informant, a mission out-school teacher, described this condition, marked by blisters and sores in the mouth, as "scurvy," which is indeed characterized by swollen gums. It is probable that he picked up the term at the mission hospital at Kalene Hill. Dr. Cahal writes that while some conditions under this heading may be scurvy, others may

[14] This term is also applied to the fermentation of beer.

well be apthous ulcers, herpetic ulcers, and so forth. For, as mentioned above, the Ndembu doctor treats symptoms not diseases.

The procedure is described thus. "First, the doctor goes to a *mwalu* tree (also called *kalukuta,* possibly *Olax obtusifolius*), collects roots, cuts them up, puts them in a pot with water, and boils them for several minutes. When he judges it hot enough he puts the pot between the patient's open legs, makes him put his head over the pot, covers him entirely with a blanket, and tells him to open his mouth directly in the path of the rising steam. To cover oneself with a cloth (so that the wind will not blow the steam away) is termed *kudibutililamu* or *kudijikililamu.* When the patient's body begins to sweat, the doctor removes the blanket or skin, takes medicine from the pot, and tells the patient to rinse his mouth out with it (*ku-mumika*—'to wash out the mouth with water' is *ku-kucha*). This treatment continues for three or four days.

"If the results are not good, the doctor goes to a *mwang'alala* tree (*Paropsia brazzeana*), takes roots, cuts them up, and warms them gently on a fire in a pot with water, then gives the medicine to the patient as a mouthwash.

"Another mouthwash is made by splitting large pieces (*nakusesa yibalu*) of the *musosu* plant (*Boscia corymbosa*) which grows on termite-hills. These laths are then soaked in warm water and the water is given to the patient to rinse his mouth with. He may do this for a week.

"Finally, roots of *kambanjibanji* are cut into pieces and warmed in water. The resultant mouthwash is retained in the patient's mouth for several minutes. He repeats this at intervals for several days."

My informants explained the treatment this way. "*Mwalu* is used because it is bitter and can kill the disease.

"*Mwang'alala* is used because it sets the teeth on edge; also it is hot (*ku-yeya*).

"*Musosu* is used because it lacks saltiness, is insipid."

One doctor said, when discussing *musosu,* that doctors test out different medicines until they find one to deaden the pain—a remark which implies some degree of rational experimentation.

"*Kambanjibanji* is used because it is hot (*ku-yeya*)." [15]

(*b*) *Toothache with mouth soreness* (*kakeleketi,* possibly from *ku-*

[15] This root is also used as a female aphrodisiac for the same reason—"to heat desire."

*keleketa,* "to gnaw"). This is a condition in which "bad teeth are left to fall out on their own," i.e. are not extracted. It is said that the following "medicines" will remove the pain and the teeth will drop out.

"The doctor cuts up the root of an *ipupa,* puts the pieces in a pot with warm water, and gives them to the patient as a mouthwash. He must rinse his mouth in the mixture frequently for several days. *Ipupa* is used because it is rather hot (*dayeya chanti*)."

to fall out on their own," i.e., are not extracted. It is said that the

(c) *Pyorrhea, chivukuta.* If the above treatment proves ineffectual and the doctor "finds blood on the front of the gums," he may suspect that the patient is suffering from *chivukuta,* "the disease that eats the gums" (*musong'u wadyang'a wushinshinyi*).

"The doctor (*chimbuki*) fetches *ileng'i* reeds and burns them into ash—often used for salt. Then he goes to the nest of a species of tiny ants called *masoha* and takes from it a ball (of organic material) known as *isoha.* Then he burns the *isoha* into ash and mixes it with *ileng'i* ash. He brings part of a calabash and makes little holes (*walokola nyiteta*) in it. Then a large leaf, such as a *mubula* leaf (*Uapaca* sp). is put into the calabash as a loose lining. The ashes are placed on top of the leaf. Next another old calabash is set beneath the first one. Water is gently poured over the ash and then strained (*ku-keleka*) through the holes of the upper calabash into the lower one. The same process is used for straining salt from grass ashes to add to food. The leaf prevents the ash itself from coming through. When the doctor estimates that enough strained liquid is in the lower calabash, he pours it off into his medicine pot. Then he goes to a *kapepi* tree (*Hymenocardia acida*), takes a root, and scrapes the outside bark (*nyemba*) into an empty *chipwepu* calabash container.

"The doctor boils the water from the strained ashes until it has all evaporated leaving only salty powder (*mung'wa*). He mixes this with the *kapepi* scrapings, then crushes the mixture very fine with a knife handle. He now adds just enough water to make the mixture into a paste.

"Taking this paste he rubs it very gently into the painful part of the patient's gums. Sometimes blood comes from the rubbing, and the patient begins to spit blood and paste. After a while the patient rubs the paste on himself, resting when the pain becomes too great. He goes on rubbing until blood ceases to flow from the painful spot. This is a very good treatment."

The treatment is explained further: "*Ileng'i* ash is used because it is very pungently salty (*ku-tukuma*). *Isoha* is used because it resembles blisters (*mabobela*) or boils (*mahuti*). *Kapepi* is used because of its bitterness (*wukawu*)."

Pyorrhea is said by the mission doctors at Kalene Hospital to be very common among the Ndembu. Some attributed its prevalence to their dependence on cassava as a staple crop—almost pure carbohydrate.

### MUSONG'U WAMPANG'A, SWELLING OF THE SCROTUM

This disease is thought to be most commonly caused by *mukayu* "medicines," used by husbands to protect their wives from adultery and by the owners of hives and gardens against thieves. White (1961, 36) discusses similar protective medicines among the Luvale and concludes that they "contain a selective power within them which enables them to function . . . medicine to keep adulterers from a wife will not injure the husband but only adulterers." It is this selective power, so it is believed, which causes the scrotum—and in some cases the *membrum virile*—of the adulterer to swell up. Ndembu are quick to point out that the disease is not invariably caused by *mukayu*—"for even a newborn infant may have it."

"The first thing the doctor (*chimbuki*) does is to go to an *ivung'u-vung'u* tree (*Kigelia pinnata*—the 'sausage tree,' with long pods) and make an address to it (*ku-shahu mpandula*). He carries his ax and hoe and says: "You, O tree, I received you from another doctor.[16] The medicine we will collect from you here must have the power of killing the diseases." (*Eyi mutondu nawutambwili kudi chimbanda mukwawu yitumbu yinukuhukaku yikali nang'ovu yakujaha nyisong'u.*)

"Then the doctor digs up a root, takes some leaves, and collects fruit from the tree. He puts one piece of root in a pot, then cuts the long pod into two parts of which one is chopped up and put in the pot. Warm water is added and the patient drinks the potion repeatedly for several days.

"The doctor next brings two potsherds, in each of which he places some *ivung'uvung'u* medicine. Then he scrapes the root and puts some scrapings in each potsherd. The leaves are pounded into pulped leaf medicine, known as *nsompu,* which is put in a third potsherd in

[16] He learned the properties and use of the tree as a therapy for elephantiasis from another doctor.

cold water. Hot water is poured in one of the original potsherds and cold water into the other. Now the patient is taken to the village ash pile (*izalelu*). The doctor then drinks *nsompu* leaf medicine, gives some to the patient, and then makes his assistant, who will tap the patient's blood (*ku-sumuna muyeji*), have a draught. That potsherd is then removed.

"The operator makes cuts on the lower half of the patient's abdomen and applies a cupping horn (*kasumu*); makes another cut just to the right of the navel and applies a horn; applies another to the right of the stomach and another just above the right hip. The operator rubs hot medicine from one potsherd into the cuts and presses it in (*ku-kanda*). After the horns have been removed, a hole is made in the ash pile, and the patient's blood is poured into it from the cupping horns and lightly covered with ashes. During the operation the patient is made to drink medicine from the pot. Afterwards the potsherds are taken away and kept for further use. The pot goes with the patient to this hut. He must go on drinking medicine after the treatment. Next day the operator and patient come back to the ash pile with the pot and three potsherds and the treatment is repeated. This continues for two or three days and after it is over the patient must go on drinking the medicine for a long time.

"The doctor afterwards goes and collects a pumpkin vine (*molu weyang'wa*), cuts a piece off it, and takes its roots. He conceals these in his hut. Then he goes to a bundle of *nsama,* used to smoke out bees. The *nsama* consists of a cone- or poke-shaped bundle of small leafy twigs (*nsonsu*) containing dry twigs and grass and tied around with bark string. A bark rope (*isosu*) is tied to its narrow top end. When a man goes to get honey, he lifts the *nsama* by this rope as he climbs the tree to the beehive or nest. He sets fire to the *nsama* and ties it to a bough above the hive so that it dangles just below the hive and smokes out the bees. Very often the rope breaks or burns through and is left hanging from the branch by the honey gatherer. It is this abandoned portion that is collected by the doctor. He then goes to a *muhwila* tree (*Strychnos spinosa*)—which produces large round fruits—and removes a fruit, a root, and some leaves.

"At his village he pounds the leaves he has collected into *nsompu* and puts it into a calabash cup (*lupanda*). Other *nsompu* is put into a small clay pot (*kanung'u*). The *isosu* rope fragment is added to this pot, also the roots of the pumpkin vine and the *muhwila* tree. This is for the patient to drink.

"Then cupping horns and medicine are applied as before, and medicine is drunk by the patient."

Further comments were these. "*Ivung'uvung'u* is used because the fruits in its pod resemble testicles (*nyisokwa* or *makutu*). *Iyang'wa,* the pumpkin, is used because it is like a swollen testicle. The fruit of *muhwila* is used for the same reason. *Isosu dansama,* the piece of rope, is a kind of *mpelu*. It is used because the *nsama* bundle hangs from it. With elephantiasis the testicles hang down because of their weight.

### MUSONG'U WAMUTU, HEADACHE

Two kinds of *musong'u wamutu* are recognized: (*a*) *Musong'u wamutu* proper, which begins when "a person feels that the skin of his temples is moving about (throbbing?). His head feels heavy and pain comes in his temples first, then spreads to his whole head." (*b*) *Musong'u wanyembu wamutu* or *Kakenka,* which starts "with a pain just above the eyes in mid-brow and spreads till it covers the whole eye, then spreads to the ears. It gives '*ku-kena,*' a word which describes the very bright light made when lightning falls on a hut—such a light comes very suddenly, it is a sharp stab of pain."

(*a*) "The doctor (*chimbuki*) goes to a *kapwipu* tree (*Swartzia madagascariensis*) and cuts from it some large chips of bark (*yitumbu yakusesa*). He then puts these in a pot and adds either hot or cold water. After a time the patient washes his whole head with it. He may do this at any time of the day or evening and continues with the washing for several days.

"If the *kapwipu* medicine fails, the doctor goes to a *chikoli* tree (*Strychnos spinosa*), carrying a flaming bundle of grass with which he burns some of its leaves. He collects burned leaves and puts them in a mortar where they are pounded into *nsompu*. This is put into a pot and warm water is added. The doctor tells his patient to wash his head in the medicine. If the patient has suffered from the disease before, he can collect these medicines himself, otherwise he must seek out a doctor. This treatment continues throughout the day. The washing is known as *ku-boba,* where the water is taken in the hollowed hand and splashed vigorously on the head. *Ku-boba* strictly refers to this splashing of the head. This treatment may last for several days.

"If *chikoli* fails, the doctor collects a root of *kambanjibanji* [see also p. 327], scrapes it, and puts the scrapings in an old potsherd. He then goes to a *lweng'i* or *lweng'eng'i* plant (*Dracaena reflexa*) and takes some leaves. These are mixed with the *kambanjibanji* bark scrapings, after having first been crushed in the doctor's fingers. He then takes his razor and makes incisions from the right temple along the hairline to the left temple. He rubs the medicine into the cut marks. This medicine is wanted so that it can fight the disease in order to kill it.

"If the disease still continues, two further cuts are made in each temple and horns are sucked onto them. No medicine is used with these *tusumu*."

Explanation for this procedure is given thus:

"*Kapwipu* is used because of its bitterness (*wukawu*) and its heat (*ku-yeya*), like that of chillies or pepper. When it is mixed with water, it can enter the whole head and fight the disease.

"*Chikoli* is used for its bitterness (*wukawu*), but also because it is a 'strong' medicine (*ku-kola*—'to be strong or well').

"*Kambanjibanji* is used because of its heat (*ku-yeya*) and slight astringency.

"*Lweng'i* smells strongly and has 'heat.' It causes pain when rubbed in. When you burn leaves this means that you burn 'a *chisaku*.'[17] When you burn leaves you burn 'insects' (*tububu*—a euphemism for witches' familiars here) and *ndumba* (witches' familiars), in fact everything with bad magical power; you make the *chisaku* go away (*wafumisha chisaku*).

"Headache is usually caused by a *chisaku;* if a patient has one it will be burned with the leaves. *Chisaku* is bad luck (*malwa*) which causes death or suffering, causes someone to be beaten to death, or makes a man break an arm or leg. It is the same as a 'grudge' (*chitela*) which a man cherishes secretly against another. One kind of *chisaku* is from familiars of witchcraft, another is from ghosts (*chisaku chikwawu chawafu*).

"*Lweng'i* grows near the edge of villages; it is used in many treatments. It is also used by sorcerers (*aloji*)."[18]

(*b*) *Musong'u wanyembu.* "The doctor goes to a *mudyi* tree (*Diplorrhyncus condylocarpon*) and splits off a portion (*chibalu*). Then he goes to a tree smitten by lightning and takes another portion. Then one from a *kapepi* tree (*Hymenocardia acida*) and another from a *kapwipu* tree (*Swartzia madagascariensis*) and from a *chikwata* tree (*Zizyphus mucronata*) and another from a *chikoli* tree (*Strychnos*

[17] According to White (1961, 38) the Luvale cognate term *chisako* "denotes anything afflicting a person, be it illness, bad luck or failure such as lack of success in hunting, or a troublesome spirit."

[18] For its use in divination, see Turner (1961, 73).

*spinosa*). All these *yibalu* are brought to the patient's hut. An old pot is then fetched. All the medicines are put into it. Then a piece of *mpemba* (white clay) and a piece of *ng'ula* or *mukundu* (red clay), already softened, are brought, and the doctor draws a line of white clay (*mufunda wampemba*) around the rim of the pot and a line of red clay (*mufunda wang'ula*) underneath it. The pot is then suspended by bark string over the patient's doorway. Sometimes a pangolin's scale is added to the medicine. Water is added to the pot, which is now called *izawu*, a 'container of medicine.'

"At dawn one of the patient's relatives comes with two ax blades. The doctor comes too and washes the patient's head, pressing on medicine where he feels pain. As he does this the relative clinks (*kukenkumwina*) the ax blades together near the front of the patient's head. When he has been thoroughly washed with medicine, his relative drops the ax heads at his feet. This treatment is repeated at sunset, and at dawn and sunset for several days, until the headache is cured."

The reasoning behind the treatment is this. "*Mudyi* is used because it was used at *Nkang'a*, the girls' puberty rites. Also because it is bitter. *Mudyi* is a strong tree (*mutondu wakola*).

"A lightning-struck tree is used because lightning is like the stabbing pain of a headache.

"*Kapepi* is used because of its bitterness (*wukawu*).

"*Kapwipu* is used because of its bitterness and heat.

"*Chikwata* (which has strong thorns) is used because it can pierce the disease.

"*Chikoli* is used because it is strong.

"The line of *mpemba* is just for purifying (*ku-tookesha*); the line of *mukundu* means blood (*mashi*) or bad luck (*ku-halwa*). The pangolin is used because it can kill the disease. It is used in many treatments. For the pangolin lies on an *isoha*, a kind of round ants' nest, waiting for the ants to come out to eat them. The clinking ax blades represent the pain of the headache. The relative drops them suddenly at his feet so that the disease may instantly leave the patient.

"When the sun comes, it brings the proper light. The sun (*itang'wa*) comes for all things, it is the elder of the country (*itang'wa wudinakwinza nayuma yejima, diyi mukulumpi wampata*). We say that (the application of) medicines must begin early just when the sun itself begins to appear. We have all found, we Africans, that if we do this our diseases become weak (*nyisong'u yetu yifomoki*). We believe, too, that diseases must die with the sun in the evening; that is why they also treat the patient in the evening.

"A long time ago the sun was said to be '*Nzambi*,'[19] (the name now given to the Deity). *Nzambi* looks after the rain, the animals, and people. Once there was a man who came from Luunda[20] called *Mweni*, 'The Owner,' or *Mweniwamatung'a*, 'The Owner of the Realms,' an important chief. He spoke personally to *Nzambi*. If he wanted more food for his people he would ask *Nzambi* for it. He reached the Lukoji River in the Congo. Now people come together to venerate *Mweni* in the *Musolu* rite—performed by chiefs when the rains are late in coming."

"Headache" is a condition that seems more clearly associated with beliefs in witchcraft and sorcery than many other diseases. Possibly this is because the head is regarded as peculiarly the seat of one's individual life. A pain in the head may be the sign of a mystical attack on one's life by a sorcerer or witch, but the treatment of headache is directed against a vague and unspecified crowd of malevolent agencies rather than a particular witch or ghost. In this respect, it falls, together with the treatment of insanity, into a borderline category between therapy and ritual. When Ndembu speak about "the bitterness," "the heat," "the sourness," "the strength," "the saltiness," or "the pungency" of medicines, it is clear that they think of them as having some empirically remedial effect on the patient's state, even though we would consider that the principles underlying their use are those of sympathetic, contagious, and homeopathic magic. When they make medicine from a lightning-struck tree to cure headache, simply because they sense an analogy between lightning and sudden headache, they would be the first to admit that the medicine was used not because of its empirically verified curative effects, but because "the disease resembles lightning" and therefore is imbued with the same sort of mystical power. Once embodied in a symbol, that power can be controlled by the doctor for the patient's benefit. A step further in the direction of ritual is exemplified by the burning of the *chikoli* leaves. This is done explicitly to destroy the harm brought on by mystical agencies. The action is directed against the malignant agency rather

[19] See H. Baumann's views (1935, 104–105) on the solar concept of death and resurrection among the Chokwe.

[20] The traditional homeland of the Ndembu in the Katanga.

than against the disease. Yet the *kapwipu* medicine, which is employed because of its "heat and bitterness" and the *chikoli* medicine which is burned "to destroy witches' familiars" are both applied in exactly the same manner—as a headwash.[21]

The distinction between "medicine" as "drug" and as "ritual symbol" is a very fine one, and it is not always possible to make it clearly. All things are felt to be charged with powers of various kinds, and it is the job both of the herbalist and of the ritual specialist to manipulate these for the benefit of society. The ritual specialist may be said to deal primarily with powers that have already come under the control of conscious and purposive beings, visible or invisible, alive or dead, who use them, in general, to afflict the living with illness and misfortune. "Diseases," although they are sometimes said to "think," are certainly regarded as "alive" but are more like animals than persons, and motiveless in their malignancy. They might almost be said to come lowest in a hierarchy of afflicting agencies and to be controlled and directed by those above them. The Ndembu theory of affliction decrees that when conscious, voluntary beings decide to afflict human beings with illness, they rarely do so alone, or in their own right, but usually with the help of another conscious being, or through an intermediary being or power. Thus, a witch has her familiar homunculi, the *tuyebela* or *andumba;* a sorcerer has his *ilomba,* the human-faced serpent, or his figurines activated by human blood; the invoker of a curse raises by it a zombie (*musalu*) to do his fell work; while an ancestral spirit, as in *Chihamba,* may afflict in association with a demigod or may assume the guise of a specific "mode of affliction" (among the Luvale known as *lihamba*[22]). The *musong'u,* the "disease," is believed to be strengthened by these intermediaries, which act on behalf of conscious beings who desire either the death or punishment of the patient.

[21] As many investigations have pointed out, it is the theoretical basis which demarcates primitive from Western medicine most clearly. It is possible that *chikoli* ash contains an ingredient that objectively reduces headache, but the ash is not used for this reason; curative medicines are epiphenomena of mystical beliefs, not the results of scientific experiment.

[22] White (1961, 47) says *Mahamba* may originally have been earth-spirits which later became syncretized with ancestral spirits and now appear as the culturally standardized mode of manifestation—in terms of illness and ill luck —of the latter.

### MUSONG'U WANSHING'U, DISEASE OF THE NECK, STIFF NECK

Ndembu say that the sufferer from this disease "feels as though the inside of his neck is broken, he has a pain in the back of his neck, and his neck is stiff and immovable."

(*a*) "The doctor first goes to a *mubang'a* tree (*Afrormosia angolensis*) and breaks off a branch retaining all its twigs. He then ties a string to its broken end and to the tip to make a small bow (*kawuta*). Next he goes to collect some grass or reeds called *nteng'wiji* (*Phragmites*); he takes two individual pieces broken off at the joints. He puts blobs of wax (*ndunda*) of the small *chilundi* bee on the tips of the grass stems. With branch for bow and grass stem as arrow, he approaches close to the spot where the pain is and releases the 'arrow.' Then he repeats the procedure at another part of the patient's neck. Next he puts the patient's arm between the bow and string and hangs the bow over his shoulder (*ku-pakatisha kawuta*).

"The doctor also takes some portions of the outer bark of the *mubang'a* tree, chews them, and spits the juice on the painful place and also on the place where there is no pain. Then the patient lifts the bow over his head and presses (*ku-kanda*) it into his neck all the way around. Afterwards the doctor puts the bow and arrow in the overhanging thatch of the patient's hut above the veranda.

(*b*) "Should the above treatment be unsuccessful the doctor goes into the bush to look for a place where a python (*mboma*) died, leaving its bones. If he is lucky, he takes three of the vertebrae and puts them on a string to form a necklace. The procedure is first to warm these bones over a fire, then to press them into the sore place, and finally to tie them on a string around the patient's neck. This treatment continues for several days."

These treatments are further explained. "A branch of the *mubang'a* tree stands stiffly; to bend it with a string means to make it yield to pressure. The disease pushes the patient's neck straight like the branch of the hard *mubang'a*—the tree against which novices urinate in seclusion after circumcision to make their wounds heal and give them a hard erection. *Nteng'wiji* grass is used because when it hits someone it is just like the pain he feels in the neck. The beeswax is soft (*yayovu*), so the disease will become soft (supple) too. A python is used in the second treatment because it is strong and supple (*mamovu*); thus the neck will become flexible instead of stiff."

MUSONG'U WACHINGONGU, SMALLPOX (WITH SEVERE CHICKEN POX)

Smallpox is not considered to be the result of witchcraft or sorcery or of ancestral affliction. It is said "to come to you in the air from Europeans." It is thought by Ndembu to be very deadly, and formerly its victims were secluded in the bush far from their villages. If a mother fell sick with smallpox, her child could accompany her, and vice versa. One of my informants, Sandombu, considered it to be the second worst disease, leprosy being the more feared. Several Ndembu know the "true" (*yalala*) medicines, but there are no great specialists, as there are for insanity and leprosy. Treatment is usually given in the bush itself.

The doctor collects bark-scrapings from the following trees: *Mufung'u* (*Anisophyllea* sp.), the "wild plum," which has reddish bark and bears either reddish or purple plumlike edible fruits; *Mukula* (*Pterocarpus angolensis*), which secretes a red gum; *Luvung'u* (*Anisophyllea boehmii*), which has round, orange colored fruits. These bark-scrapings (*nyemba*) are mixed with *museng'eleli* grass, and a European disinfectant, such as Jeyes Fluid, bought at the local store, is added. The mixture is rubbed on the pustules.

When the smallpox victim shivers with fever, the pounded leaves of the *wululu* shrub (*Khaya nyassica?*) are rubbed on his body. This treatment is continued for two successive days. *Wululu* is a legume with yellow flowers and small, round, paired leaves in a spray of light green color. The pounded leaves are also used in the preparation of fish poison. I have not been able to identify this plant: it is possibly the *mululu* of the Bemba, Yombe, Ila, Lamba, Kaonde, and many other tribes, identified by the Northern Rhodesia Forest Department as *Khaya nyassica*. Fanshawe suggests it might be a species of *Cassia*.

## *Concluding Note on Treatment of Diseases*

The above makes up the full tally of my systematic accounts of the treatment of various diseases. What follows consists of the organization of comments and remarks made to me at various times during my fieldwork by a variety of informants. Before we consider them, however, it is worth mentioning that Ndembu recognize the originators of new curative procedures under the titles "*Sayitumbu*," Father of the Medicines, or "*Sakuuka*," Father of Treatment. For example, it was said that Katontu of Kalema Village in Chief Kanongesha Ndembi's area was a Sayitumbu. A former Kanongesha, Chief Izemba, is declared to have introduced many curative techniques—and also the *Kaneng'a* rite against illness caused by witchcraft or sorcery. Although there is an element of standardization in the procedures I have listed, particularly with regard to quasi-ritual acts such as straightening a bent *mudyi* tree to cure backache, yet there is considerable variation in herbalists' recommendations of medicines to be used for particular diseases. For example, some herbalists recommended that the pounded leaves and roots of the *musenzi* (*Combretum zeyheri*) plant should be steeped in cold water for two days and then given to men suffering from dysentery (*kapokota*) rather than the *chikwata* roots mentioned in the description above of the treatment of men's *musong'u wevumu.*

Among the accounts I collected are data on some of the mechanical devices and "surgical procedures" of the Ndembu. Much of this material was collected in Mbamvu Village, in Chief Mwininyilamba's area. The villagers had come fairly recently—three years before—from the Lovwa River in Angola and were still relatively uninfluenced by the behavior and values of a changing society. Their views may fairly be said to be those of traditional Ndembu.

## SURVEY OF MECHANICAL DEVICES USED IN MEDICINE
(mainly from recent Angolan immigrants)

### *Massage*

To cure constipation, the stomach is rubbed with castor oil and then massaged gently.

### *Circular Bandages*

If muscles are displaced or joints dislocated, circular bandages, consisting of sheets of bark fibre bound round by bark strings, are tied tightly around the affected area. The bandage is called *chisesa,* a term that also denotes a split palm mat. A *chisesa* is also used in one treatment of headache. First, small incisions are made between each eye and ear, and then medicine made from the bark of the *kalayi* plant is rubbed into them. Finally, a *chisesa* is tied round the head to cover the cuts.

### *Bleeding*

To prevent bleeding, cold water is quickly applied to a wound. If the nose bleeds, it is plugged with leaves.

13. Circumcision novices dressed in their best new clothes, ready to dance *ku-tomboka* before their kin and neighbors.

14. The shrine of a great hunter: forked branches inserted to honor hunter-ancestors are interspersed with quickset *muyombu* trees planted to commemorate lineage shades.

15. An impressive array of roan and sable antelope horns adorns the ancestral shrines of a great hunter.

16. A village elder pours out a libation of "white" beer and addresses an ancestral shade at the planting of a new *muyombu* tree in honor of that shade. Note the exposure of the white inner wood by cutting at the top of the sapling. A villager will be given the name of the shade prefixed by *nswana*— "successor of."

*Abscesses* (mahuti)

Abscesses may be cut with a knife or pierced with a sharp stick and washed out with warm water.

*Snake Bite*

First, a ligature is tied at the nearest joint—below the knee or elbow as the case may be—then the flesh is cut out around the snake bite and medicine is applied to the wound. The medicine consists of: (*a*) a powder known as *ndakala;* made from the dried and pounded heads of all the poisonous snakes known to the Ndembu; (*b*) powdered root bark of the *mukeketi* (*Veptoderris nabilis*) tree—also known as *musombu;* (*c*) powdered root bark of *mupembi* (*Ekebergia arborea*); (*d*) powdered root bark of *mundoyi* (*Chrysophyllum* [*Magalismontanum*] *bangweolense*); and (*e*) powdered root bark of *mutokatoka* (*Ilex mitis*).

At the same time as the medicine is applied to the wound, the patient must chew the leaves of *musombu, mupembi, mundoyi, mutokatoka,* and *mwang'alala* (*Paropsia brazzeana*), and swallow the juice mixed with his saliva.

Next, purses (*masaku*) made from the skins of three species of mongoose (*kabunshi, mung'eli* and *kang'amba*) are tightly bound around the ligature. Before they are tied on, they are rubbed on the patient's calf and forearm. If the blood is not flowing freely from the wound as it ought to do, the doctor takes some *ndakala* medicine from a tortoise shell container (*mbachi*), chews it in his mouth, sucks the wound, then applies the medicine.

*Treatment of Severe Cuts*

Bark scrapings of *mupuchi* (*Brachystegia spiciformis*), *muvuka* (*Marquesia macrova*), *mwanda* (*Julbernardia paniculata*), *mundoyi* (*Chrysophyllum* sp.), *mwang'alala* (*Paropsia brazzeana*) and *mudyi* (*Diplorrhyncus condylocarpon*) are boiled in a pot, and the hot mixture is applied in a sheet of bark fiber to the affected part and tied over it. Then a grass hut (*nkunka*) is built for the patient outside the village where he may lie quietly until he recuperates.

*Emetics*

If a person has swallowed something poisonous, he is given root-scrapings of *mundoyi* which are mixed with thin warmed gruel (*kapu-*

*dyi*) and eaten; root peelings of *kavulawumi* (*Maprounea africana*) are also dropped in beer which is then drunk.

If a person has drunk a large amount of beer but cannot vomit, he chews leaves of any available species and swallows the sap.

*Enemas*

Enemas are made of small calabashes (*tuswaha*) with reeds inserted through the necks. They are filled with warm water and given to the patient to administer himself. They are used in cases of dysentery (*kapokota*) and, if the patient has become very thin, of hookworm.

*Splints*

Splints are used for broken limbs. They are made of mats of split palm (*yisesa*), split sugar cane, or tough reed, tied round with bark string. The patient is segregated from the village in a grass hut, as in the treatment for severe cuts. Medicine leaves are applied to the skin under the mats. The famous *Sayitumbu,* Katontu, is said to have cured broken limbs by breaking the legs of a chicken and treating patient and chicken together. When the chicken starts to walk again so (in theory!) will the patient.

*Amputation is unknown.*

*Stitches*

Stitches are never made in wounds. If a cut is deep, the doctor closes one eye "so that the medicine may sink in deeply."

*Burns*

"If someone has a burn, the doctor brings him *chitakachi* leaves (*Phyllanthus discoideus*), which are pounded, then soaked in water. He rubs this medicine on the burn. This treatment continues for two days.

"If the burn made a severe wound, the doctor burns a wild pig's bones to ash. Then he takes the patient to a *mukula* tree, rubs *mukula* gum on the wound, and finishes by rubbing bone ash (*mula*) on it. This treatment is repeated for several days.

"If the wound does not heal, the doctor goes to a *kampandi* tree (*Maytenus cymosus*), collects some pieces of bark, pounds them, and puts them in the sun to dry. When dry, they are sieved so as to form a powder. The patient is brought and his wound is well washed with water. When it is clean this powder is applied while the burn is still wet. The water and powder should meet together and form a scab. This treatment goes on for as many weeks as the burn requires to be healed.

"*Chitakachi* is *wazema* or 'tacky'; it comes off in a long string, all in one piece. Its leaves are treacly like that, just like the leaves of the relish plant *wusi;* they are difficult to separate, like honey. They are used so that the wound will not spread but will remain in one piece.

"*Mukula* is used so that the burn will form a hard dry scab, like *mukula* gum. The wild pig's bone meal, mixed with *mukula* gum, is used to make the burn hard like a dry paste.

"*Kampandi* is used to make the wound form a scab, for the bark of *kampandi* is hard."

*Steam Bath*

We have already noted the use of the steam bath in the treatment of eye disease. It is also used occasionally during the *Kayong'u* rite, which may be performed for a patient who shows signs of asthma or bronchitis, thought to be the result of ancestral affliction (Turner 1961, 5, 23–26).

*Scarification*

Scarification is a standard Ndembu therapeutic practice, as we have seen.

*Cupping*

This is employed in several rites of affliction (e.g., *Ihamba, Kaneng'a*) with the avowed aim of removing harmful objects, mystically propelled into it, from the patient's body. Cupping is also used in several kinds of therapy.

## FURTHER NOTES ON TREATMENT AND MEDICINES

*Sores* (Yilonda, *sing.* chilonda)

(*a*) The pounded leaves of *wunkomukomu* (possibly *Aphrohiza nitida*) are mixed with copper ore obtained from returned labor migrants from the Copperbelt in Zambia and are rubbed on the sores. *Wunkomukomu* is a small shrub with large lanceolate leaves.

(*b*) Either pounded *muvuka* (*Marquesia macrova*) roots mixed with salt or pounded *kapwipu* (*Swartzia madagascariensis*) leaves mixed with salt are rubbed into the sores.

*Infantile Disorders*

(*a*) If an infant is very feeble, his father collects leaves of *chikang'anjamba,* another name for the *chikoli* tree mentioned above in several treatments; the name *chikang'anjamba* means "(the tree) the elephant fails to (break)"; it is used because it is very tough and enduring. The name *chikoli* is from *ku-kola,* "to be strong, hard or healthy." The leaves are pounded and left to steep in cold water.

(*b*) If a child is slow in learning to walk, his father collects *kambanjibanji* leaves (used also as a toothache cure), pounds them, allows them to steep in cold water for three days then gives them to the child to drink.

*Hookworm*

The pounded leaves of *kuvulawumi* (*Maprounea africana*) are administered in cold water to induce vomiting.

*Lactation Troubles*

"If a woman's breast milk (*mayeli*) becomes 'red' or 'yellow,' it is called *nshidi,* 'guilt' or 'sin.' If her baby drinks it, it may die. If the creeper or vine *molu wawubwang'u* is twined around the breast that is not giving white milk, it will become white."

In the *Wubwang'u* rites, performed for a mother of twins, *molu wawubwang'u* is one of the principal medicines and is regarded as the dominant symbol of the *itu,* or streamside forest.

*Masculine Sterility*

"If the color of a man's semen is 'red' or 'yellow' he will become a sterile person (*nshinta*). But if he eats medicine made from the *mucheki* plant, mixed with thin gruel (*kapudyi*), his semen will become white. After he has finished eating *mucheki,* he must dig a little hole in the ground and urinate into it."

*Mucheki* is the dominant symbol of the *kutumbuka* or major phase of the great *Chihamba* rite (Turner 1962a), where its root is regarded as epitomizing the purest "whiteness" and all the values and ideas annexed thereto. In these two medicines, *molu wawubwang'u* and *mucheki,* we get a glimpse of the relationship between religious rite and lay treatment. Here it would seem the treatment derives from the rite, the "magical" practice from the "religious" observance.

## *Analysis and Conclusions*

It has been said (Ackerknecht 1942) that in the primitive treatment of disease, "an invisible force is dealt with visibly by means that are meant and understood to be symbolic." This formulation would account for much that goes on at Ndembu curative procedures. It seems to be the case, however, that some scope is permitted for experiment, but in the main it is held that to make visible by symbolic means is to make a disease accessible to therapeutic action, also of a symbolic character. A glance at the "Alphabetical List of Trees and Plants Used in Treatments," illustrates this point sufficiently. Sympathetic, contagious, and homeopathic magic appear to account for the employment of the majority of the "medicines." All the senses—sight, hearing, taste, smell, and touch—are enlisted in the service of association and analogy. *Mucheki* is used because its wood is white and its medicine will hence make "red" semen "white" and fruitful. The "sound" of *kung'ami* as it bubbles in a child's stomach will "drive the disease to one side." The bitter taste of *kapepi* or *mwalu* will "kill diseases of the mouth." The "nasty smell" of *mutata* will "kill stomach disease in women." The "stiffness" of *mubang'a* is communicated to a homeopathic medicine made from it which will cure stiff neck.

There is no attempt to distinguish between medicines the effect of which are thought to depend on one kind of sensorily distinguishable property and medicines dependent on other kinds, and to reserve one kind for a single curative procedure. All kinds are interlinked in a single procedure. The procedure itself may often contain actions and episodes that we in the West might consider to be "religious." I refer to the invocations made by doctors to the principal medicine trees, to the formal washings, aspersions, and anointings. The prescribed, stereotyped behavior of the curative specialists seems often to fall more within the sphere of ritual than of therapeutic action. This consideration brings me back to Ackerknecht's query with which this study began: "What are the ideas underlying these therapeutic acts, and under what circumstances (with or without ritual) are they performed?"

We have partly answered these questions in commenting on specific treatments. The central idea behind both Ndembu therapy and Ndembu ritual is that the visible world is permeated by and perhaps is

Alphabetical List of Trees and Shrubs Used in Treatments

| *Prefix* | *Root* | *Botanical Name* | *Disease or Injury* | *Reason for Use* |
|---|---|---|---|---|
| *Mw-* | *ala* | *Afzelia quanzensis* | Stomach disease | "Bitterness will kill disease" (contains a high proportion of tannins with marked astringent effect—Dr. Cahal) |
| *Mw-* | *alu* or | *?Olax obtusifolius* | Blisters in mouth (Scurvy?) | "Bitter, can kill disease" |
| *Ka-* | *lukuta* | | | |
| *Mw-* | *anda* | *Julbernardia paniculata* | | |
| *Mw-* | *ang'alala* | *Paropsia brazzeana* | Blisters in mouth (Scurvy?) | "It is hot and sets teeth on edge" |
| *Mw-* | *ang'alala* | *Paropsia brazzeana* | Snake bite | |
| *Mw-* | *ang'alala* | *Paropsia brazzeana* | Severe cuts | |
| *Mu-* | *bang'a* | *Afrormosia angolensis* | Stiff neck | "Stiff tree to bend" |
| *M-* | ***bumba yachula*** | *Landolphia rufescens* | Leprosy | "Has mottled bark like leper's skin" |
| *Mu-* | *cheki* | *Cremaspora triflora* | Male sterility | "A 'white' medicine, makes semen white" |
| *Wa-* | *dikalanziza* or | *(Memecylon flavovirens)* | Eye disease | "Bitter" |
| *Ka-* | *yiza* | *Strychnos stuhlmannii* | | |
| *Mu-* | *diansefu* | *? Craterosiphon quarrei* | Rabies | "Aperient" |
| *Mu-* | *dyi* | *Diplorrhyncus condylocarpon* | Backache | Auspicious tree (here it refers also to bent specimen—like patient's back) |
| *Mu-* | *dyi* | *Diplorrhyncus condylocarpon* | Gonorrhea | White latex resembles pus of gonorrhea |
| *Mu-* | *dyi* | *Diplorrhyncus condylocarpon* | Headache | Auspicious, bitter |
| *Mu-* | *dyi* | *Diplorrhyncus condylocarpon* | Leprosy | White like leprous spots, symbolic role in *Mukanda* rites, sanctioned by leprosy |

| | | | | |
|---|---|---|---|---|
| *Mu-* | *dyi* | *Diplorrhyncus condylocarpon* | Severe cuts | |
| *Lw-* | *eng'eng'i* | | Eye disease | "Bitter" |
| *Lw-* | *eng'i* | *Draecena reflexa var. nitens* | Headache | "Strong smell and hot" |
| *Mu-* | *fung'u* | ? *Arisophyllea boehmii* | Small pox | "Reddish fruits" |
| *Mu-* | *hanu* | *Ficus* sp. | Tuberculosis | "Grows in hole in other trees; will break obstruction in chest" |
| *Mu-* | *hotuhotu* | *Canthium venosum* | Insanity | Traditional component of medicine broom |
| *Mu-* | *huma* | *Strychnos spinosa* (*Strophanthus welwitschii*) | Eye disease | "Bitter" |
| *Mu-* | *hwila* | | Eye disease | "Bitter" |
| *Ka-* | *jing'a ludi* | ? *Apocynaceae* creeper. *Landolphia* | Gonorrhea | "Creeper with white flowers" (= pus) |
| *I-* | *kamba daChihamba* | *Cryptosepalum maraviense* | Insanity | "Clears the eyes" |
| *Mu-* | *kandachina* | (*Eriocoelum sp.*) *Rhus longipes* | Insanity | "Grows on top of termite hills; a madman goes to top of things" |
| *Chi-* | *kang'anjamba* (*see chikoli*) | *Strychnos spinosa* | Insanity | "Grows on top of termite hills; a madman goes to top of things" |
| *Mu-* | *keketi* | (*Veptoderris nabilis*) *Syzygium quineense* | Snake bite | |
| *Chi-* | *koli* | *Strychnos spinosa* | Earache | "Yellow fruits" |
| *Chi-* | *koli* | *Strychnos spinosa* | Headache | "Bitter and strong" |
| *Chi-* | *koli* | *Strychnos spinosa* | Slow infant development | "Strong tree" |
| *Mu-* | *kombukombu* | *Tricalysia angolensis* (*Leptactina*) | Insanity | Component of medicine broom |

Alphabetical List of Trees and Shrubs Used in Treatments—*continued*

| *Prefix* | *Root* | *Botanical Name* | *Disease or Injury* | *Reason for Use* |
|---|---|---|---|---|
| *Mu-* | *kula* | *Pterocarpus angolensis* | Burns | "Red gum dries like scab" |
| *Mu-* | *kula* | *Pterocarpus angolensis* | Smallpox | "Red gum like pustules" |
| *Mu-* | *kula* | *Pterocarpus angolensis* | Tuberculosis | "Red gum—spitting blood" |
| *Ka-* | *kung'ami* | | Children's stomach trouble | "Stinks, bubbles, drives disease aside" |
| *Chi-* | *kwata* | *Zizyphus mucronata* | Men's stomach disease | "Bitter" |
| *Chi-* | *kwata* | *Zizyphus mucronata* | Headache | "Strong thorns pierce disease" |
| *Ka-* | *kwema* | (*Enneastemon schweinforthii*) *Uvaria angolensis* | Stomach disease | "Its nasty smell kills disease" |
| *Mu-* | *lendi* | *Sterculia quinqueloba* | Epilepsy | "Very slippery; so disease will slip from patient" |
| *Ka-* | *leng'ang'ombi* | Thornbush of gallery forest | Insanity | "Used in *Mukanda* boys' circumcision rites" |
| *I-* | *leng'i* | (? *Uapaca sansibarica*) *cyperus* sp. | Pyorrhea | "Reeds from which salt is made. Saltiness can cure" |
| *Mu-* | *lolu* | *Anona nana* | Men's stomach disease | "Strong smell" |
| *Ka-* | *lukuta* | See *mwalu* | | |
| *Wu-* | *lulu* | (*Khaya nyassica*) *Cassia* sp. | Smallpox | |
| *Ka-* | *mbanjibanji* | | Headache | "Strong and astringent" |
| *Ka-* | *mbanjibanji* | | Blisters in mouth (Scurvy?) | "Hot" |

| | | | | |
|---|---|---|---|---|
| *Ka-* | *mbanjibanji* | | Slow infant development | |
| *Ka-* | *mpandi* | *Maytenus cymosus* | Burns | "Its bark is hard and scablike" |
| *Mu-* | *ndoyi* | *Chrysophyllum* | Severe cuts | |
| *Mu-* | *ndoyi* | (*Magalis montanum*) | Snake bite | |
| *Mu-* | *ndoyi* | *bangweolense* | Poison in stomach | Emetic |
| *Wu-* | *nkomukomu* | (? *Aphrochiza nitida*) small shrub, large lanceolate leaves | Sores | |
| *Ka-* | *nsanying'a* | (?) | Bilharziasis | "Has white roots and strong smell" |
| *Ka-* | *nshinshi* | (?) | Stomach disease of children | "Strong smell and bitter taste" |
| *M(w)* | *olu wawubwang'u* | Grows in gallery forest | Lactation disorders | "A 'white' creeper. Can make milk flow white" |
| (*Mu* | *Lu wawubwang'u*) | | Stomach disease | "Strong smell kills disease" |
| *Mu-* | *pembi* | *Ekebergia arborea* | Snake bite | |
| *Ka-* | *pepi* | *Hymenocardia acida* | Headache | "Bitter" |
| *Ka-* | *pepi* | *Hymenocardia acida* | Pyorrhea | "Bitter" |
| *Mu-* | *puchi* | *Brachystegia spiciformis* | Bilharziasis | "Red gum, like blood of bilharziasis" |
| *Mu-* | *puchi* | *Brachystegia spiciformis* | Severe cuts | |
| *Ka-* | *pumbwa* | *Ancylobothrys amoena* | Gonorrhea | "Its white gum drops on the ground, resembles pus of gonorrhea" |
| *Chi-* | *puta mazala* | *Erythrina tomentosa* | Stomach disease of children | "Strong smell" |
| *Ka-* | *pwipu* | *Swartzia madagascariensis* | Headache | "Bitter and hot" |
| *Ka-* | *pwipu* | *Swartzia madagascariensis* | Sores | |

Alphabetical List of Trees and Shrubs Used in Treatments—*continued*

| *Prefix* | *Root* | *Botanical Name* | *Disease or Injury* | *Reason for Use* |
|---|---|---|---|---|
| *Ka-* | *pwipu* | *Swartzia madagascariensis* | Stomach disease of children | "Hardness of tree = health and strength" |
| *Mu-* | *sambanjita* | *Cryptosepalum maraviense* | Stomach disease of children | "Hardness of tree = health and strength" |
| *Mu-* | *seng'u* | *Ochna pulchra* | Epilepsy | "Its leaves are curled like someone in an epileptic fit" |
| *Mu-* | *senzi* | *Combretum zeyheri* | Dysentery | |
| *Mu-* | *shokotu* | *Faurea saligna* | Earache | |
| *Mu-* | *soli* | *Vangueriopsis lanciflora* | Insanity | "To clear madman's mind" |
| *Mu-* | *sombu* | *Syzygium guineense* | | |
| *Mu-* | *song'asong'a* | *Ximenia americana* | Stomach disease of children | "Has hard wood, makes strong and healthy" |
| *Mu-* | *song'asong'a* | (*Olax obtusifolius*) | Insanity | "Bitter for the eyes. Clears them" |
| *Mu-* | *sosu* | *Boscia corymbosa* | Blisters in mouth (Scurvy?) | "Lacks salt, mild" |
| *Chi-* | *takachi* | (*Phyllanthus discoideus*) | Burns | "Stickiness of leaves coagulates burn" |
| *Mu-* | *tata* | *Securidaca longipedunculata* | Stomach disease | "Its nasty smell will kill disease" |
| *Mu-* | *tokatoka* | *Ilex mitis* | Snake bite | |
| *Ka-* | *tong'a* | *Strychnos cocculoides* | Stomach disease of men | "Very bitter" |
| *Wu-* | *totu* | *Gardenia imperialis/* | Bilharziasis | "White roots and gum resemble pus" |
| *Wu-* | *totu* | *Tabernaemontana angolensis* | Gonorrhea | "White roots and gum resemble pus of gonorrhea" |

| | | | | |
|---|---|---|---|---|
| *Ka-* | *tunya* | (*Uvariastrom hexaloboides*) *Harungana madagascariensis* | Bilharziasis | "Red roots like blood of bilharziasis" |
| *Mu-* | *tutambululu* | *Xylopia adoratissima* | Insanity | Component of medicine broom |
| *Mu-* | *vuka* | *Marquesia macrova* | Severe cuts | |
| *Mu-* | *vuka* | *Marquesia macrova* | Sores | |
| *Ka-* | *vulawumi* | *Maprounea africana* | Hookworm | "Brings on vomiting" |
| *Ka-* | *vulawumi* | *Maprounea africana* | Leprosy | |
| *Ka-* | *vulawumi* | *Maprounea africana* | Poison in stomach | Emetic |
| *Ka-* | *vulawumi* | *Maprounea africana* | Rabies | Emetic |
| *Lu-* | *vung'u* | *Anisophyllea boehmii* | Smallpox | "Round orange fruits" (like pustules?) |
| *I-* | *vung'uvung'u* | *Kigelia pinnata* | Elephantiasis of scrotum | "Fruits resemble testicles" |
| *I-* | *yang'wa* | ? *Agauria salicifolia* | Elephantiasis of scrotum | "Resembles swollen testicles" |
| *Ka-* | *yiza* | (*Memecylon flavovirens*) *strychnos stuhlmannii* | | |

but a manifestation of a series of "powers" (*jing'ovu*) assembled ultimately under the treble rubric of white-red-black and capable of being evoked by those with specialized knowledge either for good or ill. Such powers, conceived sometimes as personal, sometimes as animate but without purposiveness or rationality, may be evoked by various means. In the first place, there must be a specialist, a *chimbuki* or *chimbanda* who "knows" (*weluka*) what medicines are efficacious against a given disease, how they should be administered, and why they are used. Knowledge among the Ndembu is far more literally "power" than it is with us. To know more is to *be* more fully, and to possess greater power with respect to the field of action to which that knowledge pertains. It is also to increase in social status and authority in that field of action and knowledge. Knowledge, in short, has existential implications. It may be acquired by participation in a full-scale *rite de passage,* where the novices or candidates are taught the properties of herbal and other medicines, it may be taught by a senior relative—and this is particularly common where therapeutic knowledge is concerned—or it may be bought from another, unrelated specialist. In whatever way such knowledge may have been obtained, it confers some kind of mystical power on its possessor, gives him or her an affinity with the materia medica used, and enables the herbalist to activate the latent virtues in the herbs he uses.

However, it is not enough merely to possess power and knowledge. The herbalist must take positive steps to awaken—and here the term *ku-tonisha,* "to awaken," is actually employed—the powers hidden and slumbering in herbs. Sometimes he and his assistants do this by singing traditional songs, associated in some way with the disease, as they go into the bush to collect medicines. Sometimes the herbalist may "address" the principal medicine tree before he cuts portions from it for his special *lwalu* basket. I have given an example of such an address on p. 368: "O tree, I received you from another doctor. The medicine we will collect from you here must have the power of killing disease." After making the address (*mpandula*), the doctor often takes a leaf from the tree, places it on the back of his clenched left fist, and claps his flattened right hand down on it. The sharp report thus made—sometimes compared with a gun shot—is also intended to "wake up" the medicine or—in rites proper—the ancestral spirits who act as tutelaries to the doctor adepts.

This right-left contrast has importance in a number of ritual contexts where it may represent: male/female, husband/wife, arrow (held in the right hand)/bow (held in the left)—and indeed the "arrow" may symbolize the male genital and power of begetting while the "bow" represents female fertility.

Again, right may be associated with whiteness, while left may be associated with redness. Often they are conceptualized as a complementary pair in which the left hand is called *nkwashi,* "the helper," the one which enables the right hand to accomplish its act, just as a wife helps her husband in his activities.

In medicine it is thought that the power of a *chimbuki* passes through his right arm into his ax when he cuts medicine from a tree. This power evokes the power possessed by the tree. The smell of the slashed bark or cut root, the gum or latex oozing from the excision, these too are regarded as expressions of roused power. Each tree is felt to have its specific "virtue" which is now informed by mystical power.

Such rousing preliminaries—which may also include the use of musical instruments, such as stridulators, drums, hunting bells, and clashing bars of iron—are themselves only a part of a configuration of symbolic actions and symbolic articles, and it is the form of the total procedure which most signally evokes, contains, and controls the mystical powers employed by the healer or herbalist. It is impossible to overstate the importance of the mode of arrangement of the parts of a curative procedure. Out of the randomness and incoherence of the environment, the *chimbuki* selects certain items and arrays them in a coherent structure in accordance with his sensitivity to Ndembu evaluations and symbolism and in accordance with his intention of curing a specific, culturally defined disease. When I say that "the *chimbuki* selects" I mean no more than that he follows precedent, whether that of the doctor who taught him the medicine or of the tradition within which that doctor was working. Incidentally, it is no surprise to find that many doctors became so because they began as patients who learned the medicines and curative procedure for a particular disease in the course of being treated for it. There are more than practical considerations at work here, for Ndembu have a tendency to regard like or shared experience as creating a mystical bond between all persons (including, so Ndembu believe, the dead), things, and activities comprising the experience or closely associated with it. From the point of view of Western science, such a bond or association may be merely adventitious or superficial; from the point of view of the Ndembu, persons and things which "were together" in space and time at a moment of critical significance for an individual or a group may acquire a deep and permanent relationship of "mystical participation," to use Lévy-Bruhl's useful term.

To understand Ndembu therapy, therefore, it is necessary to turn away from an atomistic consideration of particular symbolic and pragmatic items of medicine and treatment to an examination of the principles underlying the total procedure. From this standpoint it is unimportant that a particular medicine owes its employment to a particular mode of sensory or mental association. For, behind the configuration of symbolic medicines and acts stand a few principles which articulate the separate items into a whole. This can be seen if a particular treatment is analyzed, for example, that of *musong'u wanyembu* ("splitting" headache).

In this treatment there are five components: (1) the disease; (2) color symbolism; (3) the medicines; (4) the mode of treatment; and (5) the times of treatment. These components are interarticulated by a few ruling ideas. The disease is considered in this instance to be partly the result of witchcraft or sorcery. It has, in terms of Ndembu thought, a "black" character. This gives us the key to the color symbolism, for here white and red are regarded at one level as working in combination to rid the patient of the black, deathly taint of the witch's grudge (*chitela*) or malevolent action (*chisaku*). The white decoration of the pot represents the "purification of the patient," while the red line stands for "blood" or killing. Here it may represent the "strength" desired for the patient, and would link up with the "strong" medicines used (*mudyi, chikwata, chikoli*), for Ndembu say that blood is "life," though it also stands for the taking of life. It may stand here also for the taking of the "life" of the *musong'u,* the disease, regarded as an animate being. Red is an ambivalent symbol in Ndembu ritual and here would represent both a wish for the patient's recovery of life and a wish for the "killing" of the disease and the "bad luck" (*ku-halwa*). The medicines all have a "strong" (*-kola*) aggressive character, associated with redness and the level of color symbolism. They have a "bitter" taste, they are "hot," they have thorns "to pierce (or stab) the disease." The disease itself has this very quality, for it is described as resembling "the very bright light made when lightning falls on a hut—such a light comes suddenly, it is a sharp stab of pain." It must, so Ndembu seem to think, be fought by its own weapons. Hence the use of a lightning-struck tree as medicine, "because lightning is like the pain of headache." Hence the mode of treatment by clinking ax blades together near the patient's head—not by any means a treatment that would strike us as soothing! Behind this simulation in the treatment of the supposed properties of the disease may also lie the notion (common in other aspects of Ndembu symbolic practices) that to reveal or portray is to expose, and that exposure of the "true" character of a disease or "grudge" is half the therapeutic battle, for the known is not nearly so dangerous as the hidden and unknown. Action can be taken against something visible and classified in terms of traditional thought and belief, and positive action, as has often been said, reduces anxiety and promotes confidence. Nor can we rule out of the picture the possibility that noise and shock themselves may have a therapeutic value. As Lessa and Vogt (1958, 343) have said: "The typical primitive supernatural treatment involves elements of shock or stress analogous to modern shock treatment—treatment which stimulates an internal reaction capable of returning the organism to health."

The times of performance—at sunset and sunrise—link up with the color symbolism, with the medicines, and with the disease. For the sun is considered a "white" object, and a symbol of *Nzambi,* the High God, source of all power. Here the rising of the sun seems to be associated with an increase in the effect of the medicines, while the declining sun is connected with the declining strength of the disease.

A number of symbolic actions, actually performed or implicit in the symbolism, represent the death or decline or elimination of the disease. There is the setting of the sun just mentioned—"diseases must die with the sun in the evening." Then there is the sudden dropping of the ax blades at the patient's feet, "so that the disease may instantly leave him." There is the *chikwata* thorn tree which can "pierce" the disease. Finally, there is the use of the pangolin's scale as *mpelu,* contagious magical medicine, for the reason that the pangolin eats up stinging ants, which are identified with the disease.

The symbolic contrast of "above" with "below" influences the procedure. We have noted the supposed effects of the rising and setting sun on the strength of medicine and disease. The white line above the red line on the pot may mean many things, but one of them is the wished-for ascendancy of "purification," a term that embraces the curative procedure, over "bad luck," a multivocal term that includes the disease and the witch's grudge that probably caused it. In the case of headache, it is, of course, the head (the "above") that is itself being attacked by witchcraft which, with its necrophagous attributes, is associated in many contexts with the "below." This is why the medicine pot is hung over the patient's doorway, head high, why the ax blades are clinked in front of his head, and why sun symbolism plays such a major part. Healthful powers are thus enlisted against the "disease of the head," wherein the patient's life (*wumi*) is felt to reside.

There are a number of echoes from Ndembu rites proper in the symbolic pattern of this treatment which indicate how deeply their pharmacopoeia is influenced by ritual beliefs and practices. For example, *chikoli, chikwata,* and indeed the *mudyi* tree itself, under which novices are circumcised, are important symbols in *Mukanda,* the boys'circumcision rites. *Chikoli* there represents *inter alia* an erect phallus, a tough, healthy body, and masculinity. *Chikwata* is thought to confer healing power on the boys' penes after the operation. Again, in *Mukanda,* the circumcisers' protective medicine has to be lifted above the ground or it will lose its efficacy, and when a certain song (the *ng'ung'u*) is sung by circumcisers, the novices must climb up trees or onto the shoulders of adult men, otherwise they will suffer, it is said, from incontinence of urine for the rest of their lives. Thus, what is above is auspicious and what is below or on the ground is contextually inaupicious, as in the treatment of headache. It is probable that there is here a connection between a potent and erect male member and what is above, and a slack, impotent member and what is below. Pain is certainly associated with lying on the ground, for this is the posture of circumcision. Several informants have given me this interpretation. It might not be fanciful to conjecture that Ndembu associate the head of a healthy man with the glans of the potent member, and headache (produced by witchcraft) with impotence (also produced by witchcraft).

Other symbolic links with virility are perhaps provided by the use of *kapepi* and *kapwipu* medicines, for both these trees play an important role in the symbolism of hunting rites. I have discussed this role elsewhere and here merely mention that in addition to their specific properties these trees are held to share the following characteristics: (1) string cannot be made from their bark—thus they do not "tie up huntsmanship," i.e., the hunter's power and skill in killing animals; (2) they have a tough, termite- and weather-resistant wood—the hunter should possess toughness and power of endurance; and (3) their wood is white and is thus an embodiment of the power of whiteness, supreme auspiciousness.

*Kapepi* and *kapwipu* are trees from which the most common type of shrine erected for the spirits of hunter ancestors is made: a forked branch stripped of leaves and adorned with trophies of the chase. Offerings of blood are smeared on the branches and poured at the base, and portions of internal organs of the slain animal, consecrated to the use of hunters alone, are transfixed on the sharpened points. The sharpness of the points represents the acuity of huntsmanship (*ku-wambuka kwaWubinda*).

Viewed in this wider framework, it seems likely that these medicines are not employed solely on account of their bitter taste or "heat," since they are believed to confer robustness and endurance on the person enfeebled by a splitting headache. If the connection between the treatment and hunting ritual is a valid one, there would be yet another reference to the relationship between white and red, for blood, the most direct expression of the principle of redness, is brought to the white shrine and the two are combined in the act of veneration.

The treatment of headache thus reveals itself as a formal procedure controlled by religious ideas that are expressed in symbolic actions and symbolic articles: whiteness/redness; above/below; strength/weakness; health/disease (a mode of blackness); sunrise/sunset; links between the power of God, the sun, whiteness, strength, endurance, virility; between lightning, metallic noise, stabbing headache, thorns, circumcision, the killing of animals. As in all diseases, the aim is to restore the patient from a "black" to a "white" condition (one aspect of which is purification). In the particular case of headache this process of restoration is directed towards the head (with overtones of operations on the upper parts of other extremities). The notion of lightning plays an important part here because lightning is said to strike the topknot of grass at the apex of a hut (resembling the head of a person) as well as on account of its analogy with sudden, splitting pain in the head. Lightning, in its suddenness and ferocity, is a symbol for sorcery and witchcraft, and indeed Ndembu believe that certain sorcerers use medicine (*wang'a wanzaji*, "lightning magic") to bring lightning down (even from a clear sky) to kill their personal enemies. Violent headache, spreading out into constant pain, is for Ndembu a sign that an unknown witch or sorcerer is assailing them in their most vital center. Against this assault must be mobilized medicines borrowed from rites that most signally promote health, strength and virility, and other "white" qualities: such rites as girls' puberty (with its *mudyi* tree symbol), boys's circumcision, and those of the hunting cults.

In these and other ways, ultimate and axiomatic values of Ndembu religion and ethics enter into such an everyday matter as curing a headache. The meaning existence has for a Ndembu tribesman is present in many of his minor ends as well as in the great ends of a full-scale life-crisis rite. To restore order, health, or peace the powers that make for these must be brought into play by the correct use and combination of symbols, viewed as repositories of power as well as semantic systems. For Ndembu, again unlike ourselves, to "know" something, to understand the meaning of a symbol or the use of a "medicine," for example, is to increase in "power."

After reading the above account people may ask: "Why do such treatments continue to be practiced, since it is clear that they have little empirical derivation and are based on mystical ideas?" One reason for their persistence lies, no doubt, in the very fact that they are part of a religious system which itself constitutes an explanation of the universe and guarantees the norms and values on which orderly social arrangements rest. To query the premises on which Ndembu medicine rests would be to query the axioms underlying the Ndembu *Weltbild.* Another more practical reason would be that many diseases are self-curing; in the course of time, regardless of the treatment they are given, many people recover from illness, but the recovery is attributed to the treatment. Then again, psychological considerations must play a part in the case of mild psychosomatic conditions and in the milder cases of somatic illness. Such considerations would include the authoritative air of the doctor-herbalist, the purposive structure of the procedure, the "shock treatment" aspect mentioned above, and the sense that something traditional is being done about a known and named condition. Here we have an instance of the well-known placebo effect, where medicine is given to humor rather than to cure the patient, but where improvement in health nevertheless results.

Yet when all is said, the public health situation of the Ndembu, as of most Africans, is highly unsatisfactory. Charles C. Hughes, in an admirable conspectus of the topic in nonliterate groups (1961), surveys a wide spread of literature bearing on health to reach the conclusion, with George H. T. Kimball (1960, 159), that "in the African social drama sickness has a strong claim to being arch-villain." Poor hygiene, malnutrition, dietetic imbalance (partly produced by food taboos of a ritual character), the presence of liver disease, worm infestations or other intestinal diseases which interfere with absorption or storage, famine—all these and other environmentally and culturally determined conditions maintain health at a chronically low level. The fact that a rich and elaborate system of ritual and magical beliefs and practices provides a set of explanations for sickness and death and gives people a false sense of confidence that they have the means of coping with disease does nothing towards raising the level of health or increasing the life expectancy. Only better hygiene, a bigger and well-balanced diet, the widespread use of prophylactic medicine and the extension of hospital facilities will slay the "arch-villain" disease and free the African from its ancient mastery.

## BIBLIOGRAPHY

Ackerknecht, E. H. 1942. "Problems of Primitive Medicine," *Bulletin of the History of Medicine*, XI, 503–521.

——. 1946. "Natural Diseases and Rational Treatment in Primitive Medicine," *Bulletin of the History of Medicine*, XIX, No. 5.

Baumann, H. 1935. *Lunda: Bei Bauern und Jägern in Inner Angola.* Berlin: Würfel-Verlag.

Evans-Pritchard, E. 1937. *Witchcraft, Oracles and Magic among the Azande.* London: Oxford University Press.

Goodall, E. B. H. 1921. *Some Wemba Words.* London: Oxford University Press.

Hughes, C. C. 1961. "Hygiene and Public Health in Nonliterate Societies." Paper presented at the Conference on Medicine and Anthropology at Arden House, Harriman, New York, in November, 1961.

Kimball, H. T. 1960. *Tropical Africa.* 2 vols. New York: Twentieth Century Fund.

Lessa, W. A., and Vogt, E. Z., eds. 1958. *Reader in Comparative Religion.* Evanston: Row, Peterson and Co.

McCulloch, M. 1951. *The Southern Lunda and Related Peoples.* Ed. by Daryll Forde. London: International African Institute.

Reynolds, Barrie. 1963. *Magic, Divination and Witchcraft among the Barotse of Northern Rhodesia* (Robins Series, Rhodes Livingstone Museum) London: Chatto and Windus.

Rivers, W. H. R. 1924. *Medicine, Magic and Religion.* London: Oxford University Press.

Turner, V. W. 1953. *Lunda Rites and Ceremonies* (Occasional Papers of the Rhodes-Livingstone Museum, N.S.). No. 10. Livingstone: Zambia.

Turner, V. W. 1957. *Schism and Continuity in an African Society: A Study of Ndembu Village Life*. Manchester University Press.

——. 1961. *Ndembu Divination: Its Symbolism and Techniques* (Rhodes-Livingstone Paper 31). Manchester University Press.

——. 1962a. *Chihamba, the White Spirit* (Rhodes-Livingstone Paper 33). Manchester University Press.

——. 1962b. "Three Symbols of Passage in Ndembu Circumcision Ritual," in M. Gluckman, ed., *Essays on the Ritual of Social Relations*. Manchester University Press.

White, C. M. N. 1961. *Elements in Luvale Beliefs and Rituals* (Rhodes-Livingstone Paper 32). Manchester University Press.

Wilson, M. 1957. *Rituals of Kinship among the Nyakyusa*. London: Oxford University Press, for the International African Institute.

## CHAPTER X

# A Ndembu Doctor in Practice*

THIS Chapter consists mainly of an extended case study of a Ndembu *chimbuki* (which I shall translate as "doctor," though "ritual specialist" or "cult-adept" would be equally appropriate) at work. I knew Ihembi well and during a period of six months attended a number of curative rites over which he presided. He was a member of the Ndembu tribe, a relatively conservative people as we have seen, an amalgam of Lunda invaders from the Katanga and autochthonous Mbwela and Lukolwe. They are matrilineal and virilocal; have a senior chief and about a dozen subchiefs, four of whom are recognized by the British administration under the Native Authority; and grow cassava as their staple crop along with finger millet, maize, sweet potatoes, and a variety of cucurbits and other relish plants. They have no cattle and only a few sheep and goats (though large areas are free from tsetse fly infestation). Until recently, hunting was the predominant male pursuit and was accompanied by a richly elaborated ritual system involving beliefs in the punitive and tutelary powers of hunter ancestors or "shades" (as I shall call them henceforward). Ndembu live in small circular villages each of which consists of a nuclear group of matrikin, one of whom is headman, surrounded by a fringe of cognatic and affinal kin.

These facts are relevant to the account that follows, for disease among the Ndembu must be viewed not only in a private or idiographic but also in a public or social structural framework. All societies

* First published in *Magic, Faith and Healing*. Ari Kiev, ed. (Glencoe: Free Press, 1964). Reprinted with permission of The Free Press, copyright © 1964, The Free Press, a Division of The Macmillan Company.

have, of course, a functional interest in the minimization of illness, as Parsons has pointed out (Parsons 1951, 430). The Ndembu go further in positing a social explanation for illness itself. All persistent or severe sickness is believed to be caused either by the punitive action of ancestral shades or by the secret malevolence of male sorcerers or female witches. The shades punish their living kin, so the Ndembu declare, for negligence in making offerings at their village shrines, for breaches of ritual interdictions, or "because kin are not living well together." My own observations suggest that, whenever rites to propitiate or exorcise the shades—as distinct from private treatment by herbalists—are performed, there is a factor of social conflict present. The "ritual of affliction," as I have called it (1957, 292), constitutes, in fact, a phase in the complex process of corporate life and has a redressive function in interpersonal or factional disputes, many of which have long histories. Even when a person's fault has been slight, he may be "caught by the shades," the Ndembu think, as a scapegoat for his group if it is full of "grudges" (*yitela*) or "quarreling" (*ndombu*). Therapy then becomes a matter of sealing up the breaches in social relationships simultaneously with ridding the patient (*muyeji*) of his pathological symptoms. Attributions of disease to sorcery or witchcraft are frequently made in the context of factional rivalry, especially when the factions support rival candidates for office during the old age of its incumbent, whether he be chief or village headman. All deaths are attributed to sorcery or witchcraft, but only those of structurally important individuals are singled out for special ritual attention. When minor personages die, the identities of their secret destroyers are left to speculative gossip and rumor, and no action is taken. However, in the course of lively factional struggle, the death of even an infant may precipitate accusations and counteraccusations. In villages that markedly exceed the average size of thirty men, women, and children, such accusations may precede schism—when a dissident faction leaves the parent village and builds elsewhere on the pretext that it is escaping from witchcraft, which is believed to have a limited geographical range of efficacy.

In their treatment of disease, the Ndembu, like ourselves, recognize symptoms and distinguish between diagnosis and therapy, but there the resemblance ends. Ndembu do not know of natural causes for diseases but, as we have seen, believe that either punitive shades or envious sorcerers produce them. Their diagnosticians are diviners, and their therapists are in effect masters of ceremonies.

## *Divination*

Divination is a phase in a social process that begins with a death, illness, reproductive trouble, or misfortune at hunting (for illness is only one class of misfortune that is mystically caused). It continues through discussion in the victim's kin-group or village about the steps to be taken next, the most important of which is a journey to consult a diviner (distant diviners are believed to give more reliable diagnoses than local ones). The fourth stage is the actual consultation or séance attended by the victim's kin and often by his neighbors. This séance is followed by remedial action according to the diviner's prescription. Such action may consist of the destruction or expulsion of a sorcerer or witch; the performance of ritual by cult specialists to propitiate or exorcise specific culturally defined manifestations of shades; or the application of herbal and other "medicines" according to the diviner's advice by an herbalist or medicine man.

This book contains an account of Ndembu leechcraft (pp. 299 ff.). It is sufficient to state here that whatever may be the empirical benefits of certain treatments, the herbal medicines employed derive their efficacy, according to the Ndembu, from mystical notions, and native therapy is an intrinsic part of a whole magico-religious system.

The divinatory consultation is the central phase or episode in the total process of copying with misfortune, and it looks both backward to causation and forward to remedial measures. Since death, disease, and misfortune are, as we have noted, usually ascribed to exacerbated tensions in social relations, expressed as personal grudges charged with the mystical power of sorcery or witchcraft or as beliefs in the punitive action of ancestral shades intervening in the lives of their surviving kin, diviners try to elicit from their clients responses that give clues about the patterns of current tensions in their groups of origin. Divination therefore becomes a form of social analysis, in the course of which hidden struggles among individuals and factions are brought to light, so that they may be dealt with by traditional ritual procedures. It is in the light of this "cybernetic" function of divination as a mechanism of social redress that we should consider its symbolism, the social composition of its consultative sessions, and its interrogation procedures (see Turner 1961, 18).

## *Therapeutic Rites*

The curative rites are performed by a number of cult associations, each devoted to a specific manifestation of the ancestral shades. Thus a shade that manifests itself as *nkula* afflicts its living kinswoman with menstrual disorders of various kinds, a shade that "comes out [of the grave] in *isoma*" causes miscarriages, and so forth. The patient in any given cult ritual is a candidate for entry into that cult and, by passing through its rites, becomes a cult adept. The particular shade that had afflicted him in the first instance, when propitiated, becomes a tutelary who confers on him health and curative powers for that particular mode of affliction. Although the tutelary shade is an adept's kinsman or kinswoman, cult membership cuts across membership of descent groups and territorial groups. Cult members make up associations of those who have suffered the same modes of affliction as the result of having been seized (perhaps "elected" would be a more appropriate term) by deceased members of the cults. Since there are many cults and since the focal symbols of each refer to basic values and beliefs shared by all Ndembu, it may be said that the total system of cults of affliction keeps alive, through constant repetition, the sentiment of tribal unity. Ndembu secular society is characterized by the weakness of its political centralization, by the high spatial mobility of its individual members and of its groups (due to shifting areas of cultivation and the emphasis on hunting), and by the tendency of villages to split and reassemble. This secular mobility (and lability) is counteracted to some extent by the embodiment of tribal values of unity in the cults of affliction.

## *The* Ihamba *Cult*

This necessarily truncated account of Ndembu divination and cult therapy must suffice as background to Ihembi's practice. Since this doctor specialized in the *Ihamba* cult, I shall briefly outline its characteristics. In the first place, the term *ihamba* refers among the Ndembu to an upper central incisor tooth of a deceased hunter. It forms an important element in a complex of beliefs and symbolic objects associated with hunting ritual—especially with ritual associated with those hunters who employ firearms. It is believed that the two upper front incisors of a gun-hunter (*chiyang'a*) contain much of his power to kill animals. If one of these teeth is knocked out or drops out as a result of pyorrhea, the hunter must preserve it. When a gun-hunter dies, these incisors are removed. The left incisor is said to belong to "his mother's side," the right "to his father's." The teeth must be inherited by appropriate relatives who are initiated members of the gun-hunters cult (*Wuyang'a*).

An inherited *ihamba* is carried in a pouch with a long sash of white or colored cloth. The pouch itself (called *mukata*) is made of white cloth. The *ihamba,* concealed beneath a long flap, is embedded in a paste of corn meal mixed with the blood of slaughtered game. Above it are inserted two cowrie shells (*mpashi*), which are known as "the eyes" (*mesu*). With these *mesu* the hunter's shade is said to "see animals" in the bush and to confer similar powers on their owner. The inheritor takes the *mukata* pouch into the bush with him when he goes hunting. With the carrying sash are folded strips of the dead hunter's clothing. When it is not in use, it is hung up in a shrine consecrated to hunters' shades. Women are forbidden to approach this shrine closely. Should they do so inadvertently, they are believed to develop menstrual disorders or to bleed to death after their next childbirth. This prohibition derives from a basic principle of Ndembu ritual, that "the blood of huntsmanship" (*mashi aWubinda,* from *Wubinda,* which stands for "generic huntsmanship") must not be brought into contact with "the blood of motherhood" (*mashi amama*) or the "blood of procreation" (*mashi alusemu*). For example, when a hunter's wife is about to give birth he must remove all his hunting gear from his hut and its vicinity, lest it lose its efficacy. Behind this principle lies the notion that, for a child to be born, the maternal blood must coagulate around the fetus. Hunters shed blood and cause it to gush and flow. Again, women give life, while hunters take it. The two functions are antithetical.

It is necessary to distinguish between two ritual usages in connection with *mahamba* (the plural of *ihamba*). An *ihamba* may be inherited by a renowned hunter and then be used as a charm or amulet to bring him good fortune in the chase. On the other hand, some *mahamba* are believed to afflict the living by burying themselves in their bodies and causing them severe pains. In such cases the afflicting *mahamba* are believed to be of two kinds: some are from the corpses of hunters whose incisor teeth were lost before burial; others are "escapees" from *mukata* pouches or from calabash containers in which they had been placed after extraction by *Ihamba* doctors. The *Ihamba* cult consists of male adepts, who must be initiated hunters of the gun-hunters' cult, and the purpose of the rites they perform is to extract *mahamba* from the bodies of persons afflicted by hunter shades. The *mahamba* are said to be the incisors of the afflicting shades. To remove an *ihamba,* the senior adept or "doctor" makes an incision on any part of the patient's body and applies to the cut a cupping horn (usually a goat's horn) from which the tip has been removed. After the horn (*kasumu*) has been sucked, it is plugged with beeswax. The doctor's intention is to "catch" the *ihamba,* which is believed to "wander about" subcutaneously.

What are the symptoms of *ihamba* affliction? Here are some of my informants' comments. Nyamuvwila, the aged wife of a village headman, said that she had been "eaten" (*ku-dya*) in the chest, neck, and shoulders by an *ihamba* that had "fallen" into her body. The *ihamba* came from her uterine brother, a hunter whose *ihamba* tooth had not been removed before burial. After his death, "it wandered about and went after meat." Another woman from the same village had "become sick" (*wakata*) "in the back," because an *ihamba* had "started to bite" her. My best informant on ritual matters, Muchona, in describing to me the circumstances surrounding a particular case of *ihamba* affliction, said, "Chain [the patient] comes from the village of Makumela, his mother's village. That is also where the shade of *ihamba* [*mukishi wehamba*] has come from. His grandfather is the shade, the mother's brother of his mother. He is the one who has fallen on his grandson to obtain blood from him. He has come that he may be known [remembered]. When they have sucked him out [as an *ihamba*], they should offer him the blood of an animal [smear the *ihamba* with the blood of a kill after the hunt], so that they may stay well [live in health, mutual accord, and prosperity], and that the patient, who was sick, may also stay well. They pray to him that they may put him in a pouch of cloth and sing and dance with drums for him [at a gun hunters' rite]." According to other informants, an *ihamba* can be seen moving about under the patient's skin (muscular spasms, perhaps) "like the movements of an insect (*nyisesa yakabubu*)." It is said to "catch him with its teeth," the plural form *mazewu,* "teeth," being sometimes used for the single tooth that has been extracted. It "flies in the air" to reach its victim, whose blood it demands.

Its attributes suggest that the *ihamba* epitomizes the aggressive power of the hunter. It also represents the harshness of internalized norms, since an *ihamba* only "bites" when there has been transgression of moral or customary rules. At the unconscious level of meaning, behavior associated with *ihamba*—"eating," "biting," "going after meat"—and its removal by "sucking" and anointing with blood suggests that *ihamba* beliefs may be connected with the orally aggressive stage of infantile development.

An interesting feature of the *Ihamba* cult is its comparatively recent introduction into Ndembu territory. It has been grafted onto the rites of the long-established hunters' cult and shares much of its symbolism. This cult, with many tribal variations, has a wide geographical range among the West Central and Central Bantu peoples. Certain linguistic features indicate that *Ihamba* was borrowed by Ndembu from the Luvale and Chokwe peoples in Angola. It has certainly spread rapidly in the postwar period. One major difference from the hunters' cult proper is that, while the *ihamba* is almost invariably a manifestation of a male shade, its victims include at least as many women as men, although women may not become *Ihamba* doctors since membership in the curative cult is restricted to initiated hunters.

Two further features of *Ihamba* should be noted. The cult has spread precisely where hunting has been on the decline because of the increasing scarcity of game and the increase of population. Apparently, by frequently performing *Ihamba,* the Ndembu maintain in fantasy the values, symbols, and trappings of a highly ritualized activity that is rapidly losing its economic importance. The penetration of the modern cash economy into the pores of Ndembu social organization, together with an accelerating rate of labor migration to the industrial towns of the Copperbelt in Zambia, have created new economic needs and new tensions in traditional social relationships, while new relationships based on trade and contract are insidiously undermining corporate bonds. *Ihamba* may, therefore, be seen as part of a rear-guard action whereby Ndembu culture is fighting against change. In the projective systems of modern villagers, the shades of hunters may well represent, at one level of social experience, the guilts and anxieties of those who are compelled by changing conditions to act in contravention of traditional standards.

Another sign that *Ihamba* is a response to cultural change is reflected in the fact that the rite contains its own built-in phase of divination. The traditional diviner, it is true, may well diagnose a person's illness as due to an *ihamba* affliction, but it is not strictly necessary. It is enough for someone to dream of a hunter shade when he is ill and then to consult an *Ihamba* doctor to have the rite performed for him. Furthermore, when the rite begins, the doctor divines by peering into medicated water in an old meal mortar, in which he claims to be able to see the "shadow-soul" (*mwevulu*) of the afflicting hunter. By asking questions of the patient and his kin, he declares, he can then identify the particular relative who has "come out in *ihamba*" (*wunedikili mwihamba*). He may also claim to detect sorcerers and witches who have seized the opportunity of the patient's *ihamba*-caused debility to attack him. As we shall see, part of the process of removing the *ihamba* consists in the doctor's summoning kin of the patient to come before the improvised hunters' shrine (identical with that used in the hunters' cult) and inducing them to confess any grudges (*yitela*) and hard feelings they may nourish against the patient. The tooth will "not allow itself to be caught," he will assert, until every ill-wisher in the village or kin-group has "made his liver white" (or, as we would say, purified his intentions) toward the patient. The patient, too, must acknowledge his own grudges against his fellow villagers if he is to be rid of the "bite" of *ihamba*. It is interesting how the symbolism of oral aggression pervades our own speech in the context of small-group behavior: "envy's poisonous tooth," "the bite of malice," "the mordant utterance," "back-biting," "the sting of jealousy," "being eaten up with jealousy," and so forth. There is a parallel here, too, between the Ndembu notion of the hunters' tooth preying on the living and our saying that someone is "hounded by guilt" or "a prey to remorse."

*Ihamba* (as well as other Ndembu rites that involve the sucking of objects, including bones, graveyard soil, and stones, from the bodies of patients) is a variation on that widespread theme of primitive medicine that Erwin Ackerknecht has called "the stone of the medicine man" (1942, 503–521). He quotes im Thurn that, for the Indians of Guiana at least, the foreign substance "is often if not always regarded not as simply a natural body but as the materialized form of a hostile spirit." Given this premise, im Thurn goes on to argue, "the procedure is perfectly sincere and in its way rational. An invisible force is dealt with visibly by means that are meant and understood to be symbolic." Nevertheless, I can confirm that the Ndembu—except for the doctors—do believe that the *ihamba* tooth of a specific hunter relative is actually extracted from the patient's body. The doctor confines skepticism to the issue of whether the tooth is that of a human being or of an animal (like a monkey or a pig). He leaves untouched the question that sleight of hand may have been used in making the "extraction." The doctors must themselves be aware of their own trickery, although I never managed to persuade one to admit that he had used deception. My own guess is that doctors sincerely believe that their therapy—which includes the use of washing and drinking medicines ("lotions" and "potions") and of cupping techniques—has a positive efficacy and may also believe that in some mystical fashion they actually do withdraw an influence inimical to the patient's welfare from his person. At any rate, they are well aware of the benefits of their procedures for group relationships, and they go to endless trouble to make sure that they have brought into the open the main sources of latent hostility in group life.

## *Therapeutic Procedure*

Before getting down to specific cases, I shall briefly describe the manipulative techniques of an *Ihamba* doctor. We must consider, for example, whether or not there may be certain unintended or inadvertent benign consequences for health from Ndembu practices that are overtly determined by magico-religious ideas without empirical foundation. It seems possible that the bloodletting that accompanies the doctor's efforts to "capture" the elusive tooth may have beneficial effects on some patients. There may also be in the procedure something analogous to modern shock treatment—treatment that, as Lessa and Vogt have suggested, "stimulates an internal reaction capable of returning the organism to health" (1958, 343).

It is more difficult to establish whether or not the use of "medicines" confers any physical benefit. The medicines employed are the leaves, bark scrapings, and roots of forest trees and bushes. The principles underlying their use are not derived from experiment but form part of a magical system, as is clear from a listing of the properties attributed to them by informants. I have collected a considerable body of this kind of exegetical material not only about *Ihamba* medicines but also about many other kinds of rite, and in almost every case, notions of sympathetic or contagious magic control the selection of vegetable or animal medicines.

### LIST OF IHAMBA MEDICINES

| NDEMBU TERM | BOTANICAL NAME | INDIGENOUS EXPLANATION FOR USE |
|---|---|---|
| 1. *Musoli* | *Vangueriopsis lanciflora* | a. It comes from *ku-solola,* "to make visible" or "reveal." b. It has fruit that are eaten by *duiker* and other woodland game during the early rains. Ndembu say that the name is connected with the power of the tree to draw forth |

LIST OF IHAMBA MEDICINES (*Continued*)

| NDEMBU TERM | BOTANICAL NAME | INDIGENOUS EXPLANATION FOR USE |
|---|---|---|
| | | animals from their hiding places in the bush and make them visible to the hunter. What is made visible is good, what is concealed is often bad. *Musoli* medicine is given to barren women "to make children visible."<br>c. It is the senior (*mukulumpi*) medicine of *Ihamba,* the first to be collected. The doctor addresses the *musoli* tree and says: "You *musoli* tree of animals (of huntsmanship), come quickly, may this *ihamba* come out quickly, so that the patient may get well soon." He then guesses where the tap root lies and hoes up the ground. If he finds it at once, it augurs well that the tooth will be found quickly.<br>d. *Musoli* means "to speak openly or publicly." It refers to the confession of grudges described earlier. |
| 2. *Museng'u* | *Ochna pulchra* | a. The name comes from *kuseng'uka,* "to multiply."<br>b. It has many small black fruits; it stands for "many animals" or "many children." |
| 3. *Mututambululu* | *Xylopia adoratissima* | The name comes from *ambululu,* a small bee that makes nests in the ground or in old termite mounds. Such bees come in swarms to the *mututambululu* tree to gather its nectar. In the same way, many people will come to the drum (rite) |

LIST OF IHAMBA MEDICINES (*Continued*)

| NDEMBU TERM | BOTANICAL NAME | INDIGENOUS EXPLANATION FOR USE |
|---|---|---|
| | | at which it is used, and many animals will come near a hunter who has been washed with its medicine. |
| 4. *Mufung'u* | *Anisophyllea boehmii* | From *ku-fung'a,* "to gather together a herd of animals." |
| 5. *Mutata* | *Securidaca longipedunculata* | This word means "to heat huntsmanship" (*Ku-tatisha Wubinda*). |
| 6. *Muneku* | *Randia kuhniana* | It comes from *ku-nekama,* "to sink down," which means that a *mufu* or "zombie" raised by a sorcerer's curse must "change its mind" (*ku-nekuka*) about afflicting the patient and sink down into the grave again. It will be recalled that the grudges of the living must be confessed during *Ihamba* because the Ndembu believe that protracted grudges animate the mystical powers of sorcery and witchcraft if not brought into the open. In any case, sorcerers and witches and their familiars are always likely to be present in large assemblies of people or so the Ndembu think. |

Other medicines employed in *Ihamba* have similar characteristics. They represent aspects of huntsmanship or protect the patient and the congregation from sorcery and witchcraft. Many of the medicines are borrowed directly from the hunters' cult rites and appear to represent *inter alia* the afflicting hunters' shades. At any rate, in other rites of affliction, the pieces of medicine leaves adhering to the patient's skin after he or she has been splashed by a leaf-broom are said to "stand for the shade," in that each represents a cluster of values associated with the cult of hunters' shades, and, in a sense, to identify the patient with that shade. Other antisorcery medicines in *Ihamba* include a root dug up from under a path leading into the village. This root is used because Ndembu believe that sorcerers conceal destructive medicines beside or beneath paths to injure or slay their personal enemies. The root medicine "makes known" the sorcery and renders it innocuous. The doctor thus signifies that he has exposed the hidden sorcerers and can if necessary counter their malignant magic.

The main point to note in connection with these medicines (which are pounded by the doctor and his assistants in an old meal-mortar, soaked in water, and then both splashed on the patient's body and given to him to drink) is that they are ostensibly used because, through analogy, they confer on the patient certain powers and qualities conducive to strength, good luck, and health. The semantic links of analogy may derive from the name of the object used (by a species of serious "punning") from its natural properties, as they are conceived by the Ndembu, or from both. But it is doubtful that the medicines have any pharmaceutical value at all; it is sufficient that they are not toxic.

## *Ihembi, the* Ihamba *Doctor*

This brief account of the cultural structure of *Ihamba* suggests that whatever efficacy the rite possesses—and it does have ameliorative effects on patients, as I can testify after witnessing more than a dozen performances, some of them in villages I knew really well—resides in the degree of skill wielded by the doctor in each instance of its performance. It is hardly likely to be attributable to the bloodletting and the application of medicines. We must therefore examine the form that *Ihamba* ritual takes in the light of what Radcliffe-Brown has called "the actually existing network of social relations." I propose therefore to give a few words about the personality of one *Ihamba* doctor, Ihembi, and then to describe his practice of his craft in two concrete situations.

Ihembi was a man about seventy years old, white-haired, dignified, but with a smile of singular sweetness and charm. He had the throaty voice characteristic of the Ndembu hunter, but he put it to lucid and eloquent use. I first met him at the court of a "progressive" subchief, Ikelenge, when I was collecting from the chief and his councilors the official history of his chiefdom and the royal genealogy. There was a full muster of elders from the chief's area present, and they were encouraged to contribute to the discussion. Among the most vocifer-

17. *Wubwang'u* ("Twin-Ceremony") adepts relax after "cutting medicines." My best informant, Muchona, puffs at a cigarette in the top right-hand corner.

18. *Ihamba* doctors collect medicines from trees in the bush. One plays a friction-bar, while the others sing hunting songs to "please the *Ihamba*" shade-manifestation.

19. An *Ihamba* "doctor," before performing ritual, divines into the mystical cause of his patient's affliction by gazing into the surface of medicated water in a meal mortar. Note the forked *chishing'a* shrine planted to a hunter's spirit.

20. An *Ihamba* "doctor," holding a friction-bar or "stridulator," decides on the next placement of the cupping horns. His patient's outstretched legs may be seen on the left, the forked hunter's shrine on the right.

ous was Ihembi, who tended to raise objections to the chief's narrative at crucial points. I found out afterward that Ihembi belonged to a branch of the royal lineage that had formerly supplied chiefs to the realm but had been permanently excluded from the succession several generations before after a bitter and unsuccessful dispute with another branch over the incumbency of the chieftainship. In compensation, the victors had given the defeated branch, that of Matembu, a ritual office. The members of Matembu resided in a single large village, several miles from the capital, and their headman performed important ritual functions in the installation of each new Ikelenge chief, at chiefs' funerals, and in periodically purifying the royal insignia. Ihembi thus belonged to a social group with ritual status that had nevertheless a permanently "marginal" or "outsider" quality in political terms. Within the Matembu matrilineage, Ihembi had further "dispossessed" characteristics. Although he came from a senior branch of that lineage and was chronologically senior to its headman, he did not hold political office—probably because in his youth he had migrated to another Lunda subtribe, that of Shinde in Balovale District, many miles to the south of Mwinilunga District, where he had married and raised a family. There he had also practiced as a diviner. More important for this analysis, he had become initiated into the hunters' cult and had later learned the medicines and techniques of *Ihamba,* allegedly from the Luvale people who live intermingled with the Lunda in Balovale District. At a comparatively old age he had returned to the Ikelenge chiefdom, where he found the headmanship of Matembu already occupied. He did not fall into apathy but applied himself vigorously to his practice as an *Ihamba* doctor and earned quite a substantial income, for people were prepared to pay ten shillings or even a pound for an "extraction." Chief Ikelenge, who paid careful heed to the views of the Christian missionaries in his area, on more than one occasion fined Ihembi for fraudulently exploiting the people. Nevertheless, Ihembi managed to carry on his practice and enjoyed a wide reputation. In many ways, he was typical of Ndembu doctors: capable, charismatic, authoritative, but excluded from secular office for a variety of reasons, some structural, some personal. He was the typical "outsider" who achieves status in the ritual realm in compensation for his exclusion from authority in the political realm.

It was not long before Ihembi and I were on terms of friendship that soon developed into the "joking relationship" between "grandfather and grandson." This friendship enabled us to speak very frankly to one another and to perform mutual services. I gave him gifts from time to time, and he allowed me to attend his *Ihamba* rites and explained much of their symbolism for my benefit. In this short study, I can do no more than discuss briefly two performances. They were held for the same patient and formed part of a series of seven rites performed for him, of which I was fortunate to observe three in close detail. Three of the seven were *Ihamba* rites, two belonged to the hunters' generic cult of *Wubinda* (since the patient, though not a gun-hunter, trapped and snared antelope), one was the antisorcery rite called *Kaneng'a* and one was a recently introduced rite called *Tukuka* in which the patient is believed to be possessed by the spirits of live Europeans or of alien tribesmen. The large number of these rites, all performed within a few months, indicates that the patient was seriously disturbed. Furthermore, as I have argued, it indicates that there was serious disturbance in his network of social relations.

## *Ihembi and the Case of Kamahasanyi*

It is at this point unavoidable that I should deploy the divinatory apparatus of the social anthropologist: the genealogy, the hut plan, the village census data, and the condensed life history. For the events I shall discuss fall within a social field with many dimensions, several of which must be exhibited and scrutinized if we are to make any sense at all of the observed behavior and the monologues (the prayers and invocations) and dialogues of the participants. I may say, too, that, in an intuitive or pragmatic fashion, the information and even analysis I shall submit were fully mastered by Ihembi, whose business it was to study social relationships in order to diagnose the incidence and pattern of tensions and to attempt to reduce them in his handling of the rites. We have noted earlier how *Ihamba* contains its own built-in system of divination. What I have written elsewhere of the divinatory process among the Ndembu holds true, therefore, a fortiori for the *Ihamba* doctor in his divining capacity. I wrote (1961, 18) that

> the diviner clearly knows that he is investigating within a social context of a particular type. He first establishes his clients' locale—the Senior Chief's area, then the subchief's, then the vicinage (the cluster of neighboring villages), and finally the village of the victim. Each of these political units has its special characteristics: its factional divisions, its inter-village rivalries, its dominant personalities, its nucleated and dispersed groups of kin, all of them possessing a history of settlement or

migration. An experienced diviner will have already familiarized himself with the contemporary state of these political sub-systems from previous consultations and from the voluminous gossip of travelers. Next he ascertains the relationships between the victim and those who have come to consult him. He is assisted in this task by his knowledge of the categories of persons who typically compose a village: the victim's matrilineal kin, his patrilateral kin, his affines, cognates and unrelated persons. He finds out the type and nature of the victim's relationship to the headman, then focuses his attention on the headman's matrilineage and discovers into how many sub-lineages it may be segmented. By the time he has finished his interrogation, he has a complete picture of the contemporaneous structure of the village, and of the position in its relational network occupied by the victim.

These remarks refer to diviners who are consulted by clients from distant regions and who operate by the manipulation of symbolic objects, as well as by the exhaustive interrogation that accompanies it. The clients try to trip up the diviner by feeding him false information, and it is the mark of a "true diviner" if he avoids this pitfall. The *Ihamba* doctor, however, is in the more fortunate position of operating in a village not far from his own, whose inhabitants and their interpersonal relations are known to him, and of having had full access to the patient's dreams (which induced him and his kin to call in the *Ihamba* doctor in the first place) and to the gossip and opinions of the patient's neighbors and relatives. Nevertheless, he builds up his picture of the social field and its tensions in much the same way as the specialist diviner does and acts on this knowledge in his therapeutic practice. By tactful cross-examination of the participants and by keeping his eyes and ears open, he discovers the likes and dislikes of the patient, the village headman, the members of the patient's domestic family and matrilineage, and so forth.

In the case of Kamahasanyi, which I shall describe shortly, Ihembi already knew the principal participants, and his two assistants, Mundoyi and Mukeyi, had distant patrilateral ties with the patient. What is more, before the second performance of Ihamba he spent a day and night in the patient's village, where he was able to size up the situation.

My own acquaintance with Kamahasanyi's village had been long and close, for my first camp had been in the neighborhood, and my wife and I had attended a girl's puberty ritual there. Furthermore, I had collected census and budgetary information not only in this village of Nswanamundong'u but also in many other villages of the Mukang'ala chiefdom, of which it formed a part. It was while I had been visiting Nswanamundong'u that I first became aware of Kamahasanyi's troubles. His snares had failed to catch *duiker* antelope for many weeks, and he had had the hunting rite *Mukala* performed to placate the angry shade. This shade was that of his maternal grandfather, the late chief Mukang'ala, he told me, and the same shade had "come out in *ihamba*" to afflict him "with pains in his whole body." An *Ihamba* rite was to be performed for him the day after my arrival by a Luvale doctor temporarily residing in the neighborhood. I mentioned to the villagers that I knew Ihembi well, and they immediately besought me to bring the great doctor and his assistants (who helped him with the collection of medicines and with various ritual tasks) from the Ikelenge area in my car. He could "help" the Luvale, they said, who was "only a little doctor"—they even hinted that he might tactfully take over control of the rite. They also asked me to bring to the performance a man called Samuwinu, whom they described as "the real headman" of the village. He had fled from the chiefdom at the accession of the present chief Mukang'ala Kambung'u, fearing the latter's sorcery. For Samuwinu had been a candidate for the chiefly "chair," and, indeed, the male members of the nuclear matrilineage of Nswanamundong'u belonged to a branch of the royal matrilineage of Mukang'ala chiefdom. Their village was a "royal village." The villagers told me that the shade afflicting Kamahasanyi "in *Mukala*" and "in *Ihamba*" was doing so because it was angry that a "younger man" had become headman while a member of its own generation (genealogical generation) remained alive. A member of the junior adjacent generation to Samuwinu had been appointed as headman by the villagers. The shade was incensed too, they said, because it had been slain by the sorcery of the present chief, a slaying that had been unavenged for several years. Its wrath had been manifested in other ways. Once there had been a whirlwind that had ripped the thatch from the hut of the new headman Kachimba, and people claimed that they had seen flames leaping above it. Villagers said that they had dreamed that the late chief's shade had come to reproach them. Not only was it aggrieved that it had been ensorcelled, they alleged, but also because the British authorities had a few years previously withdrawn recognition from the Mukang'ala chieftainship, which had been merged with that of Senior Chief Kanongesha. The shade, that of Mundong'u Kabong'u, blamed the people of the chiefdom and in particular those of his own village for allowing this merger to happen.

The persecution of Kamahasanyi by the late chief's shade was therefore not so much aimed at him personally as in his representative capacity. When I asked one informant why Mundong'u had not afflicted Kachimba the acting headman, he replied that the shade "wanted to shame" everyone by "catching" one of the villagers. It was not Kachimba but the village folk (*enimukala*) as a whole who had behaved irresponsibly. They should have made Samuwinu headman, and the latter should have remained in the area to represent his matrilineage fittingly. Indeed, it was Kachimba himself who begged me earnestly to bring Samuwinu to the *Ihamba* performance so that Samuwinu could invoke the shade on Kamahasanyi's behalf. The shade, he said, would listen to Samuwinu, who was his uterine brother, as well as "real headman" but might well reject his own intercession. I learned later that several villagers secretly despised Samuwinu for running away and indeed for not pressing his claim for the chieftainship with vigor while he could. As we shall see, this whole case history is pervaded by the theme of failure to undertake responsibility and failure to live up to expectation. Part of the work of a doctor is to encourage people to discharge the obligations of their status well and not seek escape from them.

While the villagers were sure that Mundong'u Kabong'u's shade was afflicting Kamahasanyi and that other misfortunes assailing them collectively at that time (like loss of crops because of wild pigs, quarrels between village sections, bad luck in hunting) could be laid at his door, it was thought highly probable that other mystical agencies were also at work. Some thought that Kamahasanyi was being bewitched by someone in the village, a line of inquiry that soon engaged Ihembi's attention and that he discussed with me. Others thought that the spirits of living Europeans were "troubling" him. Kamahasanyi himself had recently gone to Angola to consult a diviner there and had been told that his own father's shade, as well at that of Kabong'u Mundong'u, had "caught" him in *ihamba*. This diagnosis, supported by the fact that Kamahasanyi had frequently dreamed of his father's shade, opens the way for an investigation of Kamahasanyi's life history and an analysis of his character and temperament that must be postponed until our sociological analysis has been made. The point I want to make here is that, when misfortune is attributed

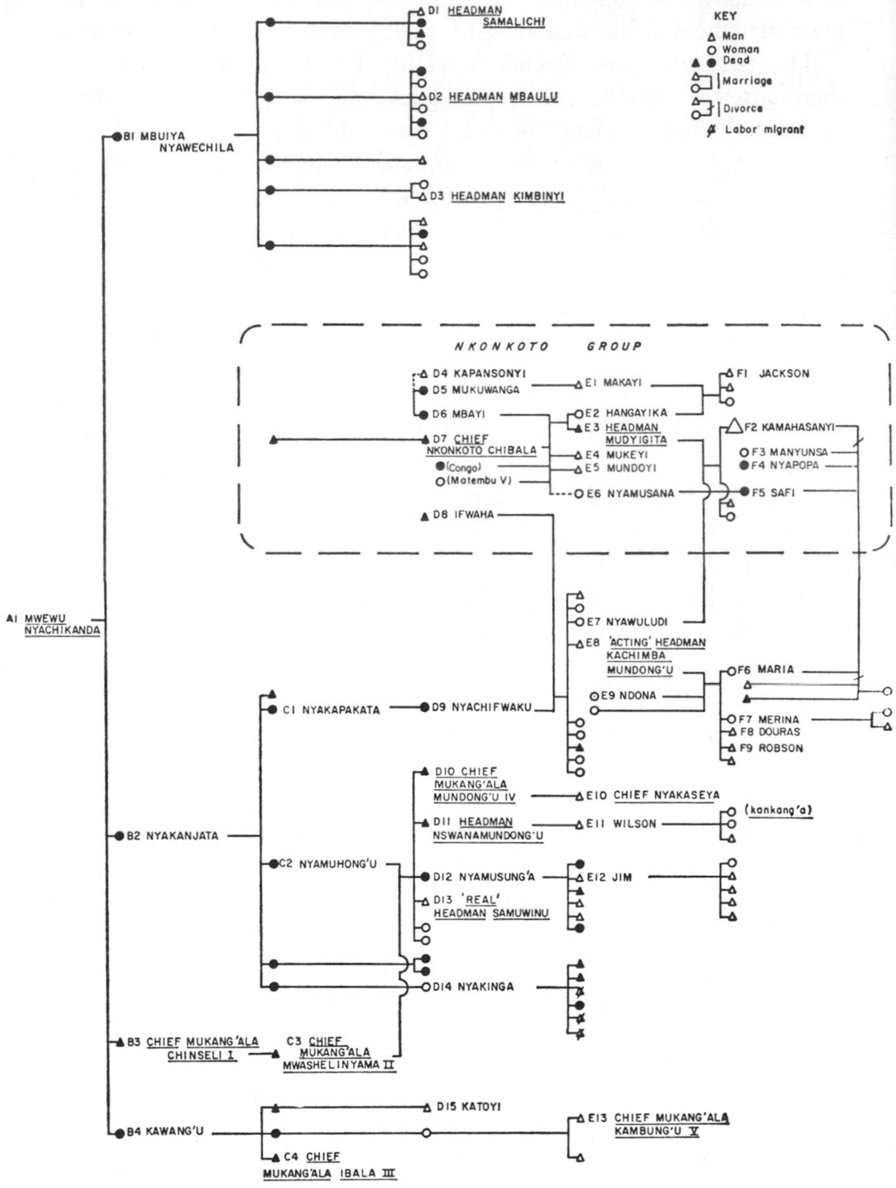


*Diagram 10.* Genealogy of Nswanamundong'u village

to mystical causes in Ndembu society, it is common for many sets of disturbed social relations to be scrutinized by the interested parties. The vagueness of the mystical beliefs enables them to be manipulated in relation to a great diversity of social situations. Eventually the crucial tension is isolated and dealt with.

## *The Structural Context of the Case of Kamahasanyi*

In order to give the reader a clear understanding of the social factors that Ihembi had to take into account in his handling of the two *Ihamba* performances he conducted for Kamahasanyi (in the first of which he removed what he claimed to be Mundong'u Kabong'u's

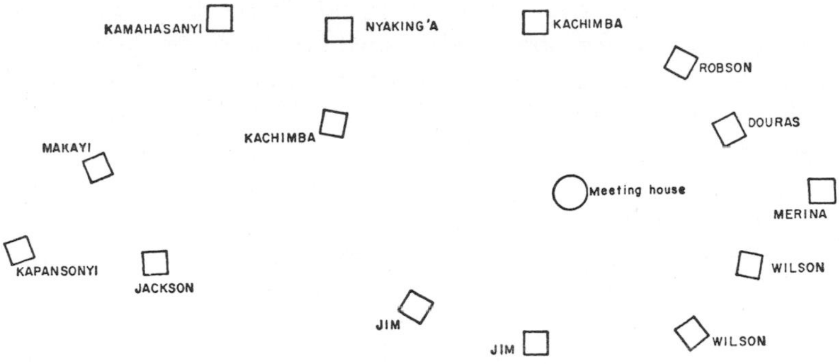


*Diagram 11.* Hut plan of Nswanamundong'u village

*ihamba* and in the second of which he removed that of Kamahasanyi's father Mudyigita), I shall have to use a genealogy and a hut plan of Nswanamundong'u (see Diagrams 10 and 11). Since the nuclear matrilineage of that village belonged to the royal matrilineage of the Mukang'ala chiefdom, I have included in the genealogy other branches of the royal lineage, for they are part of the total field influencing the behavior and ideas we are examining.

To simplify the analysis I shall subdivide the social field of Nswanamundong'u into its component social entities—various kinds of group, subgroup, category, and relationship—and exhibit them in a series of interpenetrating dimensions of relationships. These relationships consist of white-black relations, political relations between branches of the Mukang'ala royal lineage, intravillage relations, and intrafamilial relations.

### WHITE-BLACK RELATIONS

For the present analysis, this set of relations constitutes a set of perduring conditions full of chronic tension and conflict. The chieftainship of Mukang'ala had been abolished about four years before my arrival in the area. The area was in a state of seedy decrepitude. The courthouse at the capital village was falling into disrepair, as was the Mission Out-School, closed down after the abolition of the chief's chair. Those who had occupied paid positions under the Native Authority had returned to their villages of origin and reverted to the lives of peasants and hunters. Indeed, the "primitive" appearance of Mukang'ala's chiefdom was the result of regression and of "dedifferentiation," of the breakdown of the modern political structure of Native Court and Treasury with their paid officials. It was not due to isolation from modern trends of change for the chiefdom extended almost to the British Administration Headquarters. Local sources of cash income had dried up with the death of the local government. Men had either to go to the Northern Rhodesian railway 300 miles away to find paid work or to cultivate their cassava gardens and hunt in the bush—mainly with traps, snares, bows, and spears, since they had not the cash to buy guns nor the command of European and chiefly patronage to obtain licenses to purchase ammunition.

Among those who had regressed to "bush" life was Kachimba, the acting headman of Nswanamundong'u. His smattering of literacy had been enough to obtain him the post of court clerk in the days of the chiefdom's official recognition. Now he had become a shy figure who normally evaded a headmans' duty of supplying hospitality to wayfarers and, as often as not, was away in the bush when people called. His villagers and many others in the former chiefdom used to blame him for the loss of his authority. He had been brusque and uncooperative toward European officials, it was said, and many stated that he had been considered "dirty" and "unhygienic" in the way he ran his capital village.

### RELATIONS AMONG BRANCHES OF THE MUKANG'ALA LINEAGE

The abolition of black authority by white power had repercussions along several dimensions of social relations in the black sector. Among branches of the royal matrilineage, it led to widespread emigration of important men from the chiefdom. Several went to Chief Ikelenge's area to the north. This area was highly prosperous in terms of modern cash economy. Several European traders and farmers held land there and offered opportunities for paid employment. Its chief was young, progressive, literate, and in favor with the government, in contrast to Mukang'ala. The dissident Mukang'ala royals, notably Samalichi (D1), Mbaulu (D2), and Kimbinyi (D3), all prospered and became headmen under Chief Ikelenge. Kimbinyi became, in addition, a wealthy trader. Samuwinu (D13), the "real headman" of Nswanamundong'u, who had fled to Ikelenge's area before the abolition, had not prospered, but he was reckoned to be a man of weak character, who had failed to meet the crisis of his life with courage.

The defection of these royals left the Mukang'ala lineage divided into two branches: one descended from Nyakanjata (B2), the other from Kawang'u (B4). I shall call them the Nyakanjata and Kawang'u lineages. The incumbency of the chieftainship had alternated between these two lineages since Mukang'ala II—there had been earlier chiefs than those shown, but their genealogical connections are irrelevant to the present account. This alternation was never institutionalized but was the result of power struggles. Mukang'ala III, Ibala, who had fought against the British when they first came, had been slain, it is said, by the sorcery of Mundong'u Kabong'u (whose shade was believed to be afflicting Kamahasanyi). He was believed to have been ensorcelled in turn by Mukang'ala V (E13), Ibala's sister's daughter's son, of Kawang'u lineage.

It is probably because Nyakanjata lineage, most of whose members resided in Nswanamundong'u, had in the past provided so many chiefs that its members did not emigrate but continued to stay in Mukang'ala's chiefdom. I do know that they cherished hopes that the chieftainship would be restored to official favor and recognition. Among those who hoped was Jim (E12), an intelligent, enterprising young man who had worked as a labor migrant in Rhodesia. He was widely recognized as the likely heir of the present incumbent. In Nswanamundong'u, where he lived, it was Jim rather than Kachimba who took the lead in village matters and who offered hospitality to strangers. The biggest feather in his cap came when he sponsored a circumcision ceremony—a role normally performed by the chief in such a small chiefdom—at which three of his own sons were initiated. Jim's political strategy was twofold: to support the present incumbent in his frequent appeals to government for renewed recognition and to try to build up a following for himself from Nyakanjata lineage and from anyone else who could be induced to support his future claim for office. He had, therefore, a strong interest in preventing internecine strife in Nswanamundong'u and in maintaining friendly relations between it and other villages. It is hardly surprising therefore that he was among the foremost in asking for Ihembi to perform the *Ihamba* rite to propitiate his mother's brother's shade, a rite that was known to have beneficial effects on village relationships. It is also interesting that he performed the task at each ceremony of sucking the cupping horns of Kamahasanyi's body.

## INTRAVILLAGE RELATIONS

Jim's concern that Nswanamundong'u should remain united sprang from a real fear that it would split. A comparison of the hut plan (see Diagram 10) with the genealogy shows that, although the village is small, it is divided into two distinct sections. One is inhabited by Headman Kachimba (E8), his wife, and his adult children, Merina (F7), Douras (F8), and Robson (F9); by Jim (E12), his two wives, and his junior children; and by Wilson (E11), son of the late headman, and his two wives and junior children. The other is occupied by what I have called "the Nkonkoto Group," consisting of a solitary old man, Kapansonyi (D4), his classificatory sister's son Makayi (E1) and his wife, and their adult son Jackson (F1). Between these sections are the two huts of Kamahasanyi (F2) and Nyakinga (D14), Kachimba's mother's mother's sister's daughter (whom he calls "mother"). These site arrangements reflect social structure. It seems that about thirty-five to forty years before the events I record, many members of the Mukang'ala lineage fled to Chief Nkonkoto's Ndembu chieftainship in what was then the Belgian Congo, probably to escape from the forces of the British South Africa Company, which Chief Mukang'ala Ibala (C4) had opposed. There they intermarried with some Nkonkoto villagers and made friends with others. Eventually they returned and, in the course of time Mundong'u Kabong'u (D10), the senior man in Nyankanjata lineage, succeeded to the chieftainship. Some Nkonkoto people tried to exploit their ties of affinity and friendship with Nyakanjata-lineage members to obtain paid employment under the Native Authority. They sought Mundong'u's patronage to get work in the Public Works Department or the Native Court. Makayi, one of this group, sent his son Jackson to the Mission Out-School at the capital village. They built their huts beside those of Nyakanjata people. For a time, all went well, but when I knew them the Nkonkoto group, reduced in number to those I have mentioned, were a pretty disgruntled bunch. They seemed to hold their fellow villagers from the Nyakanjata lineage, especially Kachimba, responsible for the decline in fortune of the chiefdom, and they had no good word to say of Samuwinu (D13), who had defected. Relations were particularly tense between Makayi and Kachimba. Neither would sit in a group when the other was present, although both were on good terms with Jim (E12), who made it his business to be friendly with everyone.

It was into this situation of strain between the Nyakanjata lineage and the Nkonkoto Group that Kamahasanyi arrived, a short time before my own first visit to the village. He, too, had come from Nkonkoto chiefdom, where his father Mudyigita (E3) had been a great headman and a famous hunter. Furthermore, Mudyigita was the son of a former Chief Nkonkoto (D7). Since Kamahasanyi's mother, as we have seen, belonged to the Mukang'ala royal lineage, he was certainly well connected on both sides. There are several peculiarities about Kamahasanyi's life history that made it most unfortunate for him that he had plunged into a situation that exacerbated conflicts between maternal and paternal loyalties. For it was as though his endopsychic conflict had been objectivized and given social form. Through his paternal link with the Nkonkoto group, Kamahasanyi was exposed to the grievances aired by Makayi and his people. As a member of Nyankanjata matrilineage, he heard the counteraccusations of his maternal kin. As can be seen from the hut plan, Kamahasanyi built his hut between those two groups, indicating his dual allegiance. A stronger character might have acted as a mediator between his matrilineal and patrilateral kin. Indeed, I have recorded several instances of men who played this very role, but Kamahasanyi "retreated from the field" into what I can only think was neurotic illness. The key to an explanation of this illness may be found, I suggest, in the circumstances of his life and in his temperament.

## *Kamahasanyi's Life History*

Kamahasanyi was exceptional in Ndembu society for the great length of time he had resided in the village of his father's nuclear matrilineage. When he finally came to settle with his mother's kin, he was past his fortieth year, and his father had been dead for several years. It not infrequently happens that sons reside with their fathers for some years after their own marriages, especially, as in Kamahasanyi's case, when the father is a headman and can extend to his son certain privileges and assistance in economic matters. However, it is rare for a man in advanced middle life to do so, unless his mother is the father's slave (*ndung'u*). There was no evidence that Kamahasanyi's mother had been a slave, though it may well have been hushed up. If his mother had been a slave, Kamahasanyi, by matrilineal descent, would have inherited her status and would himself have been inherited by his father's matrilineal heir, unless his relatives had redeemed him by a substantial payment. Since they were too poor to have done so and since Kamahasanyi claimed to have made large payments of bridewealth for two of his wives in the Belgian Congo, he must have been a man of independent means. At all events, he seems, in his youth, to have been his father's favorite and to have received from him considerable assistance in accumulating bridewealth.

Members of the Nkonkoto group told me that Mudyigita, Kamahasanyi's father, was a man of great force of character. In this respect, he presented a sharp contrast to his son. Kamahasanyi was effeminate in manner and was reckoned to be "womanish" (*neyi mumbanda*) by his fellow villagers. He plaited his hair in a feminine style known as *lumba,* and he spent much of his time gossiping with women in their kitchens. Furthermore, although he had been married four times, he had failed to beget children. An interesting feature of these marriages is that three of them were with cross-cousins. Two of the three were with patrilateral cross-cousins, that is, with members of his father's matrilineage. Such marriages are one means, in Ndembu society, of forging closer links with one's father, since one's children thus belong to one's father's matrilineage and will inherit and succeed within it. One will then live uxorilocally in one's father's village and not move to the village of one's maternal kin. Ndembu generally consider that men of mature years who live uxorilocally or patrilocally (with their father's kin), are men who evade their responsibilities, for the major sphere of a man's struggles for status and power is the village of his primary matrilineal kin. Here it is that a man may hope to become a headman or, if he is royal, to become a chief. Here it is, also, that a man is expected to help his matrikin in legal and ritual matters and to share his economic surplus. Kamahasanyi had shirked these duties and had obviously been dominated by his successful father. After Mudyigita's death, according to my informants (Ihembi's assistants, Mukeyi and Mundoyi, who were Mudyigita's seminal brothers), Kamahasanyi's continued residence in his village aroused irritation and resentment. He had never really pulled his weight in corporate matters, and he was urged to return to "his own people," to Mukang'-ala's chiefdom. He paid several visits there, and on one visit married Kachimba's daughter Maria (F6), his first matrilateral cross-cousin. It is quite clear that unconscious incestuous drives influenced Kamahasanyi in his choice of mates. Cross-cousins are, it is true, preferred marital partners, but few Ndembu marry as many as three in a lifetime. They are the easiest partners to obtain, which would have been in accord with Kamahasanyi's tendency to take the line of least resistance. It is probable that his father and later his mother's brother had arranged these cross-cousin marriages for him. Like his father, his fourth wife Maria was a dominant personality who, both before and after her marriage to Kamahasanyi, took lovers when she felt like it. For a time she lived with her husband in Mudyigita's village, where she made large cassava gardens. The Belgian authorities paid relatively high prices for cassava meal, which went to feed the copper miners in the Katanga Union Minière belt so that Maria, and through her, Kamahasanyi, prospered for a while. When Kamahasanyi's senior wife, his patrilateral cross-cousin Safi (F5) died, his patrilateral village kin demanded a large "death payment" (*mpepi*) from him and from his matrilineal kin. The custom of paying *mpepi,* apparently introduced from the Luvale tribe, is a financially crippling one. It is connected with the notion that the matrilineal kin of the deceased have the duty of consulting a diviner about the cause of death (to ascertain whose witchcraft or sorcery was responsible for it). Diviners charge high fees, and the surviving spouse and his kin are required to hand over a large payment in cash or kind to cover diviners' fees, as well as to compensate for the loss of the deceased's services. It is unusual, however, for *mpepi* to be demanded in the case of cross-cousin marriage, for the partners are considered kin as well as affines. As Kamahasanyi had had to pay high bridewealth for his cross-cousin wives—again an unusual circumstance—so he was asked to pay a high *mpepi.* These facts indicate, I think, the villagers' dislike of the man. Kamahasanyi was dilatory in paying *mpepi,* and it was then alleged by his patrilateral kin that his wife Maria, with his connivance, had bewitched Safi to death, as co-wives are often believed to do. The result was that Kamahasanyi and Maria were virtually forced to leave Nkonkoto chiefdom and return to Maria's village in Zambia, although not before Maria had sold her cassava gardens at a profit, making Kamahasanyi more dependent upon her than ever.

Kamahasanyi had, therefore, returned at last to his own matrikin, but the fact that he was known to have been forced to do so and his reputation as a "difficult" person to have around made his welcome a rather cool one. Again, as I have said, he was confronted in Nswanamundong'u with an external duplication of his own inner conflicts, for his new village was neatly divided into groups consisting respectively of his maternal and paternal kin. The Nkonkoto group not only felt grievances against the Nyakanjata lineage as a result of the "putting down" of the chieftaincy as described, but they also shared the hostility of their Congolese kinsfolk toward Kamahasanyi.

A further complication arose. Before her marriage to Kamahasanyi, Maria had taken as her lover one of the Nkonkoto group, Makayi's son Jackson, an educated young man who had hopes of employment as a clerk in a European enterprise. On her return to Nswanamundong'u, Maria openly took up with Jackson again. So brazen was this relationship that several times when he was walking with me Jackson ostentatiously "avoided" Maria's mother Ndona (E9), rushing away from the path when he saw her advancing toward him—as though she were his mother-in-law! Kamahasanyi was said to be impotent, and to all appearances he was complaisant about the liaison. On the other hand, Maria fulfilled many of her wifely duties to Kamahasanyi. She worked beside him in his cassava gardens (indeed she did most of the work), and she brewed finger-millet beer for his guests. She even accompanied him to Angola to consult a diviner about his health and fortune. This devotion may have been tendered because Kamahasanyi occupied a structural position of some importance in the village. As may be seen by consulting the genealogy, Kamahasanyi was a full member of Nyakanjata lineage and was therefore, according to Ndembu rules, a possible candidate both for the chieftainship of Mukang'ala and the village headmanship. In view of Jim's (E12) strong claims, by virtue of blood and intelligence, to become chief in the future, it was unlikely that Kamahasanyi would succeed to the chair. On the other hand, since Jim, if he became a chief, would set up a capital village of his own, it was possible that Kamahasanyi would "continue the name" of Nswanamundong'u by succeeding to its headmanship and scraping up a modest following of matrikin, cognates, affines, and anyone else he might persuade to reside with him. At least, Maria, with her strong will and energy, might do these things with her husband as nominal headman.

Despite his disadvantages, Kamahasanyi had a strong sense of his own importance. Even in a society whose members like to stress their connections with chiefs, Kamahasanyi was more snobbish than most. For example, when I discussed the history of the Mukang'ala chiefdom with senior men like Kachimba, Jim, and Wilson (E11), he would brush aside or interrupt their accounts and tell me "what really happened." He was the only one who could tell me the full, sonorous clan formula of the Saluseki clan to which the Mukang'ala royal lineage belonged—the clan (*munyachi*) has ceased to have any political and has retained little social importance. He was also proud of his paternal link with the Nkonkoto chieftainship. He was, as I have said, conceited about his appearance, braiding his hair and oiling his body. He had brought with him from the Belgian Congo several dilapidated books in French, which he could not read but which he clearly considered to be status symbols. His attitude toward me was that we were both civilized men among barbarians, whom he despised and who could not understand him.

The symptoms of his illness consisted of rapid palpitations of the heart; severe pains in the back, limbs, and chest; and fatigue after short spells of work. He felt that "people were always speaking things against" him—though he excepted Jim from blame—and finally he withdrew from all village affairs and shut himself up in his hut for long periods. He complained to me and to Ihembi that the villagers ignored his sufferings to the extent that no one had bothered to consult a diviner to find out what was wrong with him. In the end, ill though he was, he had had to travel many miles to Angola to consult a diviner himself. I cannot say with clinical certainty whether Kamahasanyi's symptoms were real or imaginary. My own feeling is that they were mainly neurotic. At any rate, when the ritual sequence was over, Kamahasanyi was perfectly able to cultivate his gardens, to set traps for game in the forest, and to travel considerable distances to visit kin and friends. To all outward appearances there was nothing much the matter with him; he talked animatedly and at length to anyone whom, like Ihembi and myself, he considered sympathetic. It is probable that most of his symptoms were psychosomatic—with a few rheumatic pains, a common Ndembu ailment, in addition—and were an unconscious way of obtaining the attention of his fellow villagers.

## *The Performances of* Ihamba

The material I have presented—and much more—was known to Ihembi, who discussed it with me and with his assistants Mundoyi and Mukeyi, who were themselves patrilaterally connected with

Kamahasanyi and had grown up in the same part of the Belgian Congo. All of it was taken into account and put to therapeutic use by Ihembi, not only in the formalized situation of ritual performances, but also in the informal talks he held during his stay in Nswanamundong'u with Kamahasanyi, Maria, Jim, Kachimba, Makayi, and other interested parties. I would like, first of all, to present some of Ihembi's diagnoses of the causes of Kamahasanyi's illness and misfortune and then to consider his conduct of the *Ihamba* performances. Ihembi, like other Ndembu, believed that these causes were all of a mystical type. He was not at all like a Western psychiatrist working with the concept of mental illness.

After the first performance of *Ihamba,* in which he had, as anticipated, tactfully taken control of the proceedings from his Luvale colleague (with great delicacy he had first asked his permission to do so and later gave him a half share of his ten-shilling fee), Ihembi told me that, while it was true that Kamahasanyi had been "bitten" by the *ihamba* of his "grandfather" Mundong'u Kabong'u, other entities had also been at work. He had himself removed the late chief's incisor, and he had been correct, he said, in his view that the shade was angry because a proper headman had not been installed in Nswanamundong'u. He knew that he was correct, he went on, because the shade had caused the patient to "tremble"[1] (*ku-zakuka*) after Ihembi had "addressed" (*kwinka nyikunyi*) the proper questions to it. Later he had divined by gazing into a meal mortar full of pounded medicines and sprinkled with powdered red clay (with the generic sense of "blood") and white clay (which may mean "innocence," "health," "strength," certain manifestations of ancestral shades, and so forth). There he had "seen" another *ihamba,* probably that of the patient's father. Kamahasanyi, it may be recalled, had dreamed of his father's shade. Ihembi said that Mudyigita was angry with his son for having quarreled with his (Mudyigita's) matrikin. Since Kamahasanyi had dreamed on successive nights that the shade had stood between the forked branches of a hunters' shrine set up in front of his dwelling hut, Ihembi resolved to perform *Ihamba* at that very place.

In addition to *mahamba,* said Ihembi, sorcery and witchcraft were partly to blame for Kamahasanyi's troubles. When he first divined, he thought he saw in the medicated water the "reflection" or "shadow-

[1] A sort of rhythmic shuddering, indicative of possession, which begins in time with the drum rhythm and afterwards may become uncontrollable.

soul" (*mwevulu*) of Wilson. He "saw" further that Wilson had "raised a *musalu*," a kind of malignant ghost, by means of a curse, after quarreling with Kamahasanyi. I can confirm from my own information that Wilson strongly disliked Kamahasanyi and resented his coming to the village. Since he was not a matrilineal kinsman, Wilson was less constrained about expressing his hostility, for matrikin must in public maintain the fiction of amity in their relations. On going more deeply into the matter, Ihembi learned, since he was a great diviner and not easily deceived, that the "reflection" of Wilson had been "put in his *ng'ombu*" (his divining apparatus) by the "real witches." These witches were Kamahasanyi's wife Maria and her mother Ndona (E9), Kachimba's wife. They wanted to "kill Kamahasanyi for his meat," since Ndembu witches are thought to be necrophagous. They had sent their familiars (malignant little beings known as *tuyebela,* who take the forms of small domestic animals or tiny men with inverted feet) to "beat" Kamahasanyi with hoe-handles. This behavior accounted for some of his symptoms. Beside, Ndona preferred Jackson to Kamahasanyi as a son-in-law and wanted the latter done away with.

Ihembi told me that he had informed the villagers that, before he could "make another *Ihamba,*" he would have to perform a rite known as *Kaneng'a* or *Lukupu* ("splashing with medicine"), to make the witches realize that in a general way "they were known." *Lukupu* also had the effect of driving off witches' familiars. He would not mention any names openly, since "there was enough trouble in the village," but the performance of *Lukupu* would act as a sharp warning to the witches to call off their familiars, for otherwise he would expose them publicly and take drastic ritual remedial action. To perform *Lukupu* was also, in my opinion, Ihembi's way of sharply jolting the quarrelsome villagers into reconciling their differences and behaving better toward their kinsman Kamahasanyi. To imply so bluntly that witchcraft was at work in the village was the sharpest rebuke Ihembi could make and played on the Ndembu villagers' deepest fears.

Ihembi told me that it was in his mind to advise Kamahasanyi to divorce Maria and to go to reside in Chief Ikelenge's area, where his widowed mother was now living with Kamahasanyi's younger brother —not far from the "real headman" Samuwinu's hut (D13). He might thus hope to escape a horrible death. In the end, however, he decided against this course and worked to make "the livers of the Nswanamundong'u people white towards one another," to remove the state of mutual ill-feeling. This removal would "please the shade," which would stop afflicting Kamahasanyi.

In this projective guise, Ihembi was really dealing with the undercurrents of personal animosity and sectional rivalry in the village. He was also clearly trying to emancipate Kamahasanyi from the guilts and anxieties attendant upon his belated removal from his late father's sphere of influence. Kamahasanyi had to be made over, as it were, to the matrilineal sphere, which was also the arena of adult reponsibility.

I shall pass over the events of the *Lukupu* rite, which I observed, except to note that Ihembi made Kachimba (E8) throw, on behalf of the whole village, a portion of white clay (*mpemba*) into the medicines with which Kamahasanyi was washed to betoken that all had "good feelings" toward him. Makayi, too, attended the rite, which was held in the bush far away from the village.

## *The Second* Ihamba *Performance*

I shall not give a "blow by blow" account of the rite here but shall confine myself to its social implications. It is necessary to know, however, that, after certain ritual preliminaries, including the collecting of medicines in a prescribed formal manner, an *Ihamba* rite proceeds in a series of stops and starts. The "stops" occur when the cupping horns (*tusumu*) are attached to the patient's body; then follows a phase of drumming and singing, in which all present join, and the patient goes into a trembling fit. If he shakes off a horn or two in his convulsions, the doctor bids the drummers stop playing, removes the horns, and investigates them. If he finds nothing in them, he makes a statement to the congregation about why the *ihamba* has not "come out"—which usually entails a fairly detailed account of the patient's life story and of the group's inter-relations—then he invokes the shade, urging it to "come quickly" and finally invites village members to come, in order of sex and seniority, to the improvised hunters' shrine set up for the shade and confess any secret ill-feeling they may have toward the patient. The patient himself may be invited as well. Then cupping horns are affixed once more, drumming and singing commence again, and the "big doctor" passes the time until the next round of verbal behavior in dancing, purifying the village by ritually sweeping out huts and paths, or going out into the bush to bring back some new medicine plant.

Ihembi's greatest skill was in managing this stop-start routine so that, after several hours of it, the congregation felt nothing but a unanimous craving for the removal of the *ihamba* from the patient's body. The intense excitement whipped up by the drums; the patient's trembling; mass participation in the sad-sweet or rousing hunters' cult songs, which are sung to "please *ihamba,*" followed by the spate of confessions and the airing of grievances; the reverent or hortatory prayers addressed not only by the doctor but also by village elders to the shade to "make our kinsman strong"; the sight and smell of blood, which often pours in gouts from the horns: all these elements make a dialectical and dialogical pattern of activity that generates strong sentiments of corporateness, reduces skepticism, and maximizes sympathy for the patient.

Ihembi was also skilled in allocating appropriate ritual tasks to the patient's kin. For example, he asked Nyaking'a (D14) to bring in a calabash of water to be consecrated to the making of *Ihamba* medicines. Nyaking'a had been a friend of Kamahasanyi's mother while both were married out in the Belgian Congo. She was Kamahasanyi's classificatory "grandmother," and she had been ritual instructress to Maria some years earlier at her puberty rite. Because of its importance at life crises, Ndembu regard water as an "elder" (*mukulumpi*) or most venerable "thing," and Nyaking'a's friendly relationship with the disturbed marital pair was thus recognized.

Jim (E12), the tactful aspirant to the chief's chair, helped in the sucking of horns, thus demonstrating that he wanted to rid the patient (and his village) of troubles. Samuwinu was asked to invoke the shade before others did, since he was "the real headman."

Wilson was asked by Ihembi to put a piece of white clay on the fork of a hunter's shrine tree in token of his friendly and pure intentions toward Kamahasanyi, of which, as we have seen, there had been some doubt. Ihembi made the faithless Maria go into the bush to bring leaves from a *mudyi* tree (*Diplorrhyncus condylocarpon*). This tree, as I have shown elsewhere, stands for "motherhood," "matriliny," and "womanhood" (its white latex secretions are likened to mother's milk). It also stands for "auspiciousness." Maria chewed the leaves and spat the juice on her husband's temples, feet, and hands, centers of thought and activity, and tapped him smartly on the back and head with a small hand rattle—"to give him strength." By these acts, she reaffirmed her wifely duties toward the patient and her good will—the reverse of witchery.

Others too numerous to mention were assigned minor parts in this ritual drama by the old impresario Ihembi, who sought, as I have seen him do again and again in ritual contexts, to get everyone working together, despite the issues that divided them in secular life, "to please the shade," and thus to cure the patient. Once when the women attenders did not sing loudly enough, Ihembi made them come closer to the compact men's group and exhorted them to sing up. "It is very important," he said, "that you give your power to help Kamahasanyi." For, in Ndembu belief, singing is not merely a pastime or aesthetic activity but a way of generating "power," which can be used by a doctor for healing purposes.

After a number of people had admitted to ill feeling or negligence toward Kamahasanyi, the patient himself spoke out. He complained vehemently that his matrilineal kin (*akumama*) had not moved a finger to help him when he was ill. He had been forced to go to a diviner himself, although he was unwell. It was fortunate, he said, that Maria, his wife, had gone with him. But, he added, now that he had told his grudge to everyone, he thought that all would be well. His hard thoughts had kept back his cure. It was also lucky that Mundoyi and Mukeyi, Ihembi's assistants (who had performed many ritual tasks) were present, for they were Kamahasanyi's (classificatory) "fathers" (see genealogy), and it was his father who had been troubling him.

I should like to conclude my account of the performance with an extract from my field notes, written up shortly after I observed it in 1951, to convey something of its atmosphere and flavor:

Mundoyi now took the *duiker* horn out of Kamahasanyi's hair over the brow, washed it, filled it with medicine, and replaced it at the back of his head. He did the same with the blue *duiker* horn at the back, replacing it at the front. He blew his whistle twice. Kamahasanyi started to quiver again violently, and the cupping horn on the left of his neck fell off, unpleasantly spilling what looked like a small chunk of flesh. Next the horn on his temple fell off. Ihembi sat very quietly, not registering any emotion at all. I felt strongly that what was being drawn out of this man Kamahasanyi was, in reality, the hidden animosities of the village. To all appearances, Kamahasanyi was in a state of complete dissociation.

Now Ihembi fitted a long thin *duiker* horn on the little finger of his right hand, took a mongoose-skin purse in his left hand, and pointed the horn at one of the cupping horns, wiping the patient's skin just above it as he did so. The whole congregation rose to their feet as one man, and Ihembi fastened on the twitching Kamahasanyi, who fell on his side, writhing convulsively. Kamahasanyi cried out and sobbed when Ihembi removed the blood-dripping horn in a large skin purse. Mundoyi and Kachilewa (an *Ihamba* adept from a neighboring village) threw large quantities of medicine over the patient. Ihembi rushed to the small calabash (containing medicine and blood from other cuppings) and threw the cupping horn now concealed by the purse into it. He then spat powdered white clay on the really ugly bulge on Kamahasanyi's neck where the horn had been, "to cool and purify it." Kachilewa now held his hand poised over the leaf-concealed calabash while all of us waited intently. He removed the leaves and dredged with his hand in the bloody mixture. After a while he shook his head and said "Mwosi" ("Nothing in here"). We were all disappointed. But Ihembi with a gentle smile took over. He plunged his fingers into the gruesome liquid and when he brought them up I saw a flash of white. Then he rushed with what was in his fingers out of the avid circle of onlookers. From the edge of the village, he beckoned to the elders and to me. Led by Samuwinu and Kachimba, we went one by one to Ihembi. It was indeed a human tooth, we had to say. It was no bush pig's tooth, nor a monkey's. Jubilantly we told the women, who all trilled with joy. Men and women who had been on cool terms with one another until recently, shook hands warmly and beamed with happiness. Kachimba even smiled at Makayi, who smiled back. Several hours later a mood of quiet satisfaction still seemed to emanate from the villagers.

These events took place toward the end of my first field trip. More than a year later, when I visited the village again during my second tour, I found that several changes had occurred in its composition. Of the Nkonkoto group none remained in Nswanamundong'u. Old Kapansonyi had died, and Makayi had emigrated to Chief Ikelenge's area, while Maria's lover Jackson had gone as a labor migrant to the Copperbelt mining town of Chingola (where I met him by chance in the street one day—he said he was never going back to village life). Kachimba's sons Douras and Robson had built new huts elsewhere in Mukang'ala Chiefdom. Kamahasanyi was still in residence, Maria was still his wife, and indeed he had added to his personal following by persuading his younger brother and sister to reside in Nswanamundong'u. Furthermore, he had increased his prestige by becoming an adept in some of the cults into which he had been initiated through suffering, though not in *Ihamba,* for he was not a gun-hunter. In terms of social morphology, therefore, Nswanamundong'u had shed its patrilateral attachments and was reduced to its matrilineal nucleus, although it had increased in size. Kamahasanyi gave me the impression that he was enjoying life, was accepted by his fellow villagers, and was liked by his wife. He showed me with pride his new cassava gardens and told me that he was now successfully snaring game. It looked as though Ihembi's "therapy" had "worked," if only for a time!

It seems that the Ndembu "doctor" sees his task less as curing an individual patient than as remedying the ills of a corporate group. The sickness of a patient is mainly a sign that "something is rotten" in the corporate body. The patient will not get better until all the tensions and aggressions in the group's interrelations have been brought to light and exposed to ritual treatment. I have shown how complex these interrelations can be and how conflicts in one social dimension may reverberate through others. The doctor's task is to tap the various streams of affect associated with these conflicts and with the social and interpersonal disputes in which they are manifested, and to channel them in a socially positive direction. The raw energies of conflict are thus domesticated in the service of the traditional social order. Once the various causes of ill feeling against Kamahasanyi and of his ill feeling against others had been "made visible" (to use the Ndembu idiom), the doctor Ihembi was able, through the cultural mechanism of *Ihamba,* with its bloodlettings, confessions, purifications, prayers to the traditional dead, tooth-drawings, and build-up of expectations, to transform the ill feeling into well wishing. Emotion is roused and then stripped of its illicit and antisocial qualty, but nothing of its intensity, its quantitative aspect, has been lost in the transformation. Ndembu social norms and values, expressed in symbolic objects and actions, are saturated with this generalized emotion, which itself becomes ennobled through contact with these norms and values. The sick individual, exposed to this process, is reintegrated into his group as, step by step, its members are reconciled with one another in emotionally charged circumstances.

Yet, there is room within this communal and corporate process for the doctor to take fully into account the nuances and delicate distinctions of interpersonal relationships. Ihembi, for example, dealt with the idiosyncratic relationships between a father and a son, a husband and a wife, an uncle and a nephew; but his main endeavor was to see that individuals were capable of playing their social roles successfully in a traditional structure of social position. Illness was for him a mark of undue deviation from the norm. The shades punish such deviation. In this time of rapid change, the shades of old hunters are particularly likely to be sensitive to breaches of traditional norms, since hunting is for Ndembu the activity around which has formed the basic constellation of tribal values. It is therefore appropriate that hunters' shades should "bite" those who are most exposed to modern changes.

Stripped of its supernatural guise, Ndembu therapy may well offer lessons for Western clinical practice. For relief might be given to many sufferers from neurotic illness if all those involved in their social networks could meet together and publicly confess their ill will toward the patient and endure in turn the recital of his grudges against them. However, it is likely that nothing less than ritual sanctions for such behavior and belief in the doctor's mystical powers could bring about such humility and compel people to display charity toward their suffering "neighbor"!

## BIBLIOGRAPHY


Ackerknecht, E. H. 1942. "Problems of Primitive Medicine," *Bulletin of the History of Medicine*, XI.

Lessa, W. A., and Vogt, E. Z., eds. 1958. *Reader in Comparative Religion*. Evanston: Row, Peterson and Co.

Parsons, T. 1951. *The Social System*. New York: The Free Press Of Glencoe.

Turner, V. W. 1957. *Schism and Continuity in an African Society: A Study of Ndembu Village Life*. Manchester University Press.

——. 1961. *Ndembu Divination: Its Symbolism and Techniques* (Rhodes-Livingstone Paper 31). Manchester University Press.

# Index